Good Housekeeping

The
Complete
Household
Handbook

CLEANING THE RIGHT STUFF BASIC CLEANING EQUIPMENT FURNITURE FLOORS WINDOWS
AND DOORS WALLS AND CEILINGS THE KITCHEN THE BATHROOM THE NURSERY AND
CHILDREN'S ROOMS PORCHES, DECKS, AND PATIOS GARAGES AND BASEMENTS LAUNDRY
AND CLOTHES CARE LAUNDRY PRODUCTS DOING THE WASH IRONING DRY-CLEANING SEWING
LEATHER AND FUR JEWELRY CARE PACKING A SUITCASE CLOTHES STORAGE EATING WELL
SMART SHOPPING COOKING KEEPING FOOD FRESH EQUIPMENT TABLEWARE ENTERTAINING
DOING IT YOURSELF PAINTING WALL COVERINGS WINDOW TREATMENTS FLOORS FURNITURE
WALL DECORATIONS THE KITCHEN THE BATHROOM STORAGE STRATEGIES HOME OFFICE
HELP THE HOME WORKSHOP MENDING CHINA AND GLASS RESTORING WOOD FURNITURE WALL
AND CEILING REPAIRS HOW TO HANG ANYTHING DOORS WINDOWS AND SCREENS FLOORS
HEATING SYSTEMS COOLING SYSTEMS WEATHERPROOFING PLUMBING ELECTRICITY ROOF
REPAIRS GUTTERS THE YARD MANAGING YOUR MONEY EFFICIENTLY GETTING CREDIT HOW
LONG SHOULD YOU KEEP YOUR FINANCIAL RECORDS FRAUD AND IDENTITY THEFT SAFETY
BASICS CHILDPROOFING YOUR HOME SAFETY FOR THE ELDERLY THE SAFE YARD EMERGENCIES
IN THE HOME INDOOR POLLUTANTS HOME SECURITY PREPARING FOR DISASTER CLEANING
THE RIGHT STUFF BASIC CLEANING EQUIPMENT FURNITURE FLOORS WINDOWS AND DOORS
WALLS AND CEILINGS THE KITCHEN THE BATHROOM THE NURSERY AND CHILDREN'S ROOMS
PORCHES, DECKS, AND PATIOS GARAGES AND BASEMENTS LAUNDRY AND CLOTHES CARE
LAUNDRY PRODUCTS DOING THE WASH IRONING DRY-CLEANING SEWING LEATHER AND FUR
JEWELRY CARE PACKING A SUITCASE CLOTHES STORAGE EATING WELL SMART SHOPPING
COOKING KEEPING FOOD FRESH EQUIPMENT TABLEWARE ENTERTAINING DOING IT YOURSELF
PAINTING WALL COVERINGS WINDOW TREATMENTS FLOORS FURNITURE WALL DECORATIONS
THE KITCHEN THE BATHROOM STORAGE STRATEGIES HOME OFFICE HELP THE HOME WORK
SHOP MENDING CHINA AND GLASS RESTORING WOOD FURNITURE WALL AND CEILING REPAIRS
HOW TO HANG ANYTHING DOORS WINDOWS AND SCREENS FLOORS HEATING SYSTEMS COOL
ING SYSTEMS WEATHERPROOFING PLUMBING ELECTRICITY ROOF REPAIRS GUTTERS THE
YARD MANAGING YOUR MONEY EFFICIENTLY GETTING CREDIT HOW LONG SHOULD YOU KEEP
YOUR FINANCIAL RECORDS? FRAUD AND IDENTITY THEFT SAFETY BASICS CHILDPROOFING
YOUR HOME SAFETY FOR THE ELDERLY THE SAFE YARD EMERGENCIES IN THE HOME INDOOR
POLLUTANTS HOME SECURITY PREPARING FOR DISASTER CLEANING THE RIGHT STUFF BASIC
CLEANING EQUIPMENT FURNITURE FLOORS WINDOWS AND DOORS WALLS AND CEILINGS THE
KITCHEN THE BATHROOM THE NURSERY AND CHILDREN'S ROOMS PORCHES, DECKS, AND
PATIOS GARAGES AND BASEMENTS LAUNDRY AND CLOTHES CARE LAUNDRY PRODUCTS DOING
THE WASH IRONING DRY-CLEANING SEWING LEATHER AND FUR JEWELRY CARE PACKING A
SUITCASE CLOTHES STORAGE EATING WELL SMART SHOPPING COOKING KEEPING
FOOD FRESH EQUIPMENT TABLEWARE ENTERTAINING DOING IT YOURSELF PAINTING WALL
COVERINGS WINDOW TREATMENTS FLOORS FURNITURE WALL DECORATIONS THE KITCHEN
THE BATHROOM STORAGE STRATEGIES HOME OFFICE EMERGENCIES IN THE HOME INDOOR

Good Housekeeping

The Complete Household Handbook

The Best Ways to Clean, Maintain & Organize Your Home

HEARST BOOKS

A DIVISION OF STERLING PUBLISHING CO., INC.

NEW YORK

Good Housekeeping

Ellen Levine · Editor in Chief

Richard Eisenberg · Special Projects Director

Susan Leaderman · Decorating Editor

The Good Housekeeping Institute

John P. Kupsch, · P.E.Technical Director

Carolyn E. Forte · Home Care Director/Associate
Institute Director

Sharon Franke · Food Appliances Director

Delia Hammock, · M.S., R.D. Nutrition Director

Karen L. Rauen, Ph.D. · Director of Chemistry

Kathleen Huddy Sperduto · Textiles Director

Susan Westmoreland · Food Director

Gary Zukowski · Engineering Director

Project Editor
Susan Randol

Contributing Writers
Janet Allon
Richard Eisenberg
Rick Peters
Chris Peterson
Elaine Martin Petrowski
Anne Marie Soto
Dayna Winter

Book design by Renato Stanisic

Illustrations by Melanie Powell, Studio in the Woods

The Good Housekeeping Seal is a concise statement of the *Good Housekeeping* Consumers' Policy: If a product bearing the Seal proves to be defective within two years of purchase, *Good Housekeeping* will replace the product or refund the purchase price. For more information go to www.goodhousekeeping.com.

Library of Congress Cataloging-in-Publication Data
The complete household handbook : the best ways to clean, maintain, & organize your home / Good Housekeeping.
p. cm.
Includes index.
ISBN 1-58816-403-9
1. Housekeeping. I. Good Housekeeping Institute
(New York, N.Y.)
TX301.C58 2005
640--dc22
2004052389

10 9 8 7 6 5

Published by Hearst Books
A Division of Sterling Publishing Co., Inc.
387 Park Avenue South, New York, NY 10016

Good Housekeeping is a trademark of
Hearst Communications, Inc.

www.goodhousekeeping.com

Distributed in Canada by Sterling Publishing
c/o Canadian Manda Group, 165 Dufferin Street
Toronto, Ontario, Canada M6K 3H6

Distributed in Australia by Capricorn Link
(Australia) Pty. Ltd.
P.O. Box 704, Windsor, NSW 2756 Australia

Printed in China

ISBN-13: 978-1-58816-403-2
ISBN-10:-1-58816-403-9

For information about custom editions, special sales, premium and corporate purchases, please contact Sterling Special Sales Department at 800-805-5489 or specialsales@sterlingpub.com.

B4T 1/8/07

CONTENTS

Foreword

As the editor-in-chief of Good Housekeeping, I know a little bit about keeping up a house. But I learned a lot more by reading this new edition of *The Complete Household Handbook* from the authorities at The Good Housekeeping Institute. And I know you'll find plenty of useful information to outfit, maintain, and improve your home. This won't be a book you read cover to cover. Instead, you can turn to it as a trustworthy resource when a challenge arises around the house. Whether you want to buy a new washing machine, get rid of stubborn carpet stains, replace a broken doorknob, or just decorate your living room, *The Complete Household Handbook* will be your guide. I think you'll be glad to have it on your reference bookshelf. I know I'm glad that I do. Best of luck with your share of the American Dream: your home.

ELLEN LEVINE
EDITOR-IN-CHIEF
GOOD HOUSEKEEPING

Introduction

Caring for a house has never been easier—and harder. Easier because we now have so many products and services at our disposal to help clean, organize, maintain, renovate, and repair a home. Yet understanding and using these products and services takes time that we don't often have. So the job of caring for a home has actually become challenging in new ways.

That's where *The Complete Household Handbook* comes to the rescue. This book is filled with practical, easy-to-understand, easy-to-implement advice on every aspect of maintaining and managing your home. It's filled with time-, money-, and energy-saving advice on everything from cordless vacuums to wallpaper removal. It even includes up-to-the-minute information on how to prevent identity theft and the right ways to childproof your home.

Best of all, the information on these pages comes from the experts at The Good Housekeeping Institute. For more than 100 years, The Good Housekeeping Institute has evaluated household products, offered helpful advice, and championed the rights of consumers. It is also the driving force behind the Good Housekeeping Seal, the trusted icon given to products backed by a limited warranty from The Good Housekeeping Institute.

You will benefit from The Good Housekeeping Institute's expertise on every page. Institute directors in each department—engineering, chemistry, food, food appliances, nutrition, home care, and textiles—have provided guidance on every topic. Whether you're interested in stain removal, pool safety, pressure cookers, or laminate floors, you'll find their firsthand knowledge invaluable.

Throughout the book are vital hints and tips, color-coded by categories for quick reference:

- Safety First (how to be safe with appliances, furniture, and cleaning products)
- Green and Clean (how to protect the environment when using household products and supplies)
- Dollar Stretchers (tips for spending money wisely)
- DIY vs. the Pros (when to do it yourself or call in an expert)
- Time Savers (shortcuts to help you get jobs done faster)
- How to Shop for… (advice on buying specific products)
- Helpful Hints (advice on a variety of other topics)

Detailed illustrations, ranging from the best pots and pans to the anatomy of a door lock, will also help you take charge of your home.

Whether you delve into a section that particularly interests you, or simply flip to a helpful tip in a pinch, you'll find all the advice you need to make your house a happy and comfortable home.

—THE GOOD HOUSEKEEPING INSTITUTE

CLEANING THE RIGHT STUFF BASIC CLEANING EQUIPMENT FURNITURE FLOORS WINDOW
AND DOORS WALLS AND CEILINGS THE KITCHEN THE BATHROOM THE NURSERY AN
CHILDREN'S ROOMS PORCHES, DECKS, AND PATIOS GARAGES AND BASEMENTS LAUNDR
AND CLOTHES CARE LAUNDRY PRODUCTS DOING THE WASH IRONING DRY-CLEANING SEWIN
LEATHER AND FUR JEWELRY CARE PACKING A SUITCASE CLOTHES STORAGE EATING WEL
SMART SHOPPING COOKING KEEPING FOOD FRESH EQUIPMENT TABLEWARE ENTERTAININ
DOING IT YOURSELF PAINTING WALL COVERINGS WINDOW TREATMENTS FLOORS FURNITUR
WALL DECORATIONS THE KITCHEN THE BATHROOM STORAGE STRATEGIES HOME OFFIC
HELP THE HOME WORKSHOP MENDING CHINA AND GLASS RESTORING WOOD FURNITURE WAL
AND CEILING REPAIRS HOW TO HANG ANYTHING DOORS WINDOWS AND SCREENS FLOOR
HEATING SYSTEMS COOLING SYSTEMS WEATHERPROOFING PLUMBING ELECTRICITY ROO
REPAIRS GUTTERS THE YARD MANAGING YOUR MONEY EFFICIENTLY GETTING CREDIT HOW
LONG SHOULD YOU KEEP YOUR FINANCIAL RECORDS FRAUD AND IDENTITY THEFT SAFET
BASICS CHILDPROOFING YOUR HOME SAFETY FOR THE ELDERLY THE SAFE YARD EMERGENCIE
IN THE HOME INDOOR POLLUTANTS HOME SECURITY PREPARING FOR DISASTER CLEANIN
THE RIGHT STUFF BASIC CLEANING EQUIPMENT FURNITURE FLOORS WINDOWS AND DOOR
WALLS AND CEILINGS THE KITCHEN THE BATHROOM THE NURSERY AND CHILDREN'S ROOM
PORCHES, DECKS, AND PATIOS GARAGES AND BASEMENTS LAUNDRY AND CLOTHES CAR
LAUNDRY PRODUCTS DOING THE WASH IRONING DRY-CLEANING SEWING LEATHER AND FU
JEWELRY CARE PACKING A SUITCASE CLOTHES STORAGE EATING WELL SMART SHOPPIN
COOKING KEEPING FOOD FRESH EQUIPMENT TABLEWARE ENTERTAINING DOING IT YOURSEL
PAINTING WALL COVERINGS WINDOW TREATMENTS FLOORS FURNITURE WALL DECORATION
THE KITCHEN THE BATHROOM STORAGE STRATEGIES HOME OFFICE HELP THE HOME WORK
SHOP MENDING CHINA AND GLASS RESTORING WOOD FURNITURE WALL AND CEILING REPAIR
HOW TO HANG ANYTHING DOORS WINDOWS AND SCREENS FLOORS HEATING SYSTEMS COO
ING SYSTEMS WEATHERPROOFING PLUMBING ELECTRICITY ROOF REPAIRS GUTTERS TH
YARD MANAGING YOUR MONEY EFFICIENTLY GETTING CREDIT HOW LONG SHOULD YOU KEE
YOUR FINANCIAL RECORDS? FRAUD AND IDENTITY THEFT SAFETY BASICS CHILDPROOFIN
YOUR HOME SAFETY FOR THE ELDERLY THE SAFE YARD EMERGENCIES IN THE HOME INDOO
POLLUTANTS HOME SECURITY PREPARING FOR DISASTER CLEANING THE RIGHT STUFF BASI
CLEANING EQUIPMENT FURNITURE FLOORS WINDOWS AND DOORS WALLS AND CEILINGS TH
KITCHEN THE BATHROOM THE NURSERY AND CHILDREN'S ROOMS PORCHES, DECKS, AN
PATIOS GARAGES AND BASEMENTS LAUNDRY AND CLOTHES CARE LAUNDRY PRODUCTS DOIN
THE WASH IRONING DRY-CLEANING SEWING LEATHER AND FUR JEWELRY CARE PACKIN
A SUITCASE CLOTHES STORAGE EATING WELL SMART SHOPPING COOKING KEEPIN
FOOD FRESH EQUIPMENT TABLEWARE ENTERTAINING DOING IT YOURSELF PAINTING WAL
COVERINGS WINDOW TREATMENTS FLOORS FURNITURE WALL DECORATIONS THE KITCHE
THE BATHROOM STORAGE STRATEGIES HOME OFFICE EMERGENCIES IN THE HOME INDOO

Good Housekeeping

The
Complete
Household
Handbook

EANING THE RIGHT STUFF BASIC CLEANING EQUIPMENT FURNITURE FLOORS WINDOW
ND DOORS WALLS AND CEILINGS THE KITCHEN THE BATHROOM THE NURSERY AN
ILDREN'S ROOMS PORCHES, DECKS, AND PATIOS GARAGES AND BASEMENTS CLEANIN
E RIGHT STUFF BASIC CLEANING EQUIPMENT FURNITURE FLOORS WINDOWS AND DOOR
ALLS AND CEILINGS THE KITCHEN THE BATHROOM THE NURSERY AND CHILDREN'S ROOM
RCHES, DECKS, AND PATIOS GARAGES AND BASEMENTS CLEANING THE RIGHT STUFF BASI
EANING EQUIPMENT FURNITURE FLOORS WINDOWS AND DOORS WALLS AND CEILINGS TH
TCHEN THE BATHROOM THE NURSERY AND CHILDREN'S ROOMS PORCHES, DECKS, AN
TIOS GARAGES AND BASEMENTS CLEANING THE RIGHT STUFF BASIC CLEANING EQUIP
NT FURNITURE FLOORS WINDOWS AND DOORS WALLS AND CEILINGS THE KITCHEN TH
THROOM THE NURSERY AND CHILDREN'S ROOMS PORCHES, DECKS, AND PATIOS GARAGE
ND BASEMENTS CLEANING THE RIGHT STUFF BASIC CLEANING EQUIPMENT FURNITUR
OORS WINDOWS AND DOORS WALLS AND CEILINGS THE KITCHEN THE BATHROOM TH
RSERY AND CHILDREN'S ROOMS PORCHES, DECKS, AND PATIOS GARAGES AND BASEMENT
EANING THE RIGHT STUFF BASIC CLEANING EQUIPMENT FURNITURE FLOORS WINDOW
ND DOORS WALLS AND CEILINGS THE KITCHEN THE BATHROOM THE NURSERY AND CHIL
EN'S ROOMS PORCHES, DECKS, AND PATIOS GARAGES AND BASEMENTS CLEANING TH
GHT STUFF BASIC CLEANING EQUIPMENT FURNITURE FLOORS WINDOWS AND DOORS WALL
ND CEILINGS THE KITCHEN THE BATHROOM THE NURSERY AND CHILDREN'S ROOMS PORCH
, DECKS, AND PATIOS GARAGES AND BASEMENTS CLEANING THE RIGHT STUFF BASI
EANING EQUIPMENT FURNITURE FLOORS WINDOWS AND DOORS WALLS AND CEILINGS TH
TCHEN THE BATHROOM THE NURSERY AND CHILDREN'S ROOMS PORCHES, DECKS, AN
TIOS GARAGES AND BASEMENTS CLEANING THE RIGHT STUFF BASIC CLEANING EQUIP
NT FURNITURE FLOORS WINDOWS AND DOORS WALLS AND CEILINGS THE KITCHEN TH
THROOM THE NURSERY AND CHILDREN'S ROOMS PORCHES, DECKS, AND PATIOS GARAGE
ND BASEMENTS CLEANING THE RIGHT STUFF BASIC CLEANING EQUIPMENT FURNITUR
OORS WINDOWS AND DOORS WALLS AND CEILINGS THE KITCHEN THE BATHROOM TH
RSERY AND CHILDREN'S ROOMS PORCHES, DECKS, AND PATIOS GARAGES AND BASEMENT
EANING THE RIGHT STUFF BASIC CLEANING EQUIPMENT FURNITURE FLOORS WINDOW
ND DOORS WALLS AND CEILINGS THE KITCHEN THE BATHROOM THE NURSERY AND CHIL
EN'S ROOMS PORCHES, DECKS, AND PATIOS GARAGES AND BASEMENTS CLEANING TH
GHT STUFF BASIC CLEANING EQUIPMENT FURNITURE FLOORS WINDOWS AND DOORS WALL
ND CEILINGS THE KITCHEN THE BATHROOM THE NURSERY AND CHILDREN'S ROOMS PORCH
, DECKS, AND PATIOS GARAGES AND BASEMENTS CLEANING THE RIGHT STUFF BASI
EANING EQUIPMENT FURNITURE FLOORS WINDOWS AND DOORS WALLS AND CEILING
E KITCHEN THE BATHROOM THE NURSERY AND CHILDREN'S ROOMS PORCHES, DECK
D PATIOS GARAGES AND BASEMENTS CLEANING THE RIGHT STUFF BASIC CLEANIN
UIPMENT FURNITURE FLOORS WINDOWS AND DOORS WALLS AND CEILINGS THE KITCH

CHAPTER

1

Cleaning

For better or worse, we all have to clean. And cleaning a house takes a certain know-how: You need to know *what* to clean, *how* to clean, and *which equipment* to use *when* you clean. That's where this chapter comes to the rescue. It shows you exactly what to do at what time with which products and equipment to keep your house sparkling. Whether you want to remove a stain on your new couch or find out the purpose of those strange-looking vacuum attachments, you're sure to get help in these pages. Want to learn the way to remove ink from your carpet? Check out page 43. Don't know the best method for washing your Venetian blinds? You'll find the answer on page 47. Not sure how to clean your oven and all its parts? Try the advice on page 55. Here is all the important cleaning information you need, as well as clever cleaning tips and tricks from The Good Housekeeping Institute—all designed to save you time, money, and energy.

Cleaning

Saving Time

Cleaning house, while necessary for all, is a very personal issue. Some people are bothered by dirty dishes in the sink, while others are content if the dishwasher is loaded once a day. Don't worry about other people's standards. Decide what "clean" means to you, and keep house accordingly. Above all, use your time effectively. Here's how:

Establish priorities: Identify which tasks absolutely have to be done, which ones should be done, and which ones would be nice to get done. Work on them in that order, and forget about all others.

Set time limits: Keep your cleaning schedule flexible so you can change it if something unexpected comes up. You can accomplish quite a bit in several 10- or 20-minute periods. Do *what* you can *when* you can.

Delegate: Teach your kids how to fold laundry, vacuum, dust, unload the dishwasher, make their beds, and prepare their breakfasts, lunches, and snacks. Enlist teens to help with big jobs like washing windows and floors and cleaning cabinets and woodwork.

Take a walk: Make a nightly sweep of the household; it will do wonders for keeping clutter under control. Doing it just before bedtime means a fresh, clean start in the morning.

Finish tasks: Complete one project before you start another.

Bring in outside help: If the budget permits, consider paying someone else to do some of the cleaning. It could be weekly, biweekly, even seasonal. Every little bit helps!

Cutting Out Clutter

You probably spend about half your cleaning time picking things up and putting them away.

Getting rid of clutter will lighten your workload and shorten cleaning time.

- Designate one area or room where the inevitable clutter can accumulate: a place where puzzles can be left out, where the sewing machine can stay open, where model airplanes can wait for completion.
- Place containers where clutter collects: a large toy box in the playroom; a basket for newspapers and magazines in the living room; a portable file box for mail that otherwise may collect on the kitchen counter or hall table.
- Install easily accessible hooks and shelves for hats, coats, schoolbooks, and other everyday items that usually end up on the floor or on a chair.
- Sort through your belongings a few times each year. Sell, donate, or pack away anything you haven't used recently.
- Place a wastebasket in each room.

Dirt Defense

You can keep your house cleaner by preventing outdoor dirt from getting in. Use doormats and boot scrapers outside and walk-off mats inside. As needed, sweep sidewalks, steps, and stairwells leading to your home.

If you have the space, set up a mudroom where wet and soiled clothing and boots can be removed and stored. If you don't have a mudroom, keep a boot tray by the door to hold wet or muddy footwear.

To reduce airborne dust, regularly vacuum registers and radiators (see box, page 20). Change the filters in your air conditioners and furnace, following the manufacturer's instructions. If you have severe allergies, get your heating and ventilation ducts cleaned yearly by a professional. This will help keep dust and other allergens from being blown back into the air.

Keep pop-up, disposable cleaning wipes next to the kitchen and bathroom sinks so that cleaning as you go can become almost automatic.

When to Go Pro

Professional services can handle most cleaning needs, from frequent cleaning of the whole house to seasonal jobs such as carpeting, upholstery, draperies, and windows. Such services can be expensive, but they save time and energy, and may do a more thorough job than you can. Ask your friends for recommendations, and be sure to ask for and check references. Get estimates from at least 2 services before you hire.

Tips for Hiring Professional Help

- **References:** Make sure the company is reliable. Ask for references and a work history. A satisfied friend or neighbor is probably the best reference. Even if no one you know is listed as a reference, call a few names to find out what they have to say about the services that were provided. Did the person or company do a good job? Did the worker(s) show up on time and as scheduled?
- **Insurance:** If a cleaning person slips and falls while cleaning the shower, your homeowner's policy may not cover the incident. Make sure the company is insured.
- **Bonding:** Make sure the company is bonded. Some companies, if they are bonded at all, protect only themselves, not the consumer. Should a theft occur, you need to be protected.
- **Screening and hiring:** Ask if employees' references are checked and if their residence status is confirmed. A professional company will screen each employee for honesty and dependability.
- **Cleaning products and equipment:** Some independent housekeepers and cleaning services expect you to supply all cleaning products and equipment. When you are quoted a price for cleaning services, be sure to ask which supplies are included.
- **Guarantee:** Make sure the service is backed by a written satisfaction guarantee. Know what it covers and how to utilize it if necessary.
- **Taxes:** Check with your accountant to find out what your responsibilities are in terms of social security and other taxes. If you pay a housekeeper or cleaner more than a certain specified amount, the law requires you to pay social security and other taxes on that person. Many housekeeping services withhold taxes for their employees, but check to make sure.

Cleanup Calendar

Most people hate to clean house. In these busy times, it makes sense to be flexible and do only what you need to so that you can maximize and enjoy your leisure time. This timetable suggests tasks that can help you stay on top of the job.

	KITCHEN	BATHROOMS	THROUGHOUT THE HOUSE
DAILY	• Dispose of trash and recyclables • Hand wash and dry dishes or place them in the dishwasher (machine wash them when a full load has accumulated) • Wipe table, countertops and range top • Wash coffeemaker thoroughly after each use • Run food disposal and clean the sink • Sweep or vacuum floor; wipe up any spots with a damp paper towel	• Wipe fixtures, chrome, and countertops • Straighten towels • Use a squeegee or daily shower cleaner to prevent streaks and soap scum buildup	• Put clothing, books, toys, and other items where they belong • Straighten living spaces and bedrooms • Make beds • Go through the mail; handle or recycle, as needed
WEEKLY	• Thoroughly clean range top and front, drip pans, control knobs, and back splash • Wipe down microwave oven, both inside and outside • Organize refrigerator and wipe up spills; dispose of leftover foods that have spoiled • Clean items on countertop; move them away from walls to wipe under and behind them • Sweep or vacuum and wash floor • Wipe table and chairs	• Scrub bathtubs and sinks • Clean mirrors • Clean shower stalls and doors and disinfect toilets • Clean toothbrush and soap holders • Wipe tile surfaces • Vacuum and wash floors	• Dust furniture, books, pictures, lamp bases and shades, and electronics • Vacuum floors and upholstery—and wood work, as needed • Wipe smudges off walls and woodwork • Empty wastepaper baskets • Change bed linens • Clean the mirrors, if needed • Recycle or toss newspapers older than a week and magazines older than 3 months

	KITCHEN	BATHROOMS	THROUGHOUT THE HOUSE
OCCASIONALLY	• Wipe refrigerator sides and top and vacuum coils • Wash refrigerator and freezer shelves and drawers, as needed • Wash ventilating fan/hood filters • Thoroughly clean cabinets and drawers • Dust or vacuum woodwork • Wash curtains, windows, screens, blinds, and shades • Clean light fixtures • Clean the oven	• Wash throw rugs and shower curtains • Wash windows, blinds, shades, or curtains • Clean medicine cabinet and closets; discard medicines that have expired • Clean light fixtures • Dust or vacuum walls and woodwork	• Vacuum or clean curtains, draperies, and radiators • Wash windows • Dust or vacuum walls and woodwork • Clean light fixtures • Move and clean under furniture • Polish furniture • Deep-clean rugs and carpets; clean and wax bare floors, if necessary • Turn mattresses and vacuum mattresses and box springs; launder mattress pads • Straighten closets and give away unneeded items • Clean garage, basement, and attic • Clean humidifiers and dehumidifiers when in use • Clean china cabinets and bookcases and contents, as needed

The Right Stuff

Cleaning is easiest and fastest when your equipment fits your cleaning needs and is easy to store in a closet or storage space. Be sure to keep all your vacuum attachments and small items like dust cloths accessible so you can find them when you need them.

Start with the basics: a vacuum cleaner, broom, and mop. Then add specialty equipment as your needs dictate and budget permits.

Vacuum Cleaners

A good vacuum is essential for household cleaning, so always invest in a high-quality machine with optional attachments—special brushes and crevice tools—for specific jobs.

Use it not only for carpets and floors, but also for draperies and bathroom fixtures, as well as for dusting windowsills, moldings, lamp shades, wall coverings, and furniture.

Basic Vacuums

UPRIGHT VACUUM

Best for: wall-to-wall carpeting and large rugs.

Strong points: agitates and loosens dirt from carpets better than other types; it uses suction and airflow to lift the carpet slightly off the floor and rotating brushes to pick up deep dirt and dust. Most models provide a hose connection and attachment tools for above-the-floor cleaning.

Weak points: doesn't go under low areas; can be awkward and heavy to carry up and down stairs.

CANISTER VACUUM

Best for: homes with many different surfaces and stairs to vacuum.

Strong points: heavy suction; good for bare floors; hose makes it good for reaching tight spots, stairs, and above-the-floor areas. More versatile than upright vacuum.

Weak point: compact models not good for deep-cleaning pile carpets without special power nozzle attachment (see box, page 20).

BUILT-IN CENTRAL SYSTEM

Best for: all surfaces, including wall-to-wall carpeting and wood floors. Available accessories include straight and curved extension pipes, oval and round brushes, and crevice tool.

Strong points: versatile, quick, easy, and clean to use. The system consists of a network of tubes built into the walls, floors, and ceilings with inlets located throughout the house. To use it, you simply plug a long flexible hose into an inlet; dirt is sucked into a receptacle located in the basement, utility room, or garage.

Weak point: requires professional installation.

Features for Easy Vacuuming

Extra features on most uprights and canisters make vacuuming less of a chore:

- Adjustable suction
- Automatic pile-height adjuster
- Bag-change indicator
- Built-in tool storage
- Edge-cleaning feature: removes embedded dirt near baseboards and around furniture

WHAT DOES IT MEAN?

HEPA: **"High Efficiency Particulate Air" filter. HEPA filters attached to vacuum cleaners reduce dust emitted back into the air by trapping 99.97 percent of particles down to 0.3 microns in size, composed largely of dust mites, smoke, and pollen. Air purifiers with HEPA filters also are available as freestanding units that trap airborne allergens such as pollen and animal dander. Many people with allergies have a freestanding air purifier with a HEPA filter in the bedroom, a HEPA filter–equipped vacuum, or both. Filters need to be changed regularly on both freestanding units and vacuums to maintain performance.**

Bagless Vacuum Cleaners: **vacuum cleaners with a clear, removable container where dust and dirt are collected, rather than a disposable bag. On the positive side, there are no bags to purchase; on the negative side, they are not recommended for use by allergy sufferers because of the exposure to dust and allergens when the container is emptied.**

Robotic Vacuum Cleaners: **low, cordless machines that are designed to avoid obstacles and to independently work out the most efficient route around a room it has been set to clean. They are able to clean areas traditional vacuums may miss, like under low furniture and beds. Magnetic strips or special beam emitters must be placed at doorways to act as invisible walls so the cleaner stays in the room you wish it to clean. Better models have technology built in so they automatically stop instead of falling down stairs. They are helpful tools for picking up dust, pet hair, and surface debris, but they can't deep-clean carpets, so you'll still need a full-size vacuum. The best thing about the robots is that while they're cleaning, you can do something else. Be sure to move pets, children, and rugs with fringe out of the way when you use this type of vacuum.**

- Headlight
- Self-propelling feature: maneuvers the cleaner almost effortlessly
- Variable speed control: adjusts levels of suction and the brush speed; lower speed is used for delicate carpets, rugs, and bare floors
- Dirt sensors or lights to signal that an area needs more cleaning
- Automatic cord rewind
- Brush shutoff switch: a safety feature that allows you to turn off the powerful agitator brush when you use the vacuum's attachments

Good Vacuum Maintenance

Like all appliances, vacuum cleaners work best when maintained well. Be sure to follow these simple recommendations:

- Empty the dirt receptacle after every 1 to 2 uses or replace the disposable bag before it is 3/4 full. (Check it; don't rely on the indicator.) If you vacuum fireplace ashes or use powdered carpet fresheners, change the dust bag more often; the powder seals the pores of the bag, which decreases effectiveness.
- If your vacuum cleaner loses pickup power, check to see if the bag is full or the filters in the dirt container are clogged and need to be cleaned. If not, something may be blocking the hose or attachment. Gently use a straightened wire hanger to remove blockages, or, if your vacuum has an exhaust port, attach the hose and blow the blockage into a bag.
- Inspect belts frequently to make certain they are in good shape and working properly. Always keep a spare belt for replacement as needed.
- Use the type of replacement bags that are recommended by the vacuum cleaner manufacturer.
- Keep brushes clean, and replace them when worn.
- Clean or replace filters as often as recommended by the manufacturer.

Vacuum Cleaner Attachments

Upright, canister, utility, and built-in central vacuums all come with optional attachments for special cleaning needs. Most connect to a flexible hose (often 6 to 8 feet long). Rigid wands help you reach places that normally call for a step stool—ceilings, the tops of draperies, cabinets or high shelves, and lighting fixtures. Use the extension wands with any of the attachments. The following are especially useful:

CREVICE TOOL	DUSTING BRUSH	UPHOLSTERY ATTACHMENTS	WALL/FLOOR BRUSH
For vacuuming: • Between radiator coils • Cobwebs • Drawers • Filters, grilles, and air-conditioner fins • Heating and air-conditioning registers • Cracks and crevices • Automobile interiors • Refrigerator and freezer condenser coils • Underneath large appliances • Upholstered furniture crevices • Stair crevices	*For vacuuming:* • Baseboards • Blinds • Books • Carved furniture • Fireplace screens • Stereo speakers • Lamps and lamp shades • Piano keys • Shelves • Shutters • Window and door moldings • Computer keyboards	*For vacuuming:* • Automobile interiors • Carpeted stairs • Curtains and draperies • Hard-to-reach carpeted areas • Mattresses • Upholstered furniture fabric	*For vacuuming:* • Bare floors • Ceilings • Flat, low-pile rugs or carpets that may be damaged by a rotating brush (such as berber) • Walls **POWER NOZZLE** *For vacuuming:* • Pile carpets and rugs (has motor-driven brush for deep cleaning)

Specialty Vacuums

WET/DRY UTILITY VACUUM

Best for: basements, garages, workshops, and heavy-duty cleaning.
Strong points: will pick up items that would damage a standard household vacuum, such as wood shavings, nails, and broken glass; most can be used for wet spills and dry dirt; some have wet- carpet-cleaning attachments.
Weak point: not good for deep vacuuming of carpets.

HANDHELD AND STICK CLEANERS

Best for: quick pickups and light in-between cleanings.
Strong points: easy to store, can be carried up and down stairs, or to the car. Cordless (battery-operated) and corded handheld models are available. Many have tools or attachments (dusting brush, crevice tool, rotating brush) for greater versatility. Corded stick cleaners perform well on both bare floors and low carpets. Cordless models offer greater flexibility since they don't need to be plugged in.
Weak points: dust cups are small, so you have to empty them regularly. Running time on cordless models can be short, and these vacuums are usually less powerful than corded models.

CARPET SWEEPER

Best for: quick pickups of surface dirt in heavy-traffic areas, low-pile carpets, and relatively flat surfaces.
Strong points: lightweight and easy to store.
Weak point: dustbin is small, so it must be emptied regularly.

CARPET CLEANING MACHINES

Best for: removing stains and deep-cleaning soiled carpets.
Strong points: gets out ground-in dirt and soil and removes stains. The most popular type, called hot-water-extraction cleaners, spray a water-and-detergent solution onto the carpet while rotating bristles work the solution into the carpet's fibers. This solution is immediately extracted by the vacuum action of the machine. The process can then be repeated for rinsing. You can rent the equipment or call in a professional service if you prefer not to do it yourself. Small, compact versions are available for spot removal and stains.
Weak points: equipment can be heavy to use and bulky to store; can take a long time for carpet to dry; if used improperly, there is a risk of overwetting the carpet, which can cause shrinkage, streaks, or mildew.

Basic Cleaning Equipment

Although it's probably the most versatile cleaning tool in the house, the vacuum cleaner isn't always the answer. Here are some other basic cleaning products to have on hand.

Brushes

Brushes are made with either natural (animal hair or palm fiber) or synthetic (nylon or less-expensive plastics) bristles.

Natural bristles: stiffer and therefore best for scrubbing concrete, brick, and other hard or rough surfaces. Animal hair is useful for delicate fabrics.

Synthetic bristles: look better longer and dry faster.

Wash brushes in warm, sudsy water to keep the bristles clean. Always dry them with the bristles down.

SCRUB BRUSH
Use this short-bristled brush for general household cleaning.

TOILET BOWL BRUSH
Use this synthetic-bristled brush for cleaning all interior sections of the toilet bowl.

TILE AND GROUT BRUSH
Use this brush to help eliminate stains, soap scum, mold, and mildew that collects in the grout on tiled surfaces.

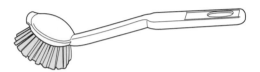

DISH BRUSH
Use this stiff-bristled brush for washing dishes and cooking utensils. Some versions come with interchangeable heads for various uses.

Brooms

Stiff-bristled brooms work best outdoors—on sidewalks, stairs, and patios—while soft-bristled brooms will last longer if used indoors. As they become dirty, rinse brooms under a hard stream of water. Shake the bristles to remove as much water as possible, then hang to dry.

 Helpful Hints

NO-BENDING DUSTPANS
Try a long-handled dustpan to save you from bending over.

WHAT TO DO WITH A WET MOP
Never put away a damp sponge mop; it can mildew and develop an unpleasant odor. Stand it upside down to dry, then hang to store.

Natural bristles (such as palm): considered best—they last longer, but are also more expensive than brooms made from the traditional corn straw.

Synthetic bristles: are often flared to pick up more dirt and are angled to reach into corners.

GENERAL-PURPOSE BROOM

Use this for general cleaning; for sweeping large areas of floor, a large broom (10 inches wide by 14 inches high) is recommended.

Clean and Safe

When not used or stored properly, ammonia, bleach, cleansers, detergents, drain cleaners, furniture polish, oven cleaners, and other common household cleaners can cause skin irritations and respiratory ailments. To avoid problems:

- Read labels carefully. They include information on how to use the product correctly. Failure to follow these instructions may be dangerous.
- Use chemically based products sparingly; a small amount will often be enough to do the job.
- Don't mix household products; some create noxious fumes when combined.
- Keep products in their original containers. Be sure caps are securely closed when the product is not being used.
- Store cleaning products in a closet or cabinet, away from food products and not accessible to young children or pets.

Safety information on household cleaning products is an important part of the label. Pay particular attention if any of the following words are used: Caution, Warning, Danger, Poison.

The words "Caution" and "Warning" are used interchangeably. They mean that improper exposure to the product is not likely to produce permanent damage, but may cause temporary difficulties such as eye or skin irritation upon contact. Adverse effects such as dizziness or stomach upset might occur if the product is swallowed. Many laundry and automatic dishwashing detergents, disinfectants, and all-purpose cleaners fall into this category.

"Danger" means that greater precautions should be taken. Accidental exposure to the undiluted product could produce permanent tissue damage. Swallowing the undiluted product could cause damage to the mouth, throat, and stomach. Some products marked "Danger" may ignite if exposed to an open flame, heat, or spark. This type of warning usually appears on specialty products intended for tough jobs, such as oven cleaners and drain cleaners.

"Poison" is the strongest indication of hazard. If improper exposure occurs, immediate and proper treatment is essential. For everyone's safety, program all phones (including cell phones) with the number for the Poison Control Center (1-800-222-1222), and post the number prominently next to every phone.

WHISK BROOM
Use this small handheld broom to remove lint and debris from clothes or upholstery. Use a second one for small amounts of dirt around plants, floors, and countertops.

PUSH BROOM
Use this square-back broom for sweeping the garage and basement floors, driveway, patio, and porch.

Mops

Wet Mops
These mops, used for washing floors, should have a wringing device to keep your hands dry and readily available replacement heads that are easy to change.

String or strip mop: more maneuverable than sponge mops; good for tight corners and behind sinks and toilets.

Rinse and thoroughly wring the mop and hang it by its handle to dry.

Sponge mop: works well on large expanses of floor, as in a kitchen. Look for "scrubber

Allergic Reactions

Many allergy sufferers are sensitive to dust mites, which live in carpets, bedding, and upholstered furniture (even clean homes have them). These microscopic creatures feed on human skin flakes that are shed every day. Mites also require moisture to survive. To lower the relative humidity in your house, use a dehumidifier (see box, right), and be sure that your clothes dryer is vented outdoors. Here are other steps to take to keep mites to a minimum:

- Dust and vacuum radiators, registers, vents, upholstered furniture, cushions, pillows, and carpets at least twice weekly if you're prone to allergies.
- Wash bedding frequently. That means washing sheets and pillows weekly; blankets, comforters, and mattress pads at least monthly.
- Consider allergen-impermeable covers if frequent laundering of pillows and comforters is burdensome. Because they're lighter and less bulky, they are more easily laundered. If pillows are not washable, put them in the dryer on the no-heat air-only cycle to eliminate the dust.
- Turn and vacuum your mattresses every 2 months.

- For bedtime buddies, choose only stuffed animals that can be laundered regularly. All others should reside in a play area in another room. For children with asthma, keep the bed free of stuffed animals.
- Replace wall-to-wall carpeting with washable throw rugs and flooring that can be wet-mopped.
- Avoid using vacuums with bagless dust receptacles. Discard disposable vacuum cleaner bags when they are half full so the suction power of the vacuum is always at its strongest for best dust pickup.
- Check to determine whether your furnace has filters and whether they need to be changed; they should be changed at least every 2 months to eliminate dust.

strips" on the sponge mop head to help remove tough stains.

Rinse and wring the mop and turn it upside down to dry.

Disposable wet-mop systems: all-in-one mopping units that have moist, disposable cloths that contain a cleaning solution, or a cleaning solution that gets sprayed directly on the floor and gets picked up, with dirt, by an absorbent pad.

When the cloth or pad gets dirty, throw it away and replace with a new one.

Dry Mops

These mops are made of synthetic or wool fibers. Both work well. Use a dry mop to dust bare floors when you don't want to use the vacuum cleaner. Spray with a dusting spray to avoid spreading dirt.

Vigorously shake the mop outdoors after each use. Remove the head and wash it with dish-washing detergent and water. Rinse thoroughly, squeeze, then air-dry before reattaching.

Wet/Dry Mop

Microfiber mop: use for kitchen floors, tile floors, and hardwood floors. Use it wet (with water only) for removing dirt and soil; use it dry for dusting.

Some versions come with a wet mop pad and a dry mop pad. The wet mop version is made from longer, coarser microfibers so it holds the water better.

Remove pad and rinse or wash to clean.

Humidifiers and Dehumidifiers

Humidifiers add moisture to the air. By doing this, they generally alleviate many of the common nuisances that are the result of winter heating: static electricity, cracks in paint and furniture, the physical discomforts of dry nose, throat, lips, and skin.

However, when you introduce excess moisture, you may also encourage the growth of biological organisms, including dust mites and mold. To prevent this, during use monitor the moisture level of the house and clean the humidifier regularly. Follow the manufacturer's recommendations to determine proper humidity and for cleaning products and disinfectants. Portable humidifiers that are in constant use should be cleaned every third day. Rinse the tank thoroughly to remove any traces of the cleaning agent before refilling the tank with water.

Central (furnace-mounted) humidifiers should be cleaned every year to remove scale, rust, and hard water marks. Follow the manufacturer's recommendations for cleaning and maintenance.

Dehumidifiers remove excess moisture from the air. They are generally used in damp basements or other areas where humidity is high and mold may be a problem. For regular cleaning, dust the grilles or louvers with a soft brush or the dusting attachment of a vacuum cleaner. Dust the cabinet or wipe it with a damp cloth. Every few weeks, scrub inside the water container with a sponge or soft cloth and a mild detergent to discourage the growth of mold, mildew, or bacteria. If the unit has a removable air filter, wash the filter with warm water and mild detergent once a month. Rinse and dry it and replace it in the unit. At least once each season, remove dust and lint from the cold coils with a soft brush.

Cleaning Product Roundup

All household cleaning products come with detailed directions on the label; read and follow them and use the products only for recommended surfaces. You should take note of any warnings on the label.

PRODUCT	GOOD FOR	HOW TO USE
Abrasive cleansers (powder)	Baked-on food residue, cooking utensils, tough stains on sinks and tubs	Wet surface and apply cleanser; rub/scour gently as needed and rinse
(liquid)	Ceramic bathtubs, sinks, toilet bowls, smooth-top ranges, tile	Apply to surface; rub gently and rinse
Air, fabric, carpet, and room fresheners, deodorizers, and odor eliminators (aerosol, spray, powder, solid, heat-dispersed)	Counteracting odors in carpets, rooms, rugs, and upholstery	Sprinkle powdered carpet freshener on and leave for 10 to 15 minutes, then vacuum; for other forms, follow package directions
All-purpose (nonabrasive) cleaners (powder, liquid)	Appliance surfaces, glass ceramic and porcelain enamel range tops/cooktops; chrome; countertops; painted walls; painted and stainless steel; small plastic appliances; resilient and masonry floors; tile; window blinds/washable shades; painted woodwork	Mix with water or use liquids full-strength according to package directions; generally no rinsing required, except for no-wax floors or when used full-strength
(spray)	Appliances (spot-cleaning and trim); chrome fixtures; countertops; small washable areas; smudges on painted walls and woodwork, doors, and around switch plates	Spray on surface; sponge or wipe to clean; dry with towel or cloth, if needed
(gel)	Appliances (spot-cleaning and trim), chrome fixtures, countertops, ceramic tile, enamel, sinks	Wet surface and apply cleanser; rub gently and rinse

PRODUCT	GOOD FOR	HOW TO USE
Ammonia*	Chrome fixtures, combs and brushes, floors (resilient, ceramic, concrete), mirrors, painted walls, stainless steel, windows, painted wood-work. Do not use to clean clear plastic windows or sur-faces and on aluminum; clouding and pitting can occur. Do not use on brass fixtures; pitting can occur	You can control the cleaning strength by increasing the ammonia from 1/2 cup to 1 cup per gallon of water as the job difficulty increases. For spray bottle use: Mix 1 part ammonia to 16 parts water. For windows and mirrors: Use 2 tablespoons ammonia per 1 quart water
Baking soda	Baked-on food and odors in utensils, chopping boards, coffeepots, food waste dis-posers, freezers, refrigerators; stains on plastic utensils and dishes, vacuum bottles; bath-tubs and sinks, countertops, chrome fixtures, fiberglass shower stalls, plastic laminate	Paste: Mix 3 parts baking soda to 1 part water Solution: Mix 4 tablespoons baking soda per 1 quart water Dry: Sprinkle straight from box. Rub with damp sponge or cloth; rinse and dry
Carpet cleaners (liquid, foam, powder)	Rugs and carpets (spots and general cleaning)	Follow package directions: Some can be applied by hand; others require equipment
Chlorine bleach*	Disinfecting cutting boards, mildew on grout and ceramic tile, patio bricks, stains on hard surfaces, toilet bowls, wooden decks (see page 64)	Mix 3/4 cup bleach to 1 gallon water; increase strength as needed
Dishwashing products (automatic dishwasher detergents)	Removing food soil from tableware and cooking and serving items in the dish-washer	Follow package directions; also available in premeasured powder and gel capsules

(continued on next page)

*Do not mix chlorine bleach with vinegar, ammonia, or a toilet bowl cleaner. Resulting toxic fumes may cause illness.

(continued from previous page)

PRODUCT	GOOD FOR	HOW TO USE
Dishwashing products (hand dishwashing liquid)	Items that are handwashed or that would be damaged in the dishwasher, such as decorated glasses, hand-painted or antique china, milk glass, pewter, nonstick cookware, wood items	Use with sponge, dishcloth, or dish brush; rinse items in warm water to remove soap film
(rinsing agents for automatic dishwashers)	Helping prevent spotting and filming	Available as a separate product or integrated into dishwasher detergent
Drain cleaners (liquid, granular)	Dissolving grease, hair, soap-scum buildup; sluggish kitchen and bathroom drains.	Follow package directions precisely
Dusting products (aerosol and pump, liquid, paste)	Furniture	Spray the product evenly on a cloth, then apply to the surface; let dry; if required, then buff with a clean cloth
Fabric refreshers	Neutralizing odors on hard-to-wash fabrics and soft surfaces such as carpets (after vacuuming), upholstery, and curtains	Apply product according to package directions and let dry
Glass cleaners (liquid, spray)	Chrome, mirrors, glass table-tops, doors, windows. Do not use on acrylic plastic doors, windows, clock face protectors, computer monitor screens	Spray directly on windows or on cloth or sponge for mirror or picture glass; wipe and dry
Mildew removers	Ceramic tile grout in showers, bathrooms (see box, page 62)	Follow package directions; use in well-ventilated areas; avoid contact with fabrics

PRODUCT	GOOD FOR	HOW TO USE
Oven cleaners (liquid, spray)	Removing charred grease and food deposits from ovens and barbecue grills	Follow package directions
Scouring pads (plain or soap impregnated)	Baked-on food, barbecue grills, broilers, cooking utensils, ovens	Wet and use; match abrasiveness of pad to surface being cleaned for safety and to avoid scratching
Toilet bowl cleaners (crystal, liquid, premeasured drop-in tablets, in-tank)*	Cleaning; some also disinfect	Follow package directions
Tub, tile, and sink cleaners (liquid, spray)	Ceramic wall tiles; fiberglass, plastic, and porcelain bathtubs, shower stalls, and sinks; toilet bowl exteriors	Apply to surface, rub gently, rinse thoroughly, and wipe dry with cloth
Upholstery cleaners (liquid, aerosol spray, powder)	Upholstery fabric	Follow package directions; test in an inconspicuous place on fabric for colorfastness
Vinegar (white)*	Automatic drip coffeemakers, appliance exteriors, chrome, glass windows and doors, mirrors, hard water deposits on bathtubs, shower stalls/curtains, sinks	Use full-strength or diluted depending on use. To clean automatic drip coffeepots, fill reservoir with vinegar and water and run through a brew cycle; follow with a cycle of clear water to rinse

*Do not mix chlorine bleach with vinegar, ammonia, or a toilet bowl cleaner. Resulting toxic fumes may cause illness.

Dusters

Dusting Cloths and Mitts

Use only clean cloths to dust. Wash or dispose of them as soon as they begin to look dirty.

Treated cloths and mitts: recommended for easiest cleaning. Chemically pretreated cloths attract dust and dirt without leaving a film on furniture.

Wash treated cloths as needed; the treatment remains on the cloth through many launderings. Never dry cloths that have been treated with wax or polish in an automatic dryer.

Microfiber cloths and mitts: fabric made from ultrafine fibers with wedge-shaped filaments attracts and holds the dirt without any chemical treatment. Can be used dry or damp on a variety of surfaces, including glass, wood furniture, and electronic equipment. When the cloth gets dirty, wash with warm, soapy water and rinse well.

Untreated cloths: use lintless cloths—cheesecloth, diapers, undershirts, or cotton flannel. Be sure to remove snaps, hooks, and buttons, which can scratch. Treat the cloth with a dusting spray. (A dry dust cloth merely spreads dust and scratches surfaces.) Wash in washing machine with detergent and hot water.

Disposable cloths and mitts: dry, disposable, chemical-free dusters that use electrostatic action to attract dust and dirt without leaving any residue.

Dusting Wands

These fluffy dusters, which resemble cotton candy on a stick, conform to the shape of the object

Time Savers

WIPE IT AWAY!

For quick cleanups, there's a cleaning wipe for almost every need.

➤ Disinfecting and scrubbing wipes for countertops, sinks, toilets, light switch covers, door handles, and other commonly touched hard surfaces where germs accumulate.

➤ Flushable bathroom wipes for cleaning toilet rims, tanks, faucets, sinks, etc. They disperse in water when agitated, just like toilet paper does, so they won't harm plumbing or septic tanks.

➤ Wipes with hand dishwashing liquid that lather up once water is added.

➤ Wipes premoistened with special cleaning solutions for cleaning and shining furniture.

➤ Dry, electrostatic disposable wipes that attract dust and soil without leaving any residue.

being cleaned. Long, telescoping versions are available for high, hard-to-reach spaces. Dust remains until duster is shaken. Shake to clean. Hand wash by swishing in a solution of dishwashing liquid and water. Rinse well, squeeze, and air-dry.

Lambswool duster: uses the natural properties of wool to attract and hold dust. Shake to clean.

Electrostatic duster: fiber "fingers" trap and hold dirt and dust. Shake to clean.

Furniture

All furniture needs frequent basic cleaning to keep it looking attractive. Treat your furniture kindly. Dust and polish wood often, vacuum upholstery before dirt weakens fabric fibers, and treat spots before they stain.

Upholstery

Many fabrics have protective finishes that resist soil and stains. Some repel water, others repel oil and water. But no fabric, treated or untreated, is soil- and stain-proof.

- Vacuum regularly with the upholstery tool to extract dust and gritty dirt from smooth fabrics.
- Use the dusting tool for napped fabrics (velvet, velour, corduroy, and plush). To thoroughly clean, remove the cushions, and vacuum the base, back, arms, and sides.

Cleaning Codes

The furniture industry has developed codes for cleaning upholstery fabrics. You will find the code on the piece of furniture and on sample fabric swatches.

W Clean the fabric with a water-based product such as foam from a mild detergent or nonsolvent upholstery shampoo.

S Clean the fabric with a solvent-based cleaner.

WS Clean the fabric with a nonsolvent or solvent-based cleaning product.

X Have the fabric professionally cleaned.

 Helpful Hints

CUSHION CARE

To help upholstered furniture wear evenly, flip and turn the cushions every few weeks. Swap the far right sofa cushion with the far left cushion; switch 2 matching chair cushions.

- Use a crevice tool in corners, areas between cushions that aren't removable, and along welted seams and in tufted surfaces.

Spots and Stains

Before cleaning upholstery, always spot test by cleaning a hidden area first. If you can, also check the cleaning code (see box at left).

- Blot up spills with absorbent towels, a cloth, or a sponge.
- Scrape up solids with a spoon or lift them off with a dull knife.
- Treat any remaining grease-based stains with a dry-cleaning fluid. Never allow dry-cleaning fluid to penetrate into furniture padded with foam rubber; it will damage it.
- For other soils, use a foam or spray upholstery cleaner. Follow the directions exactly, and test the cleaner in an inconspicuous place on the fabric for colorfastness before beginning.

Do-It-Yourself Cleaning

Vacuuming is the best cleaning method for upholstery, but there are occasions when the fabric will begin to appear soiled and you will need a further cleaning. If you use a do-it-yourself cleaner, be gentle and use as little as possible. Vacuum first to remove surface dirt and soil.

Wood Furniture Polish Roundup

Make your polish selection based on the amount of gloss you want on your furniture, the amount of protection your furniture needs, and the amount of time the method requires. Wax provides the most protection; dusting sprays the least.

PRODUCT	GLOSS	PROTECTION	COMMENTS
Paste waxes	Medium-low	Superior	Time-consuming to apply; long drying time. Buffing needed. Must remove after 2 to 3 applications.
Liquids (waxes)	High	Very good	Easier to apply than pastes. Most require some drying time and light rubbing.
(oils—for use on unsealed wood)	High	Good	Oils can smear and fingerprint if not completely dry. Waxes and oils should not be interchanged since they can build up and attract soil.
(creams)	Medium-high	Good	Same as oils.
(trigger spray—for use on sealed wood)	Medium-high	Good	Usually contains lemon or orange oil to clean and revitalize surface. Buff well to avoid smearing.
Aerosols (waxes)	Medium-high	Very good	Contain silicone for easy application and good shine. They also contain solvent to clean soil and remove previous coats of wax.

PRODUCT	GLOSS	PROTECTION	COMMENTS
Aerosols (oils)	Low-medium	Good	As with liquids, aerosol waxes and oils should not be used interchangeably.
Wipes	Medium-high	Good	Premoistened and disposable for quick cleanups.
Dusting cloths	None-low	Good	Some are embedded with dusting product, some with polishing agent.
Dusting sprays	None-low	None	Help in removing dust without leaving anything on surface. Good for frequent dusting. Reduce abrasive effects of dry-dusting.

There are various types of upholstery cleaners from which to choose: foam, liquid or spray, powdered, and dry-cleaning fluid, which has a solvent base. Different fabrics require different treatments. Select the appropriate type for your furniture and follow the package directions very carefully. Always test the cleaner in a hidden area before doing the entire piece.

Wood

Dust and grit may scratch the finish on wood furniture if it accumulates. Dust from once to several times each week, depending on your standards and the amount of dust in your home. Use the soft, round brush attachment on the vacuum cleaner for flat surfaces, chair rungs,

 Green and Clean

NUTTY SOLUTION

To camouflage a wood scratch, break the meat of a Brazil nut, black walnut, or pecan in half and rub it in.

table and chair legs. For light dusting, use cloths treated with a dust-attracting agent or a soft clean cloth and a dusting spray.

Never dry-dust. Not only do dry cloths scatter dust, but they also can scratch the surface, which will eventually dull the finish.

Start dusting at the top of each item, working down to the bottom. Remember to wipe the edges and fronts of drawers, doors, and cabinets. Follow the grain of the wood, gathering the dust into the cloth to avoid scattering it. Turn the cloth often to keep dusting with a clean section.

Polishing and Waxing

Creams, polishes, and wax not only protect and clean wood furniture, but they also enhance the wood's natural look.

Choosing the right furniture-care product, however, depends upon the wood finish (shellac, varnish, lacquer, oil, and plastic laminates) and the amount of shine you want. Read the label. Once you have found the right product, stick to it. Using more than one—especially mixing wax and oil—may damage the finish.

Before using a product for the first time, try

it out on an inconspicuous spot to make sure it won't damage the finish. Use it sparingly and apply it to a clean, dry cloth; never put it directly on your furniture.

Be sure to buff the surface dry with another clean cloth; otherwise, the finish may streak and look smeary. Always rub with the grain of the wood until all of the product is absorbed and the desired luster is achieved.

Other Materials

Acrylic (Lucite and Acrylic Plastic) and Glass

Dust the surface with a clean, damp cloth or chamois, wiping gently. The damp cloth cuts down on friction, helping reduce static electricity, which attracts and holds dust. Wash with a mild detergent and water solution for acrylic or with an ammonia and water solution or glass cleaner for glass.

Use a soft cloth or a clean sponge; acrylic scratches easily. Rinse with a clean, damp cloth and dry with a clean, soft cloth.

Chrome, Stainless Steel, and Wrought Iron

Dust with a clean, soft cloth or the dusting tool on your vacuum. Clean with a cloth soaked in a mild detergent and water solution, baking soda and water (4 tablespoons baking soda in 1 quart of water), or an all-purpose cleaner solution; rinse and dry with a clean, soft cloth.

For added protection to wrought iron, apply a thin coat of paste or liquid wax with a clean cloth.

Leather

Dust with a clean, soft cloth. Use a soft bristled toothbrush or paintbrush if the leather is tufted and has buttons or piping. Wipe with a clean, damp sponge or cloth and mild soap. Rinse with a well-wrung sponge or cloth. Dry with a clean, soft cloth.

Clean and polish sealed-leather tabletops with paste wax once or twice a year or when you do the surrounding wood.

Furniture Elixirs

In addition to the common household products you probably already have, keep the following supplies (available in hardware, paint, or home improvement stores) on hand for repairing scratches on wood furniture.

Rottenstone is a fine, abrasive limestone powder used to create a hand-rubbed finish. It can also be used to remove minor scratches and blemishes.

Pumice, a harder abrasive than rottenstone, is used for deeper, more severe scratches—it may also leave a dull spot, in which case, a paste of rottenstone and boiled linseed oil is recommended.

Boiled linseed oil, a yellowish drying oil, provides color to cover minor scratches.

Marble

Marble is not as durable as it appears. It is very porous and stains quite easily. Dust with a clean, soft cloth. Damp-dust occasionally with a clean sponge or cloth dampened in warm water. Dry the surface with a clean, soft cloth. Wipe up spills immediately.

Clean and restore marble with a marble polish, available in hardware and furniture stores. You can also apply a thin coat of paste wax and polish while the wax is moist, but be aware that paste wax will cause white marble to yellow. Greasy stains may be removed by washing with ammonia; rinse thoroughly and dry.

Vinyl and Plastic

Use a sponge dampened in a detergent and water solution to dust and clean vinyl and plastic; rinse and wipe dry with a clean cloth.

Wicker, Rattan, Bamboo, and Cane

Vacuum, using a brush to loosen dust and dirt. Sponge rattan, bamboo, and cane with a solution of water and hand dishwashing detergent; for wicker, wash gently with a soft-bristled paintbrush or toothbrush. Rinse with a clean, damp sponge, and dry the surface immediately. A light coat of furniture polish will renew natural or dark wicker, rattan, and cane. Avoid using it on white or pastel colors.

Lamps and Lamp Shades

Dust the base of the lamp, the bulb, and the shade with a soft cloth or the dusting tool on your vacuum cleaner.

Clean the base with a damp sponge or cloth and the cleaning product appropriate for the material (see pages 26–29). Do not immerse the base in water since this damages the wiring.

Washable Shades (Sewn Trim)

Fill a deep tub or bathtub with enough warm water to cover the shade. Add a mild, all-purpose liquid detergent. Dip the shade up and down in the sudsy water.

When the water gets dirty, change it. To rinse, repeat the process with clean water.

To dry, tie a string to the middle of the frame, then hang the shade over the bathtub or a clothesline (not in the sun) to drip-dry. Or put the shade in front of a fan to speed dry. To keep the metal frame from rusting, wipe it with a dry cloth and dry the shade as quickly as possible.

Fast Furniture Fix-Ups

Here are common problems with wood surfaces, along with the solutions. (For wood-polishing materials, see pages 32–33). All repair work should be done carefully, following the grain of the wood, and be finished with a coat of wax.

Alcohol stains: Alcohol has a tendency to dissolve most finishes, so blot the spot immediately, then put a few drops of ammonia on a damp cloth and wipe the area. If the spot still remains, make a thin paste of boiled linseed oil and rottenstone, and rub it into the stain with your finger. Wax or polish.

Bloom or fog (whitening): This condition is often noticeable on wooden chair arms, backs or seats, around handles on wooden cabinets, or on bed headboards when the humidity is high. To clean the area, mix 1 tablespoon of cider vinegar with 1 quart of water. Moisten a clean cloth with this solution and squeeze it dry. Gently rub the finish, and wipe dry. Rewax.

Candle wax: To harden the wax, rub an ice cube wrapped in plastic over the spill, then scrape the hardened wax off with a nonstick spatula or an expired plastic credit card.

Cigarette burn: For a burn that hasn't penetrated the wood finish, make a thin paste of pumice and boiled linseed oil, and apply it to the burned area. Wax or polish, working with the grain of the wood. If the burn is very deep and the damage too severe, professional refinishing may be necessary.

Heat mark: Blot the heat mark with a cloth dampened with boiled linseed oil and rub dry with a clean cloth. If the heat mark still remains, rub gently with fine steel wool dipped in a paste wax. Wipe off excess. Repolish.

Ink stain: Make a thin paste of rottenstone and boiled linseed oil. Apply it to the

---

Plastic, Plastic-Coated, Laminated, or Parchment Shades (Glued Trim)
Wipe the shade with a damp cloth or dampened paintbrush, and dry with a clean cloth. If the lamp has a reflector bowl, remove and wash it, using a warm water and detergent solution. You can also try a dough- or a sponge-type dry cleaner designed for use on wallpaper.

Mirrors and Picture Glass

Use a commercial window cleaner, a solution of 1 tablespoon of ammonia per quart of water, or a solution of equal parts of vinegar and water.

Dip a sponge, paper towel, or cloth in the cleaner. Never spray it directly on the mirror or picture glass; the solution may damage the picture or the mirror backing.

Wipe dry with a lint-free cloth, chamois, or paper towel.

Electronic Equipment

If possible, unplug electronic equipment before cleaning. Avoid household cleaners containing bleach since chlorine can damage the components.

Televisions
When the screen is cool, wipe it with a damp paper towel or microfiber cloth; towel dry. Dust and polish a wood cabinet as with other wood furniture (see pages 32–34). If the cabinet is plas-

stain with your finger and rub with the grain of the wood. Wax or polish.

Milk: Wipe up spilled milk or food containing milk or cream with a damp cloth and wipe dry immediately. If further attention is needed, follow the suggestions given for removing alcohol.

Nail polish: If the spilled polish is still wet, blot clean and wipe any remaining residue with mineral spirits. Avoid nail polish remover—it contains solvents that can soften and dissolve the furniture finish. Soak the stain for no longer than 5 minutes with boiled linseed oil, then scrape off the residue with a nonstick spatula or an expired plastic credit card. Repeat the process as needed.

Paint: Wipe fresh water-based paint with a cloth dampened with warm water. Scrape old water-based paint spots with a nonstick spatula or an expired plastic credit card. Remove any remaining paint using a thin paste of boiled linseed oil and rottenstone. For old oil-based paint stains, cover the spots with linseed oil, soak for 5 minutes, then gently scrape with a nonstick spatula. Then wet another cloth with linseed oil and wipe over the area. Repeat, if necessary, or use the rottenstone and oil treatment.

Scratch: First try rubbing the scratch using a thick paste of boiled linseed oil with either pumice or rottenstone, depending on the depth of the scratch. If the scratch is still noticeable, apply a paste wax and rub lightly with extrafine abrasive pad (see box, page 273) in the direction of the grain. For deeper scratches, wax touch-up sticks or furniture markers may be necessary. These are available in a selection of wood colors in paint or hardware stores.

Water mark: Wipe the water spot immediately, and rub a thin paste of boiled linseed oil and rottenstone over the spill. If this does not completely remove it, place a clean, thick blotter over the spot and press with a warm (not hot) iron; repeat this process until the mark disappears.

tic, wash it periodically with a mild detergent and water solution; rinse with a damp cloth and dry.

Clean metal or chrome trim and plastic or glass trim or doors with a soft cloth moistened with rubbing alcohol, white vinegar, or window cleaner; dry with a paper towel.

VCRs
Clean the exterior of a VCR with a soft, dry, electrostatic dusting cloth. VCR player heads need intermittent cleaning. Refer to the owner's manual for the proper method.

DVD Players
Clean the outside of the DVD player as you would a VCR, with a soft, dry cloth. Never use alcohol or solvents to clean it.

Stereo Equipment
Vacuum the ventilation louvers of your stereo components, tape deck, or CD player and speaker grilles every now and then to prevent dust buildup, which can cause overheating.

Cassette heads need to be cleaned occasionally with tapes made specifically for that. But otherwise, cassettes and compact discs are rarely exposed to dirt, so they need little cleaning.

Computers
Never use household glass cleaners on computer monitor screens. Instead, use a static-free product made for cleaning monitor screens or the same method used for TV screens. Keep static-free covers on the computer and printer when they are not in use.

Use the crevice tool on your vacuum to remove the tiny paper particles from the paper opening on the printer and to remove dust and dirt from the crevices in the keyboard. On most keyboards, you can use a cotton swab dipped in alcohol or in a window-cleaning solution to clean between the keys. Special minivacs are available from computer stores to remove dust from these hard-to-clean areas.

Telephones

Wipe the handset and base or cradle of the telephone with a damp cloth and an all-purpose household cleaner. Wring the cloth out well to prevent water from getting into the unit. If you have an old-fashioned telephone, unscrew the ear and mouth caps (if they are removable) and

Helpful Hints

SCREEN CLEAN

Never use a liquid cleaner or an aerosol product to clean the television screen. Instead, use a paper towel or soft cloth dampened with water.

wash in a detergent and water solution. Dry them thoroughly before replacing. Use a moist cotton swab to clean under the dial or between push buttons.

Wipe the mouthpiece with a cloth sprayed with an aerosol disinfectant, wrung out in liquid disinfectant solution, or dampened with alcohol.

Floors

Of all the surfaces in your home, floors probably take the hardest beating. If floors are not kept clean, dirt underfoot can mar the surface or damage carpet fibers. Dirt doesn't stick to a clean surface as readily as it does to one that is soiled or rough from wear.

Wipe up spills as soon as they occur to prevent tracking and stains. Sweep, dust, or vacuum dry soil as often as needed and before mopping, waxing, and polishing.

A variety of products are available to make floor care easier and more effective. Floors can be damaged by using the wrong cleaner, cleaning method, wax, or finish, so choose carefully and read the label.

Wood

Vacuuming and dust-mopping on a regular basis are the best care you can provide for your wood floor. Vacuuming is especially good because it lifts dirt from seams between floorboards. Other general care tips are:

- Never pour water on a wood floor because it can cause warping and stains.
- Wipe up spills as soon as they occur.
- Place glides or floor protectors under furniture legs to prevent scratches.
- Use rugs in heavy-traffic areas to protect the floor.
- Keep high heels in good repair. Worn heels can destroy a wood floor.
- Use mats and throw rugs at doorways and clean them often to prevent dirt from being tracked on the floor.

Caring for the Finish

The first step in caring for a wood floor is to know how it has been finished or sealed. To find out, try smudging the surface in a hidden area with your finger.

If there is no smudge, the floor has been treated with a "surface finish" such as polyurethane.

If you see a smudge, the floor has been treated with a penetrating wax.

Surface Finish

Most new wood floors installed today have a surface finish. **Never wax a surface finish.**

Never wet-mop a wood floor. Standing water can dull the finish, damage the wood, and leave a discoloring residue. For general cleaning, mist a small area of the floor with a solution of 1/4 cup of white vinegar to 1 quart of warm water, drying with a clean cloth as you go. It is preferable, however, to use the cleaning solution (a neutral pH cleaner) recommended by the manufacturer. Avoid oil soaps or any products that may leave a residue; they can build up and create problems when

 Helpful Hints

IS NO-WAX NO-CARE?

No-wax resilient floors require regular washing with all-purpose cleaners and rinsing to protect their finish. If you use specially formulated products to clean and shine them, and the floor has a dull appearance, it may need to be stripped (see box, page 40). If necessary, use a polish to fill in scratches, and add a protective shine.

CLEAN RINSES

Keep a sponge mop just for rinsing floors; it is almost impossible to get all the cleaning solution out of a mop.

it's time to put a maintenance coat on the floor. In addition, using an oil soap cleaner may void the floor manufacturer's warranty.

The Great Stain Rubout for Waxed Wood Floors

Always work on a stain on a waxed floor from the outer edge to the center, working with the grain, to prevent it from spreading. Be gentle. Repeat, if necessary. Never use the following methods on a floor coated with polyurethane or another surface treatment. Most spills wipe easily off these floors.

Alcohol: Rub the spot with a solvent-based wax, silver polish, boiled linseed oil, or a cloth slightly dampened in ammonia. Rewax.

Chewing gum, candle wax, and crayon: Apply ice until the material is hard and crumbles off. If the deposit remains, pour a solvent-based wax around the area (not on it) to soak under the deposit and loosen it.

Cigarette burn: Rub the burn with an extrafine abrasive pad (see box, page 273) dipped in a solvent-based wax.

Food and dried milk: Gently rub the stain with a slightly damp cloth; rub dry and rewax.

Heel and furniture caster marks: Rub the mark with an extrafine abrasive pad (see box, page 273) dipped in a solvent-based wax; buff to a shine.

Oil and grease: Saturate a cotton cloth with hydrogen peroxide and place over stain. Saturate a second layer of cotton with ammonia and place over the first. Check after a few minutes. Repeat the treatment until the stain is removed.

Water mark: Rub the spot with an extrafine abrasive pad (see box, page 273) and rewax.

If the finish is dull, buff with a clean cloth to restore the luster. If this doesn't work, it may be time for a recoating.

Penetrating Wax

Penetrating wax soaks into the wood pores and hardens to seal the wood against dirt and stains and will not chip or scratch.

If your floor has been waxed and appears dull, try buffing a small area by hand with a clean cloth to see if you can restore the luster.

If this doesn't work, apply a solvent-based wax (available in paste, liquid, or liquid buffing/wax cleaner combination) specifically for wood floors. Such waxes, which have the odor of mineral spirits, should not have water listed as an ingredient.

Do not use a wax for resilient or tile floors because it can damage the finish and leave a dirt-attracting residue.

Apply a thin coat, which creates a more protective finish than a thick coat. Wax once or twice a year, more often in heavy-traffic areas.

Complete refinishing, where machine sanding removes the old layers of finish and exposes new wood, may be necessary if a floor has been subjected to wear or neglect. This can be a difficult task and may best be left to a professional floor finishing expert

Resilient Surfaces

Clean and protect resilient floors—no-wax vinyl, conventional vinyl, asphalt, and rubber tile—regularly. There are a variety of products available for doing so. Check the product label to make sure it is appropriate for the material.

To clean: Damp-mop at least once a week before the floor is badly soiled. Mix an all-purpose cleaning solution in a bucket. Dip in a mop; sponge the floor, then wring some solution out (keep the mop damp enough to loosen dirt).

Clean the floor with slow, even strokes, using just enough pressure to loosen and pick up soil.

How to Remove Floor Polish

From time to time you need to strip polished masonry and resilient floors to prevent buildup, especially if using a new product or if you are unsure what product has been used before. Here's how:

1. Mix a solution of 1/4 cup of powdered all-purpose cleaner, 1 cup of ammonia, and 1/2 gallon of cool water in a bucket. (Cool water helps ammonia retain its cleaning power.)

2. Puddle the solution and use a sponge mop or cloth to spread the solution evenly over a 3-foot-by-3-foot area. Let it soak for 3 to 5 minutes to soften the old polish. (On tile floors, let it soak 1 to 3 minutes.)

3. Scrub briskly with a stiff nylon or natural bristle brush to loosen the softened polish.

4. Wipe up the solution and the old polish with a clean cloth or a sponge mop. Rinse with a cloth or sponge mop dipped in plain water. Repeat for the remaining floor area. Let the floor dry.

Rinse the mop or sponge frequently.

Change the cleaning solution when necessary. Rinse the floor with a mop, sponge, or cloth dipped in clean water; allow to dry.

To shine: Pour a saucer-size pool of polish on the clean floor. Use a clean sponge mop, cloth, or polish applicator to spread it evenly over a 3-foot-by-3-foot section.

Repeat until the entire floor is covered. Do not rinse. Let the floor dry for about 30 minutes.

To refresh the shine periodically, damp-mop floors with 1/2 cup of polish added to 1 gallon of warm water. After 6 to 8 applications, or at least once a year, remove the polish and apply a new coat.

To clean and shine: A product that cleans and shines combines cleaning agents for dirt removal with polish for shine and protection.

Pour a 10- to 12-inch puddle of it on the floor. Soak a damp sponge mop in the product. First mop with a scrubbing action, then with long strokes to even out the polish. For best results, rinse the mop in clean water between washing each 3- to 4-square foot section of floor. Repeat until the entire floor is cleaned and protected. Remove these products after every 6 to 8 applications (see box, left).

Laminate Floors

Dirt, which can cause scratches, is the main enemy of laminate floors. Fortunately, these floors are very easy to maintain.

- Vacuum regularly to remove loose dirt and grime.
- When a more thorough cleaning is required, damp-mop the floor, using plain warm water. Keep the mop damp, not wet, so you don't saturate the floor. Change the water frequently so that you don't transfer dirt particles back to the floor.
- Do not polish or wax a laminate floor.
- Standing water can harm the finish. Wipe up spills immediately.

- Do not use abrasive cleaners, scouring powder, or steel wool. These products all have the potential to scratch the floor.
- Place glides or floor protectors under furniture legs to prevent scratches.
- Use mats and throw rugs at doorways to prevent dirt from being tracked onto the floor.
- If scratches do occur, fill them in with a touch-up stick that is available through dealers who carry laminate flooring.

Masonry

Masonry floors—stone, marble, brick, terrazzo, unglazed ceramic tile, and quarry tile—are porous and susceptible to staining, so they should be sealed (except glazed ceramic tile) with a permanent sealer designed for use on this type of floor. Once sealed, care should be easy. Clean and vacuum them regularly. Many specific products are available for general floor cleaning and stain removal. Check with the flooring manufacturer or retailer and follow label directions. Grout, too, can stain easily, so it's a good idea to seal it also.

Rugs and Carpets

More dirt settles into your carpets than in all the rest of your house. It's essential to remove surface dirt before it becomes ground in. Too much wet cleaning, however, can also cause damage and wear.

 Helpful Hints

EASY RUG CLEANING

➤ **At least twice a year, vacuum rug padding and the floor beneath it.**

➤ **Turn rugs around now and then so they wear and soil evenly.**

Spot-Cleaning Carpets

Most spots can be treated if you attend to them as quickly as possible; the longer a stain has a chance to soak in, the harder it is to remove. Before you apply any cleaning formula, find a hidden spot and put a few drops on the carpet (or on each color if there is a pattern) and press with a white absorbent cloth or paper towel. Count to 10. If any dyes have bled onto the cloth, call a professional cleaner.

CLEANING AGENTS

Solvent=dry-cleaning solvent, available at a hardware store or supermarket	**Detergent**=solution of 1 cup warm water and 1 teaspoon of mild, hand diswashing detergent in a spray bottle	**Ammonia**=solution of 1 cup warm water and 1 tablespoon of non-sudsing household ammonia in a spray bottle	**Vinegar**=solution of 1 cup warm water and 2 tablespoons white distilled vinegar in a spray bottle

HOW TO USE THIS CHART:

Here are some common stains and ideal methods to treat them. Try the first method listed. Proceed to the second only if needed, and so on; some jobs call for using a substance twice. Remember to apply cleaner sparingly, rinse well, and blot after each method tried. Avoid using an ammonia solution on wool carpets; the ammonia will take the color out of the carpet.

Alcoholic beverages/beer/wine: detergent; vinegar. If any stain remains, apply denatured alcohol or a dry-cleaning solvent

Asphalt/tar: solvent; detergent

Berries: detergent; vinegar

Blood: sponge with cold water; detergent; ammonia; detergent (ingredients must be cold).

Butter/oil: solvent; detergent

Candy (sugar): detergent; vinegar. If any stain remains, apply denatured alcohol or a dry-cleaning solvent

Catsup: detergent; ammonia; detergent

Chewing gum: Freeze with an ice cube. Carefully remove as much as possible with a dull knife; apply solvent; wait a few minutes; work residue out of fibers; blot; repeat if necessary

Chocolate: detergent; ammonia; detergent

Coffee/tea: detergent; vinegar. If any stain remains, apply denatured alcohol or a dry-cleaning solvent

Cough syrup: detergent; ammonia; vinegar; detergent

Crayon: solvent; detergent

Dirt: detergent; ammonia; detergent

Egg: detergent; ammonia; detergent

Excrement: detergent; ammonia; detergent

Foundation makeup: solvent; detergent

Fruit juice: sponge with cold water; detergent; vinegar. If any stain remains, apply denatured alcohol or a dry-cleaning solvent

Furniture polish: solvent; detergent

Glue, model or hobby: solvent. If stain remains, carefully apply nonoily nail-polish remover

Glue, white: detergent; ammonia; detergent

Gravy: solvent; detergent

Hair spray: solvent; detergent

Hand lotion: solvent; detergent

Ice cream: detergent; ammonia; detergent

Ink, ballpoint: solvent; detergent

Ink, fountain pen: detergent; vinegar; ammonia

Ink, permanent: detergent; ammonia; vinegar; detergent

Linseed oil: solvent; detergent

Machine oil/grease: solvent; detergent

Mascara: solvent; detergent

Mayonnaise: detergent; ammonia; detergent

Mercurochrome: detergent; ammonia; vinegar; detergent

Milk: detergent; ammonia; detergent

Nail polish: apply a nonoily nail-polish remover

Paint, alkyd: solvent; detergent. If the stain remains, consult a professional cleaner

Paint, latex: solvent; detergent

Rubber cement: solvent; detergent

Rust: detergent; vinegar. If any stain remains, apply denatured alcohol or a dry-cleaning solvent

Shellac: apply denatured alcohol; blot; repeat if necessary

Shoe polish: solvent; detergent. If the stain remains, consult a professional cleaner

Soft drinks: detergent; vinegar

Soy sauce: detergent; ammonia; detergent

Urine: detergent; ammonia; vinegar

Varnish/lacquer: solvent; detergent

Wax, candle: treat as for chewing gum. If any stain remains, cover with 2 paper towels and use a warm dry iron to melt wax; rotate towels to absorb stain; if necessary, reapply solvent and blot

Vacuuming

Before vacuuming a carpet, pick up small objects, such as paper clips, coins, and buttons. Slowly move the vacuum over the carpet several times, going back and forth and side to side in parallel rows. Carefully go over areas in front of sofas, chairs, and doorways where soil from shoes collects and can be ground into the carpet.

- Move furniture as short a distance as possible to save energy and time. Tip a chair back or to the side, move the end of a table an inch or two to clean where the legs were, and then move it back.

- Once a month, vacuum the entire carpet thoroughly. Move furniture and vacuum all areas. Use the vacuum tools to clean the carpet adjacent to the baseboard, under and

Vacuuming Oriental Rugs

Oriental rugs, which are the most prized of all area rugs, can be vacuumed safely—and should be as often as other carpets to keep them in peak condition. Vacuum as usual, except when approaching the fringe. With an upright cleaner, tip up the front of the cleaner slightly and push it completely off the carpet. This cleans the fringe without catching it in the agitator. With a canister, use a floor brush or upholstery attachment for the fringe.

Deep-Cleaning Carpets

If you clean your carpets or rugs yourself, consider one of the following methods. Vacuum thoroughly before beginning. You can rent the necessary machines at your hardware store, home center, or supermarket.

FOR OVERALL CLEANING	HOW TO USE	ADVANTAGES	DISADVANTAGES
Steam-cleaning (hot-water extraction)	Use a steam-cleaning machine to inject water and cleaner into the carpet. Solution and dirt are vacuumed into machine. Vacuum when carpet is dry—usually in less than 12 hours.	Maintains appearance of pile	Overwetting the carpet may shrink or discolor it
FOR SPOT-CLEANING HIGH TRAFFIC AREAS			
Dry-cleaning powders	Sprinkle powder on (granular "sponges" absorb soil). Work it into carpet pile with special machine or brush. Vacuum.	Easy, safe, fast; no water to wet carpet; no residue remains	Machine is not available for home purchase
Shampoo	Apply with sponge, mop, hand brush, electric rug shampooer, or manual applicator as label indicates. After carpet dries, vacuum away foam and dirt.	Economical	Machine may distort pile; can leave residue to attract soil

around heating and air-conditioning units/vents, in corners, and in hard-to-reach areas.

• Check and change the vacuum cleaner bag or empty the dirt canister often.

Deep-Cleaning

Even if you vacuum carefully and consistently, heavy-traffic and heavily soiled areas may require deep cleaning every 6 months (see box, left, for methods). Areas not subject to heavy traffic should be cleaned a minimum of every 12 or 18 months before soiling is visible.

 Helpful Hints

SPOT-CLEANING STEPS

When spot-cleaning carpets, follow these guidelines:

➤ **Before treating, use a spoon or dull knife to pick up any excess solids. Always move from the outer edges toward the middle.**

➤ **Apply the cleaning formula and blot with a clean, white absorbent cloth or paper towel until dry. Never rub or scrub a stain.**

➤ **Be sure not to overwet the stain with the cleaning formula. Apply sparingly, and, once again, blot with a white absorbent cloth or paper towel. Excess amounts could damage the backing and padding.**

➤ **Continue to blot the stain until it is gone and no more moisture can be absorbed. To remove excess moisture or stain residue, place an absorbent towel, weighted with a heavy colorfast object (like a pot or vase), over the cleaned area. Leave overnight.**

➤ **Allow the cleaned area to dry before walking on the carpet. Groom the pile by hand to restore it to its original condition.**

➤ **Many stains take time to respond to a cleaning formula and may even need repeated treatments.**

 Helpful Hints

DEPRESSED CARPETS?

➤ **Carpet dents occur when heavy furniture remains in one position for a long time. Periodically shifting the location of furniture helps prevent permanent damage. Furniture coasters are an even better idea.**

➤ **After the furniture is moved, brush the dented area with your fingertips or use the steam from a garment steamer to loosen and bring up the mashed tufts.**

➤ **If depressions are still noticeable after a few days, lay a damp terry cloth towel over them and press lightly with an iron using the wool or cotton heat setting. Leave the towel in place until dry. Remove it, and the depression will be gone.**

STAIR STRATEGIES

➤ **To vacuum stairs, start at the top and work your way down.**

➤ **If you're not using a handheld vacuum with rotating brush, use the upholstery tool of your vacuum along with the crevice tool to clean the carpet where the step and riser meet.**

Often, a professional can do a more thorough job, with less risk of shrinking, fading, or staining the carpet due to overwetting. You might alternate a professional service with do-it-yourself cleaning, or use a professional only for the dirtiest or most delicate areas. Always have Oriental carpets sent out for professional cleaning.

Before hiring a service, get a reference from a friend or neighbor. Check to see if the service will give you an estimate, and if pickup and delivery services for the rug are included in the cleaning cost.

Windows and Doors

Wash windows, glass doors, and sky lights when the sun is not shining directly on the glass. Working in direct sunlight causes streaks because the cleaning solution dries faster than you can wipe it off.

Many windows can be washed by tilting in or pushing the bottom half up and the top half down, so you can reach outside. If you can reach windows from the ground, stand outside to wash them.

Window Glass

Before washing window glass, vacuum the frame, sill, or track (sliding windows and doors) with the dusting and crevice tools on your vacuum cleaner.

Wash the frame, sill, or track every few months with a sponge dipped in an all-purpose household cleaning solution. Avoid using ammonia products on aluminum—they can cause pitting. Add chlorine bleach to the solution (unless the solution contains ammonia) if the surface is stained with moss or mildew. Rinse and dry.

To clean the glass, use either a commercial glass cleaner or a solution of 2 tablespoons of clear ammonia per 1 quart of water.

Pour the ammonia solution into a pump spray bottle. Or wet a sponge or a soft, lint-less cloth with the cleaning solution.

Wipe one pane of glass at a time. Wash the

Green and Clean

PAINT POINTER

To remove paint from window glass, soften it with a sponge dipped in warm, soapy water or warm vinegar. Gently scrape with a sharp single-edge razor blade. Clean the glass, rinse, and dry.

Time Savers

SCREEN TIME

When you wash the windows from the outside each year, wash the screens, too. Before you remove the screens for the first time, use a permanent marker to write a number on the inside of the window or door frame and mark the same number on the inside frame of the corresponding screen. This makes it easy year after year to put each clean screen back where it belongs.

glass from side to side on one side. Then wash from top to bottom on the other side; this way, if there are streaks, you can tell which side to rub again.

To clean corners use a cotton swab dipped in the cleaning solution. Dry with a squeegee, chamois, paper towel, or crumpled newspaper.

Kitchen windows and skylights may require a stronger cleaner if there is a heavy accumulation of grease and dirt. Use a higher proportion of ammonia in the solution.

Screens

Clean screens outdoors or in a bathtub. Fill a large bucket with warm water and add an all-purpose (non-ammonia) household cleaner.

Dip a scrub brush into the solution, scrub both sides of the screen, then wash the screen frame with the same brush.

Rinse both sides of the screen and the frame with clean water. Let the screen drip-dry for a few minutes, then wipe it with a dry cloth; stand it up to dry completely.

Shades

At least once each year, lower your shades and dust them on both sides with a clean cloth or vacuum cleaner and dusting tool.

Most shades are washable, but test them to be sure. Also test any trims that may be attached. Wipe a small section near the roller with a sudsy cloth or sponge. Rinse with a clean cloth or sponge and wipe dry. If it looks cleaner, and the color hasn't run, proceed.

Roller Shades

Clean washable roller shades, which are usually made of plastic, canvas, or treated fabric, with a mild detergent and water solution.

Lower the shade to spot-clean finger marks and smudges. For overall cleaning, take down the shade and unroll it on a clean flat surface covered with an old sheet, an old shower curtain, or an old plastic tablecloth. Place a heavy object on both ends of the shade to hold it open while you work.

Clean one section at a time, starting as close to the top as you can get, with a sponge or cloth wrung out in a detergent and water solution. If the shade has a rough finish, scrub it lightly with a soft brush. Rinse the section with a clean, damp sponge or cloth. Wipe dry and roll up the clean section.

Repeat the process until the whole shade is clean. Turn it over and wash the other side the same way. Hang the shade back on the window and pull it down. Let it dry thoroughly before rolling it back up.

For untreated fabric shades, take them down and gently hand wash, if they are washable; if not, dry-clean them or use wallpaper dough cleaner (see page 50) to clean nonwashable shades.

Pleated Shades

Vacuum occasionally, using the dusting attachment to clean both sides of pleated shades. Most are treated to resist soil, but if the fabric looks soiled, sponge with lukewarm water and mild

suds or foam upholstery cleaner. Sponge with clear water to rinse, and dry with a clean towel. Do not immerse the shade or use commercial window-cleaning products or spot removers. Always work in a horizontal direction, parallel to the pleats. Hang the shade partially open to dry. Excessive cleaning can remove the fullness and body from the pleated fabric.

Blinds

Venetian and Mini Blinds

To dust: Use a vacuum dusting tool or a soft or electrostatic dusting cloth. Lower the blinds. Dust the slats first when they are facing downward, then upward. If you are using a pronged blind-dusting tool, leave the blinds open and slip the slats between the rollers.

To wash: Lower and open the blinds, then wash them while they're hanging. Place old cloths or newspapers under the window to catch any water drips. Remove nearby furniture.

Dip a sponge or cloth in a solution of all-purpose household cleaner and water and wring out. Start at the top and wash one slat at a time, folding the cloth or sponge around the slat and sliding it from side to side. (Or use scissors to cut halfway through a thick flat sponge and use it the same way.)

Rinse with a damp cloth or sponge, using the same method as for washing; wipe dry.

Tapes and cords: Scrub Venetian-blind tapes with a brush dipped into thick suds. Rinse with a clean, damp sponge or cloth.

Wipe each pull cord or wand with a folded sponge or cloth—first with suds and then with clean water. Leave the blind lowered and open until it is completely dry.

Bathtub method: If you prefer, take the blinds down and wash them in a bathtub half filled with a solution of warm water and a household cleaner. Pull the cord so that the slats are open. Immerse the blind in the water, spreading it out.

Wash both sides with a sponge or cloth, and scrub the tapes with a brush. Drain the sudsy water and fill the tub halfway with clean water to rinse away any dirt and suds; repeat.

Drain the water. Dry with a cloth or towel. Place old cloths on the floor under the window and put the blinds back up. Lower them and keep the slats open until they are completely dry.

Outdoors: To wash blinds outdoors, hang them over a clothesline and clean in the same way as for hanging blinds. Rinse both sides with a garden hose. Drip-dry, then hang back up on the window.

Wood Blinds and Shutters

Wood blinds and shutters may warp if you clean them with water. Instead, wipe each slat with a cloth treated with furniture polish or use your vacuum cleaner with the dusting brush attachment.

Curtains and Draperies

Frequently remove dust from curtains and draperies using your vacuum cleaner and upholstery attachment. Pull the fabric taut and use a gentle suction. Work from the top to the bottom with firm strokes. Curtains can also be "dusted" in your dryer on the "air fluff" setting (no heat) to freshen them periodically.

Most curtains are machine washable and dryable, except for those made with glass fibers (see page 78).

Draperies should never be washed unless recommended on the label. In either case, follow the care label recommendations. If there are no label directions, have your curtains and draperies dry-cleaned. Many cleaners will box-store them free of charge.

A fabric refresher can be used to remove and neutralize odors. Test first in an inconspicuous spot on the fabric. Spray the product evenly on the curtains or drapes; let dry.

Walls and Ceilings

Periodically vacuum walls and ceilings using a clean dusting or wall brush attachment or use an electrostatic duster with disposable cloths. Begin at the ceiling and work down to the floor.

Painted walls and switch and outlet plates will look presentable longer if you clean fingerprints, smudges, and other marks soon after they appear.

Always test paint to make sure it is washable before beginning. With a sudsy sponge, wipe a small spot in an inconspicuous area. If the color and finish are unaffected, proceed.

To wash: Use a sponge and an all-purpose cleaner (follow package directions) or an ammonia and water solution (1 cup ammonia per 1 gallon warm water). Wash a small section (2 feet by 2 feet) of the wall at a time, starting at the top and working down to the floor to avoid streaks and drip marks. Overlap areas as you clean. When the section looks clean, rinse with a clean, damp sponge and water. (Rinsing is always advisable, even though manufacturers of some cleaners say it is not necessary.)

Wipe dry with a clean cloth. Change the wash and rinse waters frequently to prevent redepositing the dirt.

When the walls are done, wash the ceiling with the same all-purpose cleaner or ammonia and water solution and a sponge.

Standing on a stool or stepladder, start in one corner and clean as much as you can reach comfortably. When one part is clean, rinse and dry. Proceed to the next area.

Wallpaper

Washable wall coverings include wallpaper (water-resistant or plastic-treated) and vinyl-coated or vinyl-processed coverings. The vinyls are the sturdiest.

Cleaning Your Fireplace

- When ashes are cold, remove any exceeding 2 inches. Use a fireplace shovel or vacuum cleaner.
- Wash the hearth and front of the fireplace or stove exterior occasionally with a sponge or cloth dipped in an all-purpose household cleaner and water solution.
- Clean a cast-iron exterior with a hand dishwashing detergent and water solution. Rinse with a clean, damp sponge or cloth and dry.
- Remove soot from brick or stone facing with a soft brush, then scrub with a strong solution of washing soda or trisodium phosphate (TSP) and water or all-purpose household cleaner and water. Old brick (more than 50 years old) should only be vacuumed to avoid crumbling.
- Commercial products are available for removing smoke and soot stains from brick or stone fireplaces. The cleaning product is applied and brushed briskly to create foam that removes the stains.

SCREENS
Clean the mesh every few months with a vacuum cleaner and dusting attachment. To wash, use a sponge or cloth dipped in an all-purpose household cleaner and water solution; rinse and dry.

GLASS DOORS
To remove soot and smoke residue, scrape doors with a straight-edge razor blade. Wash the glass with a sponge or cloth dipped in a solution made of equal parts of vinegar and water or 1 tablespoon of ammonia added to 1 quart of hot water; use paper towels or newspaper to dry the glass. There are also special drip-free commercial cleaners that are formulated to dissolve smoke stains.

CHIMNEY
If the fireplace is used regularly, have the chimney checked yearly by a professional chimney cleaner.

Never wash untreated paper or coverings marked "water sensitive". If you don't know how your wall covering should be cleaned, test a small spot in an inconspicuous place before beginning.

If the covering passes the test (the color did not fade, run, bleed, disappear, or the paper is not damaged), proceed.

To wash: For delicate or thin-coated paper, use clear lukewarm water. Wash vinyl and most other sturdier coverings with a well-wrung sponge dipped in a solution of hand dishwashing detergent and lukewarm water. Work from the bottom up, using as little water as possible. Clean one small area at a time and overlap your strokes. Rinse with a clean sponge dipped in cool water and gently wipe dry with a clean absorbent cloth.

USING WALLPAPER DOUGH

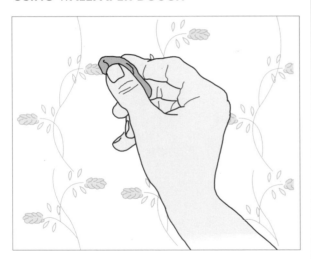

Spot-clean nonwashable coverings with a special dough available from wallpaper, paint, and hardware stores. Knead the dough in your hand until it is pliable, then rub it on the covering as you would a soft eraser. Overlap strokes and clean the soiled area. As you work, fold the soiled surface of the dough to the inside, exposing a clean surface to use on the wall.

Wall Surfaces and Fixtures

Wood Paneling

Dust and remove fingerprints and other soil from paneling using a special product designed for paneled walls. Check that any product is suitable for the finish of your paneling. Wax and oil products should not be used interchangeably. Never wet unsealed paneling, which should always be dusted instead.

To clean and polish oil-finished, varnished, or shellacked wood paneling, apply a mixture of 1/2 cup of turpentine, 1/4 cup of linseed oil, and 1 tablespoon of vinegar; let it stand for 15 minutes, then rub until all the cleaner is removed.

Brick and Stone

Scrub brick and stone with a solution of strong all-purpose cleaner and water. To remove stubborn stains, like soot (see box, page 49), scrub with an abrasive cleanser; rinse well.

Acoustical Tile

Acoustical tile should generally not be washed by wet methods. Clean tiles with a special dough, as you would nonwashable wall coverings (see left), or vacuum using the dusting brush attachment. If the tiles are vinyl-coated, they may be cleaned. Check with the manufacturer for the recommended method.

 Helpful Hints

GET OUT THE COBWEBS
Vacuum cobwebs with the crevice tool on your vacuum, or use a long-handled acrylic or lambswool duster.

CATCHING DRIPS
Tie a washcloth around your wrist to catch wall-washing drips. An athlete's terry-cloth wristband works well, too.

Fixtures

Ceiling fans: Wipe the blades often using a long-handled duster; dust and dirt build up quickly. Every 3 or 4 months, wash the blades with an all-purpose cleaner and water solution.

Light fixtures: Dust with the vacuum cleaner and dusting tool or a dusting cloth to remove dirt and cobwebs. Remove the globe or cover periodically; wash with a damp, sudsy sponge or cloth; rinse and dry. To clean lamp shades, see page 35.

Crystal chandeliers: Before cleaning, put a piece of plastic, then a layer of newspaper under the chandelier. To clean the fixture without removing all the pieces, use a premoistened glass-cleaning cloth or a small cup filled with the ammonia solution described below. After you "dip" each crystal into the cup held in one hand, towel-dry with the other hand.

If you prefer, take the chandelier apart, remove the crystal drops a few at a time, and wash them in the sink or a pan, using a hand dishwashing detergent.

Rinse in a solution of 1 tablespoon ammonia or vinegar to 1 quart of water.

Towel-dry and replace the crystal drops immediately to make sure that they go in the right places.

Repeat for all the crystals. Wipe any permanent parts of chandeliers with a damp cloth and towel-dry.

The Kitchen

While the cleaning guidelines for furniture, floors, windows, ceilings, and other surfaces on pages 31–51 apply to all rooms of the house, the kitchen needs special attention to keep it clean and hygienic, as do the bathroom and nursery (see pages 61–64).

To keep your kitchen sanitary for food preparation, wash utensils and other equipment as you use them, and wipe up spills when they occur.

Minimize open storage to keep airborne dust and grease away from dishes, boxed and canned food, and utensils—especially near the stove, where splattered food and grease are a constant problem.

Cabinets and Pantry

Clean your cabinets frequently; clean the interiors when they look dirty, but at least once a year. Use the appropriate mild cleanser for your cabinets' surface.

It isn't necessary to empty the entire cabinet—do a shelf at a time and remove only half of the items on it. Dust and wipe shelves with a damp cloth, and move the items back into place.

If the top of the cabinet is exposed, clean it first, then move to the shelves. If the shelf is lined with paper, remove the contents, remove the paper, wipe the shelf, and reline it with new paper. Wipe the inside and outside of the door. If the

 Time Savers

KEEPING UP WITH THE WOODWORK

Wash fingerprints, smudges, and marks from cabinets at least once each month; it is much easier to wash off a little dirt than to wait until a lot accumulates. Work carefully to avoid soiling or wetting the bordering wall, ceiling, or floor.

door is greasy, use an all-purpose cleaner solution or one specifically recommended by the cabinet manufacturer. Avoid overwetting wood cabinets. Rinse and dry quickly. Cabinet exteriors will need more frequent attention.

Drawers

Remove the drawer contents, then vacuum inside using the dusting brush or crevice tool. Wipe with a damp cloth. Be sure to clean the top, front, and bottom of the drawer as well as any knobs or handles. As with cabinet doors, use a mild cleaner or polish suitable for the exterior.

Countertops

Regularly move the items forward just far enough to be able to clean the counter and wall behind them. Most spills wipe up from most surface types with an all-purpose spray cleaner or a solution of soap and warm water and a sponge or soft cloth.

If food sticks, lay a damp cloth or sponge over the spot to loosen it; do not use abrasive cleansers, plastic scrubbers, or steel wool because they can scratch the surface. Move the items back and clean

 Helpful Hints

COUNTER INTELLIGENCE

Mustard, tea, coffee, dark fruit juices, and price-tag marks may stain countertops.

➤ **To remove stains, first try rubbing them with a soft, damp cloth or use a sponge and baking soda.**

➤ **If the stain persists, wipe with a cloth or paper towel moistened with a little chlorine bleach; rinse.**

➤ **For stained grout on ceramic-tile countertops, apply a bleach solution (1/4 cup liquid chlorine bleach to 1 quart of water) with a cloth, sponge, or toothbrush—or use an all-purpose cleaner containing bleach or a bleach pen. Rinse thoroughly.**

Wood Counters and Cutting Boards

Treat wood chopping blocks and counters with mineral oil several times a year. (Do not use salad or vegetable oil since they will become rancid.) Pour a small amount on the wood and rub it in with a paper towel or cloth. Let it sit for several hours until the oil is absorbed. Sand deep scratches with fine sandpaper, and lightly re-oil the surface.

After chopping onion and garlic, sprinkle wood surfaces with baking soda and rub with a damp sponge or cloth to remove the odor.

After cutting raw poultry or meat, wash the wood board with hot water, soap, and a scrub brush, and then sanitize it with a solution of 1 teaspoon chlorine bleach and 1 quart of water, or a disinfectant cleaner. If using the latter, read and follow the product label directions. Do the same for a plastic board, or put it in the dishwasher.

the rest of the countertop. Every so often clean and remove countertop items. Clean underneath and behind them as well.

Some surfaces do require extra care. For granite, use liquid dishwashing detergent or a product specifically designed to clean natural stone. Do not use an all-purpose cleaning product; ammonia and harsh detergents can dull the surface. It's a good idea to reseal stone countertops every six months with a wipe-off penetrating sealer. Sealers and natural stone cleaning products can generally be found at hardware stores and stone suppliers.

For solid surfaces, soapy water, ammonia-based cleaners, or commercially available solid surface cleaners will remove most dirt and residue. To disinfect, wipe surface with diluted household bleach (1 part water to 1 part bleach).

Rinse thoroughly with water and wipe dry. Stains can often be buffed out with an abrasive pad.

Sinks and Faucets

Kitchen sinks need gentle daily cleaning. Before doing so, rinse them thoroughly and remove any waste. With a damp sponge or cloth, rub a nonabrasive cleanser or a special product formulated for cleaning sinks over the basin, rim, and fixtures. Rinse with clean water.

Porcelain: You can remove stains from porcelain by filling the sink with lukewarm water and adding a small amount of liquid chlorine bleach. Leave the water in the sink for a while; drain and rinse. Use a rubber sink mat to avoid scratching the surfaces.

Stainless steel: To make a stainless steel sink sparkle, clean and polish it occasionally with glass cleaner, metal polish, or a baking soda paste (2 parts baking soda to 1 part water). The paste is good for removing any stubborn stains in the sink or around the rim. Towel-dry to avoid water spots.

Don't worry about scratches; stainless steel is supposed to scratch, and marks will eventually blend in. To avoid excess scratching, use a rubber sink mat.

Faucets: To remove soap and stain buildup from fixtures, dissolve 1 teaspoon of salt in 2 tablespoons of white vinegar. Rub the mixture on with a damp sponge. Be sure to rinse thoroughly and buff dry with a paper towel or clean cloth to avoid water spots.

Clog prevention: Never pour cooking grease down the drain. Once a month, pour a handful of baking soda into the drain and add 1/2 cup of vinegar. Cover the drain for several minutes, then flush with a kettle of boiling water.

Food disposal: Always use a heavy flow of cold water when operating your disposal. Cold water will congeal fats in the drain, which will aid grinding and help prevent clogging. Run the water before turning on the disposal and for 30

seconds after the grinding noise stops to make sure the disposal is completely empty and food debris has been flushed through the lines.

Once a week, flush the disposal drain by filling the sink with 3 inches of warm water and mixing in 1 cup of baking soda, then draining it with the disposal running. This should be enough to keep it clean. Never use detergent, lye, or a chemical drain cleaner.

Cooktops/Ranges/Ovens

To care for your range top, begin by reading the manufacturer's instructions. Then follow the guidelines provided below.

Porcelain enamel: Wipe up spills immediately. If the cooktop is hot, use a dry paper towel or cloth. When the surface is cool, wash it with an all-purpose cleaner; rinse and polish with a clean, dry cloth. Avoid using cleaners and harsh abrasives, which may scratch.

Stainless steel: Clean with hot, sudsy water or a paste of baking soda and water (3 parts baking soda to 1 part water). Rinse and towel-dry. To polish, moisten a cloth with mineral oil; wipe the surface and towel-dry to prevent streaks.

Anatomy of a Burner

CONVENTIONAL ELECTRIC BURNER

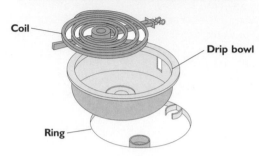

Coil

Drip bowl

Ring

CONVENTIONAL GAS BURNER

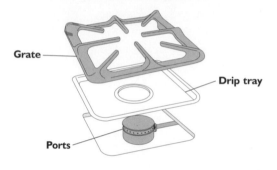

Grate

Drip tray

Ports

Glass and smooth-top glass ceramic: Clean when cool with a specially formulated cooktop cleaner. Apply sparingly directly to cooktop or a clean, damp sponge and rub lightly until the spill is no longer visible. Dry with a soft cloth or paper towel.

Do not use a soiled dishcloth or sponge to wipe the cooktop. Food particles in the cloth or sponge can scratch the surface or remain on the surface; the next time the cooktop is heated, the particles can burn into the surface.

Burned-on soil can be removed with a razor-blade scraper.

Burners

Conventional electric coil: Most are self-cleaning. Turn the burners on high to burn off spills. Porcelain drip bowls under the units are dishwasher safe or can be cleaned in a self-cleaning

oven. Wash chrome reflector drip bowls in the dishwasher or by hand.

If spills are cooked-on, the bowls require soaking in hot, sudsy water. Soap-filled scouring pads also work well to remove hardened spills. Wipe the metal rings around the surface units, or, if they're removable, wash them by hand or in the dishwasher.

Solid cast-iron electric: These units are permanently sealed to the cooktops to prevent spills from seeping underneath. Wipe the area surrounding the burners with a sponge or cloth dipped in hot, sudsy water. To avoid rust spots, heat the units on a medium setting until they are completely dry. "Season" periodically with vegetable oil and heat for 3 to 5 minutes.

Conventional gas: When food boils over or is spilled, wipe the grate, burner, drip pan, and drip tray as soon as they're cool enough to touch. Do not wash the grate or burner in the dishwasher. Clean burner caps with detergent and water or mild abrasive cleaners. To thoroughly clean the burner, lift out the parts (check your care manual for directions) and soak them in warm, sudsy water. Use a stiff brush to scrub off any burned-on food.

Clean the burner ports with a straight pin or a straightened paper clip. (Do not use a toothpick: It may break off and clog the port.)

Sealed-gas burner: These are easy to clean because the burners are sealed permanently to the cooktop so boilovers will not seep underneath. Wash burner caps and grates by hand in hot, sudsy water to prevent rusting of unfinished surfaces.

Knobs: Control knobs on most cooktops and ranges are removable for cleaning. Pull them straight off, wash, rinse, and dry well. Replace firmly in the "off" position. Water should not be allowed to drip behind the knobs.

Trash Containers

Line trash containers with plastic or paper trash bags to make garbage removal easier and to keep the container clean longer. Wipe away finger marks and residue on the outside of the container (including the lid or cover) with an all-purpose household cleaner.

To clean the interior, half fill the basket with warm, sudsy water; then scrub with a cloth or sponge. Rinse, wipe, and let dry thoroughly before using it again. Don't let water soak into cardboard or wood baskets.

Scrub the garbage can occasionally with a long-handled brush (a toilet bowl brush works well) to keep it sanitary and odorless. Use this brush only for the garbage can. If odors persist, add a little ammonia or liquid chlorine bleach to the rinse water and rinse again. Turn the can upside down to drain and dry.

Ovens

Oven-cleaning has always ranked among the least-favorite kitchen chores, but there are ways to simplify this messy job.

Racks: Soak racks in a solution of hot water and an all-purpose cleaner containing ammonia (follow the label directions for the correct proportion) or in a solution of 1/2 cup of ammonia to 1 quart of hot water. Use soap-filled scouring pads to remove stubborn soil.

Broiler pan: Clean the broiler pan after each use. Remove the grill and dispose of the grease in an old can. Fill the pan with hot water and dishwashing liquid. Replace the grill. Let stand for about 30 minutes. Then wash in hot, sudsy water; rinse and dry.

Front and sides: Remove any control dials/knobs, then wash them in hot, sudsy water or with an all-purpose cleaner. Wash the surface behind the control dials/knobs; rinse and dry thoroughly.

Periodically wash the sides of a freestanding range with an all-purpose household cleaner.

Glass doors: Use a glass cleaner, ammonia, or a solution of 1 part vinegar and 1 part water. Place a cloth or paper towel saturated with the solution (but wrung out) on the inside of the

Good Cooking Habits

GOOD COOKTOP HABITS
Foods may actually cook better on low heat, and make less mess. You need high heat only to bring foods to a boil.

Using a larger pan when cooking foods that foam—pasta, rice, milk, dried beans—will help to keep them from boiling up and overflowing.

When frying or sautéing, use a small amount of fat and medium heat to minimize spattering and to brown foods more evenly.

Keep an eye on all food while it's cooking. If you must walk away, set a kitchen timer and carry it with you.

GOOD OVEN HABITS
To prevent boilovers, do not fill pans too full. Place a sheet of aluminum foil below the pan on a low rack to catch any drips. (Do not cover the entire rack with aluminum foil; it may affect browning.)

When using glass and glass ceramic cookware, which absorb heat, set the oven thermostat 25 degrees lower than you would for metal cookware.

window with the door open; leave it for a half hour to loosen the soil. Never use an abrasive cleaner; it will scratch the glass. Use a plastic pad, if needed. Rinse well with clean water; dry with paper towels or a lint-free cloth.

Interior: Clean a standard oven by applying a commercial oven cleaner, following the manufacturer's instructions.

Remove the oven door, if it can be lifted off, to make it easier to reach inside. Then wipe the oven walls and the floor of the oven with a wet cloth or sponge. Use a soap-filled scouring pad to remove stubborn soil. Rinse the oven well, then wipe it with a clean cloth dipped in a mild vinegar solution to remove any residue; rinse with warm, clean water.

After broiling food in the oven or in a broiler compartment, wipe the walls with a hot, sudsy cloth to remove spatters.

Self-cleaning interior: Wipe the oven frame and the portion of the door liner outside the oven gasket before using the self-cleaning feature. **Never clean the gasket; cleaning can damage it.** Use soap-filled scouring pads to remove stubborn spots; rinse well.

Follow the manufacturer's instructions for setting the self-cleaning controls. During the cleaning cycle, the oven soil is reduced to light ash. When the cleaning is completed, wipe up with a damp cloth.

Fans and range hoods: Ventilating fans and range hoods exhaust cooking odors and smoke and help circulate air. All of them have filters that need periodic cleaning.

Remove the wire mesh filters and clean them in the dishwasher or soak them in the sink in a solution of hot water and an all-purpose household cleaner. Rinse well, and let dry thoroughly. Before replacing a filter, wipe the fan blades with a clean, damp cloth.

Refrigerators and Freezers

A clean refrigerator helps prevent food spoilage because it harbors no food-spoiling organisms. Spoiled and strong-smelling foods cause bad odors that are picked up by other foods.

To absorb odors, place an open box of baking soda in the back of the refrigerator or on a shelf in the door. Replace it every 2 months.

Check the refrigerator for spoiled or questionable food just before shopping, when it is the emptiest.

You can keep major cleaning to a minimum if you wipe up spills as soon as they occur. Check the inside walls for residue and wipe them off. Sponge the front, sides, handles, and top regularly with an all-purpose cleaner to remove finger marks and greasy dust.

Shelves: If you don't want to take the time to clean the entire refrigerator, do it in stages—one or two shelves at a time. Use a clean cloth or sponge dipped in a solution of 1 tablespoon of baking soda to 1 quart of warm water. Rinse the shelf and walls with clean water and wipe dry.

Condenser coils: These should be cleaned with a long brush or a vacuum cleaner several times a year. Unplug your refrigerator before cleaning the coils. Be sure to replug it when you are finished. The drip pan should be cleaned at the same time if your refrigerator has one. Check your use and care manual for the location and cleaning recommendations. On some newer models, it is not necessary to clean the condenser coils.

Drawers: Remove the drawers. Clean both inside and out using the baking soda solution described above. While the drawer is out, wipe the floor of the refrigerator and towel dry.

Gaskets and doors: Wipe the door gasket(s) and the rubber seal(s) around the door(s) with the baking soda solution, being sure to clean in the folds. If there's mildew on the gasket, use a chlorine bleach solution (1/4 cup of liquid chlorine bleach to 1 quart of water) to remove it; rinse and towel dry. Wash the door shelves and the door frames with the baking soda solution.

Freezer
Empty and clean the freezer section at least once a year. Do not touch frozen surfaces with wet

 Helpful Hints

FROST FIGHTERS

Keep the freezer section of your refrigerator at least 2/3 full to help the appliance operate more efficiently. Don't overload the refrigerator or open the door more than necessary, especially during hot weather. Cover foods and liquids and wipe moisture from the outside of containers before placing them in the refrigerator; moisture evaporates from the food and turns into frost.

or damp hands; use a sponge or clean cloth dipped in a solution of 1 tablespoon of baking soda to 1 quart of warm water.

Defrost a manual refrigerator or freezer at least once a year. Don't let more than a 1/4 inch of frost build up. Frost acts as an insulator, which makes the refrigerator use more electricity to maintain the proper temperature.

Wash the shelves and inside walls of the freezer with a solution of 1 tablespoon of baking soda to 1 quart of water. Be sure to clean the door gasket and remove any mildew with a chlorine bleach solution (1/4 cup of chlorine bleach to 1 quart of water). Rinse well and towel-dry. Return the food to the freezer when it is completely dry.

Dishwashers

Dishwashers generally get cleaned with the dishes and require minimal care. To remove lime deposits, (the white granular film that often appears in your dishwasher left behind by hard water (see box, page 315), run an empty dishwasher through the full cycle with 2 cups of vinegar or 1 cup of citrus-flavored beverage or citric acid crystals (no detergent).

To remove brown rust stains from the interior, use citric acid crystals as for lime deposits, or use a special liquid product; follow the pack-

Smart Loading

It is important to follow the manufacturer's instructions for loading a dishwasher because every model is designed differently. There's generally no need to rinse dishes, but do remove large and hard food particles before placing items in the dishwasher. Rinse dishes if they're going to sit for a while before being washed.

Store rinsed, soiled dishes in the dishwasher until a full load accumulates. Use only detergents designed for use in automatic dishwashers. Do not put detergent in the dispenser(s) until it is time to run the dishwasher; it can cake and fail to dissolve.

age directions. If staining cannot be controlled, you may need to install iron-removal equipment in your home water supply.

Some dishwashers have filters/strainers (located in the bottom of the tub), which need to be removed and cleaned periodically. Check your manual.

Occasionally wipe the outside edge or rim of the door with warm, sudsy water or a solution of 1/4 cup baking soda to 1 quart of water.

Wipe the door front with a solution of warm water and detergent; rinse and wipe dry. Avoid harsh or gritty cleaners or scouring pads that may scratch the finish.

Helpful Hints

TO PREVENT CHIPPING

➤ When loading the dishwasher, alternate plates of various sizes to prevent chipping when same-size dishes knock against each other.

➤ Leave room between glasses; secure them between the cushioned prongs in the top rack. Ensure that long stems don't interfere with the movement of the rack.

➤ Avoid nesting flatware, and be sure the spray arms aren't blocked by a fallen utensil, plate, or pot handle.

Green and Clean

HOT-WATER HINT

If the dishwasher is located a distance from the hot-water heater, turn on the hot-water faucet in the kitchen sink before starting the dishwasher to clear the line of cold water.

Small Appliances

Before cleaning, unplug all small appliances and make sure they are cool. Never immerse an electric appliance in water. To avoid major cleanups, always wipe up spills with a damp paper towel, cloth, or sponge as soon after they occur as possible.

Do not use abrasive or harsh cleaners or scouring pads; they can cause damage. Instead, use a plastic pad, a nonabrasive cleaner, or an all-purpose cleaner.

Sponge the exterior or base of a small appliance with warm, sudsy water. Polish chrome or stainless steel with a cloth moistened with white vinegar or a paste made with 3 parts baking soda to 1 part water. Rinse and dry.

To wash most electric appliances—blender, juicer, can opener, mixer, food processor—remove all parts and wash in warm, sudsy water. If recommended by the manufacturer, run them through the dishwasher. **Be careful with blender and food processor blades, can opener cutters, and other sharp objects. Don't allow them to sit in a sink of soapy water; it's dangerous to search blindly for them underwater, and they can rust.**

Microwave Ovens

If there is a turntable, remove it and wash in warm, sudsy water or in the dishwasher; then dry. While the turntable is removed, clean the oven.

To clean the interior thoroughly, boil a cup of water inside for 3 to 4 minutes. The condensation will loosen any food soil on the walls or ceiling of the oven. Then wipe with a damp sponge or cloth, and dry. **Never use a commercial oven cleaner or remove the cover in the top of the oven interior for cleaning.**

To deodorize, wash the interior surfaces every few months with a solution of 1/4 cup of baking soda to 1 quart of warm water; rinse and dry.

To clean the touch-control panel, open the oven to deactivate. Wipe the panel with a cloth dampened slightly with warm, sudsy water only;

Helpful Hints

TEAKETTLES AND LIME DEPOSITS
To remove lime deposits, boil a mixture of 1 part vinegar and 1 part water in the kettle. Simmer until the deposits disappear, then rinse thoroughly.

rinse, then dry with a paper towel or soft cloth. Do not scrub or use any sort of chemical cleaners on the panel, and avoid using too much water.

If the oven is an over-the-range model with an exhaust fan, follow cleaning directions for fans/range hoods (page 56).

Coffeemakers

Clean the serving container (percolator/drip/carafe) after each use to remove oils and residue that may affect the coffee's flavor. If recommended, put it in the dishwasher or wash it with hot water and detergent.

Automatic drip (ADC): These require periodic cleaning to remove mineral deposits. Pour 3/4 cup of white vinegar into the water reservoir or chamber; fill the chamber with cold water to the maximum fill line; brew the vinegar and water mixture. Rinse the machine twice by brewing with clean water only.

Percolator: Periodically remove the mineral and coffee stains that build up in the system. Fill the pot to the fill line with cold water and add 1 tablespoon cream of tartar. Insert the basket and pump assembly. Cover, plug in, and perk. Empty the solution and rinse well.

If you're planning to store the coffeemaker for more than a day or two, store the pot with the cover off.

Toasters and Toaster Ovens

Wipe the outside regularly. To reach crumbs lodged inside the toaster or toaster oven, unplug the appliance, release the crumb tray latch, then shake the crumbs out. Wipe the tray with a damp

Green and Clean

HOW TO CLEAN BURNED POTS

After soaking the burned pot, sprinkle baking soda (or cream of tartar if it's an aluminum pan) on the burned area, add a little water, and bring the solution to a boil. Let the pot cool, and then wash the pot as usual.

cloth. Never cover the crumb tray with aluminum foil—it can catch fire—and never clean the inside of a toaster except for the crumb tray.

For a toaster oven, wash the bake/broil pan and its rack and the crumb tray (if it's removable) in hot, sudsy water or in the dishwasher after each use. Rinse and dry. Refer to the manufacturer's instructions for cleaning the interior; different finishes require different treatments.

Helpful Hints

NO MORE DARK MARKS

When a metal utensil or object scrapes across china, it often leaves a black or gray mark. To remove it, gently rub the mark with a mild abrasive cleanser or a plastic scouring pad. (Do not use abrasives on decorations.)

NO MORE WHITE FILM

➤ If you've had a problem with etching—cloudy white deposits on glassware from the combination of high heat, dishwasher detergent, and very soft or mechanically softened water—wash glassware by hand.

➤ Ovenproof glass casseroles and dishes may have cloudy areas even when clean. This is a result of food film of protein origin (milk, eggs, cheese, meat juice). To remove, apply white vinegar to a cloth or sponge and rub. Let dry.

UNSTICK STACKED GLASSES

To separate stuck stacked glasses, fill the top or inner glass with cold water and dip the bottom or outer glass in hot water. Gently twist apart.

Dishes, Cookware, and Utensils

Cleaning dishes, silverware, and pots and pans is a daily chore. Here's help for some special items:

Aluminum

Wash aluminum utensils in clean, hot, sudsy water or the dishwasher if the manufacturer's directions indicate they are dishwasher-safe.

To brighten the interior of an aluminum pan, fill it with water and add 1 tablespoon of cream of tartar to 1 quart of water. Boil the solution for 5 to 10 minutes.

Anodized aluminum, which is found on some pie and bread pans, beverage tumblers, cookware, and covers, may be affected by high temperatures and detergent ingredients. As a rule, do not machine wash.

Cast Iron

Cast-iron utensils rust unless "seasoned" (see page 158). If your utensils are not preseasoned by the manufacturer, season them yourself before using them for the first time.

Never wash a cast-iron utensil in the dishwasher; use baking soda to remove burned-on food residue. Always be sure to hand-dry thoroughly to prevent rust.

China and Crystal

Most "everyday" china, crystal, ceramicware, and glassware can be washed safely in a dishwasher. If you're not sure a piece is dishwasher-safe,

Helpful Hints

SAFE STACKING

Store china and glassware where they are easy to remove. Store stacked plates with paper towels, napkins, or doilies between each one. Never stack glassware. Store with rims upright, not down, to prevent trapping moisture inside. Never triple-stack cups.

check for a dishwasher-safe label. You can also try washing one piece for at least a month with your regular loads.

To be on the safe side, don't wash antique china in the dishwasher. China with metal trim, hand paint, or over-the-glaze patterns may fade.

Special "china/crystal" cycles on dishwashers generally include 1 wash, 2 rinses, and a dry cycle. Depending on the manufacturer, the cycle may be shorter than the normal cycle and/or have less forceful water action.

Hand washing: Always be sure to use a plastic dishpan and sink mats to avoid chipping or breakage. When washing cold crystal, do not use water that is too hot; the glass cannot withstand drastic changes in temperature. Otherwise, rinse each piece in hot water. Air- or towel-dry.

Copper and Brass

Some brass and copper have a lacquered finish, which prevents tarnishing. Polish should be used only on tarnished (unlacquered) metals. These require more abrasive polishes than does silver. **(Never use copper and brass polish on silver.)** To clean, rinse in hot water, then apply a polish with a clean, damp sponge or cloth. Rinse and towel-dry.

Nonstick Finishes

Cookware with nonstick finishes should be washed by hand. To remove stains and deposits, fill with a solution of 3 tablespoons of oxygen bleach, 1 teaspoon of liquid dish detergent, and 1 cup of water, or 3 tablespoons of automatic dishwasher detergent in 1 cup of water. Simmer for 15 to 20 minutes; remove from the heat. Wash as usual. After washing, wipe the nonstick finish with vegetable oil.

Pewter

To prevent tarnishing, do not wash pewter in the dishwasher. Never use a harsh abrasive. Most pewter only requires washing in warm, soapy water, rinsing, and thorough drying for

 Dollar Stretchers

HOMEMADE BRASS AND COPPER CLEANER

Dissolve I teaspoon of salt in I cup of white vinegar. Add enough flour to make a paste. Apply the paste; let stand for 15 minutes. Rinse with clean, warm water; towel-dry.

regular cleaning. To polish, use silver polish (if recommended on the label), or combine 2 tablespoons of ammonia with 1 quart of hot, soapy water. Rinse in hot water and buff with a clean towel.

Plastic

Check the manufacturer's directions when you buy plastic storageware and utensils. Some types are marked dishwasher-safe. Others are marked "top-rack only" since they may not withstand the hotter, more forceful sprays of the lower rack and should be kept farther away from the heating element. Follow label recommendations.

 Helpful Hints

SILVER TARNISHERS

Know that:

➤ **Salt can corrode and discolor silver.**

➤ **Eggs, mustard, and mayonnaise are bad tarnishers.**

➤ **Contact with rubber can cause tarnish; avoid draining silver on rubber mats.**

➤ **Plastic wrap adheres to silver, which may damage the finish and create black spots that are difficult—if not impossible—to remove.**

➤ **Warm air will cause discoloration.**

➤ **Silverware and stainless steel utensils should never be washed side by side in the dishwasher. The stainless will cause the silverware to pit.**

Otherwise, wash plastic items in hot, sudsy water. To remove stains and odors, make a paste using 3 parts baking soda to 1 part water, then add 1 teaspoon to a pint of water. Soak each item in the solution for 5 to 10 minutes. Rinse and dry.

Stainless Steel and Silver

To minimize discoloration, wash items as soon as possible after use in hot, sudsy water or in the dishwasher, or at least rinse well. Separate stainless steel from silver in the dishwasher; silver will pit from contact with the stainless.

Stainless steel is not entirely stainproof. Use silver polish or a paste of 3 parts baking soda and 1 part water to remove the hazy white film some foods leave behind. To remove spots caused by minerals in the water, rinse and towel-dry immediately.

Polishing: Follow the manufacturer's directions on the silver polish container. Rub silver

Electrolytic Cleaning for Silver and Silver Plate

This method works through an ion exchange in solution rather than by cleaning or deodorizing. It is not for raised patterns since it will remove the attractive coloration on the design, and it is not for cemented pieces, such as some knives, as the required soaking could soften cement.

Place silver on aluminum foil in a nonaluminum pan; add 1/4 cup baking soda and 1 gallon of boiling water. Let stand while tarnish is removed, then rinse and dry.

gently. Rinse in clear water and wipe dry. To dry, rub each piece briskly with a clean towel, changing towels frequently.

The Bathroom

To eliminate odors, dampness, mildew, and germs, be sure to clean your bathrooms regularly. Keep them as dry and well ventilated as possible. Use an exhaust fan (vented to the outside), a ceiling heater, or an open window to help evaporate moisture.

Keep shower doors ajar and leave gaps between the ends of the shower curtain and walls to let the air into tub or shower areas. After showering, wipe down the shower walls and doors with a towel to help to reduce mildew.

Tiles

To remove soap spots or film, wipe tiles with a commercial sink, tub, and tile cleaner or a vinegar solution (1 part vinegar to 4 parts water or stronger, if needed). Rinse with clear water and buff dry with a soft towel or cloth to prevent streaking.

Clean the grout with a small stiff brush, an old toothbrush, or a nailbrush. If the grout is badly soiled or moldy, use a commercial tile and basin cleaner or apply a bleach solution (1/4 cup liquid chlorine bleach to 6 cups water or stronger, if needed). Apply the solution with a cloth or sponge to help prevent spattering on clothes or nearby fabric. After cleaning, rinse thoroughly.

A bleach pen can also be used to remove mildew from grout lines.

Using car wax on tiles will leave a shine on the surface and help prevent water spots.

Sinks and Faucets

Clean ceramic, plastic, chrome, and stainless steel with a sponge or cloth. Use a sink, tub, and tile cleaner; a mild abrasive powdered or cream cleanser; baking soda; or a diluted ammonia solution (see pages 26–29).

For a hard-to-clean faucet, soak a cloth in vinegar and wrap it around the fixture. Let it stand 5 to 10 minutes until the film loosens. Remove the cloth and wipe the fixture clean with a dampened cloth. Towel-dry the sink and faucet after each use to prevent water spots.

For brass fixtures, use a commercial cleaner recommended by the fixture manufacturer. Be aware that any type of cleaner with ammonia can ruin the finish.

Soap dish: Clean the residue by putting the soap dish in the dishwasher or soaking it in warm to hot water. To clean a built-in soap dish, place a wet sponge or cloth over it for 30 minutes. Wipe out the softened soap, rinse, and dry.

Bathtubs and Showers

Use a sponge or a long-handled brush so you don't have to stoop. If you have a sunken tub, stand in it to clean.

Porcelain and fiberglass: Clean with a sink, tub, and tile cleaner; a mild nonabrasive cleanser;

 Helpful Hints

REMOVING RUST AND MINERAL STAINS FROM TUBS AND SINKS

To remove rust spots or mineral stains, soak the area in vinegar or lemon juice; let it stand 5 minutes. Rinse; then scrub using a mild cleanser. If the stain or spot remains, swab the stain with a diluted solution of oxalic acid, available in hardware and drugstores (1 part acid to 10 parts water). Oxalic acid is poisonous; wear protective gloves.

Minimizing Mildew

Mildew is one of the biggest bathroom cleaning problems. To remove it, wet the mildewed surface with water, then spray with a bleach solution of equal parts liquid chlorine bleach and water. (Or use a commercial cleaner, according to directions, to remove mildew.)

Be careful not to get the cleaner on towels, rugs, or fabric shower curtains, because it can bleach the color out.

Be sure the room is well ventilated while using these products; noxious fumes can result. Rinse well and wipe dry.

baking soda; or a water softener, using a damp sponge. Rub or scour the entire surface, letting the cleanser remain for a minute or so to dissolve the soap film and attack the soil and stains. Rinse thoroughly and dry.

Stall shower: Once a week use a liquid disinfectant cleaner or diluted liquid chlorine bleach (see container label for proportions) to clean the floor. Take care to clean cracks and crevices, which collect soil and harbor fungi and bacteria.

Shower doors: Clean with a solution of 1/2 cup water softener and 1/2 pail of water, or vinegar and water (1/2 cup vinegar to 1 quart water). This will dissolve the cloudy film that accumulates on the doors.

You can also spray the door(s) liberally with a laundry prewash or a sink, tub, and tile cleaner. Leave the cleanser on the door for a few minutes; wipe to remove any scum. Rinse well and towel dry.

Plastic shower curtain and liner: Stretch the curtain out after each use to let it dry and to prevent mildew. Machine wash colorfast plastic curtains or liners periodically to remove built-up soap film. Use warm water and a nonprecipitating (check the label) water softener (about 1 cup) to dissolve the soap residue.

If the curtain is mildewed, add 3/4 cup of liquid chlorine bleach to the wash cycle. Set the control for a 5-minute wash on the gentle cycle. Hang the curtain on a line or shower rod to drip-dry, making sure the bottom edge is inside the tub or shower stall and the curtain is well spread.

Rubber mat: Use disinfectant. Scrub the mat on both sides; rinse well. Between uses, remove the mat from the tub or shower and hang it to dry. Rubber mats can be machine washed with bleach.

Toilet Bowls

Clean the interior with a commercial bowl cleaner, sudsy water, or mild cleanser, using a toilet bowl brush.

Scrub all interior surfaces, especially the inside rim of the bowl and the trap. The rinse holes under the rim can clog with lime deposits.

To remove mineral buildup, turn off the water and flush to drain the toilet bowl completely, and wipe out all water with a sponge. Pour in 1 gallon of a 20 percent solution of muriatic acid (available at hardware stores), following the package directions (wear goggles). Brush the solution into the rinse holes and let it stand for 2 hours. Turn the water on. Flush.

To disinfect the toilet, pour 1 cup of liquid chlorine bleach into the water. Let it stand for about 10 minutes; flush.

If you prefer in-tank cleaners, place one in the toilet tank. Most automatically release a measured amount of cleanser and deodorizer with each flush, lengthening the time between cleanings. Place these only in toilets that you use frequently.

Wipe the exterior of the bowl, base, and tank with a sudsy cloth or sponge. Do the same for the seat (both sides), the cover, and hinges.

Mirrors

Water is the most effective cleaner for mirrors; add 1 tablespoon of ammonia per quart of water or equal parts vinegar and water to increase its cleaning power. Alternatively try commercial window cleaners.

Dampen a paper towel or cloth with the desired cleaning agent rather than spraying it directly on the mirror. This prevents moisture from damaging the mirror backing. Wipe the surface thoroughly; dry with paper towel, a lint-free cloth, crumpled newspaper, or a chamois.

The Nursery and Children's Rooms

Ababy's room needs frequent cleaning to keep it hygienic. Change and launder the crib sheet, pads, and blankets weekly (more often if needed). Once a week, wipe the crib and mattress with a damp sponge and an all-purpose household cleaner that disinfects. Rinse and dry. Machine wash the bumpers.

Launder washable stuffed toys in a pillowcase in the washing machine weekly, or as needed, to keep them clean and smelling fresh.

Vacuum or wipe other toys with a damp sponge and an all-purpose household cleaner.

Empty wastebaskets often and dust furniture, windowsills, and other surfaces several times each week.

Damp-mop or vacuum floors weekly or as needed.

Organize Your Child's Room

From an early age, children can clean their own rooms. Arrange the room to facilitate this. Install low horizontal shelves, cabinets, dressers, and other units instead of tall, vertical cabinets or storage units.

Time Savers

KEEPING A LID ON CHAOS

➤ Roomy catchall storage bins and baskets—laundry baskets, modular plastic storage cases or cubes, dishpans, and milk crates—are great for storing toys. Brightly colored storage boxes make the job more enticing for children.

➤ A clothes hamper or a laundry bag makes depositing dirty clothes easy and convenient.

➤ Shoebags hung on the closet door at your children's height help them keep their shoes together.

Keep toys and books that are used constantly on open shelves and favorite toys on a low, open shelf in the closet.

Periodically, you and your child should sort out toys that are broken or no longer interesting. This will reduce the number of toys and make it easier for your child to put toys away.

Porches, Decks, and Patios

Porches, decks, and patios require basic cleaning just as interior spaces do.
- Sweep as needed.
- Scrub decks and porches, even those made from pressure-treated wood, occasionally with a chlorine bleach and water solution to remove mildew, dirt, and stains. Rinse well with clean water.

- Scrub patios, especially those paved with brick, cement blocks, slate, or stone with a chlorine bleach and water solution or a cleaner developed to remove mold, moss, or algae (available in garden centers). If mold isn't a problem, wash patios periodically with a solution of water and an all-purpose cleaner. Rinse well with clean water.

Outdoor Furniture

Lawn furniture requires care while in use and before seasonal storage.

Outdoor furniture receives a lot of abuse from the sun, rain, and wind. To protect it, read the following suggestions.

Aluminum
Although it does not rust, aluminum can become dull and pitted when left outdoors. To clean, restore the shine, and smooth the surface of unpainted aluminum chairs and chaise longues, scrub the frames with a plastic scrubber soaked in detergent or with a soap-impregnated steel wool pad; rinse and towel-dry.

Use a sponge soaked in detergent and water to wash tubular aluminum with baked-enamel finishes; rinse and dry. To maintain the luster of any aluminum surface (including baked enamel) and to make cleaning easier, wax the pieces from time to time with automobile paste wax.

Canvas
Soiled canvas seats and seat backs are usually machine washable; be sure to put them back on the furniture while they are still damp so they retain their shape.

Scrub large canvas pieces like awnings with a firm-bristled brush and a solution of water and an all-purpose cleaner. Rinse well with a hose. Air-dry.

Plastic
Wash plastic furniture with an all-purpose cleaner and water solution, then rinse with water and dry.

Wood
Scrub stubborn soil with a brush and a solution of water and an all-purpose cleaner; rinse well and towel-dry. Wood furniture may need to be stained or to have a wood preservative applied periodically for protection.

Barbecue Grills

Most grills will last many years if kept free of ashes and moisture and covered when not in use to protect them from the elements. For extra protection against rust, paint with a heat-resistant enamel available at hardware stores.

To clean the rack at the end of the season, use an oven cleaner or soak it in a household ammonia and water solution; then scrub and rinse.

For gas-fueled grills, follow the directions in the owner's manual. To clean permanent briquettes, flip them occasionally, ignite the grill, and, with the cover closed, allow it to burn at a high setting for about 15 minutes.

Garages and Basements

At least once a month, sweep or vacuum the garage floor, especially the area near the entry to the house. Put down a doormat to prevent tracking dirt into the house.

To soak up any oil spills or drippings from automobiles, sprinkle the area with kitty litter. Leave it on the spot for several hours; sweep up the litter with a broom and discard.

Sweep or vacuum basement floors every now and then. Place a doormat at the foot of the stairs to keep dirt from being tracked to other areas of the house. The stairs should be vacuumed or swept at least once a month. Clean the doormat regularly.

Keep lighting in these areas bright and in working order.

Check that items like chemicals and newspapers are stored safely.

CHAPTER

2

Laundry & Clothes Care

Although caring for clothes isn't nearly as much fun as buying them, properly washing, drying, ironing, and repairing garments is very important. Using the right equipment and cleaning products keeps your clothes looking fresh and extends the life of what you wear. This chapter explores the ins and outs of washers, dryers, and laundry products. You'll learn exactly how to wash and dry everything from bedding and down jackets to stuffed toys and vintage lace. It reveals The Good Housekeeping Institute's secrets of stain removal—did you know that you should start removing chewing gum by hardening it with an ice cube?—and explains the sewing techniques you need to know to keep your clothes in top shape. The chapter also reveals how to care for items such as shoes, handbags, belts, and jewelry, as well as the right way to pack and store your clothes and accessories. Want to learn the best methods to care for your clothes? Just turn the page!

Laundry and Clothes Care

Basic Equipment

Doing laundry is less of a chore and can fit into even the busiest schedules when good equipment is nearby. The washer and dryer can be in the basement, a bathroom, kitchen, or even a closet, as long as there is access to electricity, plumbing, and drainage, and your dryer can be vented to the outside of the house. Condenser dryers that don't need venting are available, but they take longer to dry. It's always best to vent, if possible.

Proper Installation

Each appliance must have its own circuit. Like any major appliance, both the washer and the dryer must also be electrically grounded. Consult the manufacturer, a service expert, or utility company for proper procedures.

In addition, a gas dryer must also have access to natural or liquefied petroleum gas (LPG), and venting—through a window, wall, floor, or ceiling—is necessary to carry lint and moisture outside.

If space is limited, consider a stacked washer/dryer arrangement.

Washers

Consider the following features when choosing a washer:

Capacity: If your wash loads are big, choose a "super size" washer. Newer machines without agitators (top or front loading) can also accommodate larger loads.

Water usage: To conserve water, choose a washer designed to use less water than others. Front-loading machines usually use less water than traditional top loaders. Newer top loaders are also water-saving.

Cycles: Some machines come with electroni-

cally preprogrammed cycles to take the guesswork out of laundry, as well as custom cycles, which give you more control over the washing process than ever. The most common cycles include:

Regular or cottons or whites: for most items that do not need special handling.

Color or mixed loads: has regular agitation but adds cold water to minimize wrinkling after the wash cycle and before the rinse cycle.

Delicate or handwash: recommended for lingerie, knits, and other fine fabrics. It may have a shorter wash time, gentler or intermittent agitation, and slower spin speeds.

If you have heavily soiled items, consider a machine with an automatic presoak option (not a standard cycle). A second rinse option is also helpful.

 Green and Clean

WATER-SAVING WASHING MACHINES

Front-loading washing machines use less water, less detergent, and less energy than traditional top-loading machines. Here's how they work: After you've put clothes and detergent in the machine and closed the door, the washer fills to just below the door opening. The items tumble in and out of the water as they are cleaned. Then they are spun to remove detergent and water, rinsed, and spun out.

There are now top-loading machines without agitators that also save water, energy, and detergent. They use a different wash action than front loaders: The clothes bounce and turn gently under a shower of water.

A typical energy-efficient washer uses 20 to 28 gallons of water per load, while a typical standard top-loading machine uses 40 to 45 gallons.

Green and Clean

Water controls: You can adjust water quantity when you do less than a full load.

Temperature controls: You can choose hot, warm, or cold wash and rinse water.

Bleach dispenser: This automatically dilutes and adds bleach to the wash cycle. Timed dispensers add bleach about 5 minutes after the start of the wash cycle for better cleaning.

Fabric softener dispenser: This eliminates the need to add fabric softener by hand when the final rinse cycle begins.

Dryers

Consider the following features when choosing a dryer:

Gas or electric: Both perform well, so base your decision on which hookup is more feasible inside your house and on fuel costs in your area.

Cycles: Most dryers have four basic cycles, all of which are necessary:

Regular or heavy: for items like jeans and towels.

Medium, casual, or permanent press: has an extended cool-down period that helps prevent wrinkles.

Air dry: tumbles dry without heat.

Delicate or low: useful if you dry items such as knits or lingerie.

Dryness monitors: These allow the dryer to stop when the clothes are properly dried. Every dryer works by one or more of the following systems:

Time control: lets you select the length of drying time.

Thermostat: time and temperature determine degree of dryness and length of cycle, based on whether you select more or less dry.

Moisture sensors: device inside the drum measures moisture in the load.

Venting: Dryers generally vent from more than one direction, making installation easier. For best performance, a vent duct shouldn't be too long (generally no more than about 50 feet) or have too many elbows. Check and follow the manufacturer's recommended installation instructions.

 Helpful Hints

Laundry Products

Products are available for every step of the wash process:

- Detergents for cleaning.
- Bleaches and prewash products for removing stains and whitening.
- Fabric softeners for eliminating static cling and softening clothes.
- Starches and sizings for restoring body to shapeless clothes.

Detergents

Synthetic detergents contain surfactants, which increase water's wetting ability, loosen and remove soil, and suspend the soil in the wash solution. Some heavy-duty detergents also contain one or more "builders," which increase the surfactants' cleaning efficiency.

Depending on the brand, detergents may also incorporate fluorescent whitening agents, color-safe bleach, and borax, which boost their basic cleaning power. Almost all include enzymes. Some include fabric softeners, eliminating the need to add softener to the rinse water or dryer.

Heavy-duty detergents, a good choice for very dirty clothes, can be used for all washable fabrics. Light-duty formulas are designed for laundering delicate fabrics and baby clothes.

Detergents are available in powder, liquid, and tablet form. Liquids are especially effective for oily soils and are convenient for pre-treating soil before laundering.

Bleaches

Use laundry bleaches as stain removers, whiteners, brighteners, and sanitizers to supplement detergent. Bleaches are very powerful chemicals and should never be applied undiluted directly onto fabrics. (Before use, read "Bleaching Dos

 Helpful Hints

IS IT COLORFAST?

Some dark fabrics bleed color during initial washings. Check colorfastness before washing.

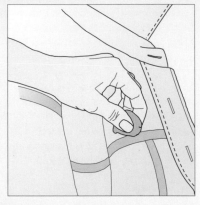

➤ **Place a drop of water on an inside seam (or a shirttail). Blot with a white cotton ball or towel.**

➤ **If the cotton ball or towel remains clean, it's safe to wash the garment with others of similar color. If it becomes tinted, wash the garment separately by hand.**

➤ **Don't hang a noncolorfast garment up to dry (the running color can streak). Roll it in a towel to blot excess moisture before ironing.**

and Don'ts," right.) Use bleach only on white and colorfast washables.

There are two kinds of bleach:

Chlorine: This is potent, fast acting, and very effective for cottons and synthetics. If not used properly, however, it can weaken fibers, causing disintegration and even holes. To avoid damage, follow label directions carefully. Never use it on silk, wool, spandex, or fabrics treated with flame-resistant finishes.

If machine washing, add diluted chlorine

Bleaching Dos and Don'ts

DO	DON'T
• Wear rubber gloves when hand washing with bleach. • Read fabric and bleach labels. • Test bleach before use: **Chlorine bleach:** Mix 1 tablespoon bleach with 1/4 cup cold water. Place a drop on a hidden area; leave for 1 minute; blot to see if there is any color change. **All-fabric/oxygen bleach:** Mix 1 teaspoon bleach with 1 cup hot water. Place a drop on a hidden area; leave for 10 minutes; blot to see if there is any color change. • Thoroughly rinse out bleach. • Keep bleach away from children.	• Let undiluted chlorine bleach come in direct contact with fabrics. • Put all-fabric/oxygen bleach directly on wet fabrics without testing for colorfastness first. • Use chlorine bleach if your household water supply has a high iron content. It can draw out the iron and deposit it as spots on clothes. • Use bleach and ammonia in the same wash. The combination can create hazardous fumes. • Use more of either kind of bleach than recommended on the package or bottle label.

bleach manually or by bleach dispenser, if your machine has one, 5 minutes after the wash cycle has begun.

All-fabric/oxygen: Milder than chlorine bleach, this bleach is for fabrics needing gentle treatment. It is slower acting and less effective in restoring whiteness, but, used regularly, it can help.

All-fabric/oxygen bleach, which comes in dry and liquid form, can be used with most washable silks and woolens—unless the garment manufacturer's label says "no bleach." Use liquid oxygen bleach to treat stains. Add oxygen bleach at the same time as detergent, before clothes are immersed in water.

Prewash Stain Removers

Use these products, which are available in pump spray, liquid, tablet, powder, stick, or aerosol forms, to pretreat heavily soiled or stained areas or add directly to the wash cycle. They are formulated to remove a variety of stains.

 Helpful Hints

IS YOUR WATER HARD?

There are several indications that you have hard water:

➤ **Fabrics look dull and gray.**

➤ **Fabrics feel stiff instead of soft.**

➤ **Soaps and detergents don't lather well.**

➤ **A "ring" settles around your bathtub (for cleaning, see box, page 63).**

➤ **A white residue appears, and remains, around drains and faucets and on glassware.**

If you do have hard water, add powdered water softener to the washing machine water with detergent or install a mechanical softener that is attached to the house water system (see box, page 315 for details). Call your local water company for more specific information on your water supply.

Cleaning Guide to Fibers and Fabrics

Here is a general guide to choosing the right cleaning method for your garments. Care varies based on colorfastness, weight, trimmings, linings, special finishes, and fabric and garment construction. Always read and follow the manufacturer's care label recommendations before cleaning garments.

Acetate: Synthetic fiber. Dry-clean.

Acrylic: Synthetic fiber. Machine wash knits in warm water on gentle setting. Wash inside out to reduce pilling. Roll in a towel to absorb extra moisture, and dry flat; or dry at low setting in a dryer. Dry-clean woven acrylic fabrics.

Blends: Fabrics of combined fibers: cotton/polyester, cotton/linen, silk/polyester, wool/polyester, and so on. Follow care guidelines for the more delicate or most prominent fiber in the blend.

Canvas: Heavy, firm, tightly woven fabric, originally cotton or linen, now also made of synthetics or blends. Machine wash in cold water and tumble dry on low setting. Dry-clean if not colorfast.

Cashmere: Undercoat hair of the cashmere goat. Treat as wool, and follow the care label. Sweaters may be hand washed with care, but it's best to dry-clean both knits and wovens.

Chiffon: Thin, transparent fabric, usually silk, but can be of synthetic fibers. Hand wash for best results.

Chintz: Glazed cotton, often printed. Dry-clean unless label states that glaze is durable and fabric can be washed; if so, wash as directed on labels.

Corduroy: Ridged-pile fabric that may be cotton, cotton/polyester, or rayon. Turn inside out and use warm water. Dry at regular setting; remove from dryer while slightly damp; smooth pockets and seams with hands. Hang until dry.

Cotton: Natural vegetable fiber woven and knitted into fabrics of many weights and textures. Hand wash lightweight fabrics, such as batiste, organdy, and voile, and hang to air-dry (or iron damp with a hot iron). Machine wash light-colored and white medium- and heavy-weight cottons with warm or hot water. Use cold water for bright colors that may bleed. Dry at regular or low setting. Remove from dryer while still damp. Iron damp with hot iron. Cottons like towels and underwear can be washed and dried on hot settings if desired.

Damask: Jacquard-weave fabric; may be cotton, linen, silk, viscose, wool, or a blend. Hand wash lightweight fabrics (see individual fiber listings for care). Dry-clean silk, wool, and all heavier-weight fabrics.

Denim: Strong, heavy twill-weave fabric, usually cotton, but can be a cotton/synthetic blend. Prone to shrinkage unless purchased preshrunk. Machine wash in warm water. Traditional blue and other deep colors bleed the first several washings, so wash separately, as necessary. Dry at low setting to avoid shrinkage. Iron while damp with a hot iron, as needed.

Down: Soft underplumage of water fowl, often combined with adult feathers (should be so labeled). Both machine-washable and dry-cleanable, but treatment depends on the fabric shell of the item; follow manufacturer's instructions carefully. Do not air dry. Tumble dry on gentle setting (temperature no higher than 140 degrees F). Fluff and turn often during drying.

Flannel: Napped fabric in plain or twill weave. Cotton and synthetics may be machine washed. Dry at low setting and remove while damp or line dry. Wool should be dry-cleaned.

Gabardine: Firm, closely woven twill fabric, originally and often worsted wool; also made of cotton and synthetic fibers. Follow label directions or dry-clean.

Lace: Open-work textile; may be cotton, linen, or synthetic. Hand wash using a detergent for delicate fabrics. Avoid rubbing. Squeeze out excess moisture; don't twist or wring. Shape by hand and hang to air-dry or dry flat; do not tumble dry. Pin delicate lace to a cloth before washing.

Linen: Natural flax fiber; light- to heavy-weight fabrics. Hand wash or machine wash in warm water if colorfast; use oxygen bleach, as needed. Iron damp on wrong side. For heavy linens, use a hot iron; for lighter-weight linens, blends, and linens treated for crease resistance, use a lower temperature. Can also dry-clean (especially heavy linens).

Microfibers (in cleaning cloths): Tightly woven polyester and nylon fibers. Machine wash separately to keep them lint-free. Never use fabric softener as it reduces the cloths' static properties and makes cleaning less effective. Line dry or machine dry on normal setting, again separately from other laundry.

Microfibers or fleece (in clothing and bedding): Small and fine polyester yarns that are tightly woven. Machine wash in cool to moderately warm water and air dry or machine dry, warm setting. If you have not purchased anti-pill fabric, turn garments wrong side out when laundering to reduce pilling. Fleece is heat sensitive, so hot dyer temperatures and ironing should be avoided to reduce pilling.

Mohair: Fiber from the angora goat. Treat as wool.

Nylon: Synthetic fiber used in fabrics of different weights, sometimes blended with other fibers. When used alone, it is both dry-cleanable and machine-washable; use warm water. Tumble dry on a low setting, or hang on plastic hanger and drip or air dry. To avoid permanent yellowing, keep away from sunlight or direct heat.

Organdy: Sheer, lightweight, plain weave cotton. Hand wash; starch to maintain characteristic crisp appearance. Iron damp with hot iron. Can also dry-clean.

Polyester: Strong synthetic fiber in fabrics of various weights and textures; often blended with cotton and wool. Does not shrink or stretch. Wash in warm water. Tumble dry and remove promptly to prevent wrinkles. Iron at low setting. If blended, follow guidelines for the more delicate fiber.

Ramie: Natural fiber from ramie plant (similar to linen), used alone or blended, often with cotton. Machine wash in warm water; tumble dry. Iron damp with hot iron. Can also dry-clean. Avoid excessive twisting.

Rayon: A generic term for a man-made fiber including viscose and cuprammonium rayon. Some garment labels identify the fabric as "rayon," some as "viscose." Follow label care instructions. Dry-clean for best results.

Rubber: A fiber found in both natural and man-made form. Used in sneakers. Remove laces (wash those separately) and machine wash warm. For best results, air-dry or dry at low setting. Using too high a temperature in the dryer will sometimes melt the rubber or shrink the canvas part of the shoe.

Satin: Fabric with a lustrous finish, traditionally silk, now also acetate and polyester. Dry-clean silk and acetate. Wash polyester satins following fiber guidelines.

Seersucker: Fabric with puckered stripes woven in during the manufacturing process; usually cotton, but also nylon, polyester, and silk versions. See specific fiber for washing

(continued on next page)

(continued from previous page)

instructions. Drip or tumble dry. Iron on low heat, if needed.

Silk: Natural fiber from the silkworm; in fabrics of various weights and textures. If recommended, hand wash plain-weave crepe de chine and thin, lightweight, and medium-weight silks in lukewarm water with mild soap or detergent or in cold water with special cold-water detergent. Do not use chlorine bleach. Rinse several times in cold water until no trace of suds remains; towel-blot. Dry flat. Iron on wrong side at warm (silk) setting. If so labeled, some silks can be machine washed; follow label directions carefully. Dry-clean heavier (suiting weight) silks, pleated silks, and those in dark colors, which may bleed.

Spandex: Generic name for stretch fibers often added to other fibers to give them elasticity. Machine wash in warm water on the delicate cycle (if exercise wear, wash after each wearing to remove body oils, which can cause deterioration). Do not use chlorine bleach. Tumble dry on low setting. Iron using low setting.

Terry cloth: Toweling fabric with looped pile made of cotton or cotton/polyester. Machine wash in warm or hot water. Tumble dry or line dry.

Velour: Napped fabric, originally wool, now also cotton, silk, and synthetics. Dry-clean unless manufacturer's label indicates it can be washed.

Velvet: Soft pile fabric, originally silk, now usually rayon or cotton. Dry-clean.

Wool: Natural fiber made of sheep fleece. Hand wash sweaters and other knits in cold water with cold-water detergent. Rinse thoroughly. Squeeze; do not wring. Towel-blot and dry flat (see Air-Drying, page 76), blocking back to original size. Machine-washable wools are so labeled; follow instructions carefully. Dry-clean woven wools and heavy sweaters.

Fabric Softeners

These make fabrics soft and fluffy, and help reduce static cling. They also reduce wrinkling and make ironing easier or unnecessary.

Liquid softeners: These should be added to the final rinse cycle by automatic dispenser if your washing machine has one, or by hand. Follow the label directions and measure carefully. To avoid buildup on towels, which reduces absorbency, use fabric softener once every 2 to 3 washings and never add more than the label recommends.

Dryer-added softeners: These paper-thin sheets are placed on top of the clothes in the dryer.

If you use a detergent that contains fabric softeners (check the label), you don't need to add extra softener.

Starches and Sizings

Starches and sizings restore body to fabrics that become limp—such as cotton and linen—when washed or dry-cleaned.

Starch
Starch comes in regular and heavy formulas. Spritz spray starch on during ironing. Let it soak into the fabric before ironing to avoid flaking.

Sizing
Lighter than starch, sizing is applied to some fabrics by manufacturers for protection and body. General wear, moisture, perspiration, and cleaning will break down sizing, but you can reapply it. Spritz it on and allow it to penetrate before ironing.

Doing the Wash

Make organizing the wash everybody's job. Each person should be responsible for gathering his or her own soiled clothes and linens, presorting them, and taking them to the laundry room.

A laundry bag or small hamper in every clothes closet helps. It is best to treat stains quickly, so ask family members to turn in their heavily soiled items as quickly as possible.

Before You Start

For best results, separate:
- Dark from white or light-colored items.
- Lightly soiled from heavily soiled garments.
- Fabrics requiring different water temperatures (see Machine Washing, right).
- Lint-shedding fabrics, such as terry cloth, from lint-attracting fabrics, such as corduroy, synthetics, and permanent-press fabrics. (Turn pile fabrics, such as corduroy or velour, inside out so they won't pick up lint.)
- Lingerie and delicate fabric from other garments; wash them in mesh bags or wash by hand.
- Any clothes in which colorfastness may be a problem. Test first (see box, page 70).

And before you wash, be sure to:
- Brush dirt and lint from the insides of pant and sleeve cuffs.
- Close zippers, hooks, and snaps to prevent breakage and snagging.
- Tie straps, strings, and sashes to prevent tangling.
- Empty pockets (remember to check children's).
- Remove nonwashable belts, shoulder pads, and trimmings.
- Mend tears and ripped seams; they are usually smaller and easier to fix before washing rather than after (see page 91).

Pretreating

Just before washing or presoaking, apply a liquid detergent; or a paste made of powered detergent and water; or a commercial prewash stain remover to stains and soiled areas such as collars, cuffs, pocket edges, and seams. Rub in (or brush with an old soft toothbrush). Some commercial prewash stain remover sticks can be applied as much as a week in advance of doing the laundry (check product label).

Before laundering, soak heavily soiled garments in a detergent solution in a sink or tub. If your washing machine has a presoak cycle, you can do this automatically. Do not soak silk, wool, or noncolorfast fabrics.

Machine Washing

First, select the appropriate water temperature:

Hot: for heavily soiled, colorfast clothes, diapers, sheets, and towels.

Warm: for cotton, blends, washable woolens and knits, and moderately soiled items.

Cold: for lightly soiled, noncolorfast, and delicate fabrics. Use cold water for rinsing to save energy and reduce the possibility of setting wrinkles in the fabrics.
- Add detergent as the washer fills.
- Add laundry aids such as bleach (according to package directions), as needed.
- Wait until the rinse cycle to add fabric softener, as needed, or use the machine's dispenser. Don't use fabric softener with other laundry products that contain softeners.
- Load the machine loosely—with enough items to fill, but do not overload. Distribute clothes evenly, balancing large and small pieces, and make sure that nothing is wrapped around the agitator.

➤ **When machine washing or drying delicate items, place them in a mesh bag or a pillowcase (tied closed or pinned with rustproof safety pins).**

➤ **When machine washing a line-dry-only item, place it in a mesh bag so it's easy to identify when the wash is finished.**

STAIN-FIGHTER SUPPLIES

Keep the following stain-removal supplies on hand and follow the label instructions:

Acetone: Pure acetone, not nail-polish remover—available at pharmacies

Ammonia: Household

Bleach: Both chlorine and all-fabric/ oxygen varieties

Color remover: Available where fabric dyes are sold

Dry-cleaning solvent: Available at supermarkets

Enzyme detergent

Glycerine: Available at pharmacies

Oxalic acid solution or rust remover: Available at pharmacies

Paint remover

Petroleum jelly

Prewash spot remover

Rubbing alcohol

White vinegar

When in doubt, try cleaner on an inconspicuous part of the garment just in case it has staining or damaging properties.

Machine-Drying

Before each wash, clean the lint filter to ensure better dryer performance.

- To dry evenly, put items of similar fabric weight, but mixed sizes, in one load.
- For recommended drying times and temperatures, read the appliance manual and follow the suggestions on garment manufacturers' labels.
- As soon as the tumbling action ends, remove items to prevent wrinkles, and hang or fold.
- If clothes or linens are to be ironed immediately, remove them from the dryer while they are still damp.

Air-Drying

Hang garments on padded hangers and line dry indoors or out. If flat drying is recommended for sweaters or garments that may stretch, roll the item in a towel to blot excess moisture, then shape the garment and place it on a towel or flat rack to dry, away from the sun, which can bleach or discolor. When dry on top, turn it over, changing towels if necessary.

Special-Care Items

Area Rugs
Some small scatter rugs of cotton or synthetic fibers are machine washable; check the manufacturer's label. Before washing, vacuum or shake out loose dirt.

If the rug is heavily soiled, use the soak cycle on your machine, or soak in a basin. Do not tumble dry if the rug has a rubber backing. Hang it on a line.

Bedding
Cotton and synthetic blankets and bedspreads can be machine washed if they are treated as delicate fabrics in both the washer and dryer. Always follow the manufacturer's recommendations.

Electric blankets should be machine washed on the gentle cycle, using a short (2 to 3 minutes) agitation time. Don't use the dryer unless the care label recommends it. Hang the blanket over

Setting Up a Laundry Room

The ideal laundry room has plenty of storage space; good lighting; venting; a no-skid, washable floor; and room for ironing, folding, and hanging and air-drying clothes. If your space is limited, try a compact, efficient, closet arrangement.

FULL-SIZE LAUNDRY

Removable hangers

Deep utility sink

Side-by-side washer and dryer

Water-resistant floor

Fold-up ironing board

Ample storage

Deep pull-out bins

Table for sorting and folding

LAUNDRY IN A CLOSET

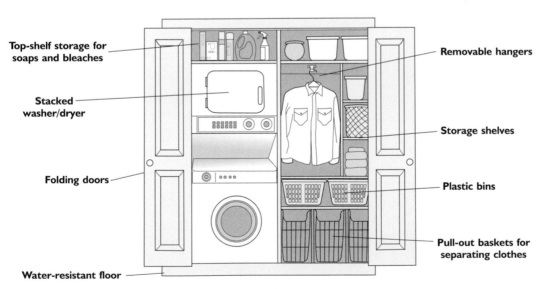

Top-shelf storage for soaps and bleaches

Stacked washer/dryer

Folding doors

Water-resistant floor

Removable hangers

Storage shelves

Plastic bins

Pull-out baskets for separating clothes

2 lines or lay it flat to dry. Never dry-clean an electric blanket because the chemicals may ruin the wiring.

Some quilts and polyester-filled comforters can be machine washed, but only if securely stitched. If the synthetic filling isn't stitched through, it will shift and become lumpy.

Wash only one large bedding item at a time, distributing its bulk evenly around the agitator, or use a front-loading machine, if possible. Tumble dry or line dry.

If line drying, hang the item over 2 lines to bear the weight better, and turn and rehang at least once.

Cotton and Synthetic Knits

Close zippers and attach hook-and-eye fasteners. Turn the garment inside out. If the label says washable, machine wash in warm water (cold water for dark colors). Tumble dry on a low temperature. Remove promptly.

Loose and open knits can be damaged by washer agitation. It is better to hand wash these and dry flat after shaping.

Don't machine wash wool knits, including sweaters, unless indicated on the care label. Follow the instructions for hand washing on page 81.

Down Jackets and Comforters

Down jackets and coats and down-filled comforters are machine-washable if their shell fabric is. Check the label.

It's especially important to mend tears and rips in the fabric before washing, since down (and feathers, if the filling includes them) can push through small holes.

Wash each item separately in warm water, distributing the bulk around the agitator. If the load is small, balance it with bath towels.

Never air-dry down garments or bedding; the down will flatten and dry lumpy. Tumble dry at a low setting (drying will be slow). Add a clean sneaker to help fluff up the down.

Down items can also be dry-cleaned if the label recommends doing so. Use a reputable dry cleaner since the wrong solvents can strip the natural oils in down and stain the shell fabric.

Glass-Fiber Textiles

Do not machine wash or dry glass-fiber textiles such as draperies. The glass particles can penetrate other fabrics. Hand wash and rinse carefully to avoid breaking the fibers. Line dry.

Helpful Hints

5 WAYS TO MINIMIZE SHRINKAGE

Always read the care label. If it indicates to dry-clean only, do so. For washable garments:

➤ Use cool or warm water, not hot.

➤ Use the most gentle wash method that achieves good results.

➤ Air-dry or dry on the lowest dryer setting.

➤ Remove clothes from the dryer before they're completely dry.

➤ Drip-dry or block into shape and lay flat to finish drying (see Air-Drying, page 76).

MYSTERY STAINS

For washable fabrics, apply pretreatment product or rub liquid laundry detergent into stain. Wash in warm, sudsy water with a few drops of ammonia added. Rinse. For any remaining stain, launder again using an appropriate bleach. For dry-cleanable fabrics, sponge stains with dry-cleaning solvent.

Label Language

Ever wonder what those symbols on garment care labels mean? This chart shows how to decode them:

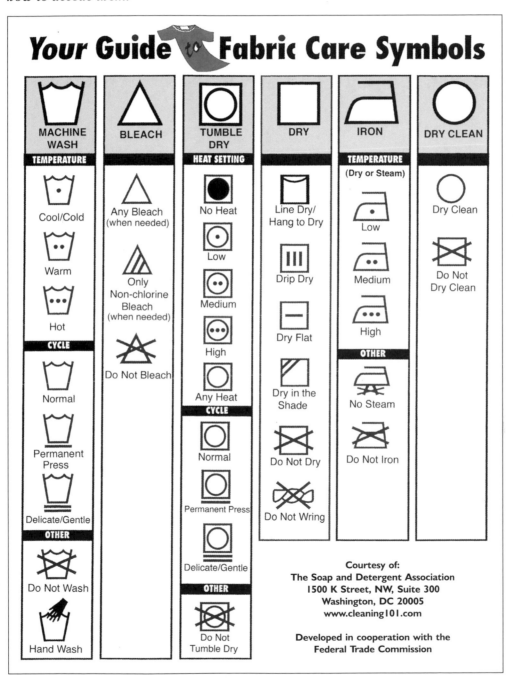

Your Guide to Fabric Care Symbols

Courtesy of:
The Soap and Detergent Association
1500 K Street, NW, Suite 300
Washington, DC 20005
www.cleaning101.com

Developed in cooperation with the
Federal Trade Commission

Laundering Vintage Linens and Lace

Before You Start

Never wash an antique or delicate quilt or textile without first showing it to a conservation or restoration specialist.

If you are washing an item with colored embroidery, consult a dry cleaner or professional hand launderer who works with vintage linens or lace about proper treatment.

If you are laundering items yourself, be sure to do the following:

- Remove any metal fasteners or decorations that might rust or discolor the fabric when wet.
- Protect small, delicate items by putting them in a mesh bag.

To Wash

If you are working with a large item—such as a tablecloth, bed coverlet, or dress—use the bathtub for soaking, placing the piece on a stack of white towels or clean white cotton cloths to support it in the water.

1. Soak the item in a solution of a commercial cleaning paste designed for vintage fabrics and water, or a solution of mild soap and water. The water can be cool or lukewarm, but not hot. Do not rub or wring the fabric while it is soaking.
2. As the water becomes dirty, change it, adding fresh cleaning paste or soap as often as necessary.

3. Rinse in fresh water several times until all traces of paste or soap are gone (any that remain can weaken the fabric). Lift the item out carefully after each rinse, holding the underside of the fabric.
4. If there are still stains and dirt, soak the item again in an all-fabric/oxygen bleach solution (follow package directions), and rinse again several times.

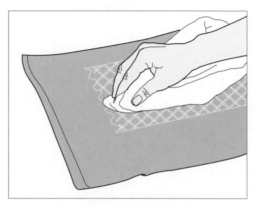

Blot fragile items dry

To Dry

Blot the item with towels, and place flat on a fresh towel or a sheet to dry, gently blotting any excess moisture and pulling the item into its proper shape.

To Press

Use a low heat setting and a pressing cloth. Place lace and embroidered pieces facedown on a towel before pressing. (Lace may not need pressing.)

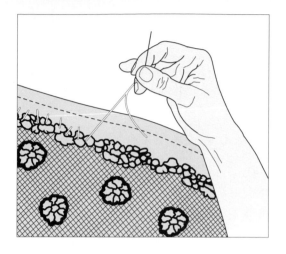

Antique Lace
To clean a fragile lace tablecloth, baste it (sew it loosely) with white thread to an old sheet before immersing it in water, and leave the two together until both lace and sheet have completely dried.

Pillows and Stuffed Toys
Before washing pillows or stuffed toys, check the manufacturer's label to see if they are machine-washable. Mend any tears or rips before washing. Place toys in a pillowcase and tie closed.

Wash 2 pillows or toys together for balance—one on each side of the agitator. Agitate 1 to 2 minutes on a gentle cycle. Rinse thoroughly.

Tumble dry polyester-filled and feather pillows; feather pillows will become lumpy if you attempt to dry them any other way. Fluff the pillows as they dry to separate lumps. Foam pillows should not be put in the dryer; air dry only.

Check to make sure stuffed toys are clean after washing, then put them back in the pillowcase, tie it shut, and tumble dry at a low setting.

Wool (Wovens and Knits)
Read care labels to determine which wool garments and blankets are machine-washable.

Follow directions carefully, and wash each item separately. Use the gentle cycle and lukewarm or cool water. Do not bleach.

Air-dry or tumble dry at regular setting (180 to 230 degrees F) for 10 to 20 minutes. Remove while the garment still contains moisture and dry flat.

Hand Washing

Always test for colorfastness (see box, page 70) before washing by hand and separate those items that run. Pretreat soiled areas such as collars and cuffs with a pretreatment product or liquid detergent, or rub with a bar of mild soap.

Dissolve detergent in warm water, or use a detergent made especially to wash delicate fabrics in cold water. Soak and swish the garment in the suds for a few minutes, then squeeze out the water. Rinse at least twice in water the same temperature as the wash water. Squeeze out water after each rinse.

Roll the item flat in a towel to blot excess water. Except for sweaters and any items whose colors may run and streak, hang on a plastic hanger to dry (never wood or wire, which can rust or discolor wet fabric). Otherwise dry flat.

If the garment is to be ironed, partially air-dry, and follow the care label.

 Helpful Hints

HOW TO CORRECT COLOR BLEEDING
If color bleeding affects a washable white fabric, use a color remover or a dye-transfer remover (available where home dyeing products are sold). Run the item through another wash cycle immediately, adding the color remover according to package instructions to restore the original whiteness.

How to Remove Stains

Always read the manufacturer's label before treating a stain. If the fabric is washable, follow the guide below. If there are any doubts, take the item to a dry cleaner (see page 88). Either way, act quickly. The longer a stain remains, the more likely it is to set permanently. Another caveat: Avoid using ammonia on silk or wool.

NOTE: Always test any method or solution on a hidden part of the fabric first. Rinse well between steps and never put a garment in the dryer until you know the stain is completely removed, or it may be permanently set by the heat.

Bleach Basics

For White Fabrics
Mix 1/4 cup chlorine bleach with 1 gallon cold water; soak for 5 minutes. Launder as usual.

For Colored Fabrics, Washable White Silk, or Wool
Apply liquid all-fabric bleach directly to stains and launder.

Alcoholic beverage: Soak fresh stain in cool water. Wash in warm suds. Rinse. For old, brown stains or any remaining stain, use the appropriate bleach.

Antiperspirant: Rub liquid laundry detergent into stain. Wash in warm suds. Rinse.

Blood: Wash stain immediately in cold running water, rubbing with bar soap, or apply hydrogen peroxide to dried blood stains. Rinse.

For old stains or any remaining stain, soak for 15 minutes in a solution of 2 tablespoons ammonia to 1 gallon cool, soapy water. Soak any remaining stain in warm water with detergent. Wash in warm suds with appropriate bleach. Rinse.

Butter/margarine: Rub liquid detergent into fabric. If a greasy residue remains after washing, sponge with or soak in dry-cleaning solvent, then rewash in warm suds. Rinse.

Candle wax: Harden the wax with an ice cube, then gently scrape off as much wax as possible with a dull knife. Sponge stain with dry-cleaning solvent to remove as much as possible. Place stain between paper towels. Press with warm, dry iron, changing towel as the wax is absorbed. Launder as usual. If stain remains, use the appropriate bleach.

Commercial candle-wax removers are also available.

Catsup/tomato sauce: Soak fresh stain in cool water. Rub in liquid laundry detergent. Wash in warm suds. Rinse. If a greasy residue remains after washing, sponge with or soak in dry-cleaning solvent. For any remaining stain, use the appropriate bleach.

Chewing gum: Harden gum with an ice cube, then gently scrape off as much as possible with a dull knife.

Soak spot with dry-cleaning solvent until remaining gum is loosened and scrape again. Wash in warm suds. Rinse.

Chocolate/cocoa: Wash stain in warm suds with a few drops of ammonia added. Rinse. If stain remains, sponge with or soak in dry-cleaning solvent, then use the appropriate bleach.

Coffee/tea: Soak fresh stain in cool water. (If the beverage contained cream, sponge stain with dry-cleaning solvent before soaking.)Wash in warm suds. Rinse. If stain remains, use the appropriate bleach.

Crayon: Place the item facedown on a pile of paper towels and spray the wax-stained area liberally with a household lubricant like WD-40; let sit for five minutes, then spritz the reverse side. Next, work in liquid dishwashing detergent, removing the top layers of towels as they absorb the stain. Wash in hot water with color-safe or chlorine bleach, followed by a warm-water rinse.

Cream/baby formula: Sponge stain with cool water. Soak in enzyme detergent solution for 30 minutes. Rinse. Sponge greasy residue with dry-cleaning solvent.

Launder as usual. Iron stains (from supplements or medicine) can be removed with a commercial rust remover.

Fruits/berries: Soak fresh stain in cool water. Wash in warm suds. Rinse. If stain remains, use the appropriate bleach. Rinse well.

Grass: Rub some liquid enzyme detergent directly on the stain. Launder as usual using the appropriate bleach.

Grease/oil: Sponge with dry-cleaning solvent. Pretreat with prewash stain remover or liquid laundry detergent. Launder as usual, using hottest water safe for the fabric.

Ice cream: Soak stain in cool water, then wash in warm suds using an enzyme detergent. Rinse. For chocolate ice cream, first sponge with dry-cleaning solvent or let soak in dry-cleaning solvent for 15 minutes. Launder as usual using the appropriate bleach.

Ink, ballpoint: Sponge stain with rubbing alcohol. Launder as usual using the appropriate bleach.

Ink, other: Rinse stain freely in cool water, then wash in warm, sudsy water and a few drops of household ammonia. Launder as usual using the appropriate bleach. (Some "permanent" ink cannot be removed.)

Lipstick: Soak stain in dry-cleaning solvent or pretreat with prewash stain remover. Launder as usual using the appropriate bleach.

Makeup: Sponge with or soak in dry-cleaning solvent. Launder as usual using the appropriate bleach.

Mascara: Rub stain with a liquid detergent. Launder as usual using the appropriate bleach. (Some waterproof products cannot be removed.)

Mildew: Take garment outside. Use a stiff brush to remove the mold spores. For fabrics that are safe to use with chlorine bleach, soak stain for 15 minutes in a solution of 2 to 3 tablespoons of chlorine bleach to 1 quart of warm water. Rinse well.

Otherwise, use oxygen bleach, and soak stain for 30 minutes. Launder as usual.

Mud: Allow stain to dry, then brush or vacuum away dirt. Rub in liquid laundry detergent. Launder as usual using the appropriate bleach, if necessary.

Nail polish: Sponge with acetone after first testing on a hidden part of the item. (Do not use acetone on fabrics containing acetate and triacetate; it will dissolve them.) Launder as usual using the appropriate bleach.

Paint, dried: Gently scrape off as much paint as possible with a dull knife. Rub petroleum jelly into stain to soften. Soak in paint remover, rubbing occasionally, until stain has dissolved. Wash in warm, sudsy water. Rinse. Launder as usual using the appropriate bleach.

(continued on next page)

(continued from previous page)

Paint, wet: Blot as much as possible with cotton cloth or tissue, then treat immediately as above. Fresh latex (water-based) paint often rinses out.

Perspiration: Rub liquid enzyme detergent into the stain and allow it to soak in a solution of enzyme detergent and water for 30 minutes to 1 hour.

Wash in warm, sudsy water using the appropriate bleach, if necessary. Rinse.

To correct any change to colored fabrics (other than wool or silk), hold stain over fumes of household ammonia, or sponge with white vinegar. To remove odor, soak 1 hour or longer in a solution of 3 tablespoons of salt and 1 of quart water.

Rust: Use a commercial rust remover or soak 15 minutes in a weak oxalic acid solution (2 tablespoons of oxalic acid to 1 quart of water). Rinse 3 times, adding a few drops of ammonia to the final rinse water.

Scorch mark: A heavy scorch that has damaged fibers usually cannot be repaired. For slight scorch stains on washable fabrics, wash in warm, sudsy water using the appropriate bleach, if necessary. Rinse.

Shoe polish: Sponge stain with dry-cleaning solvent to remove grease. Wash remaining stain in warm, sudsy water using an appropriate bleach, if necessary. (Liquid shoe polishes may not come out.)

Tar: Gently scrape off as much as possible with a dull knife. Soften the remaining stain by rubbing in petroleum jelly. Let stand 15 minutes, then soak in dry-cleaning solvent. Wash in warm, sudsy water. Rinse.

Urine: Flush stains with cold water. Launder in warm, sudsy water with the appropriate bleach. Rinse.

Vomit: Scrape to remove solids. Soak stain in enzyme detergent solution, then wash in warm, sudsy water with a few drops of ammonia added. Rinse. Launder as usual with the appropriate bleach, if necessary.

Water stains: These rings occur when a water-based stain damages a fabric's finish. To remove, dampen the entire area and let dry, or hold a steam iron over the spotted area or use a garment steamer. Press the area with a steam iron while still damp.

Wine, red: Sponge or soak the stain in cool water. Pretreat with a prewash stain remover or liquid laundry detergent. Launder in warm water. If the stain remains, launder again, using the appropriate bleach.

Wine, white: Blot excess. Sponge stain with cool water, then rub with liquid detergent. Launder as usual.

Yellowing: See Rust. For white fabrics only, use commercially available color remover or fabric whitener, available where fabric dyes are sold.

Ironing

For smooth ironing, fabrics should be damp. If possible, bring garments from the dryer or line before they are fully dry and iron them immediately. Otherwise, use the spray feature on the iron as you go.

If you use spray starch or sizing, spray each section just before ironing it, and let the starch soak in. This prevents flaking and buildup on the iron soleplate.

Let freshly ironed items cool before putting them away. If handled while still warm, they can become wrinkled. Have a rack handy for hanging warm garments and a table for stacking linens.

 Helpful Hints

HOT TIPS

➤ **Some irons have more steam vents than others (though that doesn't necessarily mean they emit more steam), and some are designed to give an extra surge or burst of steam when needed (often useful when ironing ruffles, gathers, pleats, and tucks).**

➤ **Consider cordless irons, which are available with an automatic shut-off feature. They heat up quickly, but can also cool off quickly if left off the base for too long.**

➤ **Depending on your community's water system and the steam iron you choose, you may be able to use tap water for steaming or you may need to use a mixture of tap and distilled waters.**

PRESSING MATTERS

➤ **Use a damp, lint-free cloth, such as a handkerchief, diaper, or old cotton sheet, for a pressing cloth.**

➤ **Cut your ironing time by smoothing seams, plackets, and pleats as garments dry on a hanger or line, or immediately after you take them from a tumble dryer.**

 Time Savers

NO TIME TO IRON?
Wrinkle-resistant sprays relax and smooth fabrics to help remove wrinkles, freeing you from ironing. Spray in a sweeping motion until the garment is slightly damp. Tug and smooth away the wrinkles, then hang to dry. Before using, read and follow the product label directions. You can also buy garments made from no-iron, wrinkle-resist fabrics.

Household Linens
Household cottons and linens, such as napkins, sheets, and pillowcases, may not need to be ironed if they are made of wrinkle-resistant fabrics or if you smooth them by hand immediately after drying.

If they do need to be ironed, gently pull them into shape first. To make ironing large items such as tablecloths and sheets easier, fold them first and iron in sections or drape them over a chair as you go.

Pressing

Pressing is useful for smoothing isolated wrinkles on a garment stored in a crowded closet or folded and crushed tightly in a drawer. It calls for short lowering and lifting motions, not the long gliding strokes used for ironing. Use the steam feature of your iron and select the appropriate temperature for the fabric.

Steam-press lace, silk, and wool on the wrong side, when possible. When pressing on the right side, use a dry pressing cloth. Place metallic, beaded, and sequined fabrics facedown on a board covered with extra padding, such as one or two thick towels, and steam-press on the lowest temperature setting.

Press only when and where there are wrinkles. Overpressing can take the life out of a fabric.

If your velvet or velveteen isn't wrinkled and the nap simply needs raising, steam it without pressing, moving the iron back and forth an inch or so above the fabric.

You can also hold a garment in front of a steaming kettle, hang it in the bathroom while hot water is turned on in the shower, or use a garment steamer.

Caring for Your Iron

A dirty iron or ironing-board cover can soil or damage your garments. Many irons have soleplates that wipe clean with a damp sponge or cloth. Check the manufacturer's care recommendations in your owner's manual.

Remove spray-starch deposits on the soleplate of the iron by rubbing with a damp cloth

Irons: What to Look For

The first thing to consider when buying an iron is safety. Make sure the model you choose has the UL (Underwriters Laboratories) mark, which ensures that the iron meets national electrical safety standards; any iron made by a major manufacturer will have it. Many irons are constructed largely of plastic, and are lighter in weight than those made primarily of metal. You can use virtually any iron dry or with steam.

BASIC FEATURES

Be sure to test the weight and the grip, then choose the iron that feels best to you. Any good iron should have the following:

Adjustable steam levels for different fabric needs
Adjustable thermostat with a choice of temperature settings for different kinds of fabrics
Automatic shut-off mechanism
Button grooves (indentations in the sides of the soleplate designed to fit around buttons)
See-through water tank to show how much water is left as you steam-press
Spray and burst steam controls

SPECIAL FEATURES

While fancy features aren't necessary to do a good job, they can make ironing easier and safer. Consider these:
Detachable water tank
Extra-long cord
Reversible cord (for left-handers)
Vertical steam for hanging garments and draperies

How to Iron

SHIRTS AND BLOUSES

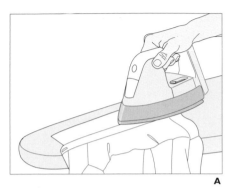

A

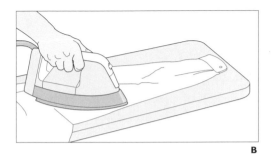

B

Start ironing at the top of a blouse or shirt. Begin or end with the collar, working toward the middle from the outer edges or points. **(A)**

Lay one shoulder over the narrow end of the board. Iron one side of the front yoke, then the shoulder, across the back below the collar line, the other shoulder, and the remainder of the front yoke, shifting as needed.

Iron the sleeves and cuffs, working down from the underarm seams. **(B)** (If you don't want a deep crease, shift the double layer of sleeve fabric and press out the crease line.)

Next, iron the body of the garment, moving from one half of the front around the back to the second half of the front.

If a blouse or shirt doesn't open, slip it over the end of the ironing board and iron front and back in turn.

PANTS

C

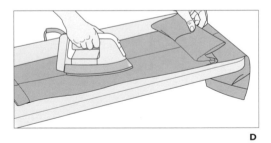

D

Turn the waistband inside out and pull the pockets out to iron first, then iron the zipper placket.

Turn back to the right side, iron the waistband and the remainder of the top all the way around. **(C)**

Put the leg seams together in the middle and fold lengthwise. Lay the pants flat on the board, fold back the top leg, and iron the inside of the lower leg. **(D)** Turn and iron the outside. Repeat the process for the second leg. Finally, iron the 2 legs (4 thicknesses of fabric) together. If the pants have creases, press heavily on the folds.

(continued on next page)

(continued from previous page)

PLEATED SKIRTS	SEQUINED GARMENTS

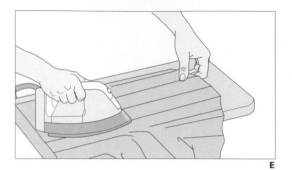

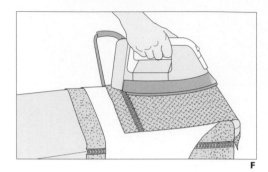

Arrange groups of pleats and hold in place or pin to the board as you iron in long strokes from top to bottom. **(E)** Don't iron over pins.

Turn the item inside out and place it carefully on the ironing board with the sequins (or beads) facedown on a towel. Put a pressing cloth on top and press with the iron on a low setting. **(F)**

sprinkled with baking soda, then wiping with a clean cloth. For stubborn starch that may have burned onto the soleplate, rub with a paste of cleanser and water, wipe clean, and steam over a cloth after cleaning and before ironing a garment.

Regularly flush steam and water through the holes to clear the iron of minerals and lint. Be sure to hold the iron over a sink while you clean it. Wipe the soleplate afterward. Always empty your iron of water after each use.

Dry-Cleaning

Use dry-cleaning solvents only for stain removal, if that is the method advised for treating a particular stain. Leave heavy-duty full-garment dry cleaning to the professionals.

The more you are able to tell your professional dry cleaner about your garment and the cause of any spots or stains, the better he or she will be able to determine the best method of cleaning.

Point out any stains and describe what they are, if you know. Even if no spots are visible but you remember spilling a beverage, show the cleaner where you think it might have landed.

If not treated, invisible spots can become visible later when it may be too late to remove them. If a garment is still stained, tell the cleaner not to press it. You may wish to try removing the stain yourself and pressing will only further set it.

Always consult your dry cleaner about:
• Clothes made of leather, fur, or suede, and clothes with leather, fur, or suede trim.

They may need the attention of a leather-cleaning expert.

- Clothes with bead, sequin, and appliqué trims. Some trims, such as polystyrene beads and imitation pearls, can melt in the cleaning process. If trim is glued on, it can loosen and fall off.

Don't dry-clean too often. Too much cleaning can weaken fibers and shorten a garment's life. After each wearing, air dresses, suits, coats, jackets, or pants before hanging them up.

Brush thoroughly and often with a clothes brush to remove lint and loose dirt. (You can even vacuum heavy fabrics.) Check for spots; if you are experienced, you may wish to try treating any you can yourself (see pages 82–84). Home stain-removal methods are not always effective on dry-cleanable fabrics, and they can sometimes even make matters worse. Proceed cautiously or consult your dry cleaner.

Bulk Dry Cleaners

Coin-operated dry-cleaning machines, in which clothes can be cleaned in bulk instead of individually, are available in some communities.

Bulk cleaners should be used as supplements to—not replacements for—professional dry cleaning.

Shrinkage sometimes occurs in these machines, and (as in laundering) dyes can be transferred when a noncolorfast item is cleaned with others, so it's best not to use bulk machines for fine clothing.

 Helpful Hints

DON'T BAG IT

Although it's tempting to keep clothing in the dry cleaner's plastic bags, the bags trap odors in clothes and the cleaning chemicals can cling to them. Remove the clothes from the bags when you get home from the cleaners. Keep the empty bags out of children's reach.

CAREFUL CLEANING

➤ Have all pieces of a suit cleaned at the same time even if only one piece needs cleaning. Cleaning fluids can affect the garment's dyes. This won't be noticeable if all pieces are cleaned together.

➤ Protect novelty and delicate buttons by covering them individually with a small piece of aluminum foil.

 Green and Clean

"WET" OR "GREEN" CLEANERS

The term "wet" or "green" cleaning refers to a professional process of cleaning clothes using methods other than the traditional perchloroethylene solvent, which is harmful to the environment and can leave a telltale odor on clothes. These green methods include a silicone-based solvent, liquid carbon dioxide and high-pressure equipment, or water and special detergents in computer-controlled machines. Although green cleaning methods are better for the environment, they may not be as effective as traditional methods at removing stains. Many traditional or "dry" cleaners are instituting environmentally friendly practices such as phasing out the use of perchloroethylene, collecting and reusing hangers, and recycling plastic bags.

Use them only for older blankets, heavy wool sweaters, and other items that don't require pressing or professional attention.

Sewing

There are times in everyone's life when buttons must be attached, seams repaired, and hems restitched. If you can make minor repairs at home, you can avoid spending money on tailors and seamstresses.

Here are the basic hand sewing techniques to get you started.

Fasteners

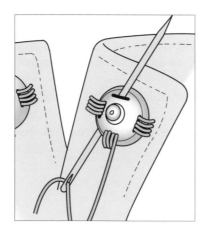

Sewing a snap fastener

Snap Fasteners

Snaps, meant to be invisible, are used where one section of a garment overlaps another. A snap has 2 parts—a ball and a socket.

1. Sew the ball half on the wrong side of the overlap section, keeping it at least 1/4 inch from the edge.
2. Take a stitch under the edge of the snap, then push the needle through the fabric and one hole.
3. Take several stitches through each hole, then secure by knotting or backstitching (see page 95).
4. Position the socket half on the right side of the underlapping fabric so that it meets the ball precisely.
5. Mark the exact spot before you begin by rubbing chalk on the attached ball and pressing it against the underlapping fabric.
6. Attach the socket as you did the ball.

Hook-and-Eye Fasteners

Use hooks and eyes for overlaps and where edges meet.

1. If attaching the fasteners at a waistband, sew the hook at the edge on the inside of the overlapping section and sew the eye on the outside of the underlap.
2. If attaching them at a neckline or other area where edges meet, sew both parts on the wrong side (inside) of the garment. Sew the hook right at the edge and the eye, if curved, with the curve extending over the edge.
3. Sew down the 2 rings at the base of the hook (forming 2 thread-covered circles).
4. Take the threaded needle in a long stitch under the fabric to the curved end of the hook and secure to the fabric.
5. Finish with a knot or backstitches (see page 95).
6. Position the eye to meet the hook properly, and sew it through the fabric and around both rings at the base.

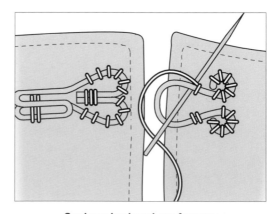

Sewing a hook-and-eye fastener

The Sewing Basket

Keep a basket in or near your laundry room with the following sewing supplies, all of which are available in most notion departments and variety stores:

Buttons: keep the extras attached to new garments by manufacturers as well as a miscellaneous selection.

Carpet thread: for sewing buttons on heavy materials or restringing beads. (You can also use dental floss.)

Chalk: for marking hems.

Fasteners: both snaps and hook-and-eyes in assorted sizes.

Needles: in different sizes, available in packets.

Needle threaders: if you have trouble guiding thread into a needle's eye. Also have on hand a bodkin—a long needle with a large eye—which is useful for threading ribbon or elastic through an eyelet or casing.

Scissors: small for cutting thread; large, bent-handled for cutting fabric; pinking shears for cutting edges that won't ravel.

Seam binding: for finishing hems.

Spools of thread: in a variety of colors and types. Both cotton-covered polyester and 100-percent polyester are all-purpose threads that can be used on all kinds of fabrics including natural and synthetic knits and wovens.

Straight pins: for most pinning tasks; also safety pins and a pin cushion.

Tape measure: for hem and other measuring.

Thimble: for protecting your finger from the needle as you sew.

Mending and Altering

Tears

Cut a piece of fabric from an inner seam, the hem, or other hidden spot. The cut piece should be slightly larger than the area of the tear.

Place it beneath the tear, matching the direction of a pattern or grain of the weave as best you can to the top surface, and secure it with pins or tape.

Working on the right side of the fabric, turn under the raveled edges of the tear and hem by hand with tiny stitches to make each one smooth. Then sew each edge down onto the patch underneath, using small slip stitches.

Patching

Apply a hidden patch on the underside of a garment, as when mending a tear. For a visible patch, hem the patch edges on the machine or by hand with a simple running stitch (see page 94).

Position the patch over the hole or tear, and pin or baste in place.

Then stitch around the edges with a plain or decorative stitch with thread that matches or contrasts with the patch or the garment. Remove pins or basting stitches.

Dollar Stretchers

NEW USES FOR OLD SCRAPS

Save bits of leftover fabric in a special box or basket. They will come in handy for making patchwork quilts, colorful patches for your children's jeans and overalls, doll clothes, sofa-pillow covers, sachets, aprons, or pot holders. Use especially pretty remnants for gift wrapping or to make drawstring bags trimmed with lace and ribbon to hold jewelry and other small gifts.

Repairing Runs in Knitted Garments

Use a narrow crochet hook to repair a run in a sweater or other knitted garment.

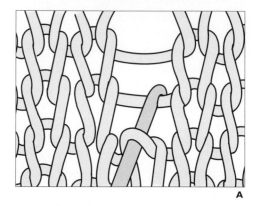

Working on the outside of the sweater, position the hook through the 2 loose stitches at the bottom of the run. **(A)**

Pull the top stitch through the loop of the bottom stitch. Then hook the third stitch in the run through the loop.

Continue this procedure to the top of the run. At the top of the run, pull the last loop and any broken yarn ends inside the garment and take tiny stitches with matching thread to sew them together.

If using iron-on patches, follow the package instructions.

Rips
A rip, which is an opening along a seam, is usually easy to repair by machine or by hand.

Turn the garment inside out and simply sew a running stitch (see page 94) along the original seam line.

Stitch an additional inch on either side of the opening to reinforce and to prevent the rip from opening again.

To make a stronger seam or to repair a seam that's hard to get to by machine, use a backstitch (see page 95).

Hemming Garments
The hemming stitch (see page 94) is the basic stitch for putting in a new hem or repairing one that has pulled out.

Stitch until the hem is completed. You may want to stitch an inch or so past the beginning stitches to reinforce them. Finish with a backstitch or a flat knot (see page 95).

Changing a Skirt Hemline
To shorten a skirt, put on the skirt and have someone else measure the fabric from the floor up to the desired new length. Mark the place all around with pins or chalk.

Then remove the stitches from the original hem and cut off any excess fabric, leaving enough extra to turn up for the new hem allowance. (A good way to decide how much extra is needed is to measure the original hem allowance.) If you own a sewing machine, finish the raw edge of the hem allowance with one of the machine's overcasting or zigzag stitches. Otherwise, finish the raw edge with seam binding.

Turn up the hem allowance along the pinned or chalked line, and pin or baste in place. Try on the garment before sewing the hem to be sure the length is correct. Sew the hem in place, then steam or press the finished hem.

To lengthen a skirt, remove the stitches in the hem, let the fabric down, and press out the crease. Turn up to the desired length, pin or baste in place, and stitch.

Sometimes the crease left by the original hem can be pressed out, sometimes not. If the mark seems to be permanent, you can camouflage it with some type of trim. Depending on the style of the garment, ribbon, rickrack, braid, and lace trim are just a few of your options. If you own a sewing machine that has built-in embroidery stitches, a row of machine embroidery is another option.

Shortening Trousers

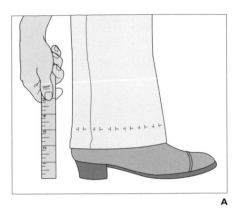

A

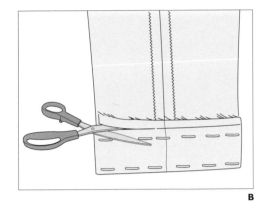

B

Measure the width of each leg's current hem; this will be your guide to an appropriate width for your new hem. **(A)**

Remove the old stitches, unfold the hem, and straighten the fabric by steam pressing over the old hemline.

While you are wearing the trousers, have a helper mark the new length by placing pins around the leg (measure up from the floor at several points to assure the line of pins is even).

With the trousers off and turned inside out, fold the fabric up at the pin line and baste to hold in place while you measure the new hem width; try on the trousers again, and if the length is correct, cut off the excess. **(B)**

If the fabric is thin, turn the cut raw edge under and stitch; if heavy, finish the raw edge with an overcast stitch on your sewing machine or with seam binding, then stitch.

Repeat for the second leg.

Simple Machine Sewing

A sewing machine is an invaluable tool for making fast and easy wardrobe repairs. And it doesn't have to be a fancy, expensive model. A basic machine that does a straight stitch and a zigzag stitch can handle most of your needs. There are many "value-priced" new machines on the market, as well as some good deals on used machines. There may even be a sewing machine lurking unused in your home.

Here are a few tips for getting the best out of your machine:

• Keep it clean. Lint and dust can clog it up, affecting the quality of the stitches. The owner's manual will tell you how to clean your particular machine. If the manual is missing, contact the manufacturer for a new one. Or you can go on the Internet and find sources for manuals, even for very old machines. Using one of the Internet search engines, type in "sewing machine manuals," and then follow the links.

• Check the needle condition. Needles that are bent, dull, or nicked will affect how your machine performs. If you can't remember the last time you changed the needle, get a new one! There may be damage that isn't visible to you, but that still may damage your fabric.

• Match the needle size to the repair. For example, if you are hemming a sheer cotton skirt, you'll need a smaller-size needle than if you are hemming jeans. Sewing machine

Basic Stitches

HEMMING

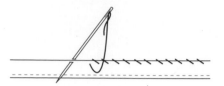

A line of small, firm stitches.

1. On the wrong side of the garment, take a stitch in the hem edge.
2. Then take a stitch in the garment, picking up only one thread of the fabric, and bring the needle up through the hem edge coming out at least 1/4 inch ahead. Continue in this manner.

BLIND HEMMING

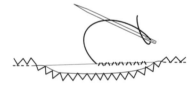

Stitches that are taken on the inside between the hem and the garment fabric, so that in the finished hem the stitches are not visible.

1. Fold back the hem edge, take a small stitch in the garment, then a small stitch in the hem edge.
2. Continue to alternate stitches from garment to hem, keeping the stitches about 1/4 inch apart.

BLANKET STITCH

Used for a decorative finish for edges.

1. Secure the thread at the left end of the edge you wish to sew by making a tiny stitch on the wrong side. Bring the needle out just under the edge.
2. Insert the needle 1/4 inch in from the edge. Hold the bottom part of the thread in a loop.
3. Bring the needle up again on the edge, catching the thread loop under the tip. Pull the needle through the loop, forming a bar at the edge.
4. Repeat, placing stitches at even intervals.

RUNNING STITCH AND BASTING

A running stitch is a line of short, even stitches used for seams. A basting stitch is a long running stitch used for gathering or to temporarily hold a hem or seam in place.

1. Push the needle through both layers of fabric, going in and out several times before pulling the thread through.
2. Keep the stitches short and close together for a seam, long and widely spaced for basting.

BACKSTITCH

Recommended for hand-sewn seams because this type of stitch is so strong. It is also used as a finishing stitch.

1. Knot the thread and pull the needle through the fabric at the point where you wish to begin sewing. Insert the needle 1/4 inch behind the point on the seam line and pull it down through the fabric.
2. Bring the needle up through the fabric 1/4 inch in front of the first stitch and insert it again at the point where the needle first came out.
3. Continue stitching in this manner, always inserting the needle into the hole made by the previous stitch.

FLAT KNOT

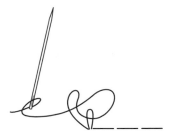

Used to finish once stitching is completed.
1. Take a small stitch at the end of your row.
2. Run your needle through the loop that forms when you pull the thread, and repeat when another loop is formed.
3. Pull the thread taut.

needles come in packs of assorted sizes. How do you know if you're using the right size? Assuming it's new and you didn't sew over a pin, if the needle breaks, it's too small; if the machine skips stitches, it's too large.

• Purchase good-quality thread. Cheap thread is made inexpensively from short fibers that will fray and deposit little bits of lint that clog up your machine.

 Helpful Hints

BUTTON, BUTTON...

➤ **Always remove good-quality buttons before you discard a garment.**

➤ **If a pulled-off button leaves a tear in the fabric, reinforce the area by stitching a little patch of fabric on the underside before resewing the button.**

➤ **If your iron doesn't have button grooves, you can protect buttons by covering them one at a time with the bowl of a spoon as you iron around them.**

Sewing Buttons

To secure a button on heavy materials such as velvet or corduroy, use carpet thread. Dental floss and clear monofilament work well, too, but are best for shank buttons, where the stitches won't show. To reinforce a button, especially on coats and suits, hold a flat button on the opposite side of the fabric and pull the thread through the holes of both buttons simultaneously.

SEW-THROUGH BUTTONS

1. Start by taking 1 or 2 small stitches at the place where the button is to be sewn.

2. Pull the thread through the fabric and 1 hole of the button and position the button over the stitches.

3. To create a thread shank that will allow smooth buttoning, slide a toothpick or matchstick as a wedge between button and fabric.

4. Continue to push and pull the needle through each set of holes at least 6 times.

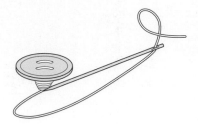

5. Remove the toothpick. With the needle on the right side of the fabric, wind the thread around the threads under the button.
6. Take a few small backstitches (see page 95) under the button to secure the thread, knot, and cut excess thread.

SHANK BUTTONS

1. Begin by taking 2 small stitches in the fabric and then take at least 6 stitches through the shank loop and fabric together.
2. Finish as for a sew-through button.

Leather and Fur

Leather, suede, and fur all need similar care. Store them in a ventilated area away from a heat source and protected from moisture. Always entrust dry-cleaning to a professional who specializes in leather or fur cleaning.

Leather and Suede

Leather

To keep leather supple, you must ensure that it isn't too dry or too wet. Give it room to breathe in the closet like other natural materials.

Drying out, which can result in cracking, is caused by the loss of natural lubricants. This happens in the course of normal wear, but it occurs much faster if the garment is exposed to heat or kept in a place where air can't circulate.

After wearing a leather garment in the rain or snow, dry it immediately; hang it on a padded hanger and let it air-dry away from a direct heat source.

If leather remains wet or damp, mildew spots can form. Sponge them lightly with a solution of equal parts of rubbing alcohol and water. Then gently wipe the area with a commercial leather cleaner or with a damp cloth and mild soap and dry with a clean, dry cloth.

Touch-ups: Between professional cleanings, you can do touch-ups at home with a barely damp cloth and mild soap. To replenish lost lubricants, treat the garment with a commercial cleaner and conditioner especially formulated for leather. Check the ingredients to make sure they don't contain alcohol or petroleum distillates, which are harmful.

Don't attempt to treat leather with products not specifically designed for leather. Instead of helping, they clog pores and interfere with leather's natural breathability. Never use solvents.

Suede

Suede is leather reversed and brushed to a nap finish. Like other leathers, it should be protected from moisture and dryness, kept from heat, and given space to breathe. To keep the nap raised, brush after each wearing with a stiff clothing brush. Try removing stains with a kneadable eraser or with jeweler's fine-grain sandpaper.

Shoes and Boots

When they are brand new, precondition leather shoes and boots.

Smooth or grained leathers: Apply a neutral polish (such as mink oil) or a silicone-based paste, liquid wax, or spray waterproofing and conditioning product.

 Helpful Hints

KEEP LEATHER COLLARS CLEAN

Like collars of other materials, the collars of leather and suede jackets and coats become dirty faster than other areas of the garment. To keep your collar clean longer, consider wearing a scarf to shield it. If the collar becomes soiled, wipe it with a commercial leather cleaner or with a damp cloth and mild soap.

REMOVE WINTER SALT STAINS

Salt stains can make shoes and boots look old before their time.

To remove winter salt stains and dirt, mix equal parts of white vinegar and water or use a commercial desalter, and lightly sponge on smooth or grained leather shoes.

HIDING SCUFFS

When scrapes happen, it is sometimes possible to glue down peeled leather. If not, cover spot with matching polish or indelible ink.

Suede: Use a silicone spray after testing on an inconspicuous area to make certain that it doesn't affect color. The silicone will resist stains and water spots.

When shoes get wet: Take them off as soon as possible. Stuff them with newspaper or paper towels and allow them to dry away from heat.

When they are thoroughly dry (24 hours for leather, a few days for suede), polish smooth leather and brush suede. If only partially wet, eliminate the possibility of a waterline by dampening the entire shoe with a wet sponge.

Shoe trees

Routine Shoe Care

- Change shoes daily, giving each pair a chance to air between wearings.
- When not in use, keep shoes in shape by inserting shoe trees. Use boot trees for boots. Wooden trees can be expensive, but they have the advantage of absorbing moisture.
- Crumpled-up tissue paper can be substituted for shoe trees, especially when trees don't fit well, as in sandals and other open-toed shoe styles.
- Keep shoes in cloth shoe bags or in boxes to avoid contact with dust.
- Keep your shoes in good repair by having

heels replaced as soon as they begin to wear down and replacing the soles when they wear thin.

- To keep leather shoes smooth and supple, polish them regularly. Begin by brushing off loose dirt. Then use clean cloths and brushes and cream polishes to enrich the leather.
- Vigorously rub the polish into the shoe until the cream penetrates. (If you run your hand over the polished surface, it should come away clean.) Liquid polishes, which contain alcohol, have a drying effect if used too often. Remove laces before polishing to avoid staining them.
- For quick emergency touch-ups of smooth leather, use applicators permeated with polish available at shoe repair shops; some are purse size.
- Rub suede with terry toweling after each use. If the nap is flattened, steam shoes by holding them over a teakettle and brush in one direction.
- Treat shoes of exotic leathers—snakeskin, lizard, alligator—with a special neutral-color conditioner that both cleans and conditions. Go with the grain of the overlapping scales.
- Clean patent leather shoes by lightly wiping with a sponge dipped in soapy water, then wipe with a dry cloth. To prevent drying and cracking, use petroleum jelly. Apply a little with one cloth; polish with a dry cloth. Avoid using wax products, which can cause cracking.

Handbags, Briefcases, and Belts

Condition new handbags, briefcases, and belts with a neutral leather polish to protect them from rain spots and bruising.

Polish regularly with cream conditioner or polish. Use only neutral polish; dark or colored polish may rub off onto clothing.

Gloves

To wash unlined leather gloves, put them on your hands, then proceed as if you were washing your hands using cool or lukewarm water and a mild soap. Give extra attention to spots by rubbing with the soap.

Rinse in clear water. Roll the gloves in a towel to blot excess water. Smooth into shape, and dry—either flat on a clean towel or hang on specially made hand-shaped glove dryers.

Gloves lined with silk, acrylic, cashmere, or fur should be professionally dry-cleaned. Between cleanings, keep gloves looking their best by pulling them back into shape after each wearing.

Fur

Keep fur in a well-ventilated area, never near direct heat. If it gets wet, shake out the excess water and hang dry. Leave repairs to professional furriers. (For fur storage, see page 103.)

Jewelry Care

Jewelry made of precious metals and/or semiprecious or precious stones is valuable and should be taken care of accordingly.

Have a jeweler do an annual check of the pieces you wear to make sure they're secure in their settings. Stones can become loosened easily, especially if you are active in sports. Also have clasps and safety chains checked on occasion. Replace as necessary.

When jewelry is not being worn, keep it in its original boxes or in other well-padded containers. Separate pieces to avoid scratching. Fasten the clasps of chains and other necklaces to help prevent tangling. Don't exercise, swim, sleep, or bathe with your jewelry on.

Jewelry Cleaning Machines
These appliances, which are a combination of ultrasonic waves and a cleaning solution, are an easy and effective way to clean most types of jewelry and are ideal if you have a lot of jewelry to clean. Although they're safe to use with most pieces, the appliances should not be used to clean delicate jewelry like pearls or soft stones like opals. Smooth jewelry is the easiest to clean;

 Helpful Hints

GETTING THE KINKS OUT

➤ If a jewelry chain becomes knotted, sprinkling it with talcum powder or cornstarch may make it easier to untangle.

➤ Or insert a straight pin into the center of the knot and, with another straight pin, gently twist and turn to loosen the snarls.

➤ If it's an especially tight knot, place it in a few drops of baby oil on a piece of waxed paper to make it easier to work with.

➤ To remove the oil, dip the chain in a warm water/detergent solution, followed by clear water. If you still can't unravel it, take the chain to a jeweler.

PEARLY WHITES

➤ Never pull or stretch a string of pearls. When pearls are freshly strung they will appear tight. Hang them up to store and eventually they will loosen.

➤ Never wear pearls while bathing or while swimming.

other pieces, depending on the amount of soil and the intricacy of the setting, may require multiple cleaning cycles. Before using any appliance, read the instructions to follow any cautions and to be certain that it is safe to immerse your jewelry in the manufacturer's cleaning solution.

Gold

Wash gold jewelry that has no stones in a lukewarm mild detergent and water solution with a little ammonia, or in a jewelry-cleaning solution. Soak for a few minutes. Rinse in warm water. Dip in rubbing alcohol for shine. Dry on a terry towel, lint-free cloth, or chamois.

Never expose gold to chlorine—either when cleaning or in a swimming pool. Chlorine can cause pitting and discoloration.

Silver

Apply silver polish, as directed on the polish container, with a dampened sponge or soft cloth (never a paper towel). Rinse, and polish with a soft cloth. For quick touch-ups or intricate pieces, cloths permeated with polish are convenient and available.

Precious and Semiprecious Gems

You can clean diamonds, emeralds, sapphires, and rubies with commercial cleaning products available at jewelry stores. However, soaking them briefly in an ammonia solution is just as effective. If necessary, scrub gently with a soft brush (such as a toothbrush), rinse, dip in rubbing alcohol, and pat dry. This treatment is also suitable for amethysts, aquamarines, garnets, jade, topaz, and tourmaline.

Pearls

Cosmetics, hair spray, and perfume have a dulling effect on pearls, so preserve their luster by putting your jewelry on last. When you remove the pearl jewelry, wipe it carefully with a soft, damp cloth or sponge to remove any traces of these substances.

Wash pearls periodically with a cloth dipped in a solution of lukewarm water and mild soap. Rinse with a cloth dipped in clear water (soaking the pearls can weaken the strings) and pat dry. Pearls are easily scratched, so never use any chemicals, abrasives, or solvents on them.

Store pearls separately, away from other jewelry. Pearls, like other beads, should be restrung frequently because strings can weaken with wear and break.

Opals

Among the most fragile gems, opals should be cleaned by wiping with a dampened cloth, then dried with a soft cloth. Composed mostly of water, opals are naturally subject to moisture loss and subsequent cracking. To restore moisture, rub the stone gently with your finger.

Changes in temperature can affect opals, causing cracks. Avoid wearing an opal when going from one temperature extreme to another. For example, if you wear an opal pin on your winter coat and go from your warm house into the cold, the fast rate of change in temperature could damage the stone. If you wear the pin under your coat, it will be protected. Also, don't store opals near a heat source or an air-conditioning unit where they might also be exposed to sudden changes in temperature.

Amber, Coral, Turquoise, and Lapis Lazuli

Avoid soaking these stones. Keep them clean by simply wiping with a soft cloth after each wearing.

Packing a Suitcase

Start with a checklist of what you want on your trip, then assemble everything. You may decide to eliminate some things as you pack if you find there's too much for your suitcases.

Have a supply of white tissue paper to layer between garments for wrinkle reduction, and plastic storage bags for shoes and cosmetics. Pack a few extra bags to carry home wet bathing suits and dirty laundry.

- Place shoes, except those you plan to wear the first day, and other heavy items in the suitcase first. Because wool fabrics are easier to free of creases and wrinkles than other fibers, they can also be put in or near the bottom of the bag.

- Pack those items you plan to wear on your first stop last so they'll be easy to find and wrinkles will be minimal. Pack the shoes you'll need first within easy reach—along the sides of the suitcase. For balance, place one at each side.

- Make as few folds as possible. Roll jerseys and other lightweight knits, as well as underwear and night clothes. After buttoning or fastening dresses, jackets, blouses and shirts, and heavy sweaters, fold them lengthwise, in thirds, turning back each side, including sleeves. Fold long garments, such as a full-length dress, crosswise only at one point to fit the suitcase. Fold pants crosswise only once.

- Pin skirt pleats so they will lie flat and unwrinkled, or pull a knife-pleated or broomstick-pleated skirt through an old cut-off stocking or panty hose leg. Some items, such as a straight skirt, pair of shorts, or sleeveless blouse, may be laid flat without folding.

- If packing more than one pair of pants, place one pair with the waist at one end of the suitcase, the next with the waist at the opposite end, and so forth. This prevents the buildup of too much bulk at one end of the suitcase and helps keep everything level.

- Stuff small things in other items to save space and help maintain the shape of larger pieces. For instance, rolled underwear and pantyhose can be stuffed in shoulders; rolled socks and belts can go in shoes.

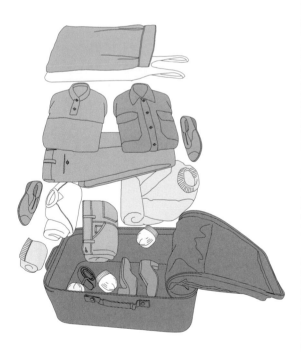

Pack in layers

 Time Savers

WRINKLE-FREE WOOLENS

Of the natural fibers, wool requires the least care. Wrinkles will smooth out if you give the garment a little time and space to air. Don't fold wool knits unless they're heavy or bulky; roll them up before packing.

Carry-On Bags

A carry-on bag is a necessity for air travel, since checked bags don't always arrive with you.

Pack in it medicines, toiletries, vitamins, an extra pair of glasses, nightclothes, extra change of underwear, blouse or shirt, folding umbrella, and a thin roll-up raincoat.

Keep jewelry, essential medication, passport and other important documents, including eyeglass and other prescriptions, in your purse or briefcase.

Keep the size of your carry-on bag small and convenient. Check with your airline concerning what items are prohibited as carry-ons.

Clothes Storage

Before storing any item, have it cleaned thoroughly. Although moths can destroy any unprotected woolens, clean or soiled, they (and other insects) are more attracted to soiled woolens and even synthetics and blends with stains.

Also, some spots, invisible when put away, can surface during the storage period. By the time they are discovered, they may be impossible to remove.

Mothproofing

The traditional method—storing in or with cedar—has yet to be improved upon. A cedar-lined closet is an ideal enclosed area.

If your house doesn't have one, attach cedar panels and planks, available at home center stores, to an existing closet interior. A cedar chest is perfect for folded items.

Although they are less effective, cedar coat hangers, drawer strips, and balls and cubes can also be tried. There are cedar chips or shavings that can be put in little drawstring bags and hung on coat hangers or from closet hooks.

Other fragrant natural moth repellents include lavender and dried orange peel.

Although mothballs contain camphor, which can be dangerous if ingested, they do repel and kill moths—unlike cedar, which simply repels them. To be effective, all repellents must remain in an enclosed space.

 Dollar Stretchers

RE-CEDARING
There's no need to replace cedar that seems to have lost its scent. Simply sand the wood.

Hang or Fold?

Keep hanging clothes clean by covering them with cloth storage bags or old sheeting. (Cut a hole at the center for the hanger hook to go through.) Cloth covers are preferable to plastic bags, which prevent ventilation that fabrics and leathers need.

- Hang a suit on a hanger made for 2 pieces. Fold the trousers along the crease and double over the hanger bar. Pad the bar with fabric, if necessary, to prevent an unwanted crease mark across the legs. Hang skirts by their loops.
- Don't hang knits, including jerseys. Their natural tendency to stretch is increased by gravity, so they soon lose their shape. Instead, roll thin knits and tuck them in the corner of a chest or drawer, just as you would when packing for a trip. Fold heavy or bulky knits.

Helpful Hints

BUCKLES AND BEADS

➤ To keep belt buckles and metal trim on bags from tarnishing, give them a coat of clear nail polish.

➤ The weight of the beads can pull and distort the shape of a beaded garment, such as a sweater or a dress. Fold and store flat instead of hanging.

Cottons and Linens

Wrap white cottons and linens—and all fragile and old fabrics—in white acid-free tissue paper or place in acid-free boxes before storing. (Acid-free products are available at most art supply stores.) Ordinary tissue paper and boxes have acidic properties that can cause delicate fabrics to deteriorate and white fabrics to become discolored.

Old bed sheets, free of their original sizing, or unbleached cotton can substitute for acid-free paper.

If possible, roll tablecloths, bedspreads, and coverlets—especially antique pieces. If you fold them, remember to refold periodically so the lines don't create permanent creases. Never starch before storing because the fabric may yellow and attract insects.

Furs

Take your fur to a furrier for summer storage at the proper temperature. Professional cleaning and routine repairs can be done at that time. If you cannot get to a furrier, cover your fur with a fabric garment bag and store in a cool, dry place.

Leather Accessories

Simply shape and smooth clean gloves and lay them flat, wrapped in tissue, in a drawer or storage chest.

Shoes, boots, and handbags should be stored clean. Brush off surface dirt, sponge off spots, and treat with a conditioner.

Use shoe trees or stuff shoes and bags with tissue paper and store, preferably in individual boxes. If you don't have boot trees, improvise with rolled and tied newspapers, magazines, or cardboard tubes, any of which will keep the boot legs straight and upright.

CHAPTER

3

Food & the Kitchen

We all know how to eat, but we don't necessarily know how to eat *well*. The first part of this chapter lays out the nutrients and foods you need, and it explains which foods to avoid in order to stay healthy. It also shows you how to shop properly, with advice on reading labels and buying the best meat, fruit, and vegetables. It covers important cooking safety information, including food preparation, grilling, microwaving, and simply cooking on your stovetop. The second half of the chapter looks at all aspects of kitchen equipment. You'll find helpful information from The Good Housekeeping Institute about pots and pans, knives, bakeware, cooking utensils, tableware, glassware, and appliances large and small. Here's what to look for when buying this equipment, including the latest features, how to use the products, and exactly which pieces a well-stocked kitchen should have. Finally, it shows you the best ways to use that knowledge as you plan and host the perfect party!

Eating Well

Food is the fuel that keeps your body running. You need about 40 different nutrients to stay healthy, though you don't need to consume all 40 every day.

Because no single food provides all the essential nutrients, choosing a variety of foods is an important part of healthy eating. This chapter is designed to give you a basic understanding of what your body needs and the nutrients that particular foods contain to help you plan your diet for optimum health as well as good taste and easy preparation.

(For more information and recommendations on putting together a healthy eating plan, look for the Dietary Guidelines for Americans at www.nutrition.gov or at www.cnpp.usda.gov)

Protein

Although we often think of protein as a single nutrient, proteins are made up of strings of individual amino acids and perform many functions, from building and maintaining tissue to forming antibodies that fight infection. Nine of the 20 different amino acids are considered essential, and they must come from food. (The other 11 are nonessential: Your body can make them if you consume enough of the essential amino acids.) Meat, poultry, fish, eggs, milk, cheese, yogurt, and soy provide all 9 essential amino acids. They are "complete" proteins. The proteins found in legumes (other than soy), nuts, seeds, grains, and vegetables are low in one or more of the essential amino acids. They are "incomplete" proteins. Soy protein is the only plant-based protein that is complete. If you don't eat foods that provide complete proteins, but you eat a wide variety of foods, your body will make complete proteins out of various incomplete ones.

Although a steady supply of protein is critical

Helpful Hints

WHAT IS A LEGUME?
Legumes are plants with seedpods that split along both sides when ripe. Beans, lentils, peanuts, peas, and soybeans are some of the most common ones. Legumes are high in protein and a staple in many vegetarian diets.

to maintain your health, you actually need to eat relatively little of it to fulfill your body's requirements. In fact, about 6¹/₂ ounces of cooked chicken breast would supply the amount of protein that men need in a day to stay healthy, and 5¹/₂ ounces would suffice for most women, but eating more is not necessarily unhealthy. According to the National Academy of Sciences, an independent organization that advises the government on nutrition, 10 to 35 percent of your total calories should come from protein.

Foods that are high in protein, such as meat, poultry, and full-fat dairy products, also can be high in saturated fat (a type of fat that can promote heart disease if eaten in abundance; see page 109 for more on saturated fats). So think lean when choosing your protein sources. Opt for leaner cuts of meat, skinless chicken, low- or nonfat dairy products, and alternative sources of protein that are naturally low in saturated fats, such as soy, legumes, and nuts.

Carbohydrates

Carbohydrates are made of sugar molecules. They come in 2 forms: There are simple carbohydrates (sugars such as sucrose and fructose) and complex carbohydrates (starches and fiber). Carbohydrates are found in many foods, but especially in fruits, vegetables, and grains.

The Truth About Low-Carb Foods

In response to dieters' demands, food manufacturers have flooded grocery stores with thousands of "low-carb" products—everything from muffins to pasta. The question: Will cutting carbs help you lose weight—or could these products sabotage your diet?

It depends. Many low-carb items contain more calories than the regular versions. And in the end, it's calories that pack on pounds. So why bother cutting carbs?

The so-called bad carbs—foods with lots of added sugar (sodas and candy) and refined starches (white bread, many crackers and cereals)—get their notoriety because they have plenty of calories but provide little long-term satisfaction. So you eat more to get full, putting on pounds in the process. Whole, fiber-filled starches (whole-wheat pasta, vegetables, beans), on the other hand, are digested more slowly, so you feel sated longer, and your blood sugar and insulin levels rise gradually.

The healthiest low-carb approach: Eat a diet rich in lean meats and vegetables, substituting whole-grain carbs for those made with white flour and lots of sugar. If you're planning on eating penne anyway, and the low-carb version has the same number of calories but fewer carbs, it may be worth buying.

Once you eat carbohydrates, your body breaks them down to form glucose, the body's main energy source.

According to the National Academy of Sciences, carbohydrates should make up 45 to 65 percent of your total calories each day. When choosing carbohydrate sources for optimal nutritional value, choose foods that are minimally processed rather than highly processed. For example, pick fresh or unsweetened, unsalted frozen fruits and vegetables over canned; opt for whole-grain foods such as brown rice, whole-wheat pasta, and whole-grain bread over refined foods like white rice, white pasta, and white bread.

Fiber

Fiber is a carbohydrate, too. It's a complex carbohydrate that your body cannot digest or absorb. Instead of being used for energy like other carbohydrates, fiber is actually excreted from the body, but on its way out it does important work.

Fiber comes in 2 forms: soluble and insoluble:

- Soluble fiber is found in fruits, some vegetables, beans, barley, and oats. Foods high in soluble fiber help lower cholesterol and thus help prevent heart disease. Soluble fiber also helps regulate the body's use of sugars, so it plays a role in managing diabetes.
- Insoluble fiber is found in fruits, vegetables, whole grains, and wheat bran. It adds bulk to the diet, facilitates digestion, and may help protect against colon cancer and other digestive disorders.

Fiber-rich foods can also keep you trim. Because they take longer to chew, fiber-rich foods help you eat more slowly, so you may eat less. They also help keep you full longer, making you less likely to feel hungry too soon after you've eaten.

Rather than rely on a single source of fiber, you should eat a wide variety of foods to ensure a balanced diet of fiber and other nutrients. Note that highly processed foods—such as white bread and pasta and many cereals and snack foods—have very little fiber. Be sure to choose whole-grain, whole-wheat products, and whole fruits and vegetables as much as possible to optimize your fiber intake. Health experts recommend you get 25 to 35 grams of fiber each day.

Fats

The term "fat" is used to refer to a class of nutrients that scientists call triglycerides, which are made of fatty acids and glycerol. Fatty acids, or fats, in moderate amounts are essential to your health. But when you consume either too little or too much fat, ill health can follow. Eat too much and you will be more prone to weight gain and possibly heart disease; eat too little and your body won't be able to perform the vital functions that require fat. You need fat to supply energy to your body, and only fat can carry the essential fat-soluble vitamins A, D, E, and K. Fat also cushions and protects your organs, and it provides insulation to help keep you warm.

 Helpful Hints

EATING RIGHT IN RESTAURANTS

➤ **If you want dressing for your salad, ask for it on the side, so you can eat the amount you want.**

➤ **Better yet, ask for undressed salads with oil and vinegar or lemon on the side.**

➤ **At salad bars, load up with fresh vegetables and limit calorie-high cheese and bacon bits, and high-fat salad dressings.**

➤ **Remember, it's not necessary to clean your plate. Take home a doggy bag.**

➤ **Order fresh fruit for dessert or order one dessert for the table and share it.**

➤ **Ask for sauces on the side.**

➤ **Order grilled and broiled foods instead of fried foods, which are less healthy.**

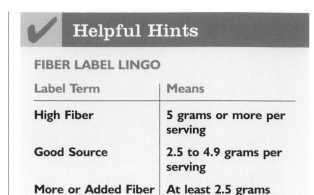

Helpful Hints

FIBER LABEL LINGO

Label Term	Means
High Fiber	**5 grams or more per serving**
Good Source	**2.5 to 4.9 grams per serving**
More or Added Fiber	**At least 2.5 grams more per serving than a standard serving size of the traditional food**

In food, fat lends certain qualities that enhance flavor. The smooth, creamy texture of ice cream comes from fat, as does the flakiness of pastry. Fat also tenderizes, emulsifies, and seals in flavor. Additionally, fat helps satisfy hunger. Because it takes fat longer to leave your stomach than either carbohydrates or protein, it helps you feel full.

The National Academy of Sciences recommends that 20 to 35 percent of your total calories come from fat, but the type of fat you choose to meet that requirement is very important. All fats are made up of fatty acids, but all fats are not created equal. There are "good" fats and "bad" fats.

- The "good" fats are the monounsaturated fats found in foods such as olive, canola, and peanut oils and in nuts and avocados. Polyunsaturated fats, also known as omega-6 and omega-3 fats, are good fats, too. They are found mainly in sunflower, safflower, soybean, and corn oils, and in seafood. Omega-3 fatty acids are a special kind of polyunsaturated fatty acid that most of us don't get enough of in our daily diets. They are essential for normal growth and development, and there's strong scientific evidence that shows they play an important role in the prevention and treatment of heart disease. Omega-3 fatty acids

Obesity

Obesity in the United States has reached epidemic proportions. More Americans are overweight than not. If you are overweight, you are more prone to certain diseases such as type 2 diabetes, hypertension, heart disease, arthritis, and some cancers.

How does someone become overweight or obese? The answer is simple. If you eat more calories than you burn, you will gain weight. That means you will gain weight if you overeat no matter which foods you are eating. Whether carbohydrates, protein, or fat. The magic formula for weight loss is this: Take in fewer calories than you burn. The best way to do that is to cut back on the amount of food you eat and increase the amount of exercise you get. It's that simple.

People often believe (incorrectly) that certain types of food make you fat, but the truth is, your body doesn't really differentiate among carbohydrates, protein, and fat. Yes, your body prefers carbohydrates and fat for energy and likes to save protein for other uses, and your body has to work harder to turn excess dietary protein or carbohydrates into body fat than it does to turn excess dietary fat into body fat. But the simple fact remains: If you consume more calories than you burn, you will gain weight. If you consume less than you burn, you will lose weight.

are found in most seafood, but they are especially abundant in fatty fish like mackerel, salmon, albacore tuna, and lake trout. There are also some omega-3 fatty acids in flaxseeds, flaxseed oil, and walnuts.
- The "bad" fats are saturated fats, which are found in foods of animal origin like meat and full-fat dairy, and trans fats, which are prima-

 Helpful Hints

CALORIE MATH

Carbohydrates, proteins, and fats all provide your body with calories (energy):

1 gram fat = 9 calories

1 gram carbohydrate = 4 calories

1 gram protein = 4 calories

One pound of body fat equals about 3,500 calories. Therefore, losing a pound requires a 3,500-calorie deficit. If you burn 125 calories by walking briskly for 30 minutes every day of the week, and you eat 125 calories less by decreasing your portion sizes at all your meals every day for a week, how much will you lose?

250 calories x 7 days = 1,750 calories, or 1/2 pound in 1 week.

rily man-made fats that are formed during the process called hydrogenation, which makes liquid oils more solid. Trans fats are found in hundreds of processed foods that incorporate partially hydrogenated oil, from peanut butter to crackers, cookies, french fries, and even salad dressing. Intake of saturated fats and trans fats should be limited (see Managing Saturated Fats, Trans Fats, and Cholesterol, page 111).

Cholesterol

The term cholesterol is used to refer to both dietary cholesterol and blood cholesterol. When it is used in discussions of blood cholesterol there is a "good" and a "bad" form.
- High-density lipoprotein (HDL) is the "good" cholesterol. It carries cholesterol from every part of the body to the liver for disposal. High levels of HDL-blood cholesterol are associated with a decreased risk of heart disease.

- Low-density lipoprotein (LDL) cholesterol, the "bad" cholesterol, carries cholesterol from the liver to other tissues. It often forms deposits on the walls of the arteries and blood vessels as it travels. High levels of LDL cholesterol are associated with an increased risk of heart disease.

Cholesterol in food is a fatlike substance found only in animal products. It is necessary for hormone and cell membrane formation. Cholesterol is an essential dietary component for children under 2. For those over 2, the body manufactures all the cholesterol it needs, and no extra intake from food is necessary.

Cholesterol is present in all meats, poultry, some seafood, dairy products, and egg yolks. Dietary cholesterol does not automatically become "bad" blood cholesterol, but eating foods that contain cholesterol does raise total blood cholesterol; furthermore, eating a diet high in cholesterol often goes hand in hand with a diet high in saturated fats. Saturated fats raise blood cholesterol levels, especially LDL cholesterol levels, more so than dietary cholesterol.

Vitamins

Vitamins are a group of organic substances present naturally in almost all foods. Additionally, many processed foods, in particular breads and cereals, are fortified with vitamins, especially B vitamins, folic acid, and sometimes vitamin C.

Vitamins perform numerous important functions in your body, including preventing disease, helping release energy from protein, carbohydrates, and fat, and facilitating hundreds of chemical reactions in the body.

If you eat a well-balanced, varied diet, you probably don't need a vitamin supplement, but all women of childbearing age should take a folic acid supplement or eat foods fortified with folic acid. Most elderly adults need vitamin D supplements. Additionally, vegans (people who do not eat meat, dairy, or eggs; see page 112) and individuals over age 50 who may lack sufficient stomach acid, which is required for B_{12} absorption, should take a B_{12} supplement or eat foods fortified with B_{12}. For others though, despite claims to the contrary, megadoses of vitamins do not have any magical effects. In fact, the overuse of some vitamins can be dangerous. Large doses of vitamins should be taken only with the advice of a physician. You should consult your physician or dietitian to decide which supplements—if any—might be right for you.

Minerals

Minerals, like vitamins, are also needed in minute amounts and are generally supplied by a balanced and varied diet. The body uses minerals to build strong bones and teeth, and to produce hemoglobin in red blood cells, as well as to maintain an optimum fluid balance and help in other chemical reactions.

Water

Water—often called the forgotten nutrient—actually accounts for most of our body weight and is the major means of transporting nutrients, eliminating wastes, and regulating body temperature. Because your body constantly loses water, you need to take in some fluids every day.

Water needs vary depending on climate, exercise, and individual differences, but drinking 8 glasses of water or other liquid daily is a good goal for most individuals. In general, the body is very good at regulating fluid balance, and thirst is a reliable indicator of water needs. But if you're exercising strenuously over long periods or in hot weather, be sure to drink regularly, even if you don't feel thirsty.

Managing Saturated Fats, Trans Fats, and Cholesterol

The National Academy of Sciences recommends that intakes of saturated fats, trans fats, and cholesterol should be minimized to prevent increases in "bad" LDL cholesterol levels. High LDL cholesterol levels have been linked to heart disease (see page 109). Simple ways to reduce saturated fats, trans fats, and cholesterol are:

- Reduce consumption of red meat. Choose lean cuts, trim fat, and keep portion sizes to about 3 ounces of cooked boneless meat.
- Have at least one meatless day per week. (Beware of meatless dishes, such as quiche, that are full of high-fat dairy products.)
- Substitute lean ground turkey for ground beef in meat loaf, burgers, and chili.
- Cook with a minimum amount of oil. Use nonstick cookware or a light coating of nonstick spray instead of oils and other fats.
- Remove skin from poultry before eating.
- Skim all grease from homemade stocks, soups, and stews.
- Avoid fried foods.
- Limit your consumption of liver and other organ meats.
- If you choose to eat eggs, try to limit your consumption of other cholesterol-containing foods that day.
- Roast, bake, or broil meats and poultry on a

 Helpful Hints

BETTER SNACKS

Between-meal snacks help optimize your energy and mental power throughout the day. Snacks also play a role in ensuring you get all the essential nutrients your body needs, especially if your snacks include fruits, vegetables, or dairy products. Try these super snacks:

➤ Crudités (fresh, cut-up vegetables such as peppers, broccoli, and carrots) with low- or nonfat dip

➤ Hummus on mini whole-wheat pita bread

➤ Fat-free or low-fat plain yogurt with fresh fruit

➤ Fresh fruit smoothies made with fruit, low-fat yogurt, and 100 percent juice

➤ Whole-grain crackers or Wasa crisps and reduced-fat cheese

➤ Low-fat bran muffins (choose muffins with at least 3 grams of fiber)

➤ Plain baked potato seasoned with herbs or topped with yogurt

➤ Rice cakes with any variety of nut butter

➤ Peanut butter–filled celery sticks

➤ Unbuttered air-popped popcorn sprinkled with Parmesan cheese

➤ Small handful of nuts

➤ Baked chips and salsa

rack or in ridged pans. Discard the fatty drippings.
- Substitute unflavored fat-free yogurt or nonfat sour cream for full-fat sour cream in dips.
- Use nonfat or reduced-fat milk (skim, 1 percent or 2 percent) instead of whole milk.
- Substitute mustard or nonfat dressings for mayonnaise as a sandwich spread.
- Buy low-fat or fat-free salad dressings or sprinkle your salad with lemon juice or balsamic vinegar and fresh herbs. (Many bottled dressing are high in trans fats.)

- Limit fatty deli meats like bologna or pastrami. Replace with roast turkey or extra-lean ham.
- Be aware that many processed and packaged foods contain large amounts of trans fats. Read labels carefully.
- Limit foods made with partially hydrogenated oils; they contain trans-fatty acids.
- Limit foods that contain coconut and palm oil, which are very high in saturated fat.

Increasing Complex Carbohydrates

The bulk of our caloric intake should come from carbohydrates—mainly from complex carbohydrates such as whole grains, vegetables, and naturally occurring sugars such as those found in whole fruit.

The best grain-based foods have not been refined. Compared to refined grains, whole grains have more antioxidants, such as vitamin E and selenium; more minerals, such as potassium, magnesium, copper, and zinc; more fiber; and more phytochemicals (protective plant chemicals). To increase complex carbohydrates, try the following:
- Include one whole-grain product in each of your 3 meals. For example, have high-fiber, whole-grain cereal for breakfast, whole-grain bread with soup for lunch, and brown rice as a side dish at dinner.
- Don't think of grains only as a side dish. Make them the base for main-dish casseroles, soups, and cold salads. Use them to extend meat entrées. Try bulgur, barley, buckwheat groats, quinoa, and wild rice as well as more common brown rice, and whole-wheat pasta or couscous.
- Keep leftover cooked whole grains in the refrigerator so you can include whole grains in meals quickly and easily.
- Thicken sauces and soups with puréed beans, brown rice, or potatoes.

Vegetarians

Strict vegetarians, or vegans, consume no animal products, including dairy and eggs. Lacto-vegetarians eat no animal flesh, but they do eat dairy products, while ovo-vegetarians don't eat meat, but they do eat eggs. Semi-vegetarians, perhaps the largest and most loosely defined group of vegetarians, eat meat, poultry, and fish only occasionally.

Vegetarians who eat dairy products or eggs have a relatively easy time maintaining a healthy, balanced diet. Even very small quantities of dairy and eggs along with alternative protein sources such as beans, nuts, and seeds, plus a variety of fruits, vegetables, and grain-based foods will provide all the nutrients needed by the body.

Vegans, however, need to guard against nutritional deficiencies. Because the majority of foods vegans eat are naturally low in calories, getting enough calories to maintain a healthy weight can be a real challenge, especially for vegan children and teens. (Vegan children must be especially careful to get enough protein while they are growing rapidly.) Other nutrients that may come up short are vitamin B_{12}, vitamin D, calcium, iron, and zinc. But planned wisely, a vegan diet can provide enough nutrients for overall good health.

- Have at least one vegetable or fruit at every meal, aiming for at least 5 a day.
- Make legumes a regular part of your diet. Add them to soups and salads, and substitute them for meat in stews, chili, and spaghetti sauce.
- Include whole fruits and vegetables as part of snacks, as well as meals. For example, have fruit and cheese or crudités and yogurt dip when you need a midday pick-me-up.

Limiting Refined Sugars

Simple sugars such as table sugar, brown sugar, molasses, maple syrup, and corn syrup provide calories but few, if any, vitamins or minerals. Moreover, some high-sugar foods, such as desserts and pastries, are also often high in fat. Remember to check the label of packaged foods, a haven for sugar. A mere 4 grams of sugar in a food equals a whole teaspoon of sugar.

Here are a few tips for limiting sugar intake:
- Brew coffee with a small piece of cinnamon stick or vanilla bean to add flavor without sugar.
- Sweeten desserts, pancakes, and waffles with pure fruit purées instead of sugar or syrup.
- Limit soft drinks that aren't sugar-free. Try mineral water or seltzer with a splash of fruit juice.
- Be aware that many processed foods contain substantial amounts of added sugar. Read labels carefully, and choose wisely.
- Limit foods with high fructose corn syrup.
- Instead of fruit flavored yogurt, have plain yogurt with fresh fruit.
- Reduce the sugar in recipes for cakes, cookies, and other baked goods. (You can often decrease the sugar by up to one-third without noticing a difference.)
- Use vanilla or other extracts and "sweet" spices like cinnamon, nutmeg, cardamom, and allspice to enhance the sweetness of a variety of foods.

Limiting Salt

Salt, while an essential part of a good diet, is usually used to excess. If you have or are predisposed to hypertension, you may need to restrict your sodium intake. A sodium intake of about 1,500 milligrams per day is considered safe and adequate for healthy young adults. One teaspoon of salt contains about 2,300 milligrams of sodium.

Here are a few tips for cutting down on sodium:
- Taste food before adding salt.
- Cook with spices and herbs as flavoring instead of salt.
- Reduce by half the amount of salt called for in a recipe. When you become used to that taste, decrease the quantity further to one-fourth.
- Try out different commercial salt substitutes, "light" salt products, and herb/spice blends.
- Be aware that many commercially processed foods contain high quantities of salt; read labels carefully.
- Limit salty snacks or buy reduced-sodium versions of your favorites.

Limiting Alcoholic Beverages

Drink alcohol in moderation. Studies show that 1 or 2 drinks daily may lower the risk of heart disease, but heavy drinking can cause many health problems. Alcohol, like other sugars, provides calories but no nutrients.

Pregnant women should abstain from alcohol.

Understanding Vital Nutrients

VITAMINS

Vitamin C and the 8 B vitamins, including folic acid, niacin, pantothenic acid, and biotin, generally are stored in the body in only small amounts, so you need to eat foods rich in them regularly. Vitamins A, D, E, and K are stored in body fat until used, but you still need a steady supply. To avoid toxicity, do not take large doses.

	WHAT IT DOES	GOOD SOURCES	USEFUL INFORMATION
Vitamin A/ beta-carotene	Essential for normal vision, gene expression, bone growth, healthy skin, hair, and nails, and resistance to infection.	Liver, egg yolks, whole milk, butter, fortified margarine, and fortified reduced fat and skim milk. Beta-carotene, which is converted to vitamin A in the body, is found in dark-green leafy vegetables, deep yellow and orange vegetables, and fruits.	Large doses of vitamin A are toxic and cause liver damage as well as birth defects if consumed during first months of pregnancy. Over time, an excess of vitamin A may also build up and weaken bones. Large doses of beta-carotene can cause skin to yellow and may increase cancer risk in smokers.
Vitamin B$_1$ (*thiamine*)	Helps body convert carbohydrates into energy and metabolize protein and fat. Promotes proper nerve function.	Whole grains, bran, wheat germ, enriched and fortified grain products (including cereal), pork, liver, dry beans, peas, and nuts.	Sensitive to heat and easily leaches into cooking water.
Vitamin B$_2$ (riboflavin)	Helps body use protein, fat, and carbohydrates to produce energy. Supports normal vision and healthy skin.	Meat, fish, chicken, dairy products, green vegetables such as spinach, broccoli, turnip greens and asparagus, whole-grain, enriched and fortified breads and cereals.	

	WHAT IT DOES	GOOD SOURCES	USEFUL INFORMATION
Vitamin B_6 (pyridoxine)	Important in metabolism of protein, fat, and carbohydrates.	Poultry, fish, whole-grain and whole-wheat products, fortified cereals, and some fruits and vegetables such as bananas, watermelon, potatoes, and spinach.	Large doses over months or years can cause toxicity with severe nerve damage, including numbness and difficulty walking.
Vitamin B_{12}	Plays role in formation of red blood cells and helps maintain nervous system. Prevents pernicious anemia.	All animal products (meats, dairy products, eggs, liver, fish, and shellfish) and fortified breakfast cereals.	Strict vegetarians (vegans) and people over 50 should take a B_{12} supplement or eat foods fortified with B_{12}.
Folate (folic acid)	Essential for normal cell division and red blood cell formation. Prevents megaloblastic anemia.	Green leafy vegetables, dry beans and peas, orange juice, asparagus, enriched and whole-grain bread and bread products, fortified breakfast cereals, and liver.	Large doses of folic acid (the supplement form of folate) can mask a B_{12} deficiency. Women of childbearing age should consume .4 milligrams from supplements or fortified foods in addition to food folate to reduce the risk of neural tube defects in newborns.
Niacin	Helps cells use oxygen to release energy in the metabolism of glucose, fat, and alcohol.	Whole grains, enriched breads and fortified cereals, meat, fish, shellfish, poultry, peanuts, and mushrooms.	Large doses can cause side effects that range from uncomfortable skin flushing to liver damage.
Pantothenic acid and biotin	Both nutrients aid in carbohydrate, fat, and protein metabolism.	Widespread in foods, especially abundant in meat, whole-grain products, and legumes.	

(continued on next page)

	WHAT IT DOES	GOOD SOURCES	USEFUL INFORMATION
Vitamin C	Prevents scurvy. Helps heal wounds by promoting collagen formation, and strengthens resistance to infection. Because of its antioxidant powers, eating foods rich in vitamin C may reduce risk of some cancers.	Citrus fruits, other fruits and vegetables, especially red and green peppers, dark-green leafy vegetables, brussels sprouts, broccoli, cabbage, potatoes, cauliflower, kiwifruit, strawberries, papaya, tomatoes, and cantaloupe. Large doses can cause side effects that range from uncomfortable skin flushing to liver damage.	Large doses can cause nausea and diarrhea, excess iron absorption, and possibly kidney stones. Heavy smokers have lower blood levels of vitamin C, and they require an additional 35 milligrams a day.
Vitamin D	Essential for proper formation and maintenance of bones and teeth. Promotes the absorption of calcium and helps to maintain blood levels of phosphorous.	Fortified milk products and margarine, fortified cereals, liver, and fatty fish; also produced by the body when skin is exposed to sunlight.	Large doses can cause calcification of soft tissue. Because the ability to synthesize this vitamin from the sun is diminished with age, people older than 50 may need supplementation.
Vitamin E	Acts as an antioxidant to protect cells against the effect of free radicals, which are potentially damaging by-products of the body's metabolism.	Nuts, seeds, whole grains, wheat germ, vegetable oils, egg yolks, and dark-green leafy vegetables.	Extremely high doses of vitamin E may interfere with blood clotting.
Vitamin K	Essential for normal blood clotting and bone health.	Dark-green leafy vegetables, cauliflower, and other cabbage-type vegetables.	Made in the body by intestinal bacteria, so dietary needs are low.

MINERALS

Minerals are nutrients that are essential to a host of vital processes in the body. Most are readily available in a balanced diet, so if you eat right, your body will receive adequate amounts. Here are some of the most important minerals:

	WHAT IT DOES	GOOD SOURCES	USEFUL INFORMATION
Calcium	Essential for building bones and teeth, maintaining bone strength and proper muscle and nerve function. Adequate daily calcium intake throughout life plays a role in preventing osteoporosis: 1000 milligrams for ages 19–50; 1200 milligrams for ages 51 and older.	Milk, cheese, and yogurt have the most calcium. Canned sardines and salmon (including bones), clams, oysters, tofu (calcium precipitated), blackstrap molasses, broccoli, kale, almonds, and calcium-fortified juices are also good sources.	Food is the best source of calcium, but supplements are acceptable too. The best supplement is one that meets your needs based on tolerance, convenience, cost, and availability. Check with your doctor or pharmacist about which ones might work for you.
Iron	Combines with protein to form hemoglobin, which carries oxygen in the bloodstream.	Meats, poultry, fish, shellfish, dark-green leafy vegetables, dry peas and beans, eggs, dried fruit, and fortified bread and grain products. Foods cooked in cast-iron cookware.	Iron deficiency is uncommon among adult men and post-menopausal women, and these individuals should not routinely take iron supplements because of the risk of iron overdose. Consuming foods rich in vitamin C in conjunction with iron-rich plant-based foods increases absorption of iron. For example, drink orange juice with your iron-fortified breakfast cereal.

(continued on next page)

(continued from previous page)

	WHAT IT DOES	GOOD SOURCES	USEFUL INFORMATION
Phosphorous	Combines with calcium to strengthen bones and teeth and helps the body convert food to energy. Maintains pH balance.	All dairy products, eggs, meat, poultry, and fish, some cereals and breads.	Dietary deficiencies of phosphorous are undetermined. Phosphorous from additives in processed foods adds significantly to intake. Excessive intake can interfere with calcium absorption.
Potassium	Helps maintain balance of body fluids. Essential for proper nerve and muscle function.	Found in all whole foods: fruits, vegetables, milk, yogurt, meat, poultry, seafood, grains, and legumes. Particularly abundant in potatoes, bananas, and acorn squash.	Diuretic (fluid-releasing) drugs can deplete the body of potassium.
Sodium	Helps maintain balance of body fluids.	Table salt, naturally occurring salt in foods, and salt added to foods during processing.	Excessive sodium can lead to edema (fluid retention), as well as aggravate hypertension.

Other important minerals: Magnesium, zinc, selenium, iodine, copper, chromium, and fluoride are found in either water or common food sources in a well-balanced diet and are needed in very small quantities.

Smart Shopping

Food is probably the most variable component of your home budget. Shop well, and you'll eat well and save money, too.

Negotiating the Market

- Make a list before you shop, and stick to it. A list saves time, and it also keeps you on track so you avoid buying items you don't need.
- Rather than handwriting a list every time you shop, type up a list on your computer of the staples you buy each week, and run off a stack. Before you head to the store, check off what you need on this weekly list, and handwrite in the extras.
- Avoid shopping when you're hungry and can be tempted to make impulse purchases.
- When you need a single item, buy it and leave the store.

 Dollar Stretchers

BUYING IN BULK

➤ Cooperative buying, where people jointly buy groceries in bulk, can save you money. You may have to contribute several hours a month to do your share of purchasing.

➤ The bulk bins in your local supermarket or health food store are also a money-saving option.

➤ Join a warehouse club and use it for groceries as well as other everyday items. You'll save the annual fee many times over.

➤ If you have storage space, buy nonfood items in bulk, such as aluminum foil, paper towels, and detergent.

➤ Be realistic about your needs; a large family can quickly consume a 5-pound bag of potatoes, but a single person will watch the spuds grow sprouts long before they're used. Don't buy more than you can use.

 Helpful Hints

COOL IT

When purchasing perishables, go directly home to unpack and refrigerate or freeze items. Many foods deteriorate quickly at room temperature.

DINE ONLINE

Don't forget about online grocers. Some are less expensive than supermarkets, and the quality of their stock often rivals that of traditional grocery stores. They can be a lifesaver for busy people.

FROZEN FOOD TIPS

➤ Pick up frozen foods just before going to the checkout counter.

➤ Buy only foods frozen solid and with no dribbles on the package, odor, or other signs of being thawed.

➤ Put all frozen foods together in one bag or in an insulated cooler so they'll stay as cold as possible for the trip home.

➤ Store frozen foods in their original wrapping. Place in your freezer as soon as possible.

➤ Cook or thaw as the label directs.

- If you can arrange it, make major shopping trips without small children. (Markets often encourage impulse buying by children by putting sugary cereals and candy at their eye level.)
- If you must take your child, bring a toy or book to keep him or her occupied.
- Take note of shelf labeling and unit pricing (price per ounce) if the market practices this policy. If not, consider investing in a pocket calculator to figure the actual unit cost of an item available in several sizes or to compare different sizes and prices of competing brands.

Buying Meat: Making the Grade

- **Prime** meats are more marbled with fat and are most tender. They are often available in restaurants and are sometimes sold to the public.
- **Choice** meats are also tender but have less fat. They are most commonly found in stores.
- **Select** refers to beef that has the least marbled fat.
- **Good** applies only to veal and lamb. These cuts are the least tender and are usually not sold retail.

GETTING LEAN
- To get the leanest cut, look for "round" or "loin" in the name when shopping for beef, and "loin" or "leg" when buying pork or lamb.
- If a label says "lean", it has less than 10 grams fat, 4.5 grams or less saturated fat, and less than 95 milligrams cholesterol per 3-ounce serving.
- If a label says "extra lean", it has less than 5 grams fat, less than 2 grams saturated fat, and less than 95 milligrams cholesterol per 3-ounce serving.

- Check expiration dates, especially of perishables such as dairy products and packaged meats and poultry. Older items are usually up front in a display case.
- Shop for unrefrigerated foods and nonperishables first to minimize potential spoilage. Most markets are laid out so that the meat, dairy, and frozen-food sections are at the end and sides of the store, so you can easily shop for these items last.
- Stock up on canned and other nonperishable foods when they're on sale.
- Double-check the cash register at the check-

out. Mistakes can be made even with computerized scanning.
- Have groceries packed with like items together. If all frozen items are in one bag, they will help keep one another cold on the trip home.

How to Buy the Best

Meat

Beef: Look for meat that is firm, slightly moist, and light to bright or dark red in color. Bones should be red and porous. Fat should not be overly thick in proportion to meat.

Lamb: Look for meat that is firm, pink to light red in color, and fine-textured. Bones should be red and porous. Fat should not be overly thick in proportion to meat.

Pork: Look for meat with a lot of grayish-

 Dollar Stretchers

SAVING WITH COUPONS

You can often save money with coupons. Here are some pointers:

➤ Check expiration dates before shopping. Some coupons have short terms; others are unlimited.

➤ Star the coupon items on your shopping list as a reminder.

➤ Don't use coupons to buy items that are more expensive than competitors' brands or that you had no intention of buying.

➤ Ask for a rain check if the coupon item is out of stock.

➤ Send in coupons for rebates. This may be time-consuming, but it can save money.

➤ The Internet can be a plentiful source for coupons. Enter the word "coupon" into your favorite search engine to bring up lots of coupon Web sites.

➤ Look for stores that double—or even triple—the value of coupons (usually up to 99 cents).

pink to light red meat in proportion to bone and fat. Smoked pork products include ham, smoked hocks, and bacon.

Hams are usually sold fully cooked except for bone-in country hams, which need to be soaked and cooked like raw pork before eating.

Veal: Look for meat that is white or very pale pink; the redder the meat, the older and tougher the veal. Fat should be thin in proportion to meat.

Poultry

Chicken: Broiler-fryers (1½ to 4 pounds) are all-purpose chickens that can be broiled, fried, braised, roasted, or stewed. Roasters are 3½ to 6 pounds and meaty and tender. Stewing chickens are older, weigh 5 to 6 pounds, and need to be cooked slowly to make them tender.

Capon (neutered roosters): These birds weigh 6 to 8 pounds and have especially tender meat.

Turkey: Although modern toms are as tender as hens, hens usually cost more per pound. Look for plump birds with substantial meat over the breastbone. Two 12-pound birds are sometimes a better choice at the market than one 25-pounder.

Duck: These birds are usually 2 months old and weigh 6 to 7 pounds. One duck will serve 3–4 people.

Goose: The tastiest and most tender geese weigh 12 pounds or less and are no more than 6 months old. Allow about 1 pound per serving.

Seafood

Fish: While most seafood on the market is safe and wholesome, it's always best to buy from a reliable source whose suppliers are equally reliable.

In whole fish, look for clean gills, clear eyes, and undamaged skin. In fillets and steaks, look for glistening flesh. Watery or dried edges indicate previous freezing or poor handling. Odor should be briny, but not pungent—no strong or fishy smells.

Shellfish: Except for shrimp and scallops, fresh, uncooked shellfish should be alive when bought, and cooked within one day.

Becoming Label Literate

The Food and Drug Administration (FDA) constantly reviews its labeling regulations to update information and make it easier for consumers to read and comprehend data. Manufacturers must note the product name, the net contents or net weight (including liquid in canned goods), and the name and address of the manufacturer, packager, or distributor.

List of Ingredients

Ingredients appear by common names in descending order according to weight. Manufacturers must list additives, but in some cases they use general language such as "artificial color" or "artificial flavor."

Nutrition Information

The FDA requires nutrition information when a manufacturer adds a nutrient (other than protein and certain vitamins and minerals) to a food or makes a claim such as "low calorie" (see page 123).

Standardized Items

The FDA has adopted standards of identity for such common foods as jams, jellies, peanut butter, and milk. Once a standard has been set, no other product can call itself by that name. For example, a beverage that is not 100 percent fruit juice cannot be called juice. Ingredients must be listed on packaging for all other foods.

Federal-Inspection Stamp

All fresh and processed meat and poultry products that are shipped interstate must bear a federal-inspection stamp showing that they meet federal standards. Meat that does not cross state lines must meet comparable state-inspection standards.

Grading

Some foods carry a label grade that is not necessarily a grading of their nutritive value. For instance, butter is usually graded "AA," eggs, milk, and milk products often are labeled "Grade A," based on FDA sanitary standards.

The U.S. Department of Agriculture (USDA) sets grades for all meat and poultry based on characteristics of taste, texture, and appearance. Grading for meat, such as prime, choice, and good, are optional. The National Marine Fisheries Service grades fish products in a similar manner.

Product Dates

Stores are not legally required to remove food products from the shelves once the expiration date has passed. The "sell by" date is the expiration date: Don't buy after this date. On the other hand, a product is still edible after the "best if used by" date has passed, but the food's flavor or quality may be diminished. The "use by" date is the last date that the manufacturer will vouch for the product's quality.

Coding

Mostly used on shelf products, coding is primarily for the manufacturer and indicates when and where a product was packaged. This is important to the consumer in the case of recall.

Nutrition Labeling

The Food and Drug Administration requires on all packaged foods a "Nutrition Facts" panel containing information on calories, fat, saturated fat, protein, carbohydrates, sugar, fiber, cholesterol, sodium, vitamin A, vitamin C, calcium, and iron content. The panel (at right) is designed to summarize what the food offers and to help you make wise food choices quickly and simply.

The Percent Daily Value

The Percent Daily Values (%DV) on the Nutrition Facts panel are designed to tell you whether the food gives you a little or a lot of the nutrients specified. You can use this information to learn more about what's in the foods you eat as well as to compare products and brands. Note that 5% DV or less is low, and 20% DV or more is high. For those nutrients you want to limit (fat, saturated fat, trans fat, cholesterol, and sodium), look for a lower percentage, and try not to have more than a total of 100 percent of each over the course of a day. For nutrients you want more of (fiber, vitamin A, vitamin C, calcium, and iron), look for a higher percentage, and try to reach 100 percent of each every day.

More Label Lingo

The government regulates nutrient content and health claims on packaged foods. Manufacturers can't use any of the words below on a package unless the food meets the criteria listed. (Go to www.fda.gov for more information on food labeling.)

Free: Means that a product has no amount (or a negligible amount) of the particular component, such as fat-free and sugar-free.

Low fat: 3 grams or less per serving.

Low saturated fat: 1 gram or less per serving.

Low sodium: 140 milligrams or less per serving.

Very low sodium: 35 milligrams or less per serving.

Low cholesterol: 20 milligrams or less and 2 grams or less of saturated fat per serving.

Low calorie: 40 calories or less per serving.

Light: Can mean two things. First, that the product contains one-third fewer calories or half the fat of the reference food. Second, that the sodium content has been reduced by 50 percent.

Healthy: Must be low in fat and saturated fat and contain limited amounts of cholesterol and sodium.

The Nutrition Facts Label

Serving sizes in familiar units like cups or piece followed by metric amount (for example, grams).

Calories are per serving, and tell you how much energy you get from that single serving.

Americans generally get enough fat, saturated fat, trans fat, cholesterol, and sodium. You should limit your intake of these nutrients; eating too much of them may increase your risk of certain chronic diseases. In addition, eating too many calories is linked to overweight and obesity.

Your daily values may be higher or lower depending on your caloric needs.

Nutrition Facts
Serving size = 1 cup (228 g)
Servings Per Container = 2

Amount Per Serving

Calories 250	Calories from fat 110

	% Daily Value*
Total Fat 12 g	18%
Saturated fat 3 g	15%
Trans Fat 1.5 g	
Cholesterol 30 mg	10%
Sodium 470 mg	20%
Total carbohydrates 31 g	10%
Sugars 5 g	—
Dietary fiber 0 g	0%
Protein 5 g	
Vitamin A	4%
Vitamin C	2%
Calcium	20%
Iron	4%

*Percent Daily Values are based on a 2,000-calorie diet.

	Calories	2,000	2,500
Total fat	Less than	65g	80g
Sat fat	Less than	20g	25g
Cholesterol	Less than	300mg	300mg
Sodium	Less than	2,400mg	2,400mg
Potassium	Less than	3,500mg	3,500mg
Total Carbohydrate		300g	375g
Dietary Fiber		25g	309g
Protein		50g	65g

Serving sizes are based on amounts people typically eat. Allows you to compare to your usual portions.

Calories from fat tell you how many of the calories per serving are from fat.

Americans often don't get enough dietary fiber, vitamin A, vitamin C, calcium, and iron in their diets. This part of the label is designed to help you understand which foods contain more of these nutrients.

The bottom part of the Nutrition Facts Panel includes language that is the same on every package. It shows dietary advice for all Americans, and is not about the specific product. The information reflects nutrition experts' advice on the nutrients specified. For example, total sodium should be less than 2,400 milligrams per day on both a 2,000-calorie and a 2,500-calorie a day diet.

Picking the Best Produce

While many vegetables and fruits are grown year-round in temperate areas, they still have a preferred buying period during which the produce is generally more flavorful and less expensive. In this buying guide, seasonal ranges (in parentheses) allow for climate variations and peak harvest times.

VEGETABLES

Artichokes (spring): Compact, plump, heavy, with thick, green, tightly closed leaves. Avoid if leaves are dry, spreading, or hard-tipped.

Asparagus (spring to early summer): Straight stalks with closed, compact tips and full green color, except for white ends. Avoid if shriveled or have spreading tips.

Avocados (all year): Shiny green or mottled purplish-black (depending upon variety); yield to gentle pressure. Ripen in a paper bag at room temperature.

Beans, green and wax (all year): Firm, crisp, bright color without blemishes.

Beans, lima and fava (late summer and early autumn): Firm, crisp, smooth skins without blemishes.

Beets (all year, but best from summer to late autumn): Firm, small to medium-size, bright colored, smooth skins; preferable with fresh green tops attached. Avoid if bruised, soft, or overly large.

Broccoli (all year): Dark green, firmly clustered buds on firm, but not thick, stalks.

Broccoli rabe (all year): Perky leaves, with thin green stalks and small bud clusters. Avoid stalks with yellowish leaves.

Brussels sprouts (autumn through early spring): Firm, tightly wrapped green heads free of black spots.

Cabbage (all year): Firm, heavy for its size, with brightly colored (green or red) outer leaves and no black blemishes.

Carrots (all year): Firm, straight, with bright orange color, preferably with fresh green leaves attached. Avoid if limp or cracked.

Cauliflower (all year): Firm heads with tightly packed creamy white clusters and fresh-looking green leaves. Avoid those with blemishes or black spots.

Celery (all year): Crisp, pale green stalks with fresh-looking leaves. Avoid stringy, bruised, or limp stalks.

Chayote (all year, but best in summer): Small, firm, unblemished.

Corn (late spring through summer): Medium-size ears with plump, milky kernels, smooth green husks, and soft silk ends.

Cucumbers (all year, but best in summer): Medium to small, with bright green color. Avoid any with soft ends, blemishes, or wax coatings.

Eggplant (all year, but best in summer): Firm, glossy purple or white with fresh green cap, heavy for its size. Avoid if soft, wrinkled, or very thick-skinned.

Endive (all year, but best autumn through spring): Small, compact, snowy white leaves edged in pale green. Avoid wilted leaves.

Fennel (autumn to early spring): Firm, unblemished white bulbs with fresh looking feathery fronds attached.

Garlic (all year): Firm, unblemished heads with tight, compact cloves. Papery skin should be soft, not brittle.

Kohlrabi (spring through late summer): Small, young bulbs with fresh-looking stems and leaves.

Leeks (all year, but best in autumn): Firm, unblemished white base with fresh-looking green leaves.

Lettuce, greens (all year): Crisp, unblemished leaves; color depends upon variety. Avoid brown edges.

Mushrooms (all year, but peak for wild mushrooms like oyster or shiitake depends on variety): Firm, plump, unblemished with tightly closed caps and fresh-looking stems. Select carefully, avoiding mold. Best bet: Buy exotic mushrooms from a good gourmet produce store.

Okra (spring through early autumn): Young, firm, tender green pods.

Onions (all year, but certain varieties best in late spring or early summer): Clean, dry, firm with papery husks, and no sprouts or soft spots.

Parsnips (all year, but best in late summer): Firm, smooth, small to medium-size. Avoid overly large roots (a sign of age) and any with gray, soft spots.

Peas, green (spring through early summer): Firm, bright or light green, with well-filled pods. Avoid swollen, wrinkled, or immature dark green pods.

Peppers (all year): Firm, shiny, thick-fleshed with bright color, green, red, orange, or yellow (depending upon variety). Avoid blemishes, soft spots, or darkened stem ends.

Potatoes (all year): Firm, smooth skinned, well shaped, with no sprouts or blemishes.

Radishes (all year): Firm, smooth, bright color, red or white, with fresh-looking leaves. Avoid blemishes or black spots.

Rutabaga (autumn and winter): Large, heavy with no soft spots. Usually coated with a thick protective wax. Also known as yellow turnip.

Spinach (all year): Bright green, fresh, tender leaves with no yellowing or wilted ends.

Squash, summer or soft-skinned, such as zucchini, yellow, straight neck, patty pan (all year, but best in summer): Smooth, bright skin, bright color, green or yellow (depending on variety), heavy for its size.

Squash, winter or hard-skinned, such as acorn, butternut (all year, but best in autumn): Unblemished, rich color, green, white, yellow, or gold (depending on variety), heavy for its size, with hard skin and stem end intact.

Sweet potatoes (all year, but best in late autumn): Firm, uniform shape with even color and no blemishes. Avoid very large ones (sign of age).

Tomatoes (all year): Firm, plump with unblemished skin; color and size depends on variety.

Turnips (all year, but best in autumn and winter): Firm, unblemished, heavy for their size with fresh-looking tops.

FRUIT

Apples (all year, but best in autumn): Firm, crisp, full color with no bruises, soft spots, or shriveled skins.

Apricots (June and July): Golden yellow to orange-yellow, plump, and firm enough to yield only slightly to pressure. Avoid soft, shriveled, or dull-looking fruit. Ripen in a paper bag at room temperature.

Bananas (all year): Solid yellow or lightly flecked with brown. If soft and with spotted or brown skin, mash and use for baking. Ripen hard green fruit in a paper bag at room temperature.

(continued on next page)

(continued from previous page)

Blueberries (June through August): Plump, firm with dusky blue color.

Cantaloupes (all year, but best in summer): Pleasant perfumelike aroma; heavy for their size; no stem at end. Rind should yield to gentle pressure. Ripen at room temperature; they're ripe when skin beneath webbing has turned from green to beige.

Cherries (June and July): Plump with bright color—red, purplish-black, or golden with a pink blush (depending upon variety); fresh stems (not discolored or dry).

Coconuts (all year, but best in late autumn): Heavy for their size, with lots of juice that sloshes when fruit is shaken. Avoid moldy or wet "eyes."

Cranberries (October through December): Plump, shiny, firm with bright to dark red color.

Figs (summer to early autumn): Smooth and yielding to gentle pressure, but not soft. Harvested ripe, thus very perishable. Color correlates with variety.

Grapefruit (all year, but best in winter): Firm and heavy for their size, with no discoloration at stem end.

Grapes (all year, but best from late summer to late autumn): Plump, colorful, from deep purple to pale green; smooth, firmly attached to fresh-looking stems. Avoid shriveled or discolored fruit.

Honeydew melons (late summer to early autumn): Firm, creamy white, smooth surface; slightly soft at blossom end; heavy for their size. Ripen at room temperature; they're ripe when they smell perfumed.

Kiwifruit (all year): Slightly firm, fuzzy, yielding to gentle pressure. Ripen at room temperature; they're ripe when they smell fruity.

Kumquats (winter): Small, bright orange, with shiny green leaves. Avoid blemished or shriveled fruit.

Lemons (all year): Firm, shiny, heavy for their size. Avoid shriveled or hard fruit.

Limes (all year): Firm, shiny, heavy for their size. Avoid shriveled or hard fruit.

Mangoes (all year, but best in spring and summer): Yellow-orange to reddish skin that may be slightly mottled, yielding slightly to gentle pressure. Avoid bruised or shriveled fruit. Ripen at room temperature.

Nectarines (summer): Plump, rich-colored yellowish to reddish skin, with slight softening on stem end. Avoid shriveled, rock-hard, or bruised fruit. Ripen in a paper bag at room temperature.

Oranges (all year, but best in winter and early spring): Firm and heavy for their size. Avoid spongy or dry-looking fruit.

Papayas (all year, but best in spring and summer): Greenish-yellow to yellow and smooth; yield to gentle pressure. Avoid shriveled or bruised fruit. Ripen in a paper bag at room temperature.

Peaches (May through September): Yellow or creamy color with red blush (depending on variety), slightly fuzzy; fairly firm, but yield to gentle pressure. Avoid shriveled or bruised fruit. Ripen in a paper bag at room temperature.

Pears (all year, but best in late summer to early winter): Color depends on variety; no discoloration at stem end; firm, but yield to gentle pressure. Avoid bruised or overly soft fruit. Ripen in a paper bag at room temperature.

Pineapples (all year): Firm fruits, heavy for their size, with fresh-looking leaves; plump and glossy eyes; fragrant aroma. The color will depend on variety, but usually dark green indicates that fruit is not fully ripe (once picked, they will not ripen further). They're ripe when you can pull out a leaf with a gentle tug.

Plantains (all year): Always eaten cooked. Green to near-yellow fruit is starchy and usually boiled. Very ripe plantains have dark brown to black skin and are good for sautéing and baking.

Plums (summer): Bright color, green to red to purple (depending upon variety); plump, slightly firm, but yield to gentle pressure. Avoid shriveled or overly soft fruit. Ripen at room temperature.

Pomegranates (September through December): Fresh-looking fruit that is heavy for its size. Avoid shriveled fruit, any with broken peel, or fruit with soft spots.

Raspberries and blackberries (summer and early autumn): Plump; dry, rich color, from red to black. Select carefully and avoid moldy or mashed fruit.

Rhubarb (April and May): Firm, crisp, fairly thick stalks that range in color from pale pink to deep red. Avoid soft stalks. Leaves are poisonous.

Strawberries (all year, but best in early spring through summer): Firm with bright color and fresh-looking leaves and stems. Select carefully, and avoid moldy or mashed fruit.

Tangerines (late autumn to early spring): Bright orange color; heavy for their size. Avoid bruised or overly soft fruit.

Watermelon (May through September): Smooth skin; rich red or yellow flesh, with no brown or black seeds; heavy for its size.

 Helpful Hints

GETTING IT RIPE

The following tips for fruit also apply to tomatoes:

➤ **Many fruits are picked well before their peak to allow for long-distance transport with the least amount of damage. Some ripen better than others once they are picked.**

➤ **To ripen fruits at home, simply place the fruit in a loosely closed paper bag, a plastic bag with holes punched in it, or a commercial ripening bowl. Do not wrap airtight, or moisture will accumulate and the fruit will spoil. Apricots, mangoes, melons (except watermelon), papayas, peaches, pears, plums, and tomatoes take especially well to this process.**

➤ **Some fruits, like tomatoes, stop ripening once they've been refrigerated, so ripen them at room temperature before refrigerating. Fresh in-season tomatoes can be stored at room temperature for a few days to retain the best flavor.**

Best Out-of-Season Buys

FROZEN	CANNED	DRIED
Blueberries	Cherries	Apples
Corn	Corn	Apricots
Cranberries	Peaches	Dates
Green peas	Pineapple	Figs
Lima beans	Tomatoes	Pears
Okra		Prunes
Raspberries (for sauces)		Raisins
Spinach		
Strawberries (for sauces)		

Herbs, Spices, and Other Flavor Enhancers

HERBS

Store fresh herbs loosely wrapped in plastic wrap in the refrigerator. Dried herbs are about 3 times as potent as fresh, but their quality diminishes over time. Buy in small quantities, and store in a cool, dry place; heat and sunlight will ruin them.

Basil: A slight anise flavor makes basil ideal for almost any Italian dish. The delicate fresh leaves bruise easily, so slice with a sharp knife or leave whole for salads. Add during the last few minutes of cooking sauces or soup. Dried basil can be added earlier.

Bay leaf: Its potent flavor mellows with long cooking, so bay leaf is a good seasoning for soups and stews. Bay leaf also adds a new dimension to poached fruit. Break dried leaves in half before adding to a recipe to release extra flavor, but remove them before serving.

Chervil: Fresh chervil has a delicate taste somewhat like tarragon, but dried chervil has little flavor. Lacy leaves, which resemble parsley, make it a classic seasoning for fish or egg dishes.

Chives: A member of the onion family, chives have far more flavor when fresh than when freeze-dried or frozen. Add chopped to egg, poultry, cheese, and fish recipes for color and taste.

Coriander: Also called cilantro or Chinese parsley, this fresh herb looks like flat-leaf parsley, but its distinctive lemony flavor is essential as last-minute seasoning in many Oriental, Indian, and Mexican dishes such as salsas. Coriander seeds are available dried but have a totally different taste

and use, chiefly in stews and soups.

Dill: Fresh dill has beautiful feathery leaves and a delicate flavor. It especially complements fish and egg dishes and makes a good seasoning for cucumbers, carrots, potato salads, and cheese sauces. Dried dill is called dill weed and may be a little bitter. The more potent dill seeds are generally used in long-cooked recipes.

Marjoram: The flavor of this herb is mildly reminiscent of oregano. It is popular in many meat and poultry dishes, bread stuffings, and potatoes.

Mint: There are dozens of types of mint, including peppermint, spearmint, and lemon mint. Most varieties have a sweet, cool, refreshing taste. Fresh mint is a standard garnish for iced tea or lemonade and is also popular as a dessert and jelly flavoring, and a classic seasoning for lamb. Dried mint is potent and should be used shortly after opening since it can lose flavor.

Oregano: A standard partner to basil, it is often used in Italian and Mexican dishes, especially with tomatoes. The dried herb has more flavor than most and thus can withstand long cooking. It's also good in salad dressings, marinades, and stuffings.

Parsley: Both the flat-leaf (also called Italian parsley) and curly-leaf varieties are available fresh so widely that it's usually unnecessary to purchase dried parsley. Though some cooks say that flat-leaf parsley is more flavorful, the 2 are interchangeable in recipes.

Rosemary: Its slightly piney, bittersweet, distinctive taste is especially good with lamb but also complements poultry, steaks, potatoes, and tomato dishes.

Sage: Its aromatic flavor is standard in poultry stuffing. Sage is also excellent with pork, liver, and cheese dishes. The plant is hardy even in cold climates, making it a favorite in a home herb garden.

Savory: Both summer and winter savory have a mild but pleasant flavor that pairs well with other herbs such as oregano or thyme. It enhances many meat, egg, pasta, and rice dishes.

Tarragon: Its pungent anise flavor is classic in many chicken, egg, and cheese dishes as well as sauces. Tarragon is also good with vegetables, especially carrots.

Thyme: Its many varieties add pleasant flavoring to soups (especially chowders), stews, meat and poultry dishes, sauces, and stuffings. Fresh or dried, it is one of the most versatile herbs.

SPICES

Most spices are sold dried and should be stored tightly covered in a cool, dark place. Whole spices retain aroma and flavor for a year or more, but ground spices lose their potency after a few months.

Allspice: Though the name indicates a blend, this berry is a spice all its own. Used in sweets and baking, it is also good in pickles, relishes, and meat dishes. It is also the predominant flavor in Jamaican jerk pork and chicken, and other Caribbean recipes.

Anise (fennel): Its distinctly licorice flavor is particularly good in tomato dishes, cakes, and cookies.

Caraway: These whole seeds are relatives of anise but have a slightly salty

Helpful Hints

HERB TIPS

➤ Cilantro, dill, and basil sometimes come with roots attached. Immerse the roots in a tall glass or jar with 1 inch water and seal in a plastic bag to prolong freshness.

➤ Because most fresh herbs are more delicate than dried, add them near the end of lengthy cooking times.

➤ To enhance the flavor of dried herbs, rub them between your fingers for a few seconds or grind in a mortar and pestle before adding to a recipe. Lightly toasting also enhances flavor.

taste. They are particularly good in savory yeast breads, cheese dishes, cabbage and other vegetable dishes, and sweet pickles.

Cardamom: Whole pods contain seeds that must be ground. A classic flavor in Scandinavian cooking, as well as cakes, breads, and cookies, it is also a pleasing seasoning for custards and sweet sauces.

Chili powder: A blend of ground chili peppers, cumin, garlic, and oregano. The proportions and other additions vary according to brand.

Cinnamon: Its sweet aroma is most commonly found in baked goods and desserts, some vegetables such as sweet potatoes, and certain Indian and Mexican savory classics. Whole cinnamon sticks can be used to stir and flavor cider or coffee.

Clove: Whole cloves are small unopened flower buds that are flavorful and attractive stuck in hams or floating in wine or cider. Ground clove is a potent seasoning in baked goods and candies.

(continued on next page)

(continued from previous page)

Cumin: Whole seeds are especially fragrant toasted for a few seconds in a hot skillet or in the oven before being ground for use in many Mexican and Indian dishes as well as in sauces and salad dressings. Cumin particularly complements chilies.

Curry powder: A blend of many ground spices, its composition varies according to brand. The namesake seasoning in certain Indian lamb, chicken, beef, and vegetarian preparations.

Ginger: Available as a fresh root, preserved, crystallized, and ground, ginger is used in Chinese stir-fries as well as in European cookies and all-American cakes. Various forms of ginger are not interchangeable, so use what is specifically called for.

Mace: This is the dried casing surrounding whole nutmeg; it has a milder flavor and is used in desserts and baked goods.

Mustard: Mustard seed is sold whole or ground; its potency varies according to brand. Whole seeds are commonly used in pickling mixtures. Ground mustard is used to add flavor and color to sauces, egg and cheese dishes, and such meats as veal and pork. The condiment includes other ingredients besides mustard. Whole and ground mustard are not interchangeable.

Nutmeg: Used in much the same way as mace, nutmeg has a more distinctive flavor, especially when it is freshly ground. Used in custards, fruit pies, and sweet vegetables such as yams.

Paprika: A bright to brick-red powder made by grinding the pods of mild sweet chiles or peppers. Its flavor ranges from mild and sweet to hot with a slight bite. Used in salad dressings, stews, and to lend color and tang.

Pepper: The most common spice, it includes whole or ground black, red, white, and green peppercorns. Since ground pepper loses potency rapidly, buy whole peppercorns, which last indefinitely, and grind as needed. Cayenne or red pepper is among the strongest while white pepper is much milder. Along with salt, pepper is added to almost all savory dishes as an all-purpose seasoning.

Poppy seeds: These little black seeds are commonly used in breads and cakes.

Saffron: Dried crocus stigmas used to flavor and give a rich golden color to rice, chicken, and fish dishes. Expensive.

Sesame seeds: Also called benne seeds in the South, sesame seeds have a nutty flavor, especially when toasted. Good in crackers and breads, they also go well in many Asian dishes. Tend to get rancid quickly; store in refrigerator.

Turmeric: Its golden color makes it a ready substitute for more expensive saffron, although its flavor is different.

Vanilla: One of the most common and versatile of dessert and baked good flavorings, it is available as an extract or in whole beans. Use sparingly; its flavor is potent.

OTHER FLAVOR ENHANCERS

Alcoholic beverages: Wine, whiskey, liqueur, and beer are commonly used in cooking to add moisture and flavor. They need not be the very best quality, but they should be good enough to drink alone.

Capers: These buds from a small Mediterranean shrub are usually sold packed in a vinegary brine. If packed in salt, rinse before using. They are especially good with seafood, in sauces, and as a flavorful garnish.

Chipotles in adobo: Dried, smoked jalapeño chiles canned in a thick vinegary purée. Used in very small amounts for hot and smoky flavor in Spanish and Latin American cooking.

Chocolate: This is sold in unsweetened, bittersweet, semisweet, and sweet forms as well as unsweetened cocoa powder. White chocolate is not really chocolate: It contains no cocoa solids. Note that various types of chocolate are not interchangeable in many recipes.

Garlic: Widely used in Mediterranean and Asian cooking, garlic is also one of the most commonly used flavorings in the United States.

Horseradish: This root can be purchased fresh, but it is more commonly available prepared, either red or white. Unlike other condiments, prepared horseradish loses potency after a few months.

Hot-pepper sauce: Brands on the market vary widely in potency, so use lightly, then add more to taste.

Lemon: Lemon juice and zest are added to many sweet and savory dishes to bring out natural flavor. The juice helps prevent discoloration of some fruits like apples, bananas, and avocados.

Salt: The world's most common seasoning, these crystals enhance the flavor of many foods. Though common table salt is specified for baked goods, kosher and sea salt may be used interchangeably in general seasoning.

Shallots: The mild-flavored cousin to the onion but with the head composed of multiple cloves. Used like onion or garlic. Choose dry-skinned bulbs with no signs of sprouting.

Soy sauce: Made from soybeans, this is a basic salty flavoring for many Asian dishes. You can buy soy sauce in most supermarkets. Look for brands that are "naturally brewed" for best flavor.

Tamari: A darker, thicker form of soy sauce with a distinctive mellow flavor. Used as a dipping sauce, for basting, and as a table condiment.

Cooking

Throughout history, traditional recipes and cooking techniques have been a constant that binds one generation to the next. In fact, mealtime is likely to be the most significant event in daily family life. This section offers helpful advice on making mealtime satisfying, healthy, and simple.

Planning Meals

One key to good meals is organization. Plan your meals ahead, bearing in mind taste, nutrition, and cost.

To save time and effort:

- Keep a grocery list in a handy place, perhaps on the refrigerator, with a pencil attached to a magnet. Noting needed supplies on an ongoing basis saves time and eliminates extra trips to the market.
- For optimum balanced nutrition, think in terms of a full day's menu. If you need help, develop meal plans on paper and balance them against a nutritional chart.
- Every week, plan to cook once for 2 meals. A large roast will yield enough meat for sandwiches or salads another night.
- Make one-dish meals such as casseroles, soups, and stews that require only a salad as accompaniment.
- Prepare foods in quantity. Bake extra potatoes expressly for another meal of potato pancakes or hash browns.

To provide variety within each meal, think about:

Color variety: An all-white meal of chicken, cauliflower, and mashed potatoes has little appeal. Change the vegetable to green beans and the starch to mashed sweet potatoes, and the plate looks much more inviting.

Flavor: Mild tastes both tame and complement the heat of fiery dishes. That's why grated mild cheese or a dollop of sour cream is the usual garnish for a spicy chili, and cool yogurt sauces generally accompany hot curries.

Richness: Follow creamed soup with a simple piece of grilled poultry or fish, then end the meal with fruit. Or balance a rich dessert with a light main course.

Taste variety: If you use a strongly flavored food, such as garlic or cabbage, avoid repeating it in another dish in the meal.

Texture: Serve soft foods with crunchy ones. Try soups with crusty breads or crackers; meat loaf with carrot and celery sticks; applesauce with pork chops.

How to Prepare, Cook, and Store Food Safely

In addition to commonsense practices such as washing your hands before fixing or eating food and after touching raw meat, poultry, seafood, or eggs, there are many other ways to ensure food safety:

Always use a clean cutting board made of hardwood, preferably maple or bamboo, which is less likely to retain bacteria than other surfaces. If you can, keep one board for produce and one for raw meat, poultry, and seafood. Replace old, very worn boards with hard-to-clean grooves. Wash the cutting board with hot water, soap, and a scrub brush, and then sanitize it with a solution of 1 teaspoon chlorine bleach in 1 quart of water.

When shopping, separate meat, poultry, and seafood from other foods in your cart, and bag them separately at checkout. Once you are home, keep meat, poultry and seafood well refrigerated, and in containers or sealed plastic bags to prevent juices from dripping on other food. Because raw meat, poultry, and seafood can harbor bacteria, wash your hands and clean work surfaces regularly and thoroughly when working with these foods.

Making Healthier Meals

Simple changes in your cooking and eating habits can improve nutrition without sacrificing taste or time.

- Reduce meat portions to about 3 ounces. Try to plan a meal so that meat is a supplement rather than the focus of a meal.
- Use lower-fat meats such as turkey or chicken. Ground turkey can often be substituted for ground beef in recipes.
- Sauté or sear meats in a nonstick skillet spritzed with cooking spray or coated with a light film of vegetable oil.
- Poach, broil, grill, or bake instead of frying whenever possible.
- Degrease all sauces, soups, and stocks by skimming off fat with a spoon, blotting with paper towels, or refrigerating and lifting off the cold, hardened fat.
- Steam vegetables until just tender to retain maximum vitamins, minerals, fiber, and flavor.
- Substitute nonfat or reduced-fat milk, sour cream, and cheese in recipes that call for full-fat versions.
- Look for recipes that use mashed bananas, applesauce, or other puréed fruits in place of some of the oil in quick breads and muffins. You'll save fat and add flavor.
- Whip evaporated skim milk instead of cream for dessert topping. (Be sure the milk and the bowl are icy cold for best volume and serve immediately.)
- Add puréed vegetables to soup instead of cream to cut fat and boost nutritional value.
- Add grated vegetables to casseroles and lasagnas to increase fiber, vitamin, and mineral intake.
- Learn to eat slowly. Doing so is more enjoyable, and you will feel satisfied with less food.

Use raw poultry, meat, fish, and shellfish directly from the refrigerator. Do not bring them to room temperature. Always marinate food in the refrigerator (at room temperature, 15 minutes is maximum), and never use a marinade from raw meat, poultry, or seafood on cooked food unless you first boil it for 2 minutes to kill any bacteria.

It is best to avoid raw meat dishes, such as steak tartare. Pork should be cooked thoroughly to avoid the potential (though now uncommon) threat of trichinosis, as should all meat, poultry, and fish.

Refrigerate or freeze leftovers within 2 hours in covered containers or tightly wrapped in plastic or foil.

Beef

Like all red meat, beef is an excellent source of essential B vitamins and of complete protein. What matters is how much beef is eaten, both in frequency and in quantity. Choose smaller portions and trim off excess fat before eating.

Well-marbled beef such as porterhouse steak contains more fat and is more tender and juicy than leaner cuts such as flank and round steaks and skirt steak. However, leaner cuts can be equally, if not more, flavorful when they are marinated or braised to tenderize and flavor them. Braised beef is done when it is fork-tender.

Whole muscle meats such as steak and roasts can be eaten medium rare, medium, or well done

Popular Beef Cuts

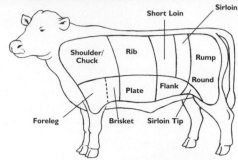

BEEF RIB ROAST SMALL END
(roast). Also called standing rib roast.

BEEF RIB-EYE ROAST
(roast). Large center muscle of rib with bones and seam fat removed.

BEEF BOTTOM ROUND ROAST
(braise, roast). Also called beef bottom round pot roast; suitable for roasting if high quality.

BEEF CHUCK SHOULDER POT ROAST, BONELESS
(braise). Also called boneless cross-rib pot roast.

BEEF CHUCK 7-BONE STEAK
(braise). Named for blade bone, which resembles number 7; also called center chuck steak.

BEEF CHUCK SHORT RIBS
(braise). Also called flanken short ribs.

BEEF SHANK CROSS CUTS
(braise). Crosswise cuts from foreshank or hindshank.

BEEF TOP LOIN STEAK
(broil, grill, panfry). Also called shell, strip, New York, club, and Delmonico steak. Also available boneless.

BEEF LOIN PORTER-HOUSE STEAK
(broil, grill, panfry). Includes tenderloin at least 1¼ inches in diameter.

BEEF RIB-EYE STEAK
(broil, panfry). Boneless steak also called fillet or Spencer steak; cut from beef rib-eye roast. Also available bone-in.

BEEF ROUND TOP ROUND STEAK
(broil, grill). Also known as London broil. Best when marinated.

BEEF LOIN TENDERLOIN ROAST
(roast). Cut from tenderloin muscle; very tender, boneless, with very little (or no) fat covering. Also called beef tenderloin.

OXTAILS
(braise). Excellent as a rich and delicious substitute for beef stewing meat; skim fat from surface of cooking liquid before serving.

Grilling

Charcoal usually takes about 30 minutes to reach the proper temperature. Wait until the coals are covered with a light gray ash before cooking. Gas grills preheat in about 10 minutes.

For successful meals, note the following:

- To lower or raise heat during grilling, adjust the racks, vents, or lid, or push coals apart or together.
- Most foods should be cooked over moderate heat several inches from the heat source. Delicate items like bread should be placed near the edge of the grill farthest from the heat source.
- Uniform thickness makes for easy timing when cooking several items together, such as burgers.
- Marinate foods in self-sealing plastic storage bags for quick cleanup.
- Brush leftover marinade on foods while grilling. Never use marinade from raw meat, poultry, or seafood on cooked food unless you first boil it for 2 minutes to destroy bacteria.
- Brush on thick marinades and sauces only during the last few minutes to prevent burning.

Be sure to follow the suggestions below for safe grilling:

- To prevent fires and smoke inhalation, place grills in the open, not in an enclosed area such as a garage or next to the house.
- Always have water nearby in case of emergency.
- Never add starter fluid after the fire is going. This can cause a dangerous flash of flame. Keep flammable liquids well away from the grill when in use.
- Never allow children to play near a grill.
- Check coals several hours after cooking to be sure they are completely burned out.
- If you're transporting food to be grilled elsewhere, keep it in a cooler at 40 degrees F or below.
- Keep coolers out of the sun both on your way to your destination and once you get there.
- Pack uncooked meat, poultry, and seafood in a separate cooler to avoid cross contamination.
- Transfer food to a clean platter and use clean utensils to serve cooked food.
- Clean grill between each use.

according to taste. Remove large roasts from the oven when the temperature on the meat thermometer is 5 degrees to 10 degrees F below the desired end point. The internal temperature will rise upon standing.

Medium rare: internal temperature of about 145 degrees F. The color is brown on the exterior, with a pink-red interior and juices.

Medium: registers about 160 degrees F, with a light pink interior and juices.

Well done: registers about 170 degrees F and is brown throughout, with little juice.

Hamburgers and ground beef mixtures such as meat loaf should be cooked to a minimum of 160 degrees F on a meat thermometer.

Pork

Today's pork is bred to be much leaner than in the past, so older recipes that require long cooking times can result in dried-out meat. Some

Helpful Hints

NO MORE CHARRING

Grilling meat at a high temperature can create potentially cancer-causing substances, but you can minimize the formation of these chemicals by taking these steps:

➤ **Remove all visible fat: it can cause flare-ups.**

➤ **Precook in the microwave immediately before grilling to release some of the juices that can drip on coals. (Don't do this if you plan to transport food to another site to grill it. Harmful bacteria can grow in the time it takes to get there.)**

➤ **Cook foods that require longer cooking times at lower temperatures—like thick pork chops or a roast—with the indicated cooking method.**

➤ **Cook food in the center of a covered grill. For charcoal, move coals to the sides to prevent fat and juices from dripping on them. For a gas grill, turn off burners directly below the food and adjust burners on both sides of the food to the same amount of heat.**

➤ **Remove charred portions of meat before serving.**

experts maintain that the new pork adapts well either to very quick cooking, such as stir-frying or sautéing, when cut thin, or to lengthy braising to tenderize the meat.

Pork tenderloin is an extremely tender cut. It is low in fat, has absolutely no waste, cooks quickly, and roasts, grills, slices, and sautés well.

Cook pork loins and tenderloins to an internal temperature of at least 155 degrees F. (Meat will still be slightly pink in center.) Larger cuts like fresh ham (leg) should be cooked to 170 degrees F. When carved, they will have some pink color near the bone, but juices will run clear. Cook ground pork until no trace of pink remains.

Lamb

With modern breeding and shipping, lamb is available year-round. Leg of lamb is a classic dish. Loin lamb chops and rack of lamb are expensive cuts. Try braised shoulder of lamb, stuffed lamb breast, and shoulder chops, which are less costly and just as flavorful.

Cook medium rare, medium, or well done, depending on individual preference.

Medium Rare: registers about 145 degrees F and has a reddish interior.

Medium: registers about 160 degrees F and is a brownish-pink tinged with red.

Well done: registers about 170 degrees F and is grayish.

Veal

Veal is the most delicate of all meats and has a subtle flavor and texture perfect for seasoning with herbs and other more distinctive ingredients. Veal comes only from young calfs. It is very lean with no marbling and only a thin external layer of fat. Like beef, better grades of veal carry federal-grade stamps.

Cuts appropriate for roasting—rump, round, loin roast, rib, and shoulder roasts—call for thorough cooking at low to moderate temperatures because of their lack of fat and the large proportion of connective tissue in the meat. Roast veal to an internal temperature of at least 170 degrees F. The exterior will be reddish-brown and the interior a creamy white.

To test panfried veal for doneness, make a small slit in the center of the meat or near the bone to check that the color is creamy white throughout. Braised veal and veal cooked in liquid should be tender when pierced with a fork.

Poultry

Chicken and turkey are excellent sources of iron, thiamine, riboflavin, and niacin, and lower in fat and calories than most other animal proteins, especially when eaten without the skin.

Popular Pork Cuts

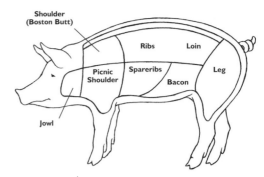

Shoulder (Boston Butt)

Ribs   Loin

Picnic Shoulder   Spareribs   Leg

Bacon

Jowl

PORK SHOULDER ARM PICNIC
(roast). **Also called picnic or whole fresh picnic.**

PORK SHOULDER ARM ROAST
(roast). **Also called pork arm roast.**

PORK LEG ROAST, BONELESS
(roast). **Also called rolled fresh ham.**

PORK LOIN CENTER RIB ROAST
(roast). **Contains loin eye muscle and rib bones; also called pork loin roast and center cut pork roast.**

PORK LOIN TENDERLOIN
(roast, broil, panfry, grill). **Very tender and lean; cut into slices for panfrying or stir-frying. Also called pork tenderloin.**

PORK SPARERIBS
(roast, bake, braise, broil, grill). **Contains long rib bones with thin covering of meat on outside of and between ribs.**

PORK LOIN COUNTRY-STYLE RIBS
(roast, bake, braise, broil, grill). **Blade end loin chops that have been split. Also called country-style spareribs.**

PORK LOIN RIB CHOPS
(braise, panfry, broil, grill). **Contain loin eye muscle and backbone. Also called center cut chops.**

PORK LOIN CHOPS
(braise, panfry, broil, grill). **Contain eye muscle and tenderloin separated by T-shaped bone. Also called loin end chops.**

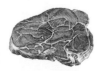

PORK LOIN SIRLOIN CHOPS
(braise, panfry, broil, grill). **From sirloin end of loin. Also called sirloin pork chops or sirloin pork steaks.**

PORK LOIN SIRLOIN CUTLETS
(braise, panfry, broil, grill). **Boneless, tender slices cut from sirloin end of loin.**

PORK LOIN BLADE CHOPS
(braise, panfry, broil, grill). **From blade end of loin. Also called pork loin blade steaks.**

Popular Lamb Cuts

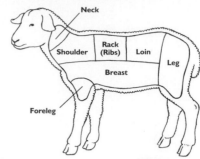

LAMB RIB ROAST
(roast). Elegant and expensive. Also called rack of lamb.

LAMB SHOULDER NECK SLICES
(braise). Cross cuts of neck. Also called neck of lamb and bone-in lamb for stew.

LAMB RIB CHOPS
(broil, grill, panfry, roast, bake). Also called rack lamb chops.

LAMB LOIN CHOPS
(broil, grill, panfry). Meaty area has both rib-eye muscle and tenderloin.

LAMB LEG SIRLOIN CHOP
(broil, grill, panfry). Includes three different muscles. Also called lamb sirloin steak.

LAMB SHOULDER ARM CHOPS
(braise, broil, grill). Cut from arm portion of shoulder. Also called arm cut chops, round bone chops, or shoulder chops.

LAMB SHOULDER BLADE CHOPS
(braise, broil, grill, panfry). From the blade portion of the shoulder. Also called lamb shoulder chops or blade cut chops.

LAMB SHANKS
(braise). Cut from the arm of the shoulder.

LAMB LEG, WHOLE
(roast). Also called leg of lamb; available bone-in and boneless.

LAMB LEG SHANK, HALF
(roast). Sirloin half removed. Lower half of leg and round leg bone included.

LAMB BREAST RIBLETS
(braise). Cut from breast, contains long and narrow ribs with layers of meat and fat.

LAMB BREAST
(braise, roast). Also called breast of lamb. Part of forequarter, containing row of ribs.

Popular Veal Cuts

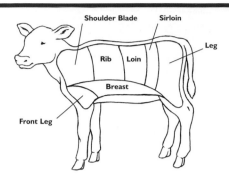

VEAL SHOULDER ROAST, BONELESS
(braise, roast). Shoulder cut with bones removed; rolled and tied to keep its shape.

VEAL BREAST
(braise, roast). Also called breast of veal. Contains lower ribs, lean meat, and layers of fat, making it juicy and flavorful.

VEAL BREAST RIBLETS
(braise). Also called veal riblets; long, narrow cuts containing rib bones with thin fat covering.

VEAL SHOULDER BLADE STEAK
(braise, panfry). Also called veal shoulder steak or veal shoulder chop.

VEAL RIB CHOPS
(braise, panfry, grill, broil). Contain big rib-eye muscle. Expensive and tasty.

VEAL LOIN CHOPS
(braise, panfry, grill, broil). Muscles include top loin and tenderloin.

VEAL TOP LOIN CHOPS
(braise, panfry, grill, broil). Same as veal loin chops except do not contain tenderloin.

VEAL CUTLETS
(braise, panfry). Very lean, thin, boneless slices from leg that are pounded thinly. Also called scaloppine.

VEAL SHANK CROSS CUTS
(braise). Cut crosswise from hindshank, usually 1 to 2½ inches thick. Also called osso buco.

Despite strict processing standards, salmonella bacteria in raw poultry still pose a threat. After handling raw poultry, wash hands, surfaces, and knives carefully with hot, soapy water. Be sure to thaw frozen poultry slowly in the refrigerator, not at room temperature. If possible, reserve one cutting board just for poultry.

Cook whole chicken or turkey until it is done. Good tests of doneness are an internal temperature of 180 degrees F in the thickest part of the meat between the thigh and the body, or 170 degrees F in the breast; juices that run clear when the poultry is pierced; and flesh that is no longer pink anywhere.

Tender boneless cuts cook in minutes, while whole birds take hours. Labels such as "old," "hen," or "stewing hen" indicate mature birds that may be on the tough side. These taste better braised or stewed rather than roasted or fried.

When microwaved, poultry can cook unevenly. Test poultry for doneness with a meat thermometer in several spots to be sure it has reached the proper internal temperature throughout.

Refrigerate leftovers promptly. Put them in shallow dishes so they cool quickly to room temperature before refrigeration. Use in a few days.

Seafood

Fish and shellfish are generally low in calories. The so-called fatty fishes—salmon, mackerel, whitefish, bluefish, shad, lake trout—contain less fat than many meats, and most of that fat is the healthy unsaturated variety. "Lean" fish—ocean perch, cod, flounder, halibut, red snapper, haddock, hake, whiting—contain less fat. All shellfish are lean.

If you're concerned about the cholesterol content of certain fatty fish and shellfish, consider this: Researchers have found that many fat fish (herring, mackerel, salmon, bluefish) contain omega-3 fatty acids that actually may help in reducing the risk of heart disease. More good news: Shellfish such as scallops, clams, oysters, and mussels have lower cholesterol levels than originally believed.

In many recipes, different kinds of similar fatty or lean fish can usually be used interchangeably. Also, frozen fish and shellfish can replace fresh fish and shellfish; just thaw them first. Shellfish are rich in minerals, contain high-quality protein, are a good source of vitamins, and are low in calories. Except for shrimp and scallops, fresh, uncooked shellfish should be alive when bought, and cooked within one day. (The Food and Drug Administration does not recommend eating raw shellfish.) Like fish, shellfish cooks quickly. Shucked clams and oysters should be plump and shiny. Always buy fish from a reputable retailer—avoid vendors who sell fish from roadside stands or the back of a truck. Don't buy frozen seafood if the packages are open, torn, or crushed.

Eggs

Salmonella bacteria may be present in eggs as well as poultry. Thorough cooking kills them.

- In the store, inspect the carton for any cracked or broken eggs. Discard any that were damaged on the way home.
- Check the expiration date on the carton to make sure it hasn't passed or isn't close.
- Store eggs in the original carton in the main section of the refrigerator. Do not remove and place them in the egg section on the door, where the temperature is higher and less constant.
- Avoid eating raw eggs in dessert mousses or meringues, homemade mayonnaises and sauces, Caesar salad, and eggnog.
- Always cook eggs thoroughly. Scrambled eggs should be firm; poached and fried eggs should be set.

Dairy Products

Dairy products are highly perishable. Quality also depends upon shipping and handling en route to your store.

- Buy from a high-volume store that replenishes its stock frequently.
- Check expiration dates on containers before buying. When in doubt, look at several packages for the latest date. Later dates are usually at the back of the case. (It's also colder there.)
- Store in the refrigerator at all times.
- Discard all dairy products that have an off odor or begin to develop mold—except mold-containing cheeses such as Roquefort or Morbier.

Produce

It is difficult to know whether produce has been treated or sprayed with chemicals, so it is safest to assume that it has. Produce can also harbor bacteria, so take care to follow these suggestions for preparing fruits and vegetables before you eat them.

- Wash all produce thoroughly under cold running tap water to remove all dirt and reduce pesticide residue. (This recommendation includes fruits that require peeling or cutting, like melons.) Don't use soap, detergents, or bleach solutions to clean produce. These products are not designed to be ingested, even in minute amounts.
- Cut away any damaged or bruised areas— bacteria can thrive there.
- Use a brush only on hard fruits and vegetables like potatoes or winter squash.
- Discard any fruit or vegetable showing signs of mold or other disease. The nutritional content will be severely diminished, and the potential for harmful bacteria is increased.

Juices

Most of the juice sold in the United States is pasteurized, but a small percentage of juice is unpasteurized and may contain harmful bacteria. For example, apple juice or cider sold at

Helpful Hints

BATTLING FOOD ODORS

To get rid of fish, garlic, or other odors lingering on your fingers, wash hands with soap, then lemon juice (and salt, if the odor is persistent). Cinnamon sticks and cloves in an open dish can cover frying odors.

health food stores or farmer's markets may be unpasteurized. These juices pose a risk, especially for children, the elderly, and people with weakened immune systems.

- If you are in one of these at-risk groups, avoid unprocessed juices, or bring juice to a boil before consuming it. (The FDA requires that unpasteurized juice carry a warning label.)
- Pasteurized juice, which is found in the refrigerated section of stores, should be kept in the refrigerator at home as well.
- Treated juice—juice that is shelf stable in boxes, bottles, or cans—must be refrigerated after opening.

Canned Goods

Foods are canned according to strict government standards, but it is still important to inspect the food before consumption.

- Most commercially canned goods have a long shelf life. Once opened, the contents should be removed, treated like fresh food, and consumed quickly, with leftovers refrigerated.
- Never eat the contents of a dented or swollen can. A dent may mean that the can has a hole, and the food may therefore be contaminated. Swollen cans may indicate that the food in the can is contaminated or spoiled.

Microwaving

Microwave ovens vary in size, power, and extra features. Smaller ovens are ideal for small

MICROWAVING FRESH VEGETABLES

Cooking vegetables is one of the things the microwave does best. Fresh vegetables cook quickly with a minimum amount of water, so they retain nutrients, taste, and color.

TIMING IS EVERYTHING

➤ **Dense foods such as lasagna will cook or heat through more slowly in a microwave than light porous foods such as cakes and breads.**

➤ **As with any cooking method, foods at room temperature will take less time to cook than refrigerated or frozen foods.**

➤ **Microwaveable foods continue to cook by internal heat after removal from the microwave. After cooking, allow them to stand 1 to 2 minutes before serving.**

kitchens or single cooks, but they're often less powerful than large models. Extra features range from preprogrammed settings for commonly cooked foods to heating elements that brown and crisp foods. Some units also do double duty as conventional or convection ovens.

Each microwave oven is different, so read the instruction manual carefully and keep it handy for reference. Most microwave recipes were developed for use in ovens with 700 watts or more of cooking power. If your oven is less powerful, recipes may require longer cooking times.

You cannot double a microwave recipe without doubling the cooking time. Microwave cooking time is in direct proportion to the amount of food to be cooked; 2 potatoes may take twice as long as 1 potato.

Microwaves penetrate food up to a depth of 1 1/2 inches, and heat is conducted from the outer edges toward the center. Therefore:

• Place denser, slower-cooking foods near the edge and quicker cooking ones in the center.
• Stir foods from the outer (hotter) edge toward the center.
• Alternate the ends of unevenly shaped foods, such as corn on the cob, and rearrange halfway through cooking.
• Place foods of uniform size in a circle.
• Prick egg yolks, sausage casings, and skins of potatoes and other vegetables before cooking to prevent steam buildup.

SAFE MICROWAVING

➤ **Never operate an empty microwave—you can damage it.**

➤ **Supervise children when they operate the microwave.**

➤ **Cover liquid foods with plastic wrap or covers to hold in heat and to prevent splattering. Carefully remove covers away from your face to avoid steam burns. Vent plastic wrap to allow steam to escape.**

➤ **Be very careful with baby food and other foods you're giving to children. There may be "hot spots." Stir before tasting; taste before serving.**

➤ **Syrups become hot quickly, and pastries with sugary fillings may quickly become hotter on the inside than the outside, so use extra caution with sugary foods.**

➤ **Follow the oven manufacturer's advice regarding the use of foil and metal containers in your microwave.**

➤ **Dinnerware with metallic trim shouldn't go in the microwave unless the dinnerware manufacturer says the dishes are designed to be used in the microwave.**

➤ **Metal twist ties shouldn't be used in the microwave.**

Adapting Recipes to a Microwave Oven

You can prepare many of your favorite foods in your microwave oven if you follow these simple directions:

- Work only with recipes serving 6 or fewer.
- Reduce liquids in braised dishes, soups, and stews. Microwaving does not cause much evaporation.
- For even cooking, chop or slice ingredients into equal size pieces.
- Shorter cooking time keeps the flavors sharper, so reduce seasonings and highly aromatic ingredients such as garlic.
- When baking, use only recipes developed for the microwave.
- Avoid recipes that call for crisply cooked or well-browned foods. They don't turn out well in microwave ovens.
- For best results, buy a microwave cookbook. When you want to convert a conventional recipe, match it with a similar one in your microwave cookbook.

A Cook's Tour of Cooking Terms

Many terms are used exclusively in cooking. You need to know what they mean in order to understand even basic recipes. Some of the most common are defined here.

Al dente: Pasta cooked until just firm. From the Italian "to the tooth."

Bake: To cook food in an oven, surrounded with dry heat; called roasting when applied to meat or poultry.

Baking powder: A combination of baking soda, an acid such as cream of tartar, and a starch or flour (moisture absorber). Most common type is double-acting baking powder, which acts when mixed with liquid and again when heated.

Baking soda: The main ingredient in baking powder, baking soda is also used when there is acid (buttermilk or sour cream, for example) in a recipe. Always mix with other dry ingredients before adding any liquid, since leavening begins as soon as soda comes in contact with liquid.

Barbecue: To cook foods on a rack or a spit over coals.

Baste: To moisten food for added flavor and to prevent drying out while cooking.

Batter: An uncooked pourable mixture usually made up of flour, a liquid, and other ingredients.

Beat: To stir rapidly to make a mixture smooth, using a whisk, spoon, or mixer.

Blanch: To cook briefly in boiling water to seal in flavor and color; usually used for vegetables or fruit, to prepare for freezing, and to ease skin removal.

Blend: To thoroughly combine 2 or more ingredients, either by hand with a whisk or spoon, or with a mixer.

(continued on next page)

(continued from previous page)

Boil: To cook in bubbling water that has reached 212 degrees F.

Bone: To remove bones from poultry, meat, or fish.

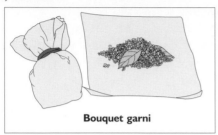

Bouquet garni

Bouquet garni: A tied bundle of herbs, usually parsley, thyme, and bay leaves, that is added to flavor soups, stews, and sauces but removed before serving.

Braise: To cook first by browning, then gently simmering in a small amount of liquid over low heat in a covered pan until tender.

Bread: To coat with crumbs or cornmeal before cooking.

Broil: To cook on a rack or spit under or over direct heat, usually in an oven.

Brown: To cook over high heat, usually on top of the stove, to brown food.

Caramelize: To heat sugar until it liquefies and becomes a syrup ranging in color from golden to dark brown.

Core: To remove the seeds or tough woody centers from fruits and vegetables.

Cream: The butterfat portion of milk. Also, to beat ingredients, usually sugar and a fat, until smooth and fluffy.

Cube: To cut food into small (about 1/2-inch) cubes.

Cut in: To distribute a solid fat in flour using a cutting motion, with 2 knives used scissors-fashion or a pastry blender, until divided evenly into tiny pieces. Usually refers to making pastry.

Deep-fry: To cook by completely immersing food in hot fat.

Deglaze: To loosen brown bits from a pan by adding a liquid, then heating while stirring and scraping the pan.

Dice: To cut food into very small (1/8-to 1/4-inch) cubes.

Dollop: A spoonful of soft food such as whipped cream or mashed potatoes.

Dot: To scatter butter in bits over food.

Dredge: To cover or coat uncooked food, usually with a flour, cornmeal mixture or bread crumbs.

Dress: To coat foods such as salad with a sauce. Also, to clean fish, poultry, or game for cooking.

Drippings: Juices and fats rendered by meat or poultry during cooking.

Drizzle: To pour melted butter, oil, syrup, melted chocolate, or other liquid back and forth over food in a fine stream.

Dust: To coat lightly with confectioners' sugar or cocoa (cakes and pastries) or another powdery ingredient.

Fillet: A flat piece of boneless meat, poultry, or fish. Also, to cut the bones from a piece of meat, poultry, or fish.

Fines herbes: A mixture of herbs traditionally parsley, chervil, chives, and tarragon, used to flavor fish, chicken, and eggs.

Flambé: To drizzle liquor over a food while it is cooking, then when the alcohol has warmed, ignite the food just before serving.

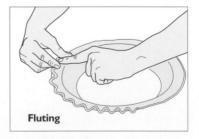

Fluting

Flute: To make decorative grooves. Usually refers to pastry.

Fold: To combine light ingredients such as whipped cream or beaten egg whites with a heavier mixture, using a gentle over-and-under motion, usually with a rubber spatula.

Glaze: To coat foods with glossy mixtures such as jellies or sauces.

Grate: To rub foods against a serrated surface to produce shredded or fine bits.

Grease: To rub the interior surface of a cooking dish or pan with shortening, oil, or butter to prevent food from sticking to it.

Grill: To cook food on a rack under or over direct heat, as on a barbecue or in a broiler.

Grind: To reduce food to tiny particles using a grinder or a food processor.

Julienne: To cut into long, thin strips, matchsticklike in shape.

Knead: To blend dough together with hands or in a mixer to form a pliable mass.

Macerate: To soak in a flavored liquid; usually refers to fruit.

Marinate: To soak in a flavored liquid; usually refers to meat, poultry, or fish.

Mince: To cut into tiny pieces, usually with a knife.

Parboil: To partially cook by boiling. Usually done to prepare food for final cooking by another method.

Poach: To cook gently over very low heat in barely simmering liquid just to cover.

Purée: To mash or grind food until completely smooth, usually in a food processor, blender, sieve, or food mill.

Reduce: To thicken a liquid and concentrate its flavor by boiling.

Render: To cook fatty meat or poultry—such as bacon or goose—over low heat to obtain drippings.

Roast: To cook a large piece of meat or poultry uncovered with dry heat in an oven.

Sauté or panfry: To cook food in a small amount of fat over relatively high heat.

Scald: To heat liquid almost to a boil until bubbles begin to form around the edge.

Sear: To brown the surface of meat by quick-cooking over high heat in order to seal in the meat's juices.

Shred: To cut food into narrow strips with a knife or a grater.

Simmer: To cook in liquid just below the boiling point; bubbles form but do not burst on the surface of the liquid.

Skim: To remove surface foam or fat from a liquid.

Steam: To cook food on a rack or in a steamer set over boiling or simmering water in a covered pan.

Steep: To soak in a liquid just under the boiling point to extract the essence—e.g., tea.

Stew: To cook covered over low heat in a liquid.

Stir-fry: To quickly cook small pieces of food over high heat, stirring constantly.

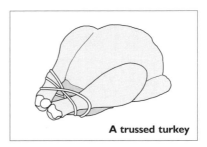

A trussed turkey

Truss: To tie whole poultry with string or skewers so it will hold its shape during cooking.

Whip: To beat food with a whisk or mixer to incorporate air and produce volume.

Whisk: To beat ingredients (such as heavy or whipping cream, eggs, salad dressings, or sauces) with a fork or whisk to mix, blend, or incorporate air.

Zest: The outer, colored part of the peel of citrus fruit.

Kitchen Equivalents

MEASUREMENTS
(For metric equivalents, see page 388)

SMALL VOLUME (LIQUID)

TABLESPOONS	CUPS	FLUID OUNCES
1 tablespoon	3 teaspoons	1/2 fluid ounce
2 tablespoons	1/8 cup	1 fluid ounce
4 tablespoons	1/4 cup	2 fluid ounces
5 tablespoons + 1 teaspoon	1/3 cup	
16 tablespoons	1 cup	8 fluid ounces

LARGE VOLUME (LIQUID)

CUPS	FLUID OUNCES	PINTS/QUARTS/ GALLONS
1 cup	8 fluid ounces	1/2 pint
2 cups	16 fluid ounces	1 pint=1/2 quart
3 cups	24 fluid ounces	1 1/2 pints
4 cups	32 fluid ounces	2 pints=1 quart
8 cups	64 fluid ounces	2 quarts=1/2 gallon
16 cups	128 fluid ounces	4 quarts=1 gallon

DRY MEASUREMENTS

1 cup=16 tablespoons
1 pound dry=16 ounces

EQUIPMENT
With a ruler, measure the length and width of the pan across its top from one inside edge to the opposite inside edge. Holding ruler perpendicular to the pan, measure the depth on the inside of the pan from the bottom to the rim.

PAN SIZE	APPROXIMATE VOLUME
2 1/2-by-1 1/2-inch muffin-pan cup	1/2 cup
8-by-1 1/2-inch round cake pan	5 cups
9-by-1 1/2-inch round cake pan	6 cups
9-by-1-inch pie plate	4 cups
8-by-8-by-2-inch square pan	7 cups
9-by-9-by-1 1/2-inch square pan	8 cups
9-by-9-by-2-inch square pan	10 cups
11-by-7-by-1 1/2 inch rectangular pan	7 cups
13-by-9-by-2-inch rectangular pan	14 cups
8 1/2 by-4 1/2-by-2 1/2 inch loaf pan	6 cups
9-by-5-by-3-inch loaf pan	8 cups
15 1/2-by-10 1/2-by-1-inch jelly-roll pan	16 cups

INGREDIENTS

Apples: 1 pound=3 medium or 3 cups sliced

Bananas: 1 pound=3 medium or 1^1/$_3$ cups mashed

Barley: 1 cup raw quick-cooking=about 3 cups cooked

Beans: 1 cup dry=2 to 2^1/$_2$ cups cooked

Blueberries: 1 pint=2^1/$_2$ cups

Bread: 1 pound loaf=16 regular or 28 thin slices

Bread crumbs: ^{1}/$_2$ cup fresh=1 slice bread with crust

Bulgur: 1 cup uncooked=3 to 3^1/$_2$ cups cooked

Butter or margarine: 1 stick=8 tablespoons or 4 ounces

Cabbage: 1 pound=4 to 5 cups coarsely sliced

Celery: 1 medium-size bunch=about 4 cups chopped

Cheese: 4 ounces=1 cup shredded

Cherries: 1 pound=about 2 cups pitted

Chicken: 2^1/$_2$- to 3-pound fryer=2^1/$_2$ cups diced cooked meat

Chocolate: 1 ounce unsweetened or semi-sweet=1 square

Chocolate chips: 6-ounce package=1 cup

Cocoa: 8-ounce can unsweetened=2 cups

Cornmeal: 1 cup raw=about 4 cups cooked

Cottage cheese: 8 ounces=1 cup

Couscous: 1 cup raw=about 2^1/$_2$ cups cooked

Cranberries: 12-ounce bag=3 cups

Helpful Hints

MEASURING UP

➤ All dry ingredients should be level with the top of the measuring cup or spoon.

➤ Measure flour as the recipe directs, either before or after sifting. To measure, lightly spoon the flour into a graduated measuring cup or spoon and level off with the flat edge of a spatula or knife. Never dip into the flour or pack the flour down or shake or tap the measuring cup.

➤ Measure brown sugar by packing it into a measuring cup.

➤ Measure liquids in a clear glass or plastic measuring cup and hold to eye level to check the line on the cup for accuracy.

➤ Weigh dry items on a kitchen scale. Be sure to allow for the weight of container if one is used.

➤ Measure the volume of a pan or bowl by filling to the rim with a known quantity of water. The number of cups needed to fill the pan equals the cup volume of the pan. If you have a pan with a removable bottom, measure with granulated sugar instead of water.

Cream: 1 cup heavy or whipping=2 cups whipped

Cream cheese: 8-ounce package=1 cup; 3-ounce package=6 tablespoons

Egg white: 1 large=about 2 tablespoons

Egg yolk: 1 large=about 1^1/$_2$ tablespoons

Farina: 1 cup regular or instant uncooked=6 to 6^1/$_2$ cups cooked

Flour: 1 pound all-purpose=about 3^1/$_2$ cups

Gelatin: 1 envelope unflavored=2^1/$_2$ teaspoons

(continued on next page)

(continued from previous page)

Gingersnaps: 15 cookies=about 1 cup crumbs

Graham crackers: 7 whole crackers=1 cup crumbs

Hominy grits: 1 cup uncooked=about $4\frac{1}{2}$ cups cooked

Honey: 16 ounces=$1\frac{1}{3}$ cups

Kasha: 1 cup uncooked=about 3 cups cooked

Lemon: 1 medium=about 3 tablespoons juice and 1 tablespoon grated peel

Lentils: 1 cup uncooked=about $2\frac{1}{2}$ cups cooked

Macaroni, elbow: 1 cup uncooked=about 2 cups cooked

Milk, condensed: 14-ounce can=$1\frac{1}{4}$ cups

Milk, evaporated: 5-ounce can=$\frac{2}{3}$ cup

Molasses: 12 ounces=$1\frac{1}{2}$ cups

Noodles: 8 ounces uncooked medium = about 4 cups cooked

Nuts: 4 ounces=1 cup chopped

Oats: 1 cup raw old-fashioned or quick-cooking=about 2 cups cooked

Onion: 1 large=1 cup chopped

Orange: 1 medium=$\frac{1}{3}$ to $\frac{1}{2}$ cup juice and 2 tablespoons grated peel

Peaches: 1 pound=about 3 medium or $2\frac{1}{2}$ cups sliced

Pears: 1 pound=about 3 medium or $2\frac{1}{4}$ cups sliced

Peppers: 1 large bell=about 1 cup chopped

Pineapple: 1 large=about 4 cups cubed

Popcorn: $\frac{1}{4}$ cup unpopped=about 4 cups popped

Potatoes: 1 pound all-purpose=about 3 medium or 3 cups sliced or 2 cups mashed

Raisins: 15-ounce box=about 2 cups

Raspberries: $\frac{1}{2}$ pint=about 1 cup

Rice: 1 cup uncooked regular=about 3 cups cooked; 1 cup uncooked instant=about 2 cups cooked

Saltine crackers: 28 squares=about 1 cup crumbs

Shortening: 1 pound=$2\frac{1}{2}$ cups

Sour cream: 8 ounces=1 cup

Spaghetti: 8 ounces uncooked=about 4 cups cooked

Split peas: 1 cup raw=about $2\frac{1}{2}$ cups cooked

Strawberries: 1 pound=about $3\frac{1}{4}$ cups whole or $2\frac{1}{2}$ cups sliced

Sugar: 1 pound confectioners'=$3\frac{3}{4}$ cups; 1 pound granulated=$2\frac{1}{4}$ to $2\frac{1}{2}$ cups; 1 pound light or dark brown=$2\frac{1}{4}$ cups packed

Tomatoes: 1 pound=3 medium

Vanilla wafers: 30 cookies=1 cup crumbs

Yeast: 1 package active dry=$2\frac{1}{2}$ teaspoons

COMMON SUBSTITUTIONS

Baking powder: 1 teaspoon baking powder=$\frac{1}{2}$ teaspoon cream of tartar plus $\frac{1}{4}$ teaspoon baking soda

Broth: 1 cup chicken or beef broth=1 bouillon cube or 1 envelope or 1 teaspoon instant bouillon plus 1 cup boiling water

Buttermilk: 1 cup buttermilk=1 tablespoon vinegar or lemon juice plus enough milk to equal 1 cup. Let stand 5 minutes to thicken. Or use 1 cup plain yogurt

Chives: Use green onion tops

Chocolate: 1 ounce unsweetened chocolate=3 tablespoons unsweetened cocoa powder plus 1 tablespoon butter, margarine, or oil

6 ounces semisweet chocolate=1 cup chocolate chips, or 6 tablespoons unsweetened cocoa powder plus 7 tablespoons sugar and 4 tablespoons butter, margarine, or oil

Cornstarch (for thickening): 1 tablespoon cornstarch=2 tablespoons flour or 2 tablespoons quick-cooking tapioca

Fish sauce, Asian: 1 tablespoon fish sauce =2 teaspoons soy sauce plus 1 teaspoon anchovy paste

Flour: 1 cup cake flour=1 cup minus 2 tablespoons all-purpose flour

1 cup self-rising flour=1 cup all-purpose flour plus 1/4 teaspoon baking powder and a pinch of salt

Milk: 1 cup whole milk=1/2 cup evaporated milk plus 1/2 cup water

Pancetta: Use sliced smoked bacon simmered in water for 3 minutes, then rinsed and drained

Pepper, ground red: 1/8 teaspoon red pepper=4 drops hot-pepper sauce

Pine nuts: Use walnuts or almonds

Prosciutto: Use ham, preferably Westphalian or a country ham, such as Smithfield

Shallots: Use red onion

Sour cream: 1 cup sour cream=1 cup plain yogurt (in unheated recipe). To prevent yogurt from curdling in a cooked recipe, you will have to stabilize it with 1 egg white or 1 tablespoon of cornstarch or flour dissolved in a little cold water for every quart of yogurt

Sugar: 1 cup light brown sugar=1 cup granulated sugar plus 1 tablespoon molasses or 1 cup dark brown sugar

Tomato sauce: 15-ounce can tomato sauce=6-ounce can tomato paste plus 1 1/2 cans water

Vanilla extract: Use brandy or an appropriately flavored liqueur

Yeast: 1 package active dry yeast=1/2-ounce yeast cake or 1 package quick-rise yeast (allow half the rising time for quick rise)

Yogurt: 1 cup plain yogurt=1 cup buttermilk

Keeping Food Fresh

Most food purchased at the supermarket has already been stored for a considerable length of time. Transit and warehousing add days, and sometimes even weeks, to the time between harvest and purchase of fresh produce.

Dairy products and meats undergo similar transport delays. So it is a good practice to keep track of labels indicating the last day of sale or use. Even canned goods, which have long shelf lives, often have expiration dates printed (albeit sometimes very small) on the can.

Refrigerating

The temperature in a refrigerator should range from 34 degrees F to 40 degrees F. Food spoils quickly when it is stored above 40 degrees F. If you have any questions about your refrigerator's temperature, check it by placing a refrigerator thermometer in the center of one of the middle shelves.

Try to minimize trips to the refrigerator since frequent opening and closing of the door causes temperature shifts.

Follow these tips for added food safety and optimal storage:

- Clean your refrigerator at least once a month.
- Periodically check your refrigerator temperature to be sure it's appropriate.
- Store milk and cream in original containers.
- Store cheese tightly wrapped or covered in a cold part of the refrigerator or in its dairy drawer.
- Use cheese promptly—especially soft cheeses, which deteriorate within a few days.
- Keep eggs in their original cartons on a shelf in the refrigerator. Don't use egg trays on the door, which is the warmest part of the unit.

Safety First

THAWING TIPS

➤ **Always thaw meats, fish, and poultry in the refrigerator or in the microwave oven. Thawing at room temperature encourages bacterial growth. After microwave defrosting, cook foods immediately.**

➤ **Partially thawed foods can be safely refrozen if the thawing has been brief and there are still ice crystals on the food.**

➤ **Never freeze or refreeze food on which you spot any indication of spoilage, such as an off-odor or an off-color.**

Helpful Hints

WHEN THE LIGHTS GO OUT

In a power failure, minimize refrigerator and freezer door openings. Protect food by placing blocks of dry ice on top of the packages. Frozen foods that have thawed completely should not be refrozen.

KITCHEN TIPS FOR LENGTHY TRIPS

➤ **Check your smoke alarm and replace the battery, if necessary.**

➤ **Clean out the refrigerator and discard whatever may spoil.**

➤ **Leave your freezer almost full. If there is a power failure, the food will stay frozen longer.**

➤ **Unplug all small appliances.**

➤ **Check to be sure your cooktop and oven are turned off.**

➤ **Refrigerate opened boxes of cereal, pasta, and other dry foods if you will be away more than a month.**

How Long Will It Last?

PRODUCT	STORAGE PERIOD	
	IN REFRIGERATOR 40 DEGREES F	IN FREEZER 0 DEGREES F
FRESH MEAT		
Ground beef	1–2 days	3–4 months
Beef steaks and roasts	3–5 days	6–12 months
Pork chops	3–5 days	4–6 months
Ground pork	1–2 days	3–4 months
Pork roasts	3–5 days	4–6 months
CURED MEATS		
Lunch meat	3–5 days	1–2 months
Sausage	1–2 days	1–2 months
GRAVY	1–2 days	2–3 months
FISH		
Lean fish (such as cod, flounder, haddock)	1–2 days	up to 6 months
Fatty fish (such as blue, perch, salmon)	1–2 days	2–3 months
CHICKEN		
Whole	1–2 days	12 months
Parts	1–2 days	9 months
Giblets	1–2 days	3–4 months
DAIRY PRODUCTS		
Swiss, brick, processed cheese	3–4 weeks	*
Milk	5 days	1 month
Ice cream, ice milk	—	2–4 months
EGGS		
Fresh in shell eggs	3 weeks	do not freeze
Hard-boiled eggs	1 week	do not freeze

*Cheese can be frozen, but freezing will affect the texture and taste.
(Sources: Food Marketing Institute for fish and dairy products; USDA for all other foods)

- Store all uncooked meats, fish, and poultry well wrapped in the coldest part of the refrigerator.
- Store fruits and vegetables in the produce drawers, which maintain the proper humidity so the food stays crisper and lasts longer.
- Do not wash produce, except leafy greens, before storing, because it will spoil more quickly.
- Wash leafy greens, dry thoroughly, and store loosely wrapped in a plastic or cloth bag.
- Inside the door, where they will be readily accessible, store condiments, soft drinks, and other foods not highly susceptible to spoilage.
- Don't leave perishables out of the refrigerator for longer than 2 hours.
- Don't overstuff the refrigerator. Cold air needs to circulate to keep food safe.

Freezing

Freezing retards the growth of microorganisms and enzymes that cause food spoilage. For best flavor and texture, home-frozen foods should be used within 6 to 9 months.

 Helpful Hints

FREEZING HINTS

➤ Freeze meatballs, berries, or cookies in a single layer on a baking sheet first, then place frozen pieces in bags for long-term storage. This way, they will freeze more quickly and won't stick together.

➤ For perfectly shaped packages that stack easily, freeze foods in a casserole dish lined with heavy-duty foil (allow enough extra foil to cover the top). After the food freezes, remove the foil-wrapped food and use the dish for something else.

SAFEGUARDING GRAINS AND CEREALS

You can store grains and cereals in the refrigerator to increase their shelf life. This is an especially good idea in warm weather.

Don't Freeze These Foods

- Salad greens and crisp raw vegetables to be used in salads and sandwiches—such as celery, onions, and sweet peppers—will lose their crispness and become limp after freezing.
- Eggs in the shell will expand and crack the shell. Hard cooked egg whites will become tough and rubbery.
- Creamed cottage cheese will change texture, becoming grainy. Freeze only uncreamed or dry-curd cottage cheese.
- Sour cream will separate when frozen and thawed.
- Heavy or whipping cream will not whip high after freezing.
- Potatoes become mushy if frozen raw, and watery and tough if boiled and then frozen.

Never store more than 2 or 3 pounds of food per cubic foot of freezer capacity at one time. Otherwise, you will overload the freezer, making it more difficult to maintain the recommended 0 degrees F temperature. Keep a freezer thermometer in the freezer and check the temperature about once a month.

An almost empty freezer is more expensive to operate than one that is nearly full. Frozen foods help keep their neighbors frozen, so keep your freezer well stocked. Here are a few more tips to make freezer storage simple and your food safe:

- Place the newest food packages in the bottom or near the back of the freezer, then move the older ones so they are next in line for use.
- Color code or label packages with different markers to help you identify foods in the freezer.
- Post a list of all frozen food (with dates) near the freezer and check off what is used.

How Long Is the Shelf Life?

Times refer to unopened products. Always check expiration dates or use-by dates on packages. Use promptly after opening. Refrigerate when indicated.

Baking powder and soda: 1 year

Cake, frosting, and cookie mixes: 1 year

Canned meats, vegetables, fruits, soups, milks, gravies: 1 year (unopened); refrigerate after opening and use promptly

Cereals: 6 months

Chocolate (chips and baking): 1 year

Coffee: 1 year; refrigerate after opening

Flour: 1 year

Frosting (canned): 8 months

Fruit (dried): 6 months

Gelatin (unflavored): 18 months

Herbs and spices (ground): 1 year; keep in a cool place; refrigerate red spices such as paprika

Honey, molasses, syrups: 1 year

Jelly and jam: 1 year; refrigerate after opening

Milk (nonfat dry): 6 months

Oils: 3 months; refrigerate if not using promptly after opening

Packaged crackers, cookies, bread crumbs: 2 to 4 months

Pancake and piecrust mixes: 6 months

Pasta and macaroni: 1 year; store airtight after opening

Peanut butter: 6 months

Pickles and olives: 1 year; refrigerate after opening

Puddings and gelatin mixes: 6 months

Rice (white): 2 years

Root vegetables such as white and sweet potatoes, onions, squash: 1 week at room temperature; store with plenty of air circulation in a dry, dark place

Shortening (solid): 8 months

Spices (whole): 1 year

Sugar (granulated): 2 years

Tea (instant): 1 year

Tea (loose and bags): 6 months

Vinegars: 1 year

Yeast (active dry): follow package date; for longer shelf date, refrigerate

Wrapping Food for the Freezer

If you're freezing food for a short time, plastic bags or wrap are adequate. Wrap foods airtight to decrease the chance of "freezer burn," which occurs when air meets frozen food. Freezer burn is not harmful but adversely affects the food's texture and color.

For longer periods, use special wrappings such as heavy-duty aluminum foil, special plastic freezer bags, or freezer wrap. You can also use heavy-duty plastic containers or jars, but never put glass containers in the freezer; the extreme temperatures may cause the glass to break. Remember to leave head space in jars or containers because foods expand during freezing. In all cases, packages should be secure, airtight, and clearly labeled with contents and date.

Fruit

When freezing fruit, wash it well, then follow a specific freezing recipe. Sometimes ascorbic acid or another antidarkening agent is called for; these products are readily available in supermarkets and pharmacies. Fruit can be packed in syrup or sugar or be completely unsweetened.

Thaw frozen fruit in its freezer container, and use it as soon as it is thawed for best flavor and texture. When fruit is completely thawed, the texture will be a bit mushy, so plan on using frozen fruit in sauces, pies, or other recipes that don't require perfect texture.

Vegetables

When freezing vegetables, wash them thoroughly, then prepare according to individual freezing recipes. For optimal taste, color, and texture, most vegetables—except peppers and onions—are best blanched before freezing (see page 143).

Times vary for each vegetable and recipe. Frozen vegetables can be cooked from the frozen state or thawed first. Remember that cooking times will be shorter, since the vegetable was partially cooked during the blanching process.

Shelf Storage

Unopened commercially canned and jarred foods can be stored safely for periods up to one year. Once opened, check the label to see if refrigeration is necessary. Many products have expiration dates, which should be noted. Organize your pantry so that all foods are rotated and used within a year or less. Use a permanent marker to date cans and packages when you purchase them so there is no question of age.

Make a plan of how to use available storage space. When building a pantry, shallow shelves are best; food is less likely to be "lost" when it can be seen easily. Lazy Susans or hinged shelves that swing out from the cupboard allow you to see and retrieve food from several angles.

Helpful Hints

IMPORTANT CANNING INFORMATION RESOURCES

For information on canning meats, poultry, fish, and other low-acid foods, or for canning all foods if you live at a high altitude, contact the Family and Consumer Sciences agent of your local cooperative extension office. You can also access the USDA's Complete Guide to Home Canning online at: www.uga.edu/nchfp

- Store similar foods together with labels facing front.
- After purchasing new items, place them behind older ones of the same type.
- At least once a year, clean the cupboard and discard any rusted, damaged, or bloated cans.
- Store flour, rice, cereals, and other dry foods in tightly covered containers to keep out moisture and prevent the spread of mealworms.
- Store food away from kitchen chemicals and refuse.

Canning

Canning preserves food by heating it hot and long enough to destroy microorganisms and enzymes that may cause spoilage and changes in color, texture, flavor, and nutritive values. It is critical that the canning process be done correctly to prevent toxin formation and foodborne illness. Use only tempered glass jars with specially designed caps or lids for canning.

Always follow the recipe and directions that come with canning equipment, jars, and lids. The U.S. Department of Agriculture also publishes advice on safe canning practices and recommended canning processes. Consult these sources before beginning to can (see box, above).

Techniques

There are 2 methods of canning, depending upon the type of food to be preserved. Timing is extremely important for safety; consult canning resources before attempting.

Acid foods: These contain natural acid, though with different degrees of acidity. Acid foods include most fruits and fruit juices, jams, and other sweet preserves. Also in this category are foods to which acid has been added to prevent spoilage, including some pickles, relishes, and sauerkraut.

These foods can be canned safely at 212 degrees F, using a boiling-water bath. Special equipment is available, but preserving can also be done in any deep kettle with a rack and a tight-fitting lid. The rack should allow the jars to remain at least 1 to 2 inches below the surface of the water. The jars must be placed so they do not touch one another during processing.

Low-acid foods: Almost all vegetables, meats, poultry, seafood, mushrooms, and soups are low in acid and need a temperature higher than 212 degrees F for safe processing. Use a special steam-pressure canner, which heats to 240 degrees F and has a lid with a safety valve, a vent, and a dial or weighted pressure gauge.

Equipment

Having the right kitchen equipment saves time and effort and is often essential to producing the right results from a recipe. High-quality kitchen equipment will give you many years of valuable service and will more than repay your investment. Start with the basics, then gradually build your kitchen around them.

Pots and Pans

Cookware is made in a variety of materials; each has different characteristics, and it is important to understand them before you buy. Many cooks purchase individual pots and pans in different materials to suit specific uses, rather than a full set in one material.

Aluminum (moderate cost; recommended for all-purpose cooking): This versatile material is the most commonly used for cookware. Cast aluminum has a thick base and thinner sidewalls. Most aluminum cookware has a nonstick finish; some has been anodized to strengthen the aluminum, making it dent and scratch resistant. The heavier the cookware, the better the heat distribution.

 How to Shop For...

QUALITY COOKWARE

What to look for:

➤ Good balance to resist tipping when empty or full.

➤ Heat-resistant knobs and handles that are easy to grasp and securely attached.

➤ Lids that fit firmly and snugly.

➤ Flat bottoms—they work best on all types of cooktops. To check for flatness, place a ruler edge across the bottom of the pan. The pan should be perfectly flat, with no space between the ruler edge and the bottom.

➤ Manufacturer's guarantee—many premium-priced nonstick lines have warranties of 10 years or longer.

Advantages: Very good heat conductor; relatively light to handle; easy to clean.

Disadvantages: Unfinished aluminum can discolor if put in the dishwasher, or pit from

Basic Pots and Pans

If you are a beginning cook or stocking a kitchen for the first time, consider these essential pieces. Before you buy, keep in mind your style of cooking, the amount of food you cook, and your storage space.

1-quart pan with lid

For heating canned soups, convenience foods; melting butter; cooking eggs; preparing sauces

2- to 2½-quart pan with lid

For cooking fresh or frozen vegetables; heating canned foods, leftovers; cooking rice, hot cereals

5- or 6-quart pan/Dutch oven

For stews, soups; slow cooking and braising

8- or 9-inch skillet with lid

For eggs, omelets; small-scale sautéing

10- to 12-inch skillet with lid

For most sautéing, braising, shallow panfrying

14-by-11-inch roasting pan

For roasting meats and poultry

8-quart stock pot

For soups, broth, and pasta, and large quantities of basic foods

Pressure Cookers

A pressure cooker uses concentrated steam, generated from the liquids included in the recipe, to cook a wide variety of foods up to 10 times faster than other methods. A pressure cooker is especially useful for tenderizing budget cuts of meat.

Sizes generally range from 4 to 8 quarts. Choose a model based on the number of family members and the kind and quantity of foods you cook. Be sure the handles are comfortable and that you can easily lift the full cooker, especially if you opt for a larger unit. Stainless steel models with an aluminum base are heavy, expensive, and durable. All-aluminum or stainless steel pressure cookers are less expensive, lighter in weight, and likely to burn foods. Most pressure cookers are designed for stovetop use, though a few manufacturers offer electric models. Look for a model with a quick-release setting that brings down the pressure swiftly to prevent overcooking.

Every pressure cooker includes a pressure regulator valve to control and maintain pressure inside the cooker. Some valves consist of a weight that sits on top of the vent pipe. As pressure builds inside the cooker, steam escapes through the vent pipe, causing the weight to rock and hiss. You need to adjust the heat level beneath the cooker to maintain steady pressure. Other cookers use spring-valve pressure regulators, which have a rod that rises as pressure increases. Marks on the rod tell you when pressure has been reached. Spring valve regulators are quieter and require fewer adjustments in heat. A rubber gasket inside the lid forms a pressure-tight seal. It will require periodic replacement. Check that the valve openings are clear and the rubber gasket is elastic and free of cracks each time you use the pressure cooker. And keep the instruction book so you can contact the manufacturer for replacement parts.

Pressure cooker

acidic foods; can discolor and impart a metallic taste to foods. Hard-water deposits may discolor aluminum, but this does not affect the use of the utensil or the food prepared in it.

Stainless steel (moderate to high cost; recommended for all-purpose cooking):

Look for stainless steel "clad" cookware. This process combines easily cleaned stainless steel on the visible surfaces with more conductive metals—such as copper or aluminum—sandwiched between. As many as 9 separate layers may be combined, but 3 or 5 is more typical. The result is a pan that cooks evenly and cleans easily.

Even manufacturers of moderately priced stainless steel cookware offer models with an aluminum disk on the bottom to provide good heat distribution.

Advantages: Exceptionally durable; smooth; scratch resistant; easy to clean.

Nonstick Cookware

Nonstick cookware offers 2 main advantages: It's generally easy to clean, and it requires no added oil or fat to keep foods (except eggs and some baked goods) from sticking and so saves calories.

Nonstick coatings have improved in recent years. Many manufacturers now use multiple coatings; the more coats, the more durable the pan is expected to be. These tough coatings are all easy to clean and offer greater resistance to heat than prior generations of nonstick coatings. Some manufacturers use metals such as titanium to reinforce the nonstick coatings. And because the finishes are tougher, many nonstick pans no longer require the use of plastic utensils. The best advice: Read the manufacturer's recommendations for utensils and cleaning on the packaging.

While nonstick cookware prevents many foods from sticking, some items, like eggs, do tend to cling. But even these are removed more easily from a pan coated with a nonstick finish.

On the downside, if food is cooked at high temperatures in a nonstick pan, residues can burn on, affecting the nonstick surface, so only medium and low heats should be used.

Disadvantages: Possible high cost; needs to be combined with other metals for good heat conduction.

Copper (high cost; recommended for browning and sauces): This is a superior cookware material. Copper reacts with certain foods, so the cookware must be lined with tin or stainless steel. Never cook or serve in unlined copper pots or pans.

Advantages: Exceptionally good looking; excellent heat conductor; durable.

Disadvantages: Needs frequent polishing; any cracks or scrapes in the lining mean the cookware must be relined.

Cast iron (low to moderate cost; recommended for even browning, especially at high heat, and for long, low simmering): Cast iron needs an initial "seasoning"—a light, even coating of vegetable oil heated in a moderate oven for 2 hours, then wiped out. A wide array of preseasoned cast-iron cookware is now available for just a few dollars more per item. Cast iron should never be scoured or washed with strong detergents. Cast iron is available with a porcelain enamel coating inside and out for rust protection and easy care.

Advantages: Retains and conducts heat evenly; relatively strong; durable. Cooking in unlined cast iron adds iron to the diet.

Disadvantages: Heavy; rusts if not thoroughly dried; may need to be periodically reseasoned to prevent foods from sticking. Porcelain enamel on cast iron is expensive and can chip or crack.

Heat-resistant glass and ceramic (moderate cost; recommended for baking and microwaving): Because this material heats slowly and unevenly, low to medium heat is best for top-of-the-range cooking.

 How to Shop For...

A GOOD-QUALITY KNIFE

Look for:

➤ **A forged blade, which tends to be more durable, better balanced, and of higher quality than a stamped one.**

➤ **A full tang—the better the knife, the longer the tang (the part of the blade that extends into the handle). The knife should be triple riveted or permanently bonded to the handle.**

➤ **A sculpted handle designed for comfort and control during use. The knife should feel well balanced in your hand.**

➤ **A lifetime warranty—a quality knife is an investment.**

THE CUTTING EDGE

➤ **Never soak knives, especially those with wooden handles.**

➤ **Hand wash knives only, in hot soapy water.**

➤ **Immediately dry knives with a soft towel and store in a wooden block or a partitioned drawer.**

➤ **Do not allow knife blades to touch one another or to touch other utensils in a drawer. Store knives in slots in specially designed wooden blocks that either fit in a kitchen drawer or sit on the countertop.**

➤ **Use knives on a wooden or plastic cutting board only, never on countertops or pot surfaces.**

➤ **Never use a knife to pry off lids or labels or for any purpose other than cutting.**

Advantages: Easy to clean; can be used directly from the refrigerator or freezer to the range top, in the oven or microwave, or for serving/storing.

Disadvantages: Poor heat conduction results in hot spots at high heat; can be cumbersome; breakable.

Enamel on steel (low to moderate cost; recommended for all-purpose cooking): Steel with porcelain enamel inside and out is used for both thin, low-cost cookware and high-quality pieces. Stainless steel rims prevent chipping. The material performs best on low to medium heat.

Advantages: Attractive enough to use for cooking and serving; easy to clean; stain resistant; doesn't react with foods or absorb odors or flavors.

Disadvantages: Thinner cookware may get hot spots and cook unevenly; can chip or crack.

Knives

No tool is more important in the kitchen than a good, sharp knife. The best-quality knives are made of high-carbon stainless steel. These have a keen, durable edge; can be sharpened easily; and won't rust or discolor. They are moderate to high in cost and should last a lifetime.

Carbon steel knives are not to be confused with stainless steel knives, which are typically less expensive. The latter are shiny and easy to clean, but because of the hardness of the steel are difficult to resharpen once dull.

Because good knives require maintenance to keep them sharp, some consumers like the convenience of serrated knives that never need sharpening. These have little teeth that saw through food rather than cut. Most of these knives cannot be sharpened. Although they stay sharp for a long time, once they are dull, they must be discarded. Never-need-sharpening knives are low to moderate in cost.

How to Sharpen Knives

To keep high-quality knives in good working order, care for them on a regular basis by steeling and sharpening.

Steeling: An old-fashioned metal chef's "steel" (the rod-shaped implement you may have seen the butcher in your local supermarket use) does not actually sharpen a dull knife. Rather, it realigns and maintains the edge on an already sharp knife by smoothing away tiny ridges and chips that occur during normal everyday use. Regular use of a steel lengthens the time between sharpening.

Safety First

KNIFE SAFETY

While it seems contradictory, sharp knives are actually safer to use than dull blades because they require less pressure to cut and don't slip as easily. Sharp knives are more predictable and thus are easier to control. Don't wait to sharpen until knives are completely dull. And, until you are confident of your sharpening skills, practice—but not on your best knife.

Essential Knives

When buying a knife, always get the best quality you can afford. A few well-chosen knives will serve you well and prove a worthwhile investment. The knives shown below are standard equipment in most well-stocked kitchens.

TYPE	USES
8- or 10-inch chef's knife	For chopping and cutting—the most commonly used kitchen knife
Paring knife	For peeling and small cutting jobs
Serrated or bread knife	For slicing bread, delicate cake, and tomatoes
Boning knife	For boning meats, poultry, and some seafood
Carving or slicing knife	For carving cooked meats and poultry
Cleaver	For large chopping jobs, cutting through bones, and pounding meat
Santoku	For mincing, dicing, slicing vegetables, meat, and even bread; multipurpose, versatile

Chef's steel

The easiest way to use a steel is to place it perpendicular to a table or countertop. Hold the base of the knife against the top of the steel (at about a 10- to 20-degree angle, depending on the original factory-set bevel of the knife blade). With just a bit of pressure, pull the knife down and back toward you until the tip is near the bottom of the steel. Alternate sides of the knife, making sure the whole edge contacts the steel as you pull.

On an already sharp knife, you'll need only a few light strokes to maintain an edge. A dull knife might require heavier pressure and as many as 15 to 20 strokes on each side of the blade.

For best results when buying a steel, choose one that it is several inches longer than your longest knife. Many manufacturers offer steels packaged in sets with their knives.

Sharpening: You'll find a wide array of sharpening devices, ranging from old-fashioned manual methods (like whetstones), to diamond-coated ceramic sticks or rods, to 2- and 3-stage automatic sharpeners—some electric powered. All do the same job: remove a bit of metal from the blade of a knife to restore a fine edge. Unlike automated sharpening devices, manual sharpening methods allow the user to choose the angle that is ground on the blade. While this allows you to replicate the factory edge on the knife without removing too much metal, it requires skill to hold and pull the knife steadily at a precise angle. Automatic knife sharpeners are easy to use and produce a finely honed blade. Some models work on fine-edged knives; others work on serrated knives. A few models work on both.

The most affordable and versatile sharpening method is a natural or man-made sharpening stone. You'll find these in fine, medium, and coarse grits. Some models combine 2 or 3 grits on different sides of one stone. Once you have chosen a stone, use either oil or water to lubricate it. And once you have chosen a lubrication method, do not switch.

- Place the water- or oil-lubricated stone on a damp cloth to stabilize it.
- Hold the knife at a 10- to 20-degree angle to the stone.
- Push the knife away from you. Hold the handle firmly to maintain the angle; lock your wrist, and move only your arm, as if you were shaving a paper-thin slice from the top of the stone.

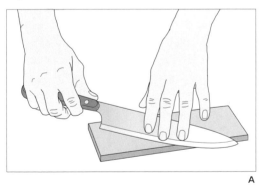

A

- Pull the knife back toward you at the same angle. Use your free hand to exert even pressure on the blade from tip to hilt. **(A)**
- Keep the pressure light on the knife and maintain the same angle through the entire stroke from base to tip.

 Helpful Hints

SHARPER SCISSORS AND SHEARS

To hone a dull scissors edge, use an aluminum oxide bench stone (available at hardware stores). Put a little household lubricating oil on the stone, then place the open scissors blade on the stone's coarsest face. Slant the blade slightly so that it tips back toward the stone at a 10-degree angle. Draw the scissors blade firmly from end to end on the stone until the edge has been sharpened. Turn the scissors and repeat with the other blade. (If the scissors still do not cut smoothly, tighten the screw that holds the blades together.) As an alternative, manual and electric scissors sharpeners are available in stores.

- Repeat the push and pull strokes several times.

How sharp you make the knife depends on a number of factors, including the quality of the steel the knife is made from and your ability to maintain the correct angle on the blade through the sharpening process. To test sharpness, try slicing a ripe tomato. The weight of the knife should be able to pierce the tomato without applying force. Do not check sharpness with your fingers.

As an alternative to the stone, you can use a manual or electric sharpening tool. Always follow the manufacturer's guidelines carefully.

Bakeware

As with cookware, it's possible to find bakeware in all shapes and sizes and in a dizzying array of materials. These different materials affect heat distribution, conductivity, and browning of the food as well as cost and the ease of cleanup.

Choose bakeware based on your cooking style and the items you bake most frequently. Consider buying items individually rather than in sets so you can mix and match different materials to suit varying needs, selecting perhaps a glass pie pan, nonstick tube or loaf cake pans, and shiny aluminum cookie sheets. If perfectly golden, optimally browned gourmet dishes are your aim, select high-grade aluminum or stainless steel–clad aluminum bakeware. If you're baking muffins from a mix for the kids in between sporting events on the weekend, or using cookie sheets to turn out a once-a-year batch of holiday cookies, nonstick properties might be of greater importance to you.

Shiny aluminum bake pans are lightweight, durable, do not rust, and consistently produce the most even baking results.

Nonstick bakeware features one of a variety of nonstick coatings applied generally to steel or aluminum pans. Nonstick pans clean easily and need not be greased. However,

 Helpful Hints

BAKING TIP

When using a glass baking dish, lower the oven temperature by 25 degrees F, since glass retains heat longer than metal.

because of their dark color, they absorb heat and can overbrown or even burn baked items. Consider reducing oven temperatures slightly or cut cooking times by a few minutes for optimum results.

Insulated bakeware is made from 2 sheets of shiny aluminum with a cushion of air sandwiched between the layers. The air layer protects the bottoms of cookies and cakes from direct heat and results in light, even browning with no burning.

Glass bakeware does not require any special care and is ideal for oven-to-table use but may get too hot and bake too quickly or unevenly, so keep a close eye on items baked in glass. Glass is good for pies and cobblers.

Black steel is an excellent conductor of uniform heat. It browns food well and produces thicker crusts. This bakeware must be thoroughly dried and lightly oiled after washing, or it will rust.

Stainless steel is durable, shiny, and easy to clean. However, since it is a poor conductor of heat, it alone is not recommended for bakeware. Some manufacturers offer bakeware that features an aluminum core wrapped in easy-to-clean stainless steel.

Manufacturers claim that the newest member of the bakeware family, silicone, needs little or no greasing; that pans cool to the touch in as little as 2 minutes; and that cookies and cakes pop out so cleanup is easy. But the Good Housekeeping Institute has found that items do not brown as evenly as they do with aluminum. Look for silicone bakeware with smooth interiors and handles that provide a secure grip.

Basics for Bakers

Baking (cooking with dry heat) is a delicate art, and not one that can be successfully undertaken without the proper equipment. The following tools will allow you to create and embellish dishes both from scratch and from mixes.

Cake pans: Two 8-inch round pans, two 9-inch round pans, two 8-inch square pans, a 13-by-9-inch rectangular pan, a 10-inch tube pan, a 12-cup Bundt pan, and a 9-inch springform, all in aluminum or with a non-stick finish

Cookie cutters: Metal or plastic, in assorted sizes

Cookie press: With several cutter shapes

Cookie sheets: At least 2 large, flat sheets, in aluminum, shiny or with a nonstick finish

Cooling wire rack: Large, stainless steel

Decorating tubes and pastry bag

Jelly-roll pan: Aluminum, shiny or with a nonstick finish, 15$1/2$-by-10$1/2$-by-1-inch

Loaf pans: Two 9-by-5-inch in aluminum pans, shiny or with a nonstick finish, or glass

Muffin pan: Aluminum, shiny or with a nonstick finish, in 12-mold standard size

Pastry blender

Pastry brush

Pastry wheel: Plain edge for trimming; fluted for cutting decorative strips

Pie pans: 9-inch, glass or aluminum

Pie weights: Small metal or ceramic pellets; prevent pie shells from bubbling up during baking

Pizza pan: Aluminum, shiny or with a nonstick finish

Rolling pin: Hardwood

Spatula: Metal in several sizes, for icing; plastic or rubber, for scraping and folding

Small Appliances

Small electrical appliances offer convenient ways to prepare foods and save time. Here's a list of some basic small appliances.

Coffeemakers: Drip models come with cupcake or cone-shaped filter baskets in 8- to 20-cup capacities as well as compact 1-, 2-, and 4-cup models. While this familiar-style coffeemaker remains the popular standard, manufacturers now offer a wider variety of brewing options. These include electric vacuum brewer machines that make a single cup at a time using pods or capsules of coffee and espresso machines designed for home use. Some combination units allow you to grind the beans and brew both coffee and espresso in the same machine.

Look for these features in a coffeemaker:
- Automatic shutoff
- Drip stop to interrupt the coffee flow when the carafe is removed (so you can pour a cup during the brew cycle)
- Dual carafes—ideal for serving a crowd or simultaneously brewing caffeinated and decaffeinated
- Programmable timer so you can wake up to freshly ground and brewed coffee

Useful Cooking Utensils

There are so many different cooking utensils that not even the largest kitchen could hold them all. It is best to outfit your kitchen slowly with high-quality durable items as your needs and cooking interests develop. Consider the following:

CUTTING, PEELING, AND GRATING

8- to 10-inch chef's knife

serrated utility knife

serrated bread knife

paring knife

carving knife

boning knife

knife sharpener/sharpening steel

kitchen shears

poultry shears

swivel vegetable peeler

can opener

4-sided grater

garlic press

pepper mill

cutting boards

rotary grater

MICROWAVE EQUIPMENT AND UTENSILS

glass-ceramic cookware

microwave-safe dinnerware

microwave-safe cooking rack

microwave-safe glass bake-ware, bowls, casseroles, custard cups, measures

microwave-safe glass or plastic storage containers

microwave-safe plastic bowls, casseroles, bakeware

paper plates

paper towels

plastic wrap

waxed paper

MIXING AND MEASURING

blender

electric mixer

food processor

immersion blender

graduated measuring cups for dry ingredients

liquid measuring cups (1-, 2-, and 4-cup)

ladle

rubber spatulas

ruler

slotted metal cooking spoon

wire whisk

mixing bowls

food scale

measuring spoons

large metal cooking spoon

wooden spoons

OTHER USEFUL COOKWARE

long-handled meat fork

large and small metal spatulas

skillets (10-inch, 12-inch)

saucepans (1-, 2-, and 3-quart)

Dutch oven (5- to 8-quart)

saucepot (5- to 8-quart)

glass and metal baking pans (13-by-9-inch)

steamer rack

strainer or sieve

colander

salad spinner

heat-and-serve covered casseroles

large roasting pan

potato masher

instant-read thermometer

omelet pan

ramekins

soufflé dish

steamer

wire rack

metal tongs

custard cups

- Built-in charcoal water filters
- Vacuum-sealed thermal carafes

Toaster and toaster oven: In addition to toasting bread, most wide-slot toasters also handle bagels and other breakfast foods. Cool-touch exteriors protect against burns, and models with electronic controls ensure consistent toast color cycle after cycle. Some manufacturers offer convenience features such as a warming rack for buns, a lift that removes small toast slices, special settings for toasting bagels on one side, and a defrost setting.

Toaster ovens do not toast bread quite as well, but operate as mini ovens for baking, broiling, and top browning. They are energy efficient and ideal for small cooking jobs.

Can opener: Some models are taller than standard size, or adjust to accommodate tall cans. A cutting assembly that removes for easy cleaning is important.

Blender: This is the best machine for blending liquids, puréeing, mixing drinks, and crushing ice. Blenders come with glass, plastic, or metal containers. Although many models have 12 to 14 speeds, 2 to 5 speeds are all that are necessary. Look for:

- Large-capacity containers
- Easy disassembly for cleaning
- Ice-crushing mode
- Touch-pad controls, which are easier to clean than push buttons

Manufacturers now offer lightweight, handheld, push-button immersion blenders, designed to purée foods like soups right in the pot they are cooked in. This appliance works most efficiently if it fits your hand and is easy to hold, offers one-touch control, variable speeds, and a long electrical cord.

Food processor: This machine can chop, slice, shred, grind, mix, and knead dough. Gourmet cooks and large families will need a mid- to full-size (7- to 20-cup capacity) heavy-duty unit while a compact model or mini chopper (3-cup capacity) that handles tasks like grating cheese and chopping onions or herbs might

Helpful Hints

USE AND CARE OF APPLIANCES

➤ **Read and follow the manufacturer's instructions for all cookware and appliances.**

➤ **Do not use electrical appliances when floor or counters are wet.**

➤ **Unplug small appliances when you're not using them.**

➤ **Use a separate grounded electrical circuit for each major appliance.**

➤ **Never allow small children to touch or operate kitchen appliances.**

➤ **Keep a working fire extinguisher and smoke detector in the kitchen (see box, page 373).**

satisfy those with small families or limited cooking needs.

A large opening on the feeder tube will save time by eliminating preslicing. Look for dishwasher safe bowls and smooth control buttons to make cleanup easier. Consider buying more than one bowl so that bowls needn't be cleaned between tasks, plus a storage case for blades, disks, and other accessories.

Mixer: Handheld and stand mixers are the 2 choices. Hand mixers are portable and easy to store. They are perfect for light mixing jobs like cakes and whipped cream; some heavy-duty models can handle cookie dough and even bread dough.

Stand mixers are more powerful and can do all kinds of heavy mixing jobs, and they are recommended if you often make bread. Because of their size and weight, stand mixers usually sit out on the counter.

Slow cooker: This appliance maintains a low, even temperature. Slow cookers are ideal for stews, soups, and anything that requires long cooking times.

Ice cream maker: Electric models produce up to 1$\frac{1}{2}$ quarts of your favorite flavor of ice cream, yogurt, gelato, sherbet, or sorbet. While some electric models require that you pack the bucket with ice water and salt, others use a bowl or canister that you prechill in the freezer. For best results, prechill the ingredients and carefully follow the manufacturer's instructions for freezing the bowl or canister up to 24 hours ahead in a 0 degree F freezer. Buy an extra mixing bowl to keep in the freezer so you can mix a batch on short notice.

Rice cooker: This device perfectly steams white, brown, or wild rice, as well as other grains. Cookers handle the process automatically, removing the risk of water boiling over or rice burning. Some models come packaged with an insert that converts the rice cooker to a steamer for meats and vegetables or an option that allows you to cook rice and other foods together. The most common features include a nonstick cooking pot, a preprogrammable timer, a keep-warm setting, a see-through lid so you can keep an eye on the cooking progress, and built-in cord storage. Capacity generally varies from 3 to 10 cups, depending on the model.

Tabletop grill: This handy appliance makes it possible to enjoy flavorful and healthy grilling indoors all year round. Models vary by manufacturer, but most consist of an electric heating element concealed behind a grooved or ridged, nonstick cooking surface that drains off fat and imparts the characteristic grill marks to foods like fish, vegetables, and meats.

 Helpful Hints

APPLIANCE TIPS

➤ **Never inspect, clean, or work on an appliance until it is unplugged.**

➤ **Keep all appliances clean.**

➤ **Read the manufacturer's directions for all appliances, and keep them in one accessible place.**

➤ **If an appliance doesn't work, check to make sure it is plugged in and all controls are properly set before calling for service.**

Contact grills, which open and close like a waffle iron to accommodate foods of varying thickness, feature 2 cooking surfaces and are ideal for grilling items like burgers and panini.

Features to look for include a nonstick cooking surface, several temperature settings, an indicator light that glows when the unit is on, some type of grease-disposal system, and handles that stay cool to the touch. Be sure to choose a model that accommodates the amount of food you need to cook at one time.

Juice extractors: These produce fresh fruit and vegetable juices. Pulp ejection models feature a bin designed to collect pulp. Other models employ filters to collect pulp right in the grinding chamber to produce clearer juices. A large opening on the feed tube helps save time and eliminates some of the chore of cutting fruits and vegetables into small pieces before adding to the juicer. Other features to consider: easy disassembly for cleaning, how much counter space the model requires, and how noisy it is while operating.

Major Appliances

One of the most important purchases you make for your home is a major appliance. Here are some tips:

- Do your research ahead of time.
- Talk to friends about their experiences, good or bad, with various brands.
- Decide which capacity or size you need.
- Decide which special features you want and will really use.
- Ask the dealer to show you the use and care manual for the appliance you are interested in. Look it over before making your purchase.
- Ask about the warranty. What is covered and for how long?
- Ask about delivery charges and servicing availability.

Once the appliance is in your home, try each feature and control. Most defects show up during the first few uses, and you want to know of any problems before the warranty expires.

Ranges, Ovens, and Cooktops

There have been many technological developments reflected in the design of cooking appliances.

Ranges: A range is a freestanding appliance that combines a cooking surface with an oven. Models that drop in and slide into a countertop provide a built-in look. Ranges are fueled by either gas or electricity. Dual-fuel ranges combine a gas cooking surface and an electric oven. Other models pair a gas or electric cooking surface with an oven that combines thermal and convection (air moved by a fan) technologies. All but the least-expensive models have self-cleaning ovens.

Many new ranges feature smooth ceramic glass tops. On gas models the burners are fused to the glass, and on electric models the coil or element is concealed under the glass. This prevents spills from seeping into the burner box or under the coils. Cleanup is easier, provided spills are wiped up promptly. Carefully follow the manufacturer's instruction for upkeep, and do not use steel wool or abrasive cleaners.

Wall ovens: These are available in single- and double-oven configurations. Most are electric and self-cleaning. Some models offer a combination of cooking modes, primarily conventional and/or convection.

The newest generation of speedcook wall ovens combine more than one energy source—such as thermal, microwave, and convection, or microwave and halogen light—in a single unit. The combined energies cook foods many times faster than a conventional thermal oven. They can be switched from one cooking energy to another so that they can microwave at breakfast, speedcook at lunch, and serve as a traditional thermal oven at dinner.

Cooktops: Built into the kitchen counter or an island, these offer a great deal of flexibility in kitchen design. Cooktops are fueled by either gas or electricity and are available in ceramic glass, porcelain enamel on steel, or stainless steel surfaces. They are usually offered with 4, but sometimes as many as 6, burners. The heat output of each burner may vary so that one or more will provide a steady simmer and others will quickly bring water to a boil.

Gas-fueled cooktops are sought by many because of the instantaneous response of the flame and the infinite heat settings. Like ranges, the newest models feature sealed burners that are fused to the cooktop surface to make cleanup easier. Continuous grates on gas cooktops make it easy for the cook to slide, rather than lift, full pans. If the surface is ceramic glass, spills must be wiped up at the end of each cooking session or they will bake onto the surfaces.

The most popular electric cooktops (like ranges) feature heating elements fused into or concealed under a smooth, ceramic glass surface.

Surface-Cooking Options

Below are some of the pluses and minuses of various cooktop features that you should keep in mind before choosing a unit.

TYPE	ADVANTAGES	DISADVANTAGES
GAS		
Conventional burner	Generally inexpensive to buy. Easy to control heat. Any type of cookware can be used.	Difficult to clean. Open flame. Few models to choose from.
Sealed burner	Prevents food from getting beneath burners, making cleanup easy. Any type of cookware can be used. Easy to control heat.	Open flame. Only one burner may be designed for low heat.
ELECTRIC		
Coil element	Least expensive to buy. Any type of cookware can be used.	Less responsive than gas. Difficult to clean.
Glass ceramic (smooth top)	Spills stay on top. Cleans easily if attended to promptly.	Less responsive than gas. Remains hot to the touch even when turned off. Requires flat-bottom pans.

Microwave Ovens

Microwaves vary in size from compact countertop models (with interiors as small as 0.5 cubic feet) to full size (with up to 2.2 cubic feet of interior space).

A microwave's cooking power is measured in output wattage, which varies from about 500 watts to 1,350 watts. Higher-wattage ovens cook foods faster than lower-wattage ovens. Low-wattage ovens (under 700 watts) are suitable for small tasks like popping corn, defrosting meats, and reheating foods, and are ideal for the infrequent user. If you intend to cook part or all of most meals with your microwave oven, choose a high-power mid- or full-size oven.

A convection/microwave oven can be used as a microwave oven alone, convection oven alone, or as a combination oven. It offers the speed of microwave cooking and the browning and crisping capabilities of convection.

Microwave ovens are also available in units that take the place of a range hood, or as part of a double wall oven. Some of these units are as large as 1.9 cubic feet.

Before you buy a microwave oven, be sure to visit the Web sites of several manufacturers.

They can help pinpoint precisely which models will suit your needs best, based on your answers to a series of questions.

Refrigerators

Some top- and bottom-mount refrigerators are equipped with doors and handles whose swing can be reversed with a few basic tools. This is particularly useful if you plan to move and take the refrigerator with you. Look for these other features:

- Energy efficiency. Look for the yellow-and-black Energy Guide label on the refrigerator. The guide will give you the estimated average annual operating cost. Compare these with costs for models of the same size and type. Today's refrigerators are the most energy efficient ever built. A refrigerator that costs less to run but has a higher purchase price may be the best buy. See box, page 69, for Energy Star information.
- Adjustable shelves/bins for maximum storage flexibility; also look for shelves that slide out for easy access to foods
- Water filter if there is an ice and water dispenser
- Easy to read and access controls
- Interior lighting in both freezer and refrigerator
- Exact temperature display
- Automatic ice makers
- Clear bins
- Dispensers for crushed ice, cubes, and water, some large enough for a pitcher
- Electronic systems to monitor functions
- Extra-deep door shelves
- Humidity controls on crispers
- Rollers that allow the refrigerator to be moved easily for cleaning
- Tempered glass shelves that hold spills
- Enclosed condensers that don't have to be cleaned

These are the choices in refrigerator styles:

Top mount: This model has 2 doors with the freezer on top. Available in a wide range of models and sizes, most are now self-defrosting,

How to Shop For...

A MICROWAVE

Consider these features when buying a microwave:

➤ **Quick defrost**

➤ **Browning capability**

➤ **Keep-warm or simmer setting**

➤ **Add-a-minute key**

➤ **Cook sensors that adjust time and power levels automatically, depending on the food**

➤ **Safety lockout feature if you have children in the home**

➤ **Multilingual keypads**

which is the most commonly used option and a good choice if you use the freezer often. One disadvantage: If you use fresh fruits and vegetables frequently, you will bend down often to reach for the produce drawers.

Side by side: This style has 2 doors with full-length refrigerator and freezer sections. It also comes in built-in models that fit flush to cabinets. It has more total freezer space than other styles and more up-front visibility of food. The doors require less aisle space for opening. This type is most likely to offer ice and water dispensers in the door, making it a good choice for people who are disabled.

The style costs more to buy and operate than a top mount, and narrow shelves in the smaller capacity sizes may limit storage of bulky or wide items. All are no-frost.

Bottom mount: This model has 2 doors with a freezer at the bottom. It is convenient since more of the fresh food space is at eye level. Some offer freezer lights and rollout wire bins. Look for one with a door that pulls out for easy access to the contents as opposed to a door that opens on one side. This model is not as convenient if you use your freezer frequently.

Single door: This has one outside door with a small inner freezer compartment for short-term storage only. It is the least costly to buy and operate and has limited capacity. All models must be manually defrosted.

Freezers

Freezers are fairly simple units designed to keep food at 0 degrees F or below. For maximum cooling efficiency, keep a freezer close to full but avoid overloading (for more on freezing, see pages 152–154). Choose a model that does not greatly exceed your storage needs. Temperature alarms that sound if the freezer temperature rises above a certain level (depending on the model) are a useful feature, and so are safety locks to keep children out.

Upright freezers permit more food to be visible, but they are less efficient than chest freezers since cold air is lost each time the door is opened. They are available in manual defrost and no-frost models.

Chest freezers with several bins and shelves can be almost as convenient as upright models, but they take up more floor space and it is more difficult to organize the contents and find items. All defrost manually.

No-frost freezers are more expensive to buy and operate, but they are much more convenient than manual defrost versions. A hidden advantage of manual-defrost is that it forces you to take an inventory of freezer contents. Choose a model with a drain in the bottom to make the defrosting chore easier.

Automatic Dishwashers

When it comes to convenience and saving time, it is hard to beat a dishwasher. Prerinsing is not necessary with today's dishwashers due to better technology.

When shopping, check the Energy Guide label on the dishwasher for the estimated annual operating cost. Look for an energy-efficient model.

Features

- Adjustable racks and fold-down shelves for flexibility in loading
- Delay start
- Electronic control for cycle readout
- Electronic system to diagnose problems
- Flush control panels that blend with your kitchen cabinetry
- Hot-water temperature booster
- No-heat drying option
- Special cycles for pots and pans, light wash, or rinse and hold
- Special insulation for quiet operation

Gas Grills

Choosing a Gas Grill

When buying a gas grill, consider the following:

- The amount of space you have.
- The types of foods you grill and the number of people you cook for. A grill that can handle 2 dozen burgers is unnecessary for a small family unless you do a lot of entertaining.
- Wheels make it easy to move a grill that is not permanently installed.
- An easy-to-access drip tray makes cleaning the grill less of a chore.
- Stainless steel grills cost more, but will weather better than less-expensive painted grills.
- Side shelves give the cook somewhere to put hot foods, hamburger and hot dog buns, and serving plates.
- Side burners are useful if you plan to cook sauces and side dishes on the grill.
- Dual heat controls allow you to control burners separately.
- Wide cooking grate bars are easier to clean and allow fewer foods to fall into the flames.
- Plan for out-of-season storage, and make sure the model you're considering fits where you intend to store it.
- Consider if you will really use expensive extras like rotisseries, smokers, warming racks, built-in thermometers, and side burners.

Gas Grilling Safety Tips
- When lighting a gas grill, always keep the grill's lid open to prevent a flash fire from built-up gas.
- Do not lean over the grill when igniting the burners or cooking.
- Never use a grill indoors. Use the grill at least 10 feet away from any building. Do not use the grill in a garage, breezeway, carport, porch, or under a surface that can catch fire.
- If a burner doesn't ignite, turn off the gas. Leave the grill lid open and wait 5 minutes before trying to light again.
- If the burners go out during operation, turn all gas valves to off. Open the lid and wait 5 minutes before attempting to relight, using lighting instructions.
- After a period of storage and/or disuse, check the grill for gas leaks, deterioration, proper assembly, and burner obstructions.

Safety Checks
To reduce the risk of fire or explosion, routinely perform the following safety checks:
- Check the tubes that lead into the burner for any blockage from insects or grease.
- Use a pipe cleaner or wire to clear blockage and push it through to the main part of the burner.
- Check grill hoses for cracking, brittleness, holes, and leaks. Make sure there are no sharp bends in the hose or tubing.
- Move gas hoses as far away as possible from hot surfaces and dripping hot grease.
- Check for gas leaks, following the manufacturer's instructions. Never use a flame to check for gas leaks. If you detect a leak, immediately turn off the gas and don't attempt to light the grill until the leak is fixed.
- Keep lighted cigarettes, matches, and open flames away from a leaking grill.
- Follow the manufacturer's instructions that accompany the grill.

Propane
Liquid petroleum (LP) gas, or propane, used to fuel many gas grills, is highly flammable. Be sure to follow the manufacturer's instructions for handling the cylinders. In addition:
- Never use an LP cylinder if it shows signs of dents, gouges, bulges, fire damage, corrosion, leakage, excessive rust, or other forms of external damage; it may be hazardous and should be checked by an LP supplier.
- When the LP cylinder is connected, the grill must be kept outside in a well-ventilated space.
- Always keep containers upright.
- Never store a spare gas container under or near the grill or indoors.
- Never store or use flammable liquids, like gasoline, near the grill.
- To avoid accidents while transporting LP gas containers, transport the container in a secure, upright position.
- Never keep a filled container in a hot car or car trunk. Heat will cause the gas pressure to increase, which may open the relief valve and allow gas to escape.
- Keep in mind that there are limits on how much propane fits into an LP cylinder. Do not ask the propane supplier to overfill the container.
- When not in use, the LP valve must be turned to the off position.
- When storing a gas grill indoors, the LP cylinder must be disconnected, removed, and stored outdoors. Never store an LP cylinder indoors.
- Never attach or disconnect an LP cylinder when the grill is hot or in operation.

Cleaning a Gas Grill
Before or after each grilling session, burn off any residue on the cooking grates by turning the grill on high and running it until the smoke stops. Then brush the grates with a brass wire grill brush.

Clean up grease drippings on warming racks, control panels, and all exterior surfaces as soon as possible. Use mild, soapy water and rinse thoroughly. Harsh cleaners can ruin the paint finish.

Change the drip pan. Buy replacement pans at a grill retailer or hardware store.

Clean the bottom tray. Remove the bottom tray from under the grill and place it over a trash can. Carefully scrape the inside with a one-inch putty knife, then wash the tray in warm, soapy water. (Never line the bottom of this tray with foil because grease can accumulate in the creases and cause a fire.)

Tableware

To make the most of your tableware, choose patterns that look good together and that are versatile enough to be dressed up or down according to the occasion. Always look at tableware together in a place setting before you buy it.

China

The word "china" is used as a convenient shorthand for any ceramic dinnerware. It's common to choose a set of good china, usually bone china or porcelain, and a set of everyday dinnerware, usually in stoneware or earthenware. All are generally dishwasher safe except those with decorations over the glazing that are not fired on. Check with the manufacturer or test wash a piece.

Bone china: This fine china, made with bone ash, is prized for its translucency and whiteness; it is usually expensive.

Porcelain: This is a hard, translucent china similar to bone china, known for its richness of pattern. It's usually safe to put porcelain in dishwashers, but confirm this with the manufacturer.

Stoneware: Less expensive than bone china and porcelain, this hard, opaque china holds heat well, so it makes good servingware and dinnerware. Colors tend to be earthy. Stoneware is safe in dishwashers and microwave ovens. It can go

 Helpful Hints

MIX-AND-MATCH GLASSWARE
Barware and stemware don't have to match. Cordial glasses and brandy snifters also do not have to match your stemware pattern.

PERFECT TABLE SETTINGS
➤ Use ornate silver with contemporary linens and china for unusual settings.

➤ Try a Victorian cookie box or bonbon dish to hold cheese sticks or vegetables on the dinner table.

➤ For a child's birthday, cover the table with Sunday comics. Use Chinese newspapers for a Chinese feast.

➤ Make a tablecloth out of a designer sheet or a folk-art rug. Stitch napkins from sheeting.

➤ Make a centerpiece of dollar-store toys or small collectibles, like a group of circus animals or glass balls.

➤ Try a layered look. Use 2 or more tablecloths in contrasting colors or coordinating prints.

from oven to table to refrigerator and is usually inexpensive.

Ironstone: This is a hard, heavy white pottery similar to stoneware, and moderately priced.

Traditional Place Setting

The standard formal 5-piece place setting consists of a dinner plate, a salad/dessert plate, a bread-and-butter plate, and a cup and saucer. A table setting, however, can have many variations. The one below is a traditional formal arrangement, including a service plate, wine and water glasses, and utensils for several courses.

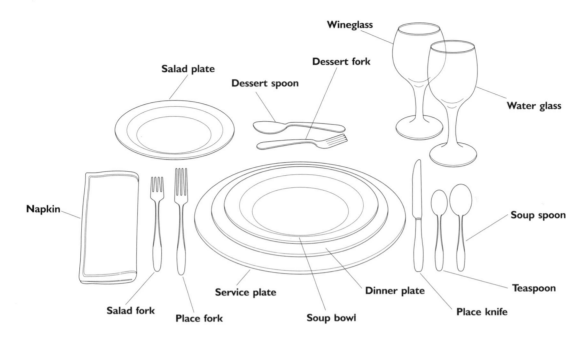

Earthenware: This inexpensive pottery is not as strong as other types of china. Its lower firing temperature permits more brilliantly colored glazes, making unusual patterns possible.

Flatware

Sterling, silver plate, and stainless steel flatware (in descending order of cost) are all beautiful and durable.

Serving pieces needn't match flatware in either pattern or material. You can mix ornate place settings and simple serving pieces, or the other way around.

 Helpful Hints

METAL DETECTOR
Overglazed metallic-trim china can't go into a microwave oven or dishwasher, so it isn't as versatile as other china.

CARING FOR BREAKABLES
To avoid chipping precious china and crystal, place a kitchen towel in the bottom of the sink before hand washing them.

Tableware Glossary

From simple to specialized, here is a range of table and serving pieces.

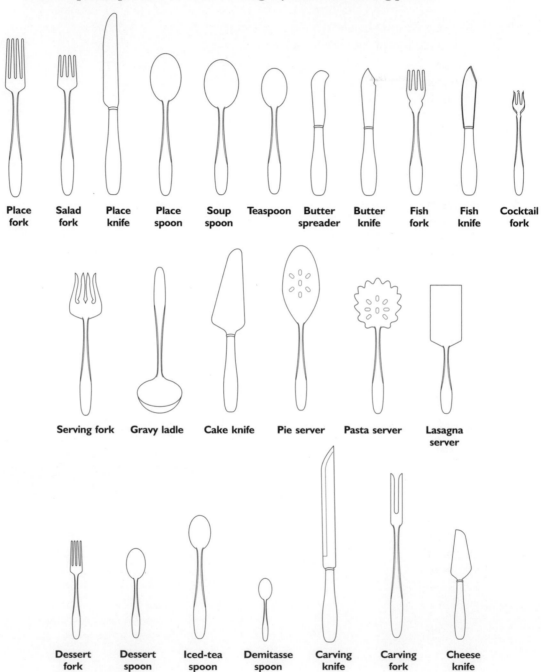

Place fork | Salad fork | Place knife | Place spoon | Soup spoon | Teaspoon | Butter spreader | Butter knife | Fish fork | Fish knife | Cocktail fork

Serving fork | Gravy ladle | Cake knife | Pie server | Pasta server | Lasagna server

Dessert fork | Dessert spoon | Iced-tea spoon | Demitasse spoon | Carving knife | Carving fork | Cheese knife

Glassware Glossary

The following are the most common types of glasses and are fine for a range of drinks.

Short tumbler

A 5- or 6-ounce capacity with straight or slightly sloping sides. Used for fruit juices, water, old-fashioneds, whiskey on the rocks, and soft drinks.

Tall tumbler

A 10- to 12-ounce capacity with straight or slightly sloping sides. Used for drinks mixed with fruit juices, exotic tropical drinks, highballs, soft drinks, iced tea, and other drinks that require lots of ice cubes.

Wineglass (white)

About 4-ounce capacity on a stemmed base. The typical wineglass for white wine has a smaller bowl and taller stem, so the warmth of your hand won't reach the bowl and destroy the wine's crisp flavor.

Wineglass (red)

Varying capacity; should be large enough to be filled only one-third full, so the wine can be swirled to bring out its full flavor.

Cocktail glass

About 4-ounce capacity, with a wide-rimmed top and a stemmed base. Used for martinis, Manhattans, and other mixed cocktails.

Tall flute or tulip glass

About 4-ounce capacity, with a tall, narrow bowl on a stemmed base. Used for Champagne, sparkling wines, and Champagne cocktails.

Liqueur glass

About 1$\frac{1}{2}$-ounce capacity on a short-stemmed base. Used for small amounts of liqueurs and cordials.

Brandy snifter

Varying capacity with large, round, wide-bottom bowl that narrows to a slightly inverted rim and a short-stemmed base. Made to be cradled in the hand so that the brandy may be warmed and swirled to release its bouquet.

Easy Napkin Folding

Follow these steps for an elegant "lily."

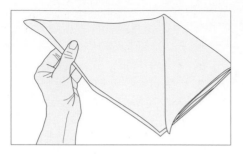

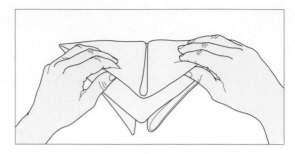

1. Form a triangle from an open square napkin. Fold the right corner to the center. Take the left corner to the center, making a diamond.

2. Keeping the loose points at the bottom, turn the napkin over. Then fold downward in half to form a triangle.

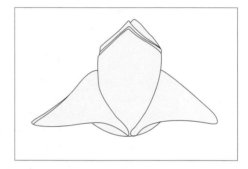

3. Tuck the right corner into the left. Stand the napkin up; turn it around, then turn the petals down.

4. You now have a lily.

Sterling

Solid sterling silver offers luxury plus the value of a precious commodity. Prices vary depending on the pattern's detailing, complexity of handwork, and silver content.

Sterling won't wear out. If you use it regularly, you will have to polish it only rarely, and it is dishwasher-safe. But load the basket carefully so the silver isn't crowded. Be sure to remove the flatware before the dry cycle and dry by hand if hard water spotting is a problem. The intense heat can loosen the blades from some older hollow-handle knives.

Silver Plate

Silver plate has the look of solid sterling, and it is an economical alternative when you don't want to pay sterling prices.

Some brands have a very thick coating of silver, measured in microns, over the undermetal (usually nickel and steel). Others have a thinner coat. The thicker coating looks better and lasts longer.

Look for a manufacturer's warranty that utensils are dishwasher-safe. Avoid putting silver plate with worn spots where the base metal is exposed in dishwashers. This intensifies the deterioration of the silver coating.

Contact between silver and stainless steel items in the dishwasher can cause pitting. Make sure these materials do not touch, especially in the flatware basket.

Stainless Steel
Prices range widely for stainless steel flatware. Better pieces usually have more chromium for stain resistance and more nickel for luster and strength. Utensils with a numerical rating of 18/8, for example, have 18 percent chromium and 8 percent nickel and are considered durable. Stainless steel flatware is dishwasher-safe, and good-quality brands last many years.

Glassware

Clarity and flawlessness are marks of high-quality glassware. Both attributes are enhanced when lead is added to the formula—up to a maximum of about 32 percent. If you opt for a cut-glass pattern, hand cutting is preferred to machine cutting, though it is more costly.

While all kinds of glasses are available for all kinds of drinks, the only necessary types are tall and short tumblers and stemmed wineglasses. In general, choose glasses with a

Safety First

CRYSTAL CARE
Crystal containing up to 30 percent lead is safe for serving food (but not for strongly acidic foods). Rinse lead crystal containers prior to use. Do not store wine or whiskey in lead crystal containers.

graceful shape that are comfortable to hold.

Stemmed glasses vary in size and shape according to the type of drink to be served. An all-purpose glass for red and white wine, a Champagne flute, and a water goblet are the 3 most useful types.

You may want to opt for at least 2 sets of wineglasses: one for red and one for white wine.

Caring for Fine Crystal
Hand washing is usually best for all crystal, especially for gold-trimmed, hand-painted, or antique glasses. Rinse glasses thoroughly to remove soap. Although you can wash heavy crystal in a dishwasher, place it only in the top section and make sure glasses don't touch or become dislodged.

When wine has left sediment in a decanter, fill it with a room-temperature solution of half water/half white vinegar and allow it to soak. A bit of rice can be added to provide mild abrasion. If you gently swish it around, it won't scratch the crystal.

Avoid drastic temperature changes when handling crystal. Extreme changes in temperature may cause the glass to crack.

Entertaining

Whether the party is large or small, casual or formal, advance planning ensures a success.

- Invitations, whether issued by hand, mail, e-mail, or telephone, should always be specific about time, date, location, and dress.
- To keep track of guests, request an RSVP by a date. Provide an e-mail address as well as a phone number to respond to.
- Be realistic as to your time, cooking ability, and budget. Unless you're hosting a kitchen party with a few close friends, it is best to go with your most reliable favorites dishes. Don't attempt complicated new recipes for guests.

 Helpful Hints

PARTY EXTRAS THAT MAKE A DIFFERENCE

➤ Use real linen, china, and flatware.

➤ Make personal place cards for seated meals.

➤ Spend time with each guest. Plan potential topics of conversation if guests don't know one another well.

➤ Be sure to introduce newcomers to at least 2 guests before leaving them alone.

➤ Send guests home with a tiny party favor such as a minibox of home-baked cookies or a single flower.

➤ Ask a good friend to listen to your party plans and to help you brainstorm ideas. Offer to return the favor.

➤ To save time, plan part of the menu around make-ahead or store-bought foods, such as a great dessert from the best bakery in town.

➤ Don't work so hard that you can't be a guest at your own party.

- Decorations set the stage, but they need not be elaborate. Candles and flowers are always reliable as well as elegantly simple.
- Plan guest seating, music, lighting, and menu. Conceptualize the party from start to end. Details often make the difference between a good party and a great one.

Parties for Adults

From anniversaries to holidays, each party depends on some general guidelines:
- For a cocktail party, be sure to provide plenty of food for nibbling.
- For large groups, set up 2 bars if possible, so guests don't jam one area.
- Always offer nonalcoholic beverages in addition to alcohol.
- Allow about 30 minutes to 1 hour for drinks if a full meal is to be served afterward.

Parties for Teenagers

Planned independence guarantees successful teenage parties. Plan carefully with your teen, then be home and occasionally in evidence, but let your child be the host.
- Provide lots of things to do: music, games, dancing, yard sports, videos. It's hard to know which will be the hit of the party.
- Make plenty of food, especially food that guests can put together themselves. Try sandwich fixings and oversize rolls, chili with a dozen condiments, or top-your-own pizzas.
- Fruity, highly garnished punches are festive, but also offer an array of soft drinks. Be firm on the rule for no alcohol.
- Warn neighbors ahead of time that music may be loud, particularly if the party is outdoors. Check to see if local ordinances require the music to stop at a certain hour.

Party Timetable

Use this timetable as a checklist to plan a big party.

4 WEEKS AHEAD
- Mail or deliver the invitations. Do not rely on the telephone or word of mouth.
- Keep a written guest list.
- Plan the menu.
- Check on cooking and serving equipment. Rent or buy what may be needed.
- If needed, arrange for help with parking, serving, or cleanup, and rent coat racks.

3 WEEKS AHEAD
- Buy nonperishables, disposable items, liquor, nonalcoholic beverages, and mixers.
- Plan traffic flow and table service.
- Clean and iron the linens.
- Order any grocery or butcher items.

2 WEEKS AHEAD
- Cook and freeze foods such as desserts, breads, and casseroles.
- Check the condition of the garden if the party is to be outdoors.
- Do any major housecleaning.
- Polish silver if needed.
- Begin making ice.
- Order flowers.

2 DAYS AHEAD
- Set the buffet table.
- Set up the bar.
- Set up the music.
- Clean the rooms where the party will be held, and rearrange furniture as necessary.
- Begin making food or portions of recipes such as pasta or potato salads, crudité dips, and some desserts.
- Post a last-minute itemized checklist.
- Label platters and set out serving utensils.

1 DAY AHEAD
- Draw a timetable of what needs to be cooked and served when.
- Shop for perishable foods.
- Do bulk of cooking.
- Pick up and arrange flowers.
- Call all helpers and give each explicit instructions.
- Make the punch base.

DAY OF THE PARTY
- Finish cooking.
- Arrange ice and fruit for the bar.

Parties for Children

Include the guest of honor (the "host") in the planning. Listen carefully to his or her wishes, but know the child. A shy child may love the idea of a big birthday bash but will probably be happier with a smaller party with a few good friends. For very young children, a general rule of thumb: Invite one more guest than the birthday child is in years so as not to overwhelm the child with too many guests; thus a party for a 5-year-old would include 6 guests. Be sure to have at least one other adult on hand to help out.
- Have the host draw the invitations.
- Childproof the party area. Roll up rugs or move furniture as needed.
- Kids love to participate. Supply a sturdy white paper tablecloth, lots of washable markers and pens, glitter, and crayons, then have the guests make the table decor. Leave the cupcakes unfrosted, and set out an array of icings and

sprinkles. Provide cups full of ice cream; then let the guests garnish their own.

- Plan more activities than might fill the time in case one planned event does not work out or moves faster than anticipated.
- Set firm time limits for each activity; attention spans are short.
- Be clear on the invitation about when the party begins and ends.
- Make sure at least one adult is in the party room at all times. Accidents or mishaps can occur very quickly.
- Have inexpensive party favors for guests.
- Take photographs.

Planning a Big Party

At one time or another, everyone hosts a big party, whether it's a wedding reception, anniversary party, or holiday open house for the office. This kind of party may be intimidating, but careful planning makes it easier to pull off.

- Think the party through, and invite only as many as can be accommodated by your space. You don't want to jam 30 people into a 15-foot-by-12-foot living room.
- Consider parking, restrooms, and coat storage. Arrange for some chairs, but you don't need one for every guest.
- Keep food and drink simple.
- Plan for enough food. It's better to have too much food than too little.
- If necessary, hire help (teenagers or professionals) for kitchen preparation, serving, and cleanup. Include this in the budget. Only those of legal drinking age can bartend.

- Rent any necessary glasses, tableware, and serving equipment.
- Shop at club stores for paper goods.
- Choose appropriate music at a listening level to enhance but not dominate conversation.
- If absolutely necessary, have a separate well-vented area for die-hard smokers.
- Take photographs.

Menu Planning

For a large party, buffet service is easiest. Foods can be prepared ahead and served with minimum last-minute fussing.

Consider foods that can be served at room temperature. These are easiest to handle, and they stay at peak flavor. Avoid delicate hot sauces and soufflés. Opt for roasts, hams, and turkeys that serve large numbers and are attractive and easy to manage. If guests will eat standing up or with plates on their laps, precut meats so knives won't be necessary.

- Make several salads ahead of time. You can also buy salads at a high-quality take-out store or delicatessen. Salads are also good for friends to bring, should they offer.
- Put out rolls, pickles, olives, and an array of condiments.

Uncorking Champagne

1. Hold the bottle in one hand with the neck facing away from you and remove the wire muzzle with the other.

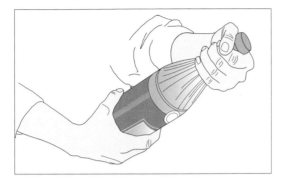

2. Tilt the bottle at a 45-degree angle and hold the cork firmly while rotating the bottle.

3. Pull the bottle down gently and slowly to reduce internal pressure. The cork will come out with a soft "pop." There should not be a loud explosion at uncorking.

• Self-serve finger desserts are easiest to manage. Cookies, petit fours, tartlets, and brownies are good choices, as are fresh fruits such as grapes, apples, and orange slices. Avoid frozen desserts.

Planning a Small Dinner Party

These days, most people host small dinner parties without professional help, so simple preparation and presentation are essential. Invite only as many as can be seated comfortably at a single table. Usually 6 or 8 is a manageable number.

• Plan 1 or 2 hors d'oeuvres to be served with drinks. One should be simple and light.
• Plan the menu for ease of preparation, minimum last-minute work, and general appeal.

Serve dishes you know you do well. Avoid delicate sauces and tricky garnishing.

• Be sure there is enough oven and stovetop space for cooking.
• Prepare some dishes ahead that will reheat well in a microwave oven in serving bowls or pretty casseroles.
• Plan the seating arrangement in advance and direct guests to their places or have place cards.
• Keep the first course simple, such as a salad or soup that can be prepared in advance.
• For an outdoor grilling or a kitchen party, let guests participate in some food preparation.
• Assemble plates in the kitchen or serve food family-style at the table.

Fun and Affordable Party Ideas

Breakfast: An easy inexpensive meal for entertaining small groups of early risers. Offer a selection of cereals, fresh muffins and bagels, and fruits as well as juices, coffee, and tea.

Brunch: An informal meal, for groups of mixed ages and interests; good for a buffet with make-ahead casseroles, breads, and fruits. Try organizing it around a theme, such as Creole.

✔ Helpful Hints

WINE TIPS

➤ **Acidic foods such as salad with vinaigrette dressing are best served between wine courses. The acids may fight—rather than complement—the wine.**

➤ **When cooking with wine, use one you would also enjoy drinking.**

➤ **When pouring red wine to another container, be sure to leave any sediment in the bottom of the bottle.**

➤ **White, blush, and sparkling wines should be served before they lose their chill or sparkle.**

➤ **Champagne goes with almost anything. It's also served as an aperitif and a dessert wine.**

The Well-Stocked Bar

There are no rules when it comes to stocking a bar. Follow your preferences and those of your most frequent guests. Stock your bar with the following items, and you should be able to handle any occasion.

ALCOHOL

Beer

Blended whiskey

Bourbon

Brandy

Champagne

Gin

Liqueurs (coffee, orange, and herbal)

Rum

Scotch

Sherry (dry and sweet)

Sour mash whiskey

Tequila

Vermouth (dry and sweet)

Vodka

Wine (red, white, and sparkling)

MIXERS

Club soda

Fruit juice

Soft drinks

Sparkling and still waters (flavored and plain)

Tomato or seasoned vegetable juice

Tonic water

GARNISHES AND FLAVORINGS

Bitters, for old-fashioneds

Citrus (lemon, lime, and orange) whole, slices, wedges, or peels

Coarse salt, for margaritas

Cocktail onions, for Gibsons

Cream of coconut, for piña coladas

Hot-pepper sauce, for Bloody Marys

Ice (preferably coarsely crushed)

Maraschino cherries, for Manhattans and old-fashioneds

Olives, for martinis

Simple syrup, for sweet cocktails and punches

Worcestershire, for Bloody Marys

EQUIPMENT

Blender

Bottle opener

Citrus squeezer

Coasters

Cocktail napkins

Cocktail shaker or pitcher

Corkscrew

Cutting board

Dish towel

Drink stirrers

Ice bucket

Jigger

Paring knife, for fruit peels

Strainer

Tea: An old-fashioned custom enjoying a revival and an easy meal to make ahead and serve. Small sandwiches are simple to prepare, and finger desserts can be purchased from a bakery. Concentrate on quality tea service and attractive presentation. Use good linens and silver. Try a Victorian theme with lots of ribbons and lace, and scones and jam.

Cocktail party: An occasion for plenty of attractive finger food to be passed around and laid out on tables. Whoever tends the bar should control alcohol consumption and offer nonalcohol alternatives. Enlist someone to monitor cleanup of glasses and plates if it's a large party. Indicate definite beginning and ending hours.

Dessert party: A simple but elegant affair for groups large and small. Provide homemade and bakery-bought cakes, pastries, and cookies, as well as wine, soft drinks, juices, and coffee. If you have friends who like to bake, let them show off at a potluck dessert party.

Picnic: An occasion for easily transportable foods such as salads and cold meats. Take plenty of ice or coolers to keep food fresh. Remember to pack trash bags for cleanup.

Potluck: An easy meal; the host assigns courses or sides to each guest. Noncooks can bring beverages, flowers, or bakery desserts. The host provides all serving and eating utensils. Service should be buffet-style.

After-event supper: A meal to follow the theater, Christmas caroling, or a game. Keep it informal and relaxed. Casseroles, hearty soups, or sandwiches and salads are appropriate. Serve family- or buffet-style.

Setting Up a Bar

Bar needs vary greatly according to the party's size and budget. The general rule is 1½ ounces (1 jigger) hard liquor and 3 or 4 ounces of wine equal 1 cocktail serving. Most liquor stores allow returns of unopened bottles providing that the wine has not been refrigerated. Every bar should

Helpful Hints

BAR TIPS

➤ **If possible, chill cocktail and beer glasses ahead of time.**

➤ **Handle glasses by the stem to avoid leaving finger marks and warming the contents.**

➤ **Add carbonated beverages at the last minute, even to punches.**

➤ **To avoid spills, don't fill glasses to the brim.**

➤ **Keep a kitchen towel handy; making drinks can be messy.**

➤ **Don't overserve.**

➤ **Never allow an inebriated guest to drive.**

have a supply of soft drinks, bottled water, and fruit and vegetable juices.

If you are serving only wine, offer red, white, and perhaps even sparkling. If wine is part of a more complete bar setup, white wine is the most commonly requested. Don't serve red wine if you are concerned about spills.

For a meal, tradition says that white wine goes with white meats, fish, and seafood; that red wine accompanies meats and richly sauced dishes; and that blush and sparkling wines go with anything. Today, the rules are less strict. The best guide is your own taste.

- In general, light wines, both white and red, best complement light and delicate foods. Bolder wines of both colors stand up better to richer, more assertive foods.
- Red wines are generally best when uncorked and allowed to "breathe" for about 15 minutes before serving at room temperature.

Liqueurs are usually served after dinner. Brandy and cognac are the most common types. Fruit, coffee, and herbal flavors are also popular. The best-quality liqueurs can be expensive but have almost unlimited shelf life.

CHAPTER

4

Decorating

A well-designed and handsomely decorated home often looks as if it were put together without planning or effort. But interior designers—and people who have successfully decorated their houses—know that color, style, furniture arrangement, lighting, flooring, and window treatments must all work together to create a harmonious setting. This chapter explains the basics of home decorating and design so you can make every room in your house a designer's dream. You'll learn the ABCs of painting: which type of paint and painting equipment to use, the right way to prepare a surface, and exactly how to paint. Plus, the chapter offers a guide to smaller but equally important topics such as how to choose the right type of lightbulb for a particular space. Want to know how to wallpaper a den? Choose curtains for a sun-filled room? Buy durable carpeting for high-traffic areas? You'll find all this and more—including the specifics of decorating a kitchen and a bathroom—in this information-packed chapter.

Doing It Yourself

Decorating is one of the most satisfying aspects of caring for your home. Choosing paint colors, fabrics, and new furnishings is not only enjoyable and creative, but it also helps you learn how to make the most of what you already have.

If you are new to decorating, try starting with some simple changes. Even small touches—new lamp shades or colorful throw pillows, for example—can make a surprising difference in a room.

Then move on to more ambitious schemes. To start, familiarize yourself with the decorating basics: color, style, furniture arrangement, and lighting.

Color

Color is probably the single most powerful element in a decor. It can set a mood, provide interest and accents, and even compensate for architectural problems by altering the perception of depth and space.

Because color has specific attributes, it is easy to make the right shade work for you. For example, warm colors—red, orange, yellow, and their various tints—attract attention, increase the apparent size of objects, and tend to soften their outlines. Walls painted in warm colors appear to move forward and make a room seem smaller and cozier.

By contrast, cool colors—blue, green, and their various tints—are soothing, decrease the apparent size of objects, and make their outlines appear crisp. Walls painted in cool colors appear to recede and make a room seem larger.

Colors also react to other colors in very specific ways. Against a dark background, light shades appear darker. Against a light background, dark colors are more intense. A medium tone appears light when placed against a

4 Steps to Success

To save time and money in any decorating project, plan ahead by following these simple hints from the pros:

1. **Take inventory:** Make a list of your existing furnishings. Note what you want (or need) to keep and what you'd like to replace. Then plan to add any new pieces in order of priority.
2. **Keep a loose-leaf notebook:** Give each room or project its own section and insert an envelope behind each divider to hold product literature, clippings from home design magazines, paint chips, and fabric swatches. Jot down the names of recommended professionals and craftspeople and tips from friends.
3. **Window-shop:** Spend time in decorating, fabric, and department stores and home centers. Note what you like and what things cost, so you can plan a budget.
4. **Develop a floor plan:** Sketch a plan of the room or rooms you want to decorate, and experiment with furniture arrangements (see pages 192–193).

dark background, and looks dark against a light background.

Working with Bold Colors

Bold, vivid colors allow you to express yourself like no other element in your home's decor. Using bold colors, however, involves following some simple rules to ensure that your color choices don't overwhelm the space. (Rules, of course, are meant to be used as a starting point. If you have a creative urge, feel free to explore it.)

Do:

• Limit risk. If you're considering integrating a dynamic new color into your interior, start by painting a wall, which can easily be

 Helpful Hints

DECORATING FOR EASY CARE

➤ **Minimize clutter:** The fewer decorative objects in your decor, the easier it is to clean rooms and keep them tidy.

➤ **Choose soil-camouflaging patterns** rather than solids, which tend to show spots more easily.

➤ **Use washable slipcovers** to help protect good upholstery and keep cleaning bills down.

➤ **Place washable area rugs** in front of your easy chairs, in the entry hall, and in other heavy-traffic spots to protect carpets and wood floors from wear and soil; then stash them out of sight when company comes.

➤ **Use semigloss paint** for door and window frames; the smooth surface allows for easy cleanup of fingerprints.

➤ **Choose high-resin, stain-resistant flat or velvet paints** for high-traffic areas such as kids' rooms. Stains will easily scrub off without removing the paint.

 Helpful Hints

PUTTING COLOR TO WORK

➤ **Emphasize interesting architectural features,** such as Victorian moldings, by painting them a color that contrasts with the wall.

➤ **Camouflage unattractive features,** such as old radiators, by painting them the same color as their background.

➤ **Fool the eye:** Make a long, narrow room appear wider by painting the end walls a warm color or the side walls a cool color. In a small house or apartment, paint or carpet all the floors in the same color (a medium or light shade) to make the floor area seem larger.

COLOR CONTROL

Unless you are really sure of yourself, avoid extremes; too much of one color can be distracting, and you may tire of it sooner than you would of a subtler mix.

changed if the color is overwhelming or creates the wrong mood. Once you feel comfortable with a color, you can safely incur the greater risk of window treatments, furniture, or flooring in that color.

• Don't overdo the use of a single color. Even if you are in love with a color, overusing it can create a visual fatigue in the space. For instance, if you're painting a wall in a bold color, paint the floor and ceiling in more muted colors. If you add a boldly colored piece of furniture, bracket it with pieces that are neutral or complementary.

• Create continuity in a room. A great way to work with bold color is to use it as a thread throughout the decor. For instance, you might mount a fabric panel on a wall, then carry the same color through throw pillows on the couch, and in the shade for a standing lamp in the corner.

Decorating Checklist

Keep in mind that space can be flexible. Think about how room use might change over time; 2 young children who sh factors. If you anticipate that climbing stairs will become a problem, you may wish to consider shifting room use so that you can primarily use one floor. To focus on your needs, ask yourself the questions below; if you are using a decorator, this information will be particularly useful to him or her.

- How old is each household member, and how long will he or she live in the house?
- Where will each person sleep?
- Where will each person spend time alone?
- Where will the family gather for leisure activities?
- Where do household members like to eat—in the kitchen, in the dining room, or in front of the TV?

- Do you need an all-purpose family room, including a kitchen, dining area, and sitting area? The family room might also include a media center, a laundry area, a play space, or a home office.
- Do you need specialized rooms—a home office, a workshop, an exercise area, or a playroom?
- Do you need specialized storage for books, collectibles, music, videotapes, or sports equipment?
- Which entry doors get used the most?
- Which part of the house receives the most sun and natural warmth?
- How do you usually entertain—with sit-down dinners, buffets, or living-room get-togethers?

- Stick to the color wheel (see page 189). The guidelines of the color wheel are especially important in using bold color. You can balance bold colors by using complementary colors, such as blue and gold, or analogous colors, such as 2 yellows that sit next to each other on the wheel. Safer still, use a supporting cast of whites or neutrals.

Don't:
- Clash. Creating successful bold color combinations requires a very practiced eye. Stick to one bold color in a space for best results.
- Go big. Painting a whole room in a bold color can be overwhelming. Painting one wall will still create immense visual impact, while maintaining balance through the

room. The same is true of furniture. Rather than a whole dining room suite in a bold color, consider using a sideboard or one or two chairs to make the color statement.

How to Choose Colors
Choose colors that you know you like instead of risking an untried combination.

As a rule of thumb, restrict the main colors in a room to 3 or fewer; these will be most noticeable on the walls, fabrics, and floor coverings. Then introduce accent colors with accessories, flowers, and artwork.

If you aren't decorating from scratch, start with the elements you are not planning to change—the carpet or wallpaper, perhaps—and select new accent colors to go with them.

If you are decorating your entire house, select

The Color Wheel

The color wheel is a popular decorating tool that is used as a guideline for selecting coordinating colors to help plan a room's color scheme. The 12-color wheel shows the relationship of primary, secondary, and tertiary colors based on how they appear in the spectrum. Colors on opposite sides of the wheel produce vibrant and contrasting schemes, while colors on the same side of the wheel form harmonious color combinations.

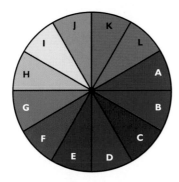

The color wheel with 12 primary, secondary, and tertiary colors

The **primary colors** are red, blue, and yellow and are the colors from which all other colors are derived. (A, E, and I on the wheel.)

Secondary colors are achieved when you mix 2 primary colors in equal proportions. There are 3 secondary colors (C, G, and K on the wheel):
- Red and blue mix to create violet.
- Blue and yellow mix to create green.
- Red and yellow mix to create orange.

Tertiary colors or intermediate colors are achieved when a primary color is mixed equally with the secondary color adjacent to it on the wheel. There are 6 tertiary colors: red-orange, red-violet, yellow-green, yellow-orange, blue-green and blue-violet. (B, D, F, H, J, L on the wheel.)

The wheel arranges the warm colors (red and yellow combinations) on one side and cool colors (blue and green combinations) on the other. A tint of a color is made by adding white. A shade of a color is made by adding black.

By following the wheel's guidelines, you can come up with workable color combinations for your room:

A monochromatic color scheme uses various tints and shades of a single color. This scheme looks clean and elegant and produces a soothing effect, especially with blue or green hues. The chosen color is often integrated with neutral colors, such as black, white, or gray.

An analogous color scheme uses colors that are next to each other on the color wheel, such as red, red-orange, and red-violet. One color is used as a dominant color while the others are used to enrich the scheme.

A complementary color scheme is made of 2 colors that are opposite each other on the color wheel, such as red and green. Using the wheel also helps you figure out the best combination of warm and cool colors. Complementary colors are high-contrast: When they are placed beside each other, they both seem brighter and more intense. When using the complementary scheme, choose a dominant color and use its complementary color for accents.

A triadic color scheme uses 3 colors equally spaced around the color wheel. This scheme is not as contrasting as the complementary scheme, and looks more balanced and harmonious. The best known of the triadic color schemes are: the primary colors red, yellow, and blue; the secondary colors orange, green, and violet; and tertiary colors, like red-orange, blue-violet, and yellow-green.

one color scheme, then vary the individual colors from room to room. If your scheme is a mix of yellow, blue, rose, and white, for example, the yellow could dominate in the bedroom, the blue in the living room, and both rooms would incorporate smaller touches of rose and white.

Neutrals

Neutrals, which include white, tan, gray, brown, and black, are technically not colors. A neutral scheme makes an effective backdrop because it helps the color stand out. Neutrals also make good accents and a completely neutral theme is soothing to the eye.

Style

There is an enormous range of decorating styles—from traditional to ultra contemporary—and choosing one is entirely a matter of your personal taste. However, if you live in a period home, it's safest to stick to a decorating style that complements the architecture. A Victorian with traditional detailed molding and accents would look strange decorated with sleek postmodern furniture. Consult books, magazines, and even museums to get an idea of different styles and to find one that you really like.

You can select one style for your whole house, or do some rooms one way, some rooms another. The key is common sense. If you have young children, for example, you would logically want to use washable fabrics and sturdy furniture in rooms where kids roam. You can even mix styles—18th-century paneling with modern furniture, for example—for an eclectic look.

Whatever the style, it will likely fall into one of 2 categories: formal or casual.

As a rule, a formal decor is elegant and reserved. It is best suited to rooms that have less traffic, or that you use for special occasions.

In a casual decor, where styles and pieces tend to be mixed, there is more room for flexibility; any element will work as long as it contributes to the overall effect.

A casual decor with comfortable hard-wearing furniture suits the rooms that you use the most for leisure activities, such as the TV or family room.

Arrangement

Good furniture arrangement relies on 3 basic elements: scale, balance, and placement.

Scale and balance: These affect how furniture pieces relate to one another and to the room they are in. Seek balance overall, but don't be

How Long Will It Last?

WHAT	HOW LONG
Carpet, rugs	With care, at least 15 years
Interior paint	5 years
Upholstery	With care, if upholstery is made of tightly woven fabric in a long-wearing fiber, at least 15 years
Wallpaper	10 years
Wood furniture (tables, dressers, desks, etc.)	With care, generations

Helpful Hints

TRAFFIC LANES

For easy access and an uncluttered look, leave:

➤ **At least 3 feet of open space to allow adequate walking room**

➤ **At least 3 feet of space behind dining and desk chairs**

➤ **2 to 3 feet of space between furniture pieces; 1 1/2 feet between a sofa or chair and a coffee table**

➤ **2 feet of open space around a bed**

➤ **3 feet in front of a bureau or cabinet to open drawers.**

➤ **A 3-foot arc of space around a door.**

afraid to experiment with eclectic mixes of small and large pieces.

Two delicate chairs placed across from an overstuffed sofa can make for an interesting juxtaposition. The idea is to ensure that no one piece overwhelms the design scheme and sticks out like a sore thumb.

To determine whether furnishings are balanced, try to think in terms of size and weight across the room. If all the large pieces are on one side of the room, the space will appear unbalanced.

Similarly, if a piece is too small to fill an area such as an alcove, you need to build weight. You can do this by adding smaller elements to fill in, such as a side table, a grandfather clock, or even tall potted plants. Built-in features, such as a wall of bookshelves, can also function as part of the balance equation.

How to Work with Design Professionals

The right experts bring valuable insight to your home-decorating projects, and can save you time and energy.

If you're puzzled about where to start with your home design, you may want to consider hiring an interior decorator or designer. Decorators generally have experience with color and style, and can advise you on compatible design choices for the home. Interior designers have more training and more in-depth expertise, and can create floor plans, suggest renovations, oversee workers, design custom furnishings, and provide advice on color schemes and furniture placement.

Typically, both charge a fee or a percentage of the cost of goods they order for you. However, many will tailor their services; for example, charging an hourly rate for a preliminary consultation.

Many home-design stores have in-house designers who often come at a discount if you are buying a certain amount of merchandise from the store. Chances are, if you like and trust the store, you can rely on its designer.

The best place to find qualified design help is through the American Society of Interior Designers (ASID). ASID designers have passed the group's written test and have given proof of their experience and skills in decorating. Find them on the web at www.asid.org.

How to Make a Floor Plan

A floor plan is a simple diagram of a room drawn to scale. Making one is an easy and effective way to try different arrangements for furniture and large appliances—without having to move the pieces themselves. To make a plan, follow these easy steps:

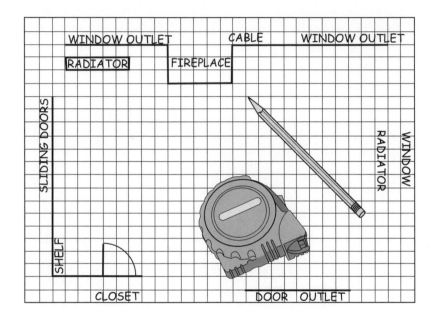

1. Using a retractable tape, measure the perimeter of the room at floor level, indicating door, window, and fireplace size and placement, and mark the dimensions to scale on graph paper. Use one (or more) graph square(s) to represent one foot of actual space. Be sure to measure and mark the direction and distance of door swings.
2. Measure and mark the location of built-ins, radiators, and heat registers, as well as any outlets, switches, phone jacks, and antenna connections.
3. Photocopy your completed plan.

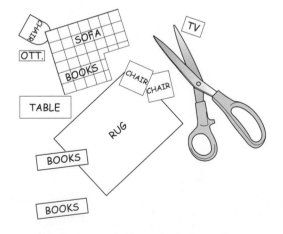

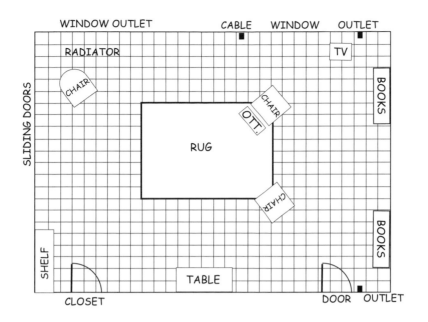

4. Measure your furniture (or large appliances) to the same scale on a separate piece of graph paper and make cutouts. Place the cutouts on the photocopied plan according to the arrangement you want. Check to see whether the outlets, switches, and any hookups are located conveniently (and not blocked), and adjust your layout accordingly.

5. When you are pleased with a layout (or layouts), trace around the cutouts. You may want to keep a scheme or two on file, especially if you'd like to rearrange a room for a change of season.

 Safety First

SAFE PASSAGE

When placing your furniture, always watch for potential hazards—for example, exposed lamp cords that can cause tripping. Be sure that small area rugs are secured to the floor (with nonskid pads or strips of adhesive tape) and that vases and other fragile items are in safe spots, away from high-traffic areas and the reach of children or pets.

 How to Shop For...

COLORED PAINT AND FABRIC

Because colors look different under different light conditions, always bring home fabric swatches and paint chips and check them— during both day and night—under typical lighting conditions in your house. (Remember that pastels look best in sunlight and tend to fade at night.)

Placement: Evaluate traffic patterns and arrange furnishings so there is a clear pathway in and out of each room, and from one area to another (see box, page 191). Don't crowd a small room with big pieces of furniture that make it difficult to move around or visually overwhelm.

Do, however, consider the special features or attributes of a room. For example, you might wish to plan groupings that will make it easy for people to draw close to a fireplace, to enjoy the view from a picture window, or to have intimate conversations.

You can also place furniture to "manipulate" space: 3 small groupings instead of one large one will make a big room seem more inviting and comfortable and will help define smaller spaces within it. A long sofa positioned across a space effectively divides the area into 2 sections.

Lastly, there are practical considerations in placing furniture. Keep furniture and upholstered pieces out of direct sun, and don't place them up against radiators or heating ducts.

Lighting

There are 3 basic types of home lighting:

Ambient: This general lighting provides overall illumination (often a ceiling light).

Task: This puts a concentrated pool of light where you need it for close work, such as reading, stovetop cooking, or sewing.

Accent: This is subtle lighting that emphasizes one feature or surface, such as lighting for a piece of art or a mood-setting "wall wash" of light.

In most rooms, you will want some combination of these, although there is no one way to do it. In a dining room, for example, many people prefer an overhead fixture on a dimmer (rheostat), supplemented only by candles.

However, if you have enough individual lights placed around a room, you may not need a ceiling light; several standing and table lamps set by sofas and chairs in a living room can work together to create the ambient lighting.

Keep in mind the nature of the room and its function, and choose your lighting accordingly. Follow these guidelines:

Entrance halls and stairways: ambient light, so people can see where they are going.

Public spaces, such as living and dining rooms: overall ambient lighting combined with softly lit areas for comfortable living and entertaining.

Kitchen: bright overall lighting and direct task lighting.

Bedrooms: soft, intimate lighting, and an ambient source that's equipped with a bulb simulating natural light.

Libraries, studies, and work spaces: good task lighting to enable maximum comfort and efficiency, and bookshelf or other accent lighting to play up interesting features in the room.

Bathrooms: good lighting around the mirror and in the tub and shower area.

Making Lighting Work for You

To determine where you want to place your lights, experiment with different schemes using a clip-on work light and a long extension cord; move the light around the room and observe the effects.

The following placement suggestions will also help ensure a successful lighting scheme:

- Place table lamps at or below eye level so they don't shine in people's eyes.
- To augment a ceiling fixture, put an additional fixture on top of a high cabinet or shelf

 Helpful Hints

DIMMER SWITCHES

Use a rheostat, or dimmer, to brighten or subdue light in a room as the occasion may suggest. Dimmer switches come in many styles to suit taste and decor style, including dial, standard switch, slide, and push pad.

Basic Bulb Shapes

Bulbs come a range of shapes for different fixtures. A reflector bulb works for track lighting or recessed fixtures, for example, while decorative or flame shapes are used in sconces and chandeliers.

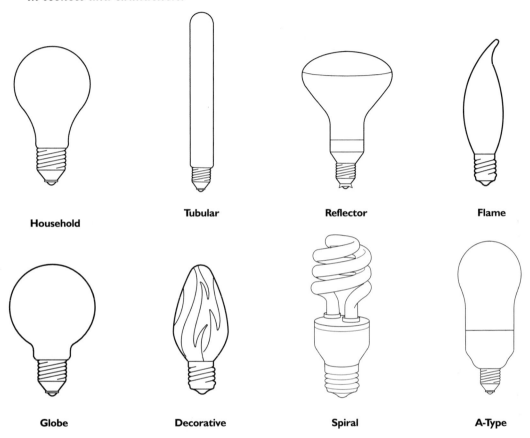

Household

Tubular

Reflector

Flame

Globe

Decorative

Spiral

A-Type

and angle in at the ceiling for additional ambient light.

- Use a strip of small bulbs hidden behind a valance to provide a soft, suffused accent light; this can be a pleasing effect for floor-length draperies.

- Light a work area from more than one direction to prevent distracting shadows.

- Place a ceiling fixture in the center of a room or over a major piece of furniture, such as a dining table or piano.

 Helpful Hints

LIGHT READING

➤ **Table lamp: 20 inches to 25 inches from where you hold your book.**

➤ **Floor lamp: 20 inches from where you hold your book.**

➤ **Wall lamp: 15 inches from where you hold your book.**

Which Bulb Is Best?

Different bulbs can dramatically change the look of a room, affect the quality and brightness of the light, and even influence your mood. A 3-way bulb gives you flexibility if more than one person will use a lamp at various times. Some household members might want more light for an activity or task than others.

Some light fixtures take only 1 of the 3 basic bulbs described here; others can take any, which should be specified on the fixture and in some cases will be obvious by the type of receptacle. Never exceed the wattage (w) rating of any fixture. Using a bulb that is not appropriate for a fixture can shorten the life of the bulb or pose a potential fire hazard.

Incandescent: These are the most common all-purpose bulbs. They provide a flattering light and are easy on the eyes. They are relatively inexpensive, easy to find in stores, and easy to install, but they can be short-lived and hot to the touch. Versions include long- life, energy-saving, pastel, soft white, and daylight styles, in all sorts of shapes (see box, page 195).

Standard incandescent bulbs come in standard wattages: 40, 60, 75, and 100. The larger the wattage, the greater the energy efficiency. Two 60-watt bulbs, for example, are less efficient than one 100-watt bulb. Wattage ratings are generally much lower for other types of bulbs.

Always check the fixture to be sure that you are not overloading the socket. Never, for instance, put a 100-watt bulb into a fixture that specifies a 75-watt one. If you prefer a dimmer light you can always use a lower wattage than specified. If no wattage is specified, you can use any standard incandescent bulb.

Halogen: There are 2 basic types: screw-in (similar to incandescent) and special shapes with different connector styles (double-ended, bayonet, miniature thread). They produce a bright white flattering light that casts a sparkle, and are good for accent and track lighting. They feature a focused, intense beam. Low-voltage versions are popular for task lighting, bookcase lights, and decorative fixtures. Halogen bulbs are relatively expensive, but they provide about one-fourth more light than incandescent bulbs for the energy they consume.

Halogen bulbs get extremely hot, so keep all liquids away from the bulb and never touch the bulb or fixture if the light is on— or even if it has been on recently. Don't touch a halogen bulb with your bare hands—use gloves or a cloth to avoid getting natural oils on the bulb.

Fluorescent: Once used primarily for workshops and commercial applications, fluorescents now come in a range of bulb shapes and lights. These include soft white, natural (full spectrum), and daylight. Tubular shapes use bi-pin connectors, while other bulb shapes feature screw-in bases. They are good for high levels of general lighting in the kitchen, bath, and family room.

Standard fluorescent bulbs are long-lasting and very energy efficient; they provide about 5 times more light than incandescent bulbs for the amount of energy they consume (and can last 10 times longer).

Compact fluorescents are some of the most popular bulbs, offering the same light choices as incandescent bulbs with as much as 8 times longer life and a quarter of the energy use. Although more expensive than most other bulbs, their long life span usually makes this type of bulb the better value.

7 Classic Lamp Shades

When shopping for a lamp shade, measure the height of the base and of the metal harp that holds the shade. As a general rule, the shade should measure about half the total height of a table lamp. Here are 7 classic styles:

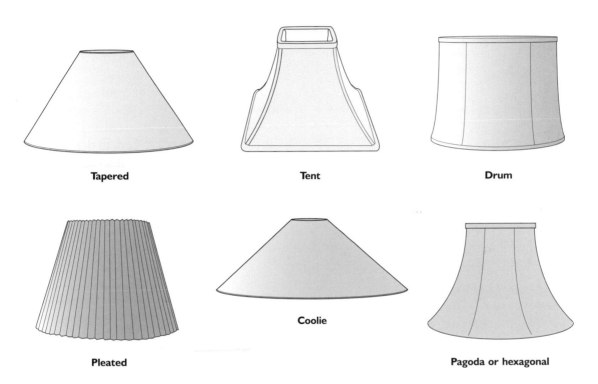

Tapered

Tent

Drum

Pleated

Coolie

Pagoda or hexagonal

There are many variations on these shapes (tapered drum, for example), offering a range of choices for your lamps. Shades come in a variety of materials, including silk, paper and parchment, and synthetics. You can also have shades custom made out of fabric you already own.

The shape of a lamp shade affects the way it casts light:

Wider at the bottom: casts a wider arc of light on a desk or over a chair for reading.

Straight sides: good for all-purpose lighting.

A dark-colored lampshade may work best for a certain lamp style, but it will let out less light; a light neutral shade lets out the most light.

Box

Painting

Painting is one of the easiest and least expensive ways to bring new life to a room. Even if you've never painted, you'll achieve good results if you understand the basic paint types and finishes, and prepare your room properly.

Choosing Colors

Any paint store or home center displays racks of free color samples called paint chips. These chips are arranged in strips of similar colors and related tones to show you the range of a particular hue.

After selecting some chips, take them home and look at them during the day in natural light (and at night under artificial light) alongside your fabrics, furnishings, and flooring materials.

Once you've narrowed the choices, buy a quart or a sample packet of the color you like and try it out on a sizable section of the wall. Evaluate it with your fabric, furnishings, and flooring materials in both daylight and at night under artificial light.

Paint and Primer

There are 2 types of paint: primer and finish paint. Use primer to prepare a surface so it holds the finish coat well. This is especially important for new drywall, plaster, and wood.

A type of primer called primer/sealer also seals cracks, stains, and wood knots that might otherwise show through, and inhibits rust on metal surfaces.

Priming is always a good idea, but it is essential if you have done any patching or scraping or if you are painting an unfinished surface. You should also use primer if you are applying a light color over a dark color or a matte finish over a glossy coat. Tinted primer allows for a more vibrant finish.

Latex vs. Alkyd

Both primer and finish paint, which is more opaque than primer, come in 2 basic types:

Latex: This is an easy-to-use water-based paint that is generally less expensive than alkyd. It produces a slightly rough finish and dries in a few hours. Relatively odor-free, this paint emits nontoxic fumes and needs only soap and water for cleanup.

Alkyd: This is an oil-based solvent-thinned paint that takes about 24 hours to dry completely. Alkyd resists moisture better than latex and offers a somewhat more attractive surface finish. However, it has strong-smelling fumes that can be toxic if inhaled over a sustained period, so it is important to wear a face mask and work in a well-ventilated area when using it.

Cleanup also requires time and patience because you must use mineral solvents like turpentine to get the paint off you and your brushes. Because these solvents are flammable, you must separate your rags from other refuse. Ask your garbage collector about disposing of them properly.

How Much Paint to Buy?

A gallon of paint covers about 450 square feet. To figure how much you need for a wall, multiply the length and height; for a ceiling or floor, multiply width by length. Be sure to subtract the area taken up by doors, windows, fireplace, or other spaces that won't be painted. When applying 2 coats (the paint label will tell you whether to plan on 1 or 2 coats) just double the figure.

For example, consider a 12-foot-by-18-foot room with an 8-foot ceiling, with 2 windows each on one long wall and one short wall, and a doorway on the second long wall:

1. The 2 long walls measure 144 square feet each (8 feet by 18 feet) for a total of 288 square feet. The 2 short walls measure 96 square feet each (8 feet by 12 feet) for a total of 192 square feet.
2. Add these sums for a total of 480 square feet.
3. Now subtract the windows (3 feet by 4 feet each) and the doorway (3 feet by 6½ feet), for a total of 68 square feet (rounded up from 67½ feet).
4. The result is 412 square feet. Therefore, the walls can be covered by 1 gallon of paint per coat. For the ceiling area, calculate the corresponding floor area.

The Right Equipment

Using a good applicator will help your job go faster and smoother. The better the quality, the better the results. Don't cut corners; cheap brushes and rollers can cause your paint to smudge and streak.

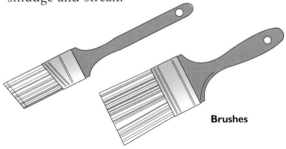

Brushes

Brushes: These are typically used for trim and for "cutting in" (painting edges around windows, doors, and wall and ceiling joints that a roller can't reach).

A good brush has flagged (split) ends for even spreading and dense bristles that bounce back to shape when you tap them against your hand. Natural bristles are traditionally used for alkyd paint because they hold the paint better but swell when used with latex; nylon and polyester are preferred for latex and can also be used with alkyd. High-quality brushes of any type have a

Helpful Hints

HOW LONG WILL IT TAKE?

A 12-foot-by-18-foot room with 8-foot ceilings should take 6 to 7 hours of actual painting time for primer, paint, and a finish coat of latex paint; more for alkyd. Add a couple hours to that if you have no experience painting, or if the room features a lot of intricate molding. When calculating the time a room will be unusable, remember to add drying and prep/cleanup time.

wood handle and strong ferrule (the metal part that holds the bristles to the handle).

Use the largest brush possible to avoid streaking. A 1- or 2-inch angle-cut sash brush is recommended for window frames and moldings, a 3- or 4-inch brush for cupboards, doors, and cutting in.

Pad

Pads: Inexperienced painters often find these easier to use and control than brushes and rollers, especially for hard-to-reach places such as corners or for intricate work such as railings and window frames. They combine the speed and smoothness of a roller with the precision of a brush, but without the brush marks. They come in a variety of shapes for different uses and in an array of materials for different finishes. Foam, for example, is good for flat surfaces while mohair will smoothly cover walls with a rougher texture such as stucco. A long handle can be attached to a pad to reach high surfaces.

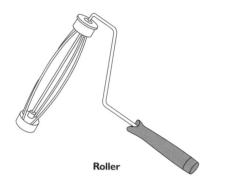

Roller

Rollers: The workhorses for painting interior walls, rollers are the best tools for covering a large area smoothly. Sizes range from about 2 inches wide, for woodwork, to 18 inches wide; a 9- or 10-inch roller is customary for walls, ceilings, and floors.

Roller sleeves: Purchased separately, these paint applicators are slipped on the roller, and then discarded after the painting is done. The best rollers hold the sleeve securely without requiring a wing nut. A short nap, or pile, is good for smooth surfaces or a soft matte finish.

A thick pile works best for rough surfaces like stucco and brick. Lamb's wool sleeves are recommended for alkyd paint, but synthetic nap is preferable for latex.

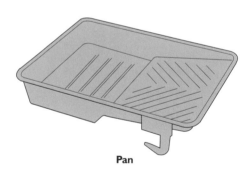

Pan

Pans: If you plan on painting regularly, a heavy-duty metal pan is a good investment; less expensive plastic types should be sturdy molded plastic so they don't bend out of shape. Make sure the size of the pan matches the size of your roller. Consider buying a pan with a cover; the cover provides an air-tight seal that allows you to reuse the paint later.

Getting Ready

Careful preparation is crucial to a good paint job. First, you need to get the room itself ready. Remove as much furniture as possible. Roll up the rugs. (This is a good time to send them out for cleaning and refurbishing.)

Cover the floor with plastic or canvas drop cloths and make a path on top with old newspapers to help soak up wet paint. Place any remaining furniture in the middle of the room and cover it with drop cloths tied down with clothesline.

Remove any hardware you don't want painted, including switch plates, doorknobs, latches and locks, curtain rods and brackets, picture hooks, and light fixtures. Use masking tape to cover anything you can't remove, such as thermostats.

Then get yourself ready for painting. Paint splatters everywhere, so it's is a good idea to wear old clothes, old shoes or sneakers, a head covering, and surgeon's rubber gloves.

How to Prepare a Surface

No matter how great your paint job may look, it won't last if you haven't prepared the surfaces before you start.

If the walls and ceiling are grimy, wash them. This is especially important in the kitchen or bathroom, where film from grease or soap residue can build up, making it difficult for new paint to adhere.

Use a powdered floor cleaner or trisodium phosphate (TSP) and work from the top down to avoid streaks. Special fungicides can wash off mildew and prevent it from returning. Allow

 How to Shop For...

DROP CLOTHS

Canvas drop cloths absorb paint and are less slippery than plastic. Although they are more expensive, they can be reused. (You can also use old sheets as drop cloths.)

all surfaces to dry thoroughly before painting.

You also need to clean out cracks, holes, and nail pops (where nails have risen and become visible) and fill them with spackle or plaster (see page 277) and scrape away any loose paint. You can use a standard scraper or try one of these specialized tools:

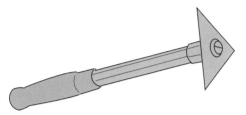

A hook scraper takes paint off windowsills and door frames.

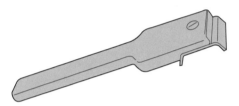

A triangular shave hook gets at paint and dirt embedded in woodwork.

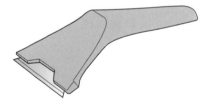

A razor scraper takes paint off moldings and window muntins (the strips of wood that separate panes of glass).

A putty knife handily separates softened paint and wallpaper from a surface.

A heat gun quickly softens paint so it can be easily scraped off.

How to Paint

To avoid drip spots, paint the ceiling first, then the walls, beginning at one corner and working your way around the room.

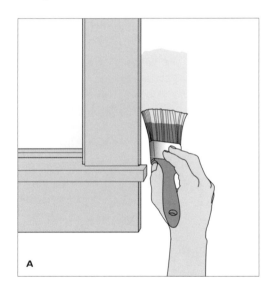

1. Do your cutting in first, brushing a narrow strip of paint where the walls and ceiling meet, along door and window frames and trim, and anywhere else a roller will not reach. (A)
2. Cutting in against an area that is painted a different color requires a steady hand to make a clean line between the 2 areas. This is a simple skill to develop with a little practice, but many people prefer to tape the adjacent area to ensure a crisp line. If you do this, use

blue painter's masking tape, which is the easiest type to remove. Once you're done painting, remove the tape immediately, before the paint dries.

B

3. Then fill in the large areas with a roller, working in one 3-foot-square area at a time. Make several zigzag strokes upward and downward in the shape of a W, then smooth them out with horizontal strokes. **(B)** Finish with the windows, doors, moldings, and trim, doing the baseboards last.

Drying Time

Drying time varies depending on humidity levels. Even though latex paint is formulated to dry almost on contact, it's generally better to paint on a dry, mild, windless day, so the paint will dry more quickly, and you can leave the windows or doors open wide for good ventilation.

Decorative Techniques

Decorative finishes create unusual, often textural, effects that provide interest and dimension to a surface. Many are called faux finishes because they imitate the look of a specific material, such as the mottled colors and distinctive graining of marble.

Most specialty finishes involve applying a base-coat color, then a glaze or opaque finish on top to make an interesting pattern. These methods include sponging, ragging, stippling, spattering,

Helpful Hints

STOPPING SPLATTER

A roller shield is an easy and inexpensive way to stop paint on rollers from getting on you or other surfaces. This appliance simply clips onto the roller and stops paint from splattering while you roll.

COLOR CONTINUITY

➤ When using more than one gallon of a colored paint, "box" the paint before using to eliminate color variations. Pour paint from all the containers into a 5-gallon bucket and then mix thoroughly.

➤ Since different batches of paint can vary slightly in color, it is best to buy more than you need, allowing a little extra for spills and touch-ups. Many paint and hardware stores take back unopened cans of paint—ask first. Store extra paint in pint jars and label them by room for quick touch-ups.

Safety First

PLEASANT DREAMS

If you are painting a bedroom, you will want to sleep somewhere else until the paint dries, so you can avoid fumes.

SAFETY STEPS

Keep ladders away from closed doors so others won't hurt themselves or you by barging in (see page 264 for information on ladder safety).

and marbleizing. They are fun to do but can be rather complicated.

Follow the directions in a book, video, or the pamphlets offered at paint stores and home centers, and experiment on a sample board or a section of the wall before you actually begin painting a surface.

Which Paint Finish Where?

Interior paint (latex and alkyd) comes in a variety of finishes, from flat to a shiny high gloss. Each has its uses:

FINISH	RECOMMENDED FOR	APPEARANCE	CHARACTERISTICS
Flat/matte	Little-used rooms like dining rooms and guest bedrooms	Soft matte; slightly porous and soft	Absorbs grease and moisture; not easily washable
Eggshell	Hallways, family rooms	Soft matte with a slight sheen	Absorbs grease and moisture
Satin	Hard-wear rooms like children's bedrooms, kitchens, bathrooms, hallways	Slight sheen; reflects light	Scuff- and scratch-resistant; sponges clean easily
Semigloss	Woodwork, trim	Shiny; reflects light	Highly scuff- and scratch-resistant; sponges clean very easily
High gloss	Cabinets, woodwork, trim	Glossy sheen	Highly scuff- and scratch-resistant; sponges clean easily

 ## Time Savers

QUICK OPTION

Paint large areas more quickly with the help of a power roller. Controlled by a trigger, a pump forces paint through the roller from a large canister, letting you finish large flat surfaces in a fraction of the time.

 ## Helpful Hints

STENCIL STRATEGIES

➤ **When working with an intricate stencil pattern, glue a sheet of fine dressmaker's netting onto the back to hold it together while you paint.**

➤ **Use waterproof drafting tape to repair stencils that become damaged.**

Painting Dos and Don'ts

DO

- Wait until you are ready to start painting before mixing the paint, since the paint will separate as it stands.
- Line your roller tray with aluminum foil or a disposable plastic liner to give it a longer life.
- Thoroughly clean brushes after you are done painting for the day. If using alkyd paint, put the brushes in a plastic bag and store them in the freezer away from food. This will keep them soft and ready for painting the next day.

Metal drip wire

PROFESSIONAL COATINGS

EGGSHELL

- Put a metal drip wire over the open paint can when you are painting to wipe excess paint off the brush (you can make one from a wire hanger). This will prevent drips on the can and give you just the right amount of paint on your brush.

DON'T

- Assume machine-mixed paint will stay mixed until you get it home. Instead, pour a third of the paint into another container, and mix the remainder. Pour back the reserved third, continuing to stir.
- Leave brushes in a paint container during breaks. Instead, lay the brush flat on a wire grid over the open can or wrap the brush in a plastic bag or aluminum foil.
- Dip more than a third of the brush into the paint, or the brush will become too saturated.
- Leave the roller in the tray when you're finished, or it may get stuck for good.

Special Paints

In addition to standard wall and ceiling paint, there are a number of paints and finishes for specific situations. Some are practical; some are decorative.

FINISH	WHAT TO USE IT ON	WHAT IT DOES
Aluminum paint	Metal, painted wood, masonry	Gives surfaces a silvery aluminum color. Reflects heat on radiators.
Epoxy paint	Plaster, masonry, concrete, cinder block, wood, metal, porcelain	Gives surfaces such as refrigerators, sinks, and bathtubs a hard, ceramic appearance.
Glaze (clear or tinted)	Special effects on interior walls	Produces a rich, semi-transparent finish. Adds depth to wood grain and solid colors underneath.
Masking stain	Wood	Provides an even color on mismatched woods.
Penetrating stain	Wood, concrete	Helps floors and stairwells withstand heavy traffic.
Porch and floor paints	Wood	Brings out color gradations and markings.
Textured paint (white or tinted)	Plaster, wood	Creates a sandy (finely grained), rough (pebbly, randomly grained), or stuccolike (heavily grained) finish that adds texture and masks imperfections on a surface.
Waterproofing paint	Unpainted concrete, cement, brick, stone, stucco (especially good for basement walls)	Helps prevent moisture from seeping through.

Step-by-Step Stenciling

Stenciling, which involves creating a repeated paint design with a cutout pattern, is a simple, inexpensive way to transform a room with distinctive decoration.

Favored for both borders and overall designs, this fail-safe decorating technique, which requires no freehand work, has a long tradition in this country, where it was originally used to imitate more expensive printed wallpapers.

You can use it to create an all-over pattern or a border around a door or window, near the ceiling or baseboard on a wall, or at the edge of a floor.

And you can use a stenciled design over a textured paint finish for an interesting effect.

You can also use stencils to liven up old furniture and add interesting details to white or beige lamp shades.

Buy ready-made stencils (and complete stencil kits) in craft stores or home centers, or make your own from stencil card—a heavy treated paper also available in craft stores—cutting the design out with a sharp utility knife.

To create a pattern with more than one color, you will need a stencil for each color. Clean the cards periodically with a damp sponge to prevent paint buildup on them.

Paint stores sell stenciling brushes with stiff, tight bristles and flat heads, but you can use any brush that produces an effect you like.

Fast-drying Japan paints are often used for the stencil colors, as well as the special creamy acrylic paints sold with stencils and stencil materials.

1. Prepare the surface with flat finish paint (latex or alkyd).
2. If you have more than one stencil, start with the largest. Begin in a corner—or wherever the design starts—lightly penciling the position for the stencil on both the horizontal and the vertical. **(A)**

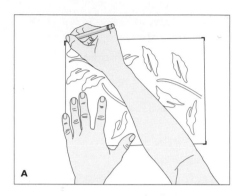

A

3. Tape the card to the surface—or attach it with mounting/positioning spray—following the pencil mark.
4. Dip the brush into the paint, wiping off excess paint with a paper towel so the brush is almost dry.

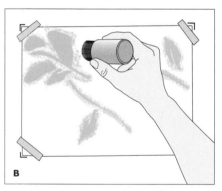

B

5. Apply the paint in a circular motion, or use a dabbing, pouncing motion for more interesting mottled effects within the stenciled design. **(B)**
6. Repeat the process, moving across the surface to continue the pattern.
7. Let the paint dry thoroughly and repeat for additional colors.
8. Carefully remove the stencil after all paint has dried.

Wall Coverings

Wall coverings can make a strong decorative statement in a room, adding pattern, texture, and color. They can also be useful problem solvers, disguising uneven plaster or an old paint job.

Next to paint, wallpaper is probably the most common and economical wall decoration. Other popular choices include fabric, tile, paneling, and stucco.

All About Wallpaper

This versatile wall covering comes in standard paper as well as washable synthetics that are great for baths, kitchens, and children's rooms. Most home-decorating stores supply sample books; you can order from these or buy ready-stocked rolls right off the shelf.

Designer patterns are also available through decorators. A specialized paper can easily be triple the cost of mass-produced versions, so shop carefully. The average roll is around 35 feet, but cutting the paper so that the pattern matches at the seams and corners of the room brings that down to about 27 feet—so keep your eye on the price tag when choosing papers.

Some wallpapers are offered with coordinating fabrics, window treatments, and even lamp shades.

 ## How to Shop For...

WALLPAPER
You should check that all the rolls of wallpaper you buy come from the same dye and run lots. Dye and lot numbers are printed on each roll. Different dye lots can produce differences in color from roll to roll, and you should record these numbers in case you have to purchase more paper.

If you're the type to redecorate regularly or if you think you may want to change the paper sometime in the future, buy strippable or peelable types. Don't forget to prime your walls properly before you put up the paper; it will help the paper come off more easily when you want to change it. Strippable paper can be pulled right off the wall, but leaves a paper backing that generally needs to be removed. (For advice, see page 208.) Peelable paper can be pulled completely off the wall, leaving little or no residue.

Types of wallpaper include:

Vinyl-coated: one of the most common and easy-to-use papers. It is washable, but scrubbing can remove coating and damage the paper underneath.

Solid vinyl: waterproof and scrubbable; a good choice for kitchens, baths, and children's rooms. Because they don't breathe, vinyls must be pasted to the wall with a fungicidal adhesive to prevent mold from forming underneath.

Uncoated: less durable and harder to work with than vinyls, these can be machine printed or hand printed (as in the case of more expensive varieties).

Flocked: has a velvetlike raised pattern that stands out in relief. This fragile paper should be used in low-traffic areas. Flocked papers require special care in hanging since the wallpaper paste can spoil the decorative surface. Vinyl flocks are less delicate.

Foil and Mylar: shiny covering with a metallic plastic film or Mylar coating on a paper base; some also have a printed pattern. Not recommended for walls with imperfections, which the shiny surface exaggerates. The metallic finish can conduct electricity, so it's important to cut around light switches and sockets and to avoid tucking the wall covering under face plates.

Paper Power

- Create interest by pairing 2 different wallpaper patterns in the same room. At the bottom of a wall, place one pattern to chair-rail height and put a paper with another pattern in the same color family above it (try stripes and a floral); paste a border where the 2 coverings meet.
- To achieve some of the visual effect of wallpaper without all the work, consider a wallpaper border. Placed along the top of a plain painted or papered wall, borders add detail to rooms and hallways. They generally come in strip form, but are also available as part of the wallpaper itself.
- Choose large geometric patterns for visual punch in a large room; use small geometric patterns to create the illusion of subtle textures in a small room.
- Use vertical stripes to make a ceiling seem higher.
- Paper the ceiling of a large room to make it seem smaller and cozier; leave the ceiling of a small room unpapered to create a sense of height.

Embossed: durable, with a stamped relief pattern on the surface. Offered in white and off-white, these papers are paintable, allowing for great control of color and style. The dense surface pattern makes this covering excellent for flawed walls.

Fabric: made of woven cloth and easy to hang because there is no pattern to match. Hard to clean and difficult to handle.

Grass cloths: made of natural grasses woven into a mat and glued onto a paper backing. Adds texture, but is delicate, hard to hang, and hard to clean. Synthetic look-alikes are less fragile and cheaper.

Think about what kind of effect you want to achieve before you go to the store or showroom; that way you won't be overwhelmed by the variety once you get there. When you decide on a pattern, order all you'll need at once. If you don't, discrepancies between different batches may show up on your walls (see box, page 207).

Hanging Paper

Hanging your own wallpaper is a challenge; unless you are experienced, it is probably best to turn the job over to a professional. This is especially true if you are considering uncoated, fragile designer papers.

If you are a beginner and want to give it a go (see box, right), try a prepasted, pretrimmed medium-weight covering with an allover pattern so you don't have to worry about matching from strip to strip; you can also avoid the trimming often necessary to make matched patterns fit a room.

Papers used in a moist environment like the bathroom need an especially tight fit so that mildew won't creep in behind the paper.

Preparing Your Walls

Whether you're wallpapering or hiring a professional, you will save time and money—and ensure good results—by preparing your walls properly.

Most experts recommend removing old paper before applying new—but if the existing covering is very smooth and tight, you may opt to put the new wallpaper right over the old.

Be sure to secure loose seams in an existing covering using vinyl glue, and use a razor to cut a small X over any bubbles. Smooth over any uneven places with spackle (see page 277) and apply a primer/sealer.

If the walls are in bad shape, you can use a liner paper. This is a thick wall covering made

How to Hang Prepasted Wallpaper

For best results, first remove all wall accessories and hardware, including light switches and plates. Paper the walls, then put the wall accessories back. Cut your paper to fit angles; if there are too many odd-shaped surfaces, don't try the job yourself. A standard roll of wallpaper will cover about 36 square feet of wall surface. Measure the surfaces in the same way you measure for painting (see page 198).

YOU'LL NEED THIS BASIC EQUIPMENT:

- A long table to measure, cut, trim, and book (or fold) wallpaper strips. Improvise with sawhorses and boards, or rent a table if necessary
- Stepladder
- Measuring tape
- Spirit level or plumb line to align paper
- Water tray
- Wallboard taping knife
- Utility knife
- Smoothing brush
- Sponge

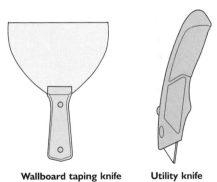

Wallboard taping knife   **Utility knife**

Smoothing brush

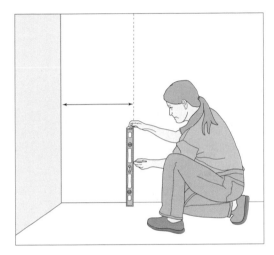

Establishing a plumb line with a level

1. Decide where to start and stop. It is almost inevitable that the pattern will mismatch at your stopping/starting point, so choose an inconspicuous place (behind a door, for example). If there is a floor-to-ceiling breaking place, such as a bookcase, start there.
2. Measure out from the stopping/starting point to the width of your wallpaper, then mark with a pencil. Draw a vertical plumb line at this point, using the level as a straight edge and vertical guide.

If you are starting at a corner, move your plumb line 1/2 inch away from the corner.

(continued on next page)

3. Measure the wall height, then add 2 inches to the top and to the bottom. Cut a strip to this length.

4. Loosely reroll your strip inside out. Soak the strip in water, according to the manufacturer's directions.

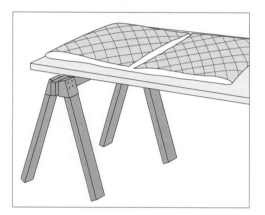

Booking a strip

5. Pull the strip slowly from the water and fold it loosely on the table, glue side to glue side, so the two ends meet in the middle of the strip—known as "booking" the strip. Wait for the paste to activate, according to the time indicated in the manufacturer's instructions.

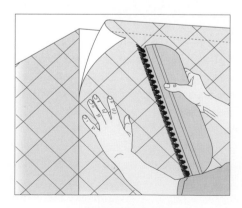

Papering a corner

6. Unfold the top part of the strip and place it glue side down on the wall, alongside your starting line, letting the top overlap 2 inches on the ceiling. If starting in a corner, fold the extra 1/2 inch of paper in or around that corner.

Smoothing on the paper

7. Unfold the bottom and smooth the strip onto the wall with a smoothing brush, working out large air bubbles from the center angling down to the sides. Avoid horizontal strokes except at the ceiling line.

Trimming wallpaper

8. Trim off any excess paper at the top and bottom of the strip by running a utility knife along the edge of a wallboard taping knife.

9. Cut the next strip, adding one pattern repeat to the length for matching. Repeat the soaking and application process, butting strip edges together without overlapping them. Align the pattern of the old strip to the new.

10. Repeat for all remaining strips. When you come to a corner, measure the distance from the edge of the last strip to the corner and add 1/2 inch to it. Cut your next strip to this width. Hang the strip, wrapping the 1/2 inch around the corner; it will cover any bare wall that might have shown from turning the corner. Hang the remaining strip on the next wall butting the corner and covering the overlap.

    When you are done, wipe the paper down with a damp sponge to remove any glue residue.

to go under other papers, hiding imperfections in the wall surface. It is applied horizontally to ensure seams don't align with the top paper's.

Removing Old Paper

To remove a strippable wall covering, grip a corner of the paper from the baseboard and pull until the entire strip comes off. Strippable paper will leave a paper backing behind; if it is tight, you can leave it on and hang the new paper right on top of it without using a sealer or primer. Otherwise, use a scraper (available at paint and hardware stores) to take off the backing. Some strippable wallpapers are easier to remove than others. Peelable paper should come completely off the wall, leaving only a small amount of adhesive that is easily scraped off. If the adhesive is stubborn, soak it with removal solution and then scrape it off.

You'll need to work harder to remove other types of wallpaper. First, cover the floors with a drop cloth. Next, score the wallpaper with one of the many scoring tools offered at home centers and paint stores. These tools help you avoid cutting through the paper and into the wall. You can also use a utility knife to make a series of small Xs across the paper's surface. Make sure you score the paper thoroughly, including into the corners. Sponge on or spray the wall with a commercial wallpaper removal solution and allow the solution to soak into the paper for the time indicated on the package label. Or make your own solution by pouring a capful of fabric softener into a gallon of warm water.

Resoak one strip of paper at a time and remove it with a wallpaper scraper. Thoroughly remove any residue.

If the wall covering is extremely stubborn, you may need to use a steamer, which you can rent at a hardware, paint, or home-decorating store.

Paint ceiling and moldings before applying new paper.

Window Treatments

Depending on their material and style, window treatments can block out unwanted light, provide privacy or enhance a view, insulate drafty windows, and make a room look and feel warmer. You can also use window coverings to unify windows of different sizes or to make small windows seem more impressive.

Curtains and Draperies

Curtains and draperies are the most common types of decorative window coverings. The terms are interchangeable; however, "curtain" is sometimes used to describe an informal treatment in which fabric is gathered or tied onto a rod or pole, while "drapery" suggests a more formal window treatment.

Traditional or highly decorated rooms will probably call for curtains or drapes, while more contemporary or streamlined rooms might benefit from blinds or shades (see boxes, pages 215–218).

If you buy curtains: The most economical option, ready-made curtains, come in standard stock sizes that fit within most windows.

If you have curtains custom-made (or make them yourself): Full floor-length curtains can use a surprisingly large amount of fabric—as much as 22 yards for a pair of very full, gathered curtains.

Helpful Hints

ALL THE TRIMMINGS

If you are making curtains and using washable fabric such as polished cotton, make sure your trims are also washable; many trims, such as satin grid lace, must be dry cleaned.

How to Shop For...

RODS AND FINIALS

If you're hanging curtains or drapes from a rod, you should take advantage of the great selection of decorative rods and finials (the ornaments that fit on the ends of the curtain rod, including glass balls and filigreed metal designs). Match the style of the rods to the curtain or drape—wrought iron or metal for dark colors and dramatic fabrics such as velvet, wood for lighter colors and fabrics such as cotton and taffeta.

Since the fabric is usually a significant portion of the total cost of curtains, shop for closeouts to find yardage at a bargain price. At the same time, don't compromise the look of the curtain by skimping on fabric.

Allow enough yardage so the window treatment will appear as full as possible. Double the fabric width for each curtain or drapery panel, and triple it for very lightweight fabrics.

Lining
Lining lengthens the life of curtains and draperies by protecting them from fading. Lining also reduces street noise, helps block sunlight, and increases insulation. Lined curtains also have more body, so they hang better.

Line a moderately priced silky cotton fabric, and it will look almost as luxurious as more expensive silk taffeta.

You can also use interlining, a layer of padding between lining and curtain that gives curtains extra body. Thermal fabric is a good idea for unusually drafty windows. Blackout liner fabric effectively blocks out light.

Classic Curtain Styles

Select curtains according to the amount of privacy you need. Sheer fabrics filter daylight, but are see-through from the outside at night, when your lights are on. If this concerns you, opt for a medium-to-heavy fabric. Or try using heavier curtains with sheer, unattached liners.

Side drapes and valance

Double-tier café

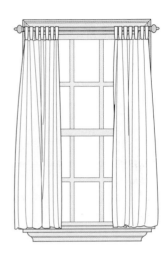

Tab

Priscilla with ruffle

Swag and cascade

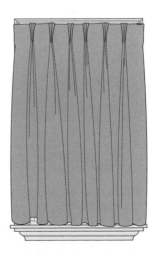

French (or pinch) pleat

Measuring a Window for Curtains

Before buying curtains, you need to measure carefully. Use an extendable steel tape; it won't stretch. The 3 most common curtain lengths are to the sill, to just below the sill (apron), and to the floor. Before measuring, install the curtain rod. The rod should extend at least 6 inches on either side of the window—more if desired. However, if the window is recessed, drapes can be fitted within the recess. Take the basic measurements to your salesperson.

FOR STANDARD CURTAINS
Width A = rod
B = stacking space (for pulling open)
Length C = rod to sill, or
D = rod to apron, or
E = rod to floor

FOR CAFÉ CURTAINS
(Curtains hung from mid-window to the sill. Double-tier café curtains cover both the top and bottom halves of the window.)

Width F = casing to casing
Length G = rod to meeting rail
H = meeting rail to sill

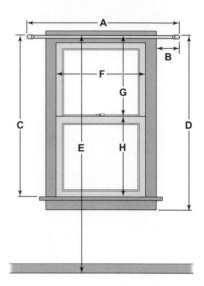

Measuring a Window for Shades or Blinds

Shades and blinds can be mounted inside the window recess (an inside mount) or outside the window (an outside mount.) For either mount, measure the inside opening's width and height. For an inside mount, make sure that the window is deep enough to contain the mounting equipment so the shades or blinds do not project out of the opening. For an outside mount, add at least 3 inches to each side of the window opening, and at least 2 inches to the height. If you are uncertain which mount to choose, take the measurements—including the depth of the window casing—to your salesperson for suggestions.

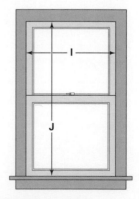

FOR SHADES OR BLINDS
Width I = casing to casing
Height J = casing to casing

Window Shades

Simple, inexpensive, and versatile, shades let in maximum light when open and cover the entire window neatly when closed. They are available in stock sizes and can also be custom-made. Many types of shades and blinds are available in top-down, bottom-up versions, which can be opened from the bottom, the top, or both. They can, for instance, maintain privacy while allowing light to enter through an open space at the top of the window. Below are some classic types:

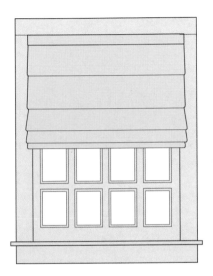

Roller shades: Shades that pull down from a tensioned roll and hold their places automatically; a light downward snap makes them roll up again. Typically come in a durable material known as shade cloth, sometimes with a vinyl coating; they may also be made of canvas or other fabric. Most retail outlets cut to fit the width of your window.

Roman shades: Overlapping folds stack when closed to allow for maximum window exposure. One of the most elegant blinds, when open, the fabric construction provides a look similar to drapes. Available in teardrop (or hobbled) or flat folds. Roman flat-fold shades hang smooth while the teardrop style hangs in rows of looped fabric and are excellent for use as blackout shades.

(continued on next page)

Curtain Rods

There are two basic types of curtain rod: simple solid rods and those with a hidden channel concealing a pulley system. Both are installed on brackets, usually sold with the rod. To install the brackets, position them where you want them, mark the holes, and drill starter holes. Then just screw in the brackets. In addition to the basic brackets that mount on the outside of the window molding or wall, you can purchase special brackets to mount the rod on the inside of the window molding. These are also screwed into place.

(continued from previous page)

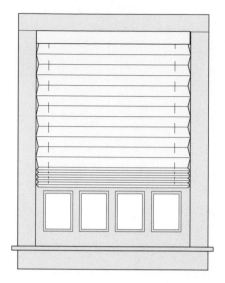

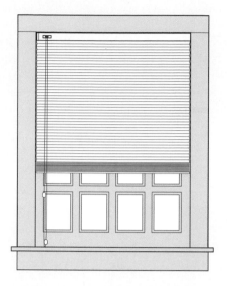

Pleated shades: A look that combines the softness of curtains with the clean lines of a shade. Usually made of permanently pleated polyester fabric and can be sheer or opaque.

Honeycomb (or cellular) shades: Synthetic shades with lightweight horizontal pleats created by "cells" when open. Closes tight to allow for maximum view. Available in styles from sheer to blackout; modern sophisticated look.

Balloon (or Austrian) shades: Fabric shades that pull up by means of tapes or cords threaded through rings sewn into the fabric. When the shade is raised, horizontal folds or bellows form, one on top of the other.

Blinds and Shutters

Blinds and shutters, available in stock sizes, are slatted window coverings that offer insulation, superior light control, ventilation, and excellent privacy when they are tightly closed. The slats can be tilted at a range of angles to provide ventilation and minimize glare while letting you enjoy the view.

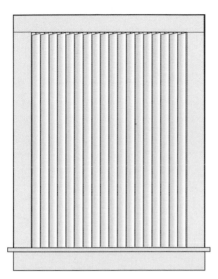

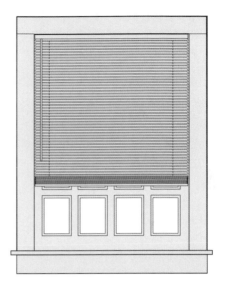

Vertical blinds: Made of vinyl, aluminum, wood, and fabric; draw completely to one side and are a good choice for sliding glass doors or large picture windows. Some accommodate wallpaper or fabric inserts; 2-toned treatments available.

Miniblinds (slats of 1-inch or less): Offer unobtrusive alternatives to wider slats; available in metal or vinyl.

(continued on next page)

 Safety First

CORDLESS ADVANTAGE

If you have children, consider buying cordless blinds or shades. Some use adjustment knobs, eliminating hanging cords in which young children can become entangled and hurt, or even strangle, themselves.

 Helpful Hints

OPEN WIDE

For sliding or French glass doors, use a curtain rod wider than the window. When fully open, the curtains will have space to pull all the way back and not cover the doors.

(continued from previous page)

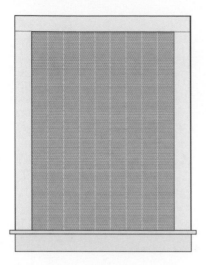

Matchstick blinds: Inexpensive natural fiber (usually reed); roll up. Roman versions, which close in folds, are also available.

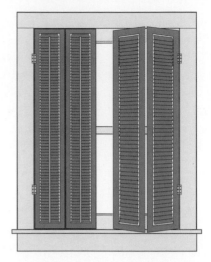

Folding shutters: Wood; hinged to the window frame. Open and close easily and fold up, so they take little room. Offer privacy and ventilation.

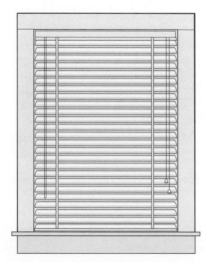

Venetian blinds: Wood, metal, or vinyl (available in colors and in natural finish wood); tapes can contrast or blend with the slats.

Plantation shutters: Wood; hinged to the window frame. Open like doors instead of folding; thicker than folding shutters, with wider louvers. Colonial style is similar, but with narrower louvers.

Floors

Floors are often overlooked, but because they are the single largest expanse in a room, they actually have a powerful effect on the decor.

One type of floor or covering is rarely suitable for every room in your house, so it is especially important to do good research. If possible, visit showrooms so you can compare different materials in person.

Looks are only one consideration; comfort underfoot, cost, noise and energy insulation, and washability and durability are also important.

Be sure to bring your floor measurements to a salesperson so you can get a cost estimate; most materials are sold by the square foot or the square yard, which can add up fast. (For example: a 12-foot-by-18-foot room measures 216 square feet, or 24 square yards.)

Carpeting

Carpeting is a wall-to-wall floor covering that is tacked down to a floor or subfloor. Soft underfoot, it is usually easy to care for, and helps unify and bring warmth to a room. (For advice on carpet cleaning, see pages 18–21.)

Carpet is a serious investment, but it will last a long time if you select a good-quality, stain- and wear-resistant brand. Different manufacturers offer different stain- and wear-resistant treatments under trademarked names, but a good baseline for comparing carpets is to check the warranty for each feature. Typically, wear- and stain-resistance warranties are 15 to 20 years on good-quality carpets.

When shopping for carpet, bring along fabric samples and paint chips so you can coordinate colors and designs. After making a preliminary selection, take a large sample—at least 1 or 2 square feet—and live with it for a few days.

Try walking on it, test to see if your doors swing over the pile easily (don't forget to include the depth of padding), and check the texture and color during daylight, and at night under different types of artificial lighting.

How to Measure

Carpet is priced by both the square yard and square foot, usually in a standard 12-foot width, although some carpets are offered in 9-, 15-, and 18-foot widths. If the carpet has a pattern, you need to order extra to match the pattern at the seams.

 DIY vs. the Pros

MEASURING SUCCESS

Measuring carpet is a complicated science. Carpets come in standardized widths, and measuring entails how to plan for the fewest seams while keeping waste to a minimum. For best results, follow these guidelines:

➤ **Don't use your own measurements.** Any shortages will involve the cost of ordering more carpet and having an installer return at a later date.

➤ **Consider hiring an installer to do the measuring.** A pro will usually deduct the cost of measuring from the overall installation fee.

 Helpful Hints

CARPET BACKING

Carpet backing is typically made of a natural fiber, like jute, which should not be used on damp areas, or a synthetic, which is less expensive. Ask what type it is before you buy; a latex coating increases durability.

Avoiding Hidden Costs

Always check with a salesperson to see if installation is included in the price. Ask about the underlay pad, too. Check to see if the dealer will remove old carpet and move furniture for you. Carpet layers may also need to remove doors; will the store charge extra for this?

Understanding Your Options

Judging a potential carpet involves looking at several factors, but the first decision is fiber. Carpet is available in wool and synthetic fibers. Wool is natural, warm, and strong, but can be significantly more expensive than synthetic fibers, and is not as resistant to stains and soil.

Nylon is the most popular carpet fiber; it is the strongest, has good stain resistance, and holds its color well. It can also be cleaned easily. Polyester has many of the same characteristics of nylon, but doesn't feel as nice underfoot and tends to mat—especially PET, a type made of recycled plastics. Polypropylene, or olefin, resists moisture and stains, and is used in indoor-outdoor carpeting or in areas below grade, such as basements.

Carpet Construction

How a carpet is made will determine how long it lasts and how good it looks over time. Density is a key aspect of construction, and is described as the "face weight." This represents how much fiber was used per square yard, and, generally, the higher the weight the better the carpet.

Twist refers to the preparation of cut pile carpets in which each fiber is twisted and heat sealed. The greater the twist, the more wear-resistant the carpet, but loop piles are not twisted, so the measure applies only to cut-pile carpets.

Carpets are either tufted or woven. In woven carpet, the pile is woven with the backing to form a single fabric. A quality woven carpet can last decades and, while much more expensive (up to twice the price of tufted carpet), can hold more detailed patterns.

Tufted carpet accounts for the vast majority of home-carpet sales. The yarn is mechanically attached to adhesive-sealed primary and secondary backings in loops, which are either left as they are or cut and twisted. A wide variety of surface textures are offered.

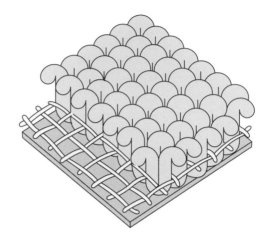

Tufted carpet

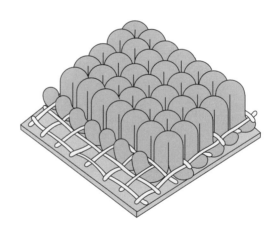

Woven carpet

Patterns and Solids

A color pattern may be woven into the carpet, or printed on the carpet's surface. Small patterns—florals, pin dots, and geometrics—are safe choices because they don't compete with other patterns in a room. If you choose a large pattern, consider whether the motifs

Pile Possibilities

Pile type is the key difference between carpets, and the one that determines how the carpet will withstand wear and tear and show signs of traffic.

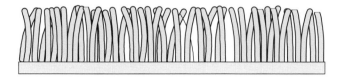

Cut pile: the most common and popular type, this creates a velvety look.

Looped pile: creates a smooth surface with an informal look; great for high-traffic areas.

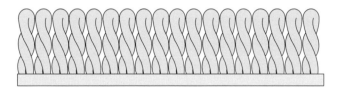

Twisted loops: provides more texture and firmer surface.

Cut and loop: combining both styles creates interesting surface textures and durability.

Carpet Style

Berber: Traditionally crafted of wool with a dense, thick, multilevel loop surface, Berbers are considered superior carpets. Contemporary Berbers are available in nylon, olefin, and blends, in addition to wool, and the traditional beige color is now accompanied by offerings in a wide range of shades.

Frieze: Tightly twisted yarns that form a curly surface. Good for high-traffic areas.

Plush: A cut-pile carpet made from untwisted yarn that yields a luxurious feel underfoot; it tends to show footprints and vacuum marks and is usually best for formal areas such as dining rooms, which see less traffic.

Saxony: A denser cut pile than plush, and subsequently more durable, but still shows signs of traffic.

Sculptured: Made with a cut-and-loop technique that produces a multilevel surface pattern. It looks elegant and is more durable than plush carpet.

Shag: Longer, twisted yarns that create a loose 3-dimensional look. Good for casual areas.

Textured: Suitable for high-traffic areas, the highly twisted tufts cut to different heights create a dense surface that masks footprints and doesn't show dirt as much as other styles do.

 How to Shop For...

QUALITY CARPET

When shopping for carpet, fold a sample back on itself. If the backing is visible, the weave may be too loose. The pile should be dense with tight twists and the backing hard to fold. Check, too, for loose strands, snags, and any uneven coloring.

 Helpful Hints

STANDARD AREA-RUG SIZES:

➤ 2 feet by 3 feet

➤ 3 feet by 5 feet

➤ 4 feet by 6 feet

➤ 9 feet by 12 feet

➤ 12 feet by 15 feet

will look odd if they get cut off by a corner or door.

Patterns tend to camouflage dirt and are good for areas subject to food stains, such as the dining room, or traffic, such as the foyer. They also don't show footprints or vacuum marks as clearly as do solid colors. If you prefer a solid, consider a medium tone, which will hide dirt and lint better than a very light or dark shade.

Buying a Pad

All carpeting except foam-backed carpet needs a good-quality underlay pad. A pad helps carpet look and feel better underfoot and protects it from wear, in addition to providing heat and sound insulation.

There are several types of padding. Prime urethane padding, the most common type, is a good insulator and usually used for residential carpeting. This springy material comes in various thicknesses and densities. Bonded urethane (made from pieces of prime urethane) is less expensive and of lower quality.

Felt padding made of hair and jute is another good insulator. It is especially durable and more expensive than urethane. However, it can cause reactions in people with allergies.

A less-expensive alternative is the foam-rubber or sponge-rubber padding generally used for area rugs. However, it can disintegrate quickly and is not generally a good choice for wall-to-wall carpeting.

In addition to the type of pad, you need to determine thickness and density (measured in pounds). For high-traffic areas or lower-pile heights, you generally want a thinner, denser pad—for example, a 3/8-inch, 6-pound one. In areas such as a bedroom, where a lush feel underfoot is important, you can go thicker. To test the feel of the padding, place a large carpet sample on top of each pad sample and try it out, preferably in stocking feet.

Area Rugs

An area rug is a rug that doesn't reach wall to wall and has finished edges—hemmed or trimmed. Unlike carpeting, area rugs can be rolled up and moved, so they offer more flexibility. They can warm a room while still showing off a beautiful floor; you can also layer them over carpeting to break up a large space, tie together a furniture grouping, or add more pattern. A room-sized rug can give the appearance of carpeting.

Here are some common types:

Aubusson: ornately patterned from France with decorative floral, scenic, or scroll designs, made in a flat tapestry weave.

Braided: reversible rug made from braids of narrow fabric strips.

Dhurrie: loosely woven, handmade, flat reversible Indian wool or cotton rug; often pastel colored with geometric patterns.

Kilim: tightly woven wool rug with geometric patterns; traditionally made in the Middle East. Colored with natural dyes.

How to Shop For...

TRADITIONAL ORIENTAL RUGS

➤ Oriental rugs are made up of a series of knots: the more knots per square inch, the better the quality. A good rug has 800 knots per square inch; a better rug has more than 1,000. Besides the number of knots per inch, the vibrancy of color and clarity of pattern determine the quality of the rug.

➤ Characteristic regional patterns once were produced only in that region. Today copies, which can be almost as good as the real thing, are likely to be made almost anywhere. For example, Belgium produces very fine copies of Oriental rugs.

➤ Although handmade originals can be extremely expensive, machine-made versions in synthetic materials re-create the detailing and color of more expensive types with a durability that makes them appropriate even in high-traffic areas.

➤ Authentic Oriental rugs are woven from wool or from silk, which is more expensive.

Needlepoint: hand-stitched wool rug with decorative floral patterns or scenes. Portugal is known for its fine needlepoint rugs.

Oriental: knotted rug in colorful designs made of hundreds of knots per square inch. Traditionally handwoven in the Middle East, but many Oriental-design rugs are now machine made. Genuine Oriental rugs are of natural fibers; others may be synthetic.

Shag: includes Rya, a shaggy Scandinavian wool rug hand-woven in bright abstract patterns; flokati, a Greek shag rug made with soft wool; and simple shags made in a range of fibers.

Sisal: rug of sisal hemp fabric, tightly woven, and displaying geometric or herringbone designs. Sisal-look rugs are now being made in wool.

Wood Flooring

Wood is a classic flooring that complements virtually any decorating style. It is versatile, relatively inexpensive, and takes well to refinishing when the floor gets old and worn-looking. Stained or polished to a new shine, many a beautiful floor has emerged from underneath a layer of old carpet or vinyl.

Hardwoods, including oak, maple, beech, birch, hickory, walnut, mahogany, and teak, offer rich colors and durability, but are expensive. Softwoods, typically pine, are less expensive, but more prone to scratches and denting. (See pages 38–40 for care of wood floors.)

Wood floors come in 3 types:

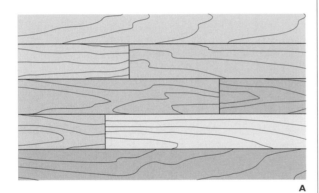

A

Strip: the most common type of wood flooring; is made up of 2- to 3-inch wide boards usually laid lengthwise, crosswise, or on a diagonal. **(A)** It gives linear perspective to a room and shows off the natural beauty of wood.

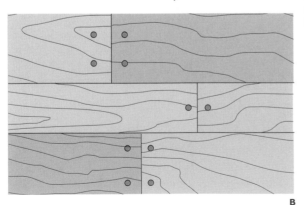

B

Plank: composed of strips installed in random widths. **(B)** It is reminiscent of Colonial-era design, and can be ordered with wooden plugs at the end of each board to simulate the pegged floors of that time.

C

Parquet blocks: squares of wood strips, typically measuring 12 inches by 12 inches. **(C)** They are more decorative than strip or plank flooring and create strong patterns underfoot.

When selecting a floor type, there are two cost factors to consider: the type of materials used and the installation. For instance, while the cost of materials used in a strip wood floor may be similar to the other options, the installation is easier and therefore likely to cost less. Make sure to get competitive bids from installers.

Wood Grades

Wood flooring is graded according to its appearance. The highest grades have the fewest knots and surface variations in color and grain. Strength and durability do not diminish in lower grades of the same wood. You may prefer a lower grade with more surface variations and knots, which can add interest to the grain pattern. There are 3 basic grades.

Clear: the highest grade; indicates heartwood (the best-quality wood from the tree heart), generally free of defects.

Select: the next highest grade; also high quality but has some knots and color variations.

Common: the lowest grade; has more knots,

burls, and streaks than the above grades, but is sometimes chosen for this very reason to add character.

Costs vary depending on the type and grade of wood, the finish, and the region of the country in which you live.

Resilient Flooring

Resilient flooring includes types that flex and give. The 2 basic forms are tile and sheet. Sheet flooring has fewer seams to attract dirt, but installation is difficult and best left to a professional. Both types can be laid directly over smooth concrete, wood subfloor, or an existing floor that is properly prepared.

The types of resilient floor coverings are vinyl sheet, vinyl composite tile (VCT), solid vinyl tile, linoleum sheet and tile, and laminate.

Vinyl sheet flooring is available in a vast array of colors and patterns. The best consist of a durable wear layer over a printed or inlaid pattern, with cushion backing. Vinyl sheet is highly water- and stain-resistant, comfortable underfoot, and will withstand wear and tear. New innovations in surface treatments ensure that the surface remains attractive over time and is easy to clean.

Vinyl composition tile, made of vinyl resins, fillers, and color pigments, is generally less expensive than other vinyl flooring. Solid vinyl tile is considered more durable. Either option allows you flexibility in floor design because you can customize borders and designs. Vinyl tile is also easier to change than sheet flooring. The self-stick variety is well suited for do-it-yourselfers. Both vinyl sheet and tile are available in faux wood and ceramic and stone finishes, in addition to a wealth of solid colors and patterns.

Although many people use the term generically for all resilient flooring, real **linoleum** is an all-natural product offered in a wide range of colors and patterns. It provides a comfort-able cushion to walk on and ages well, with the added advantage of providing an antistatic surface. Linoleum needs to be sealed with a quality floor polish, and its porous surface makes it a bad choice for bathrooms.

Laminate flooring is quickly becoming the most popular type of resilient flooring. Created by layering synthetic materials, laminates are offered as tiles, planks, or strips. They are notable for their extremely realistic surface finishes, mimicking the look of popular hardwoods, stone surfaces, and ceramics. Many include special backings to create the "walking sound" of wood or stone.

These flooring options are very durable and easy to clean. They don't fade in sunlight and are water-resistant. Most manufacturers offer substantial warranties against wear, and the engineered structure of laminates is more resistant to scratching and denting than any other type of resilient floor.

Laminate floors are installed in one of two ways: with adhesive, or snapped together in a "locking" system. Locking types create a precision fit with little effort or expertise, making them popular do-it-yourself options. They also allow for easy replacement if the floor is ever damaged, or if styles or tastes change.

Nonresilient Flooring

Floor materials that are hard and do not give underfoot, such as slate, marble, granite, brick, and tile, are called nonresilient.

Though these materials do not offer the comfort of wood and vinyl, they are extremely durable. In temperate climates, most nonresilient materials can be laid outdoors as well as indoors and are, therefore, ideal for extending indoor-outdoor living and entertaining areas.

Nonresilient flooring can be relatively expensive due to both the cost of the material and the cost of labor to install it properly. (It is possible to install these types of flooring yourself, but it is difficult and time consuming, and the margin for error is very small.) If you find the look appealing, you can bring costs down by limiting such materials to a small area, such as a foyer.

Stone and Brick

Stone flooring comes in a remarkable range of colors, so you can find one to go with virtually any color scheme. It can be laid in irregular patterns, which tend to look casual, or regular patterns, which establish a more formal ambience.

Marble and granite, which come in tile form, are the most elegant; you can also use slate. While some experts recommend sealing stone floors for protection, the sealant can cause marble to discolor.

Brick, which can be laid in a variety of graphic patterns, needs a polyurethane sealer to prevent staining.

Ceramic Tile

Since ceramic floor tile, typically laid directly on a subfloor with adhesive and finished with grout, is impervious to water, it makes a particularly good choice for bathrooms, entry halls, and sun rooms. Unglazed tile is a good choice for patios, because it is not slippery like glazed tile.

Grout is readily available in a wide variety of colors to match any color or pattern of tile.

Glazed ceramic tile cleans easily and does not need to be sealed, but the grout does. Pat-

terns and themed groups of tile are popular; although more expensive, they can create a unique look for a floor or high-profile areas such as a kitchen backsplash or tub surround.

Mosaic tiles are tiny ceramic tiles that offer a different, more ornate look. Until recently, using mosaic meant painstaking installation, but these tiles are now offered attached as groups to a webbed backing, in 12-inch-by-12-inch squares for easy handling.

Quarry Tile

This is usually unglazed with a matte finish. It comes in the various earthy tones of clay as well as with decorative finishes in a wide range of colors. Unglazed quarry tile must be finished with a sealer after it is laid or it will stain. It, too, is secured with grout.

Terra-cotta: plain, unglazed ceramic tile that sometimes comes decorated with relief or inlaid designs. Be aware that it can stain.

Color-glazed floor tile: useful for bathrooms if small tiles are specified; the small size keeps the floor from being slippery, and the glazing keeps water from seeping into the tile.

Glass Tile

More homeowners are turning to glass tiles to add an eye-catching element to kitchens or baths. The material is almost as strong as ceramic, and won't break unless something hard and heavy is dropped directly on the tile.

Colored glass: The color is part of the structure of the tile and won't fade or wear off. Sections of a single color are quite impressive, or you can use individual tiles as accents in a ceramic tile surface. For best effects, the tile should be laid on a white, thin-set mortar designed for use with glass tile.

Fused or cast glass: Special glass treatments allow for customized effects such as images or surface relief. These are generally expensive and best used sparingly as special focal points in a larger tiled area.

Furniture

There is no single rule for choosing furniture. Some people prefer using old family pieces, adding new items as needs or tastes change.

Others prefer to start from scratch, buying all the pieces for a room at one time to make sure that everything is coordinated precisely. Your choices depend entirely on your personal taste, budget, and decor.

If you decide to buy a new piece, it pays to invest in the best quality you can afford. A cheap upholstered piece will probably lose its shape and pop its springs in a few years, while a better version can last for generations.

Opt for classic styles and durable fabrics, and avoid fad styles that soon look dated. If the structure is sound, you can always revitalize a chair or sofa with new upholstery or a slipcover when the upholstery wears out.

Shopping on a Budget

You don't have to buy cheap furniture to buy furniture cheaply. There are lots of ways to get the pieces you want—from high-style designs to antiques—at prices you can afford.

Familiarize yourself with good-quality pieces: Browse in better stores, even if your budget is tight; a sale may bring the price of a

 How to Shop For...

FURNITURE

Department and large furniture stores offer these advantages:

➤ **One-stop shopping for furniture and accessories.**

➤ **Design service: In-store professionals offer advice and consultations.**

➤ **Delivery; check for the cost. Is it extra?**

➤ **Good-quality merchandise with warranties.**

➤ **Return policy.**

better piece down to one you can afford. Some department stores have special plans to delay or spread out your payments without charging you interest.

Shop for floor samples: Most stores hold regular sample sales. Even if a sale isn't on, a lower price is often available for the asking.

Try ready-to-assemble (RTA) furniture: A full range of pieces, from tables to sofas to lighting, is available from ready-to-assemble manufacturers. Browse large warehouse stores or go online for a greater diversity of manufacturers. Most styles are European or simple contemporary, but when mixed with antiques they can create a warm and inviting decor. A big advantage to RTA furniture is that you can sometimes paint, stain, and customize the furniture to suit your tastes and decor.

Shop for used furniture and antique pieces at flea markets and estate sales: Don't fool yourself; choose pieces that don't need repairing and refinishing if you will be unhappy undertaking those types of projects. Check for wear and scratches.

Buy from a decorator show house at the end of its run: You get high style at a fraction of the usual cost.

Buy direct from North Carolina outlets: Much of the furniture manufactured in this country comes from North Carolina, and some of these manufacturers sell direct through outlet operations. You'll find them on the Internet, and you can save hundreds of dollars. But buyer beware applies here—check with the Better Business Bureau about any company you're considering buying from direct, and make sure they have a return policy in case the piece is not what you expected once it has been shipped to you.

Antiques

Any piece of furniture that is over 100 years old is considered an antique. It takes considerable expertise to make serious investments in antiques, but not all purchases have to be major. You can still find bargains at auctions and flea markets. Many moderately priced antiques are cheaper than a similar new piece bought off the showroom floor.

When buying an old piece, check to see whether it is stable. Doors should swing smoothly and quietly, hang evenly, close and remain closed. Drawers should slide freely.

How to Shop For...

CHAIRS OR A SOFA

Before you buy an upholstered chair or sofa, make sure the cushions:

➤ **Have the same firmness.**

➤ **Are identical on both sides so you can reverse them.**

➤ **Have zippers for easy cleaning.**

➤ **Are covered under the upholstery with durable fabric.**

Anatomy of an Upholstered Chair

Every aspect of upholstered furniture is important—especially parts you cannot see.
The elements that make for good construction are fabric, frame, padding, and springs.

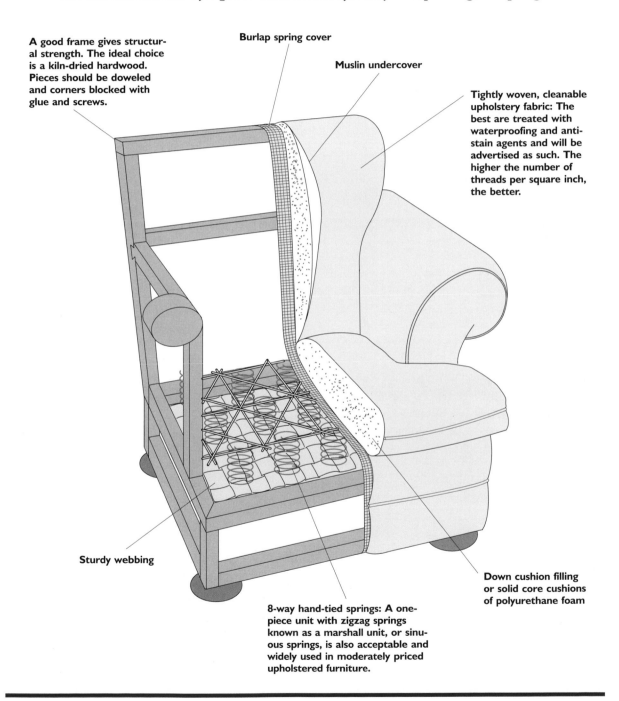

A good frame gives structural strength. The ideal choice is a kiln-dried hardwood. Pieces should be doweled and corners blocked with glue and screws.

Burlap spring cover

Muslin undercover

Tightly woven, cleanable upholstery fabric: The best are treated with waterproofing and anti-stain agents and will be advertised as such. The higher the number of threads per square inch, the better.

Sturdy webbing

Down cushion filling or solid core cushions of polyurethane foam

8-way hand-tied springs: A one-piece unit with zigzag springs known as a marshall unit, or sinuous springs, is also acceptable and widely used in moderately priced upholstered furniture.

Slipcovers

Slipcovers expand your decorating options for upholstered furniture. Use them to cover a threadbare sofa or chair, for a seasonal change, or to protect pieces from heavy use.

Chair without a slipcover

Same chair with a slipcover

- Consider buying an upholstered sofa that also comes with a set of slipcovers; you'll get twice the longevity out of the upholstery and 2 different looks for your sofa.

- Slipcovers can be custom-made or bought ready-made. Custom-made covers fit best and cost the most. You can save money if you're handy with a sewing machine by stitching your own custom covers. Look for patterns in fabric stores.

- Ready-made covers are sold in chain stores. Or try draping an upholstered piece with sheets or remnants and tuck and tie the fabric into place. Use double-faced tape to secure the material.

CUSHIONS

Avoid shredded foam cushions; the foam eventually mats and the cushions become lumpy.

FURNISHINGS

➤ **Multipurpose pieces such as drop-leaf and extension tables, nesting side tables, sleep sofas, and futons can be tucked into place when not in use.**

➤ **Check to see if the back of a large case piece—such as a hutch, bookcase, or bureau—is finished. Some manufacturers use low-grade wood for the back to reduce the price. This is okay if you plan to place the piece against a wall.**

STURDY UPHOLSTERED FURNITURE

To test for quality, lift an upholstered piece from one end; you shouldn't hear any creaking sounds. Check for reinforcement blocks at points of structural stress, such as corners, and ask your salesperson what type of wood the frame is. It should be made of a hardwood, such as oak or maple.

Look for interlocking dovetail joinery and a uniform finish. Even hard-to-reach areas near joints or in carvings should be evenly stained and free of glue.

Alterations and any refinishing of the original piece reduce the value of an antique, so it is wise to check for repairs and patching if you consider your purchase an investment.

Otherwise, choose an old piece for the same reason you would a new one: because you love it.

Buying a Mattress

Unless you have a platform bed that doesn't require a box spring, always buy a mattress and a box spring together. If you are buying the mattress from a showroom, the only way to determine comfort and firmness is to lie down and try the bed. Some luxury manufacturers have even added "nap rooms" to their showrooms so you can more thoroughly test the mattress. If you are going to share it, be sure to shop with your partner. If you are buying your mattress directly from the manufacturer, make sure there is a money-back guarantee if you are dissatisfied with the product after you've tried it at home, and make yourself aware of the company's return policies.

Innerspring mattress on a box-spring foundation: the most popular choice. Both units have tempered-steel wire coils covered with layers of padding. Different companies make different coil configurations, but generally look for 300 coils in a double-, 375 in a queen-, and 450 in a king-sized mattress.

Signs of a good-quality mattress include polyester, polyester-cotton, or damask ticking (the outer layer of fabric). A quality mattress will also have handles that go all the way through the sides of the mattress and connect to the springs, and at least a 15-year warranty (warranties are excellent indicators of quality in mattresses).

In an effort to make mattresses more com-

How to Shop For...

A MATTRESS

Mattresses and box springs come in these standard lengths and widths (always measure to make sure you have room for a new bed):

➤ **Daybed (33 inches by 76 inches)**

➤ **Twin (39 inches by 76 inches)**

➤ **Double (54 inches by 76 inches)**

➤ **Queen (60 inches by 80 inches)**

➤ **King (76 inches by 80 inches)**

Beds purchased from European retailers such as IKEA may not match standard mattress sizes. Always measure a new bed to ensure your mattress set will fit.

The Well-Dressed Bed

Bedclothes, which come in numerous variations, can dramatically change the look of your bed—and your bedroom. The set here has all the essentials, plus some popular decorative touches. Instead of a floor-length bedspread, many people prefer a dust ruffle or skirt, which fits around the box spring, topped by a comforter or duvet (with a removable cover for easy washing).

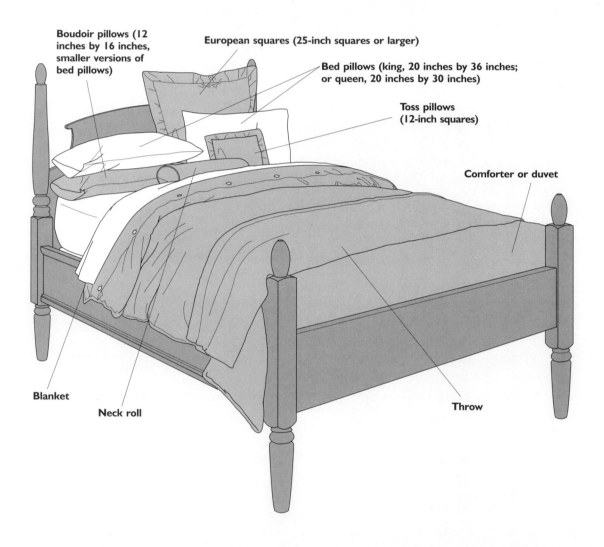

Boudoir pillows (12 inches by 16 inches, smaller versions of bed pillows)

European squares (25-inch squares or larger)

Bed pillows (king, 20 inches by 36 inches; or queen, 20 inches by 30 inches)

Toss pillows (12-inch squares)

Comforter or duvet

Blanket

Neck roll

Throw

Pillow Talk

Fine bed pillows are usually closed by a hand-sewn seam with muslin ticking. Choose a pillow based on the feel that you prefer, which is determined by the type of stuffing. The stuffing itself might be one of the following:

- **Down:** tiny feathers; very soft and plush; the most expensive pillows are 100 percent down.
- **Down/feather mixture:** soft, but not as soft as pure down.
- **Down with polyester fiberfill:** similar to down and feathers but less expensive.
- **Polyester fiberfill:** good for allergy sufferers.
- **Foam:** firm; typically less expensive than other types; more expensive types conform to the shape of your head and neck, and return to pillow shape when not being used. Many preformed shapes available for different neck and head positions.
- **Natural hulls:** buckwheat or other seed hulls provide firm support for head and neck, although lacking in softness.
- **Cotton batting:** soft and unsupported; least expensive pillow, quick to wear.

fortable, manufacturers have added layers of padding; as a result, thicknesses have increased from an average of 8 inches to an average of around 12 (with many high-quality mattresses measuring more than 14 inches thick). This means you'll probably have to buy new deep-pocket sheets for your new mattress—which can be an opportunity to try out new colors in the bedroom.

Foam mattress (without coils): completely different feel than spring mattresses because the foam conforms to your body without creating movement elsewhere on the mattress. The latest advances include high-quality "memory" foam that cradles your body and returns to original shape when you get up. Again, a long warranty is the sign of a good foam mattress.

Air mattress: a mattress that adjusts to your body's shape and weight and allows you to select the firmness of your choice. Foundations designed specifically for air mattresses are available.

Wall Decorations

Few rooms seem complete without wall decorations. Paintings, prints, posters, photographs, textiles, and drawings are obvious choices, but you can also use autographs, maps, children's artwork, awards, diplomas, old advertising art, and decorative plates to great effect.

Before hanging a group of wall decorations, lay them on the floor or draw the wall and grouping to scale on a piece of graph paper. You can also get an idea of how a room will look by tracing the framed artwork on paper, then making cutouts and taping them to the wall.

If you want to assemble a composition slowly over a period of time, start with the largest picture you have in the center and fill in around it as you go.

Framing

The best way to try out different frames and mats for a work of art is to bring the piece to a frame shop.

Deciding on mat size and color is usually a matter of eyeing the art, mat, and frame together. Put different combinations in each corner and stand back to judge the effect. Some people prefer a mat that is slightly wider on the bottom to add substance and weight. Art dealers and collectors recommend:

Acid-free matting and museum-quality adhesives: Ordinary paper and adhesives can cause discoloring.

Museum-type frames: These separate the artwork and glass to allow for air circulation.

Ultraviolet-resistant glass if exposure to excessive sunlight is anticipated: Too much sun can fade pigments under ordinary glass.

 Helpful Hints

THE BIG PICTURE
A mix of small pictures and other items mounted in a group can substitute for a single large picture.

 Dollar Stretchers

GETTING FRAMED
Custom framing can be surprisingly expensive. You can save money by using ready-made frames, available in art supply stores and through catalogs, and following simple instructions. Many larger art stores even carry a selection of precut mats, with a variety of opening and trim sizes.

Glare-free glass: Use if you are hanging a picture in a very sunny or brightly-lit area.

Since needlework and textiles are particularly fragile, have them mounted in a way that they

Caring for Framed Art

NEVER
- Spray cleaner directly onto the glass. It can stain the mat or art if it drips behind. Instead, spray the cleaner onto a cloth before wiping.
- Hang or store art over a radiator or heat register. If you hang a piece over a fireplace, there should be a mantel to deflect heat, soot, and smoke, all of which can damage a work rapidly.
- Hang valuable art in a bathroom or kitchen where moisture or grease can harm it.

- Direct a bright light onto a piece of art. If you are using a picture light, make sure it is not stronger than 25 watts.
- Expose art to direct sunlight, which can badly fade prints and paintings.

ALWAYS
Inspect your framed artwork periodically. If you notice deterioration, stains, or other changes anywhere on the art or on the frame, have a professional framer check them..

How to Hang Pictures

For most pictures and art, a simple picture hook is sufficient. These hooks are nailed into the wall at an angle, and the pull of gravity on the picture works to secure the hanger. You'll find picture hooks sized and rated by the weight they support, up to 100 pounds. (For heavier objects and more secure hangings, see pages 280–282.) When hanging heavier objects, be sure to secure the nail and hook into a wall stud so that the object doesn't fall.

Keep these design tips in mind when hanging pictures:

- Hang pieces at eye level. In groups, the centerpiece picture should be at eye level.
- If you are hanging small pieces, such as a group of family photos, place them on a wall where people can easily examine them.
- A busy background, such as strongly patterned wallpaper, needs strong pictures.

However, avoid highly ornate frames for walls with very busy wallpaper. Such a frame looks much better against a simpler background or a solid color.
- Experiment with shapes. A circle, oval, or diamond introduced among the usual squares and rectangles of picture frames will make a dramatic statement.
- Try using all the same size and type of frame and group the pictures together to make a grid with clean lines.

can later be unmounted without harm. Have your frame shop do this or ask them for guidelines.

Mirrors

A beautifully framed mirror can have as much decorative effect in a room as a painting and is often a less-expensive alternative. It will also add sparkle and make the room seem larger.

There are as many different types of mirror frames as there are picture frames. You can also use picture molding—wood or plaster framing usually used for posters or art—to hold a mirror. Glass-framed Venetian mirrors and mirrors with carved baroque frames are such powerful decorative elements that they can be used as focal points. Also consider stars, sunbursts, tiny mirrors in very large frames, round mirrors, and mirrors in unusual shapes or made of smoked glass. Antiqued glass mirrors are a popular look, one that goes well with many different furniture styles.

You can add mirrors to a mixed group of wall decorations or hang several framed mirrors in various sizes and shapes together.

 Helpful Hints

HANGING A MIRROR

To hang a mirror, use hardware made specifically for that purpose (see pages 280–281). Check the package to be certain that it is adequate for the weight it will bear. Make sure that the fastener is securely attached to both the wall and the mirror. You can also use one of the many adjustable hangers on the market, which makes leveling and securing the mirror easier.

FLOWER POWER

A shadow-box frame has a very deep interior so that 3-dimensional items such as dried flowers and family keepsakes can be displayed.

Flowers

Cut flowers enliven any room with their color and beauty, and those with a strong scent, such as hyacinths, lilies, and gardenias, also impart a lovely aroma to the air.

Like potted plants, however, cut flowers need special care.

- Cut garden flowers early in the morning or after sundown, rather than in the midday heat. Bring a bucket with a few inches of lukewarm water with you and place each stem in it as soon as you cut it. When you return to the house, refill the bucket with cold water and leave it in a cool, dark place overnight, or at least for several hours. This conditions the flowers and provides moisture. (Purchased flowers also need a water bath for a few hours before they are arranged.)
- Flowers with woody stems, such as roses,

💲 Dollar Stretchers

IN FULL FLOWER
Keep flower arrangements out of bright light; they will last longer this way. Also, change the water every day. And, yes, an aspirin added to water will lengthen the life of the flowers. Or add $1/2$ cup of seltzer or carbonated water and 1 teaspoon sugar to the water.

chrysanthemums, and lilacs, last longer if you scrape and split the stem ends with a knife, so they can absorb more water. If a stem exudes a milky substance, as poppies and poinsettias do, seal the end by dipping it in boiling water or singe it with a candle.
- Recut the stems of cut flowers and then strip the bottom leaves before placing them in the vase's water.

How to Arrange Flowers

If you are using a shallow container to arrange flowers, you need a holder, such as a wire frog or the spongy material called floral foam (which should be soaked in water for 15 minutes before use). Anchor the frog with tape or wedge the floral foam in place. You can also use marbles or stones for support.

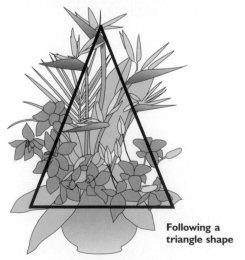

Following a triangle shape

Professional flower designers offer these secrets to success:
- Build the arrangement so it echoes the shape of the container or roughly follows the form of a circle, arc, or triangle.
- Use larger foliage and flowers to form the basic shape. Place the tallest items first. Then place additional items to make the outline of your design. Fill in with more flowers and foliage.
- In general, the flowers in tall arrangements should be $1^1/2$ to 2 times the height of the vase; in short arrangements, the

flowers should spread 1¹/₂ to 2 times the diameter of the container.

- Imagine a centerline running up through the middle of the vase and the space above. There should be the same weight of flowers and foliage (though not necessarily the same number of flowers) on either side of that imaginary line to maintain proper balance in the arrangement.
- Dark colors often look best at the base or center of the arrangement, with lighter colors near the edges.
- Single-color arrangements are popular and can be very powerful focal points in a room.
- For the best effect, floral centerpieces should be 2 inches lower than eye level of seated guests.

- Don't discount the power of a single flower. Placed in a slender bud vase or attractive bottle, a sunflower or a large rose can create a beautiful, delicate display on its own.

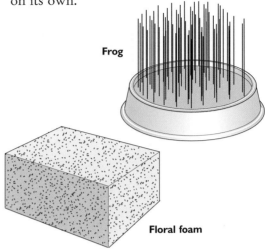

Frog

Floral foam

The Kitchen

While the general design guidelines in this chapter apply to any room in the house, some rooms need special consideration. First and foremost is the kitchen.

The kitchen has become the center of the home, where people gather as a family or even to entertain in an intimate social environment. How you arrange your kitchen affects how well the space suits these many roles. You can improve an existing kitchen plan or design a new one by following these simple rules for space usage:

- Add an island or a peninsula with drawers and cabinets to increase storage space.
- Store the utensils and appliances you use the most where they are easily accessible.

- Use tilt-out bins and pull-out bins to squeeze more storage out of a small space.
- Keep your work areas clear and reserve plenty of room to put away utensils, tableware, cleaning supplies, and food.
- Designate a snack-preparation area—perhaps with a microwave oven—to help keep traffic out of the main work space. If you cook or entertain a lot, consider a 6-burner stovetop and an extra sink. Many families also like to have a place for informal meals in the kitchen.
- Add lazy Susans—available in full circles, D-shapes, pie-cut, and half-moon shapes—in corner cabinets.
- Use the work triangle to plan your kitchen to suit your needs and the room's structure.

The Work Triangle

A traditional kitchen planning device, the work triangle is an invisible triangle connecting the refrigerator, sink, and stove so that there is the shortest walking distance among them. If the stove and refrigerator are side by side, use extra insulation between them for energy conservation. The complete triangle perimeter should total less than 26 feet, measured from the center front of each appliance. No single leg of the triangle should be shorter than 4 feet or longer than 9 feet. Here are 4 classic plans:

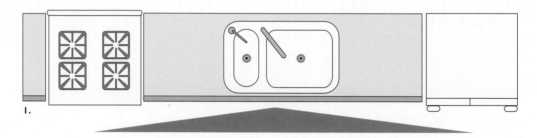

Galley: most efficient in long, narrow spaces

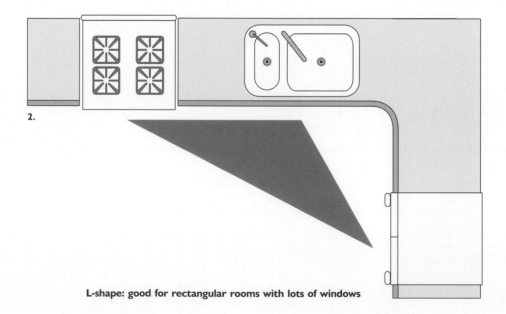

L-shape: good for rectangular rooms with lots of windows

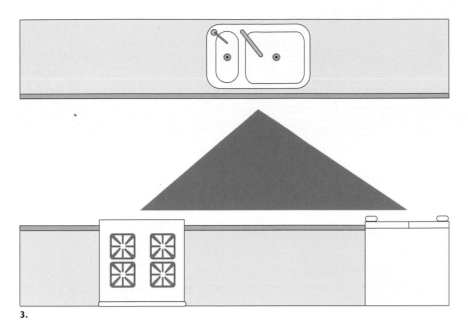

3.

Straight line: allows a straight run of cabinets for maximum storage space

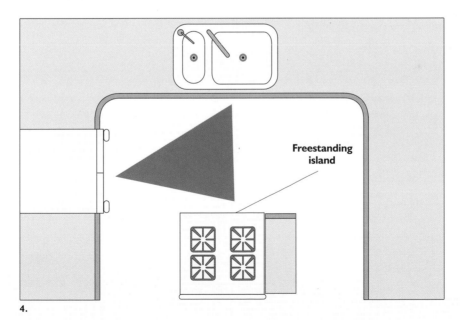

Freestanding island

4.

U-shape with island: makes distances shorter in large kitchens

Space Strategy

TO SAVE SPACE:

- In a narrow corridor kitchen, group all the appliances on one side and keep the counter depth to 24 inches. Keep the counter depth on the opposite side to 18 inches and gain 6 inches of floor space for easier movement around the room.
- Install a fold-down work surface.
- Use top cabinets that extend to the ceiling for more storage space.
- Install corner shelving to make use of space that is usually wasted.
- Hang pots and utensils from an iron rack or use a pegboard.

FOR ENOUGH SPACE:

- Reserve 2 to 3 feet of counter area for food preparation in a small kitchen, and 3 to 4 feet of counter area in a large kitchen. In the cooking area, 3 feet of counter space is also recommended.
- Standard counter height is 3 feet.
- Do not place service or cooking islands closer than 3 feet from any wall cabinets.
- Reserve 3 feet of counter space for dishwashing and drying.

Cabinets

Cabinets are the main design element in a kitchen and usually the biggest expense. To save money, you might simply refinish the cabinets you have; painting or replacing the fronts or even the hardware can also give them a brand-new look.

Replacement choices include factory-made stock units and custom-made woodwork. Stock cabinets offer a huge range of colors, finishes, and door designs, as well as storage options, such as pull-out doors and divided tray racks, and are usually available sooner than custom designs (in about 6 to 8 weeks).

Custom designs generally take longer and cost more, but not always. If you want a simple design, a contractor or carpenter may be able to build cabinets for less than the price of stock models.

Inspect your cabinets thoroughly before you have them installed to be sure they have arrived as ordered and are in perfect condition. Look for consistency of paint color or wood grain. Professional installation is recommended; if you don't want to use a contractor or a carpenter, local home stores now offer the services of a professional to install cabinets at a better price. After the cabinets are installed, make sure the drawers ride smoothly, the doors hang evenly, and clearances are adequate.

Countertops

The ideal countertop is impervious to stains, scratches, and moisture; won't scorch; and is easy to clean. Unfortunately, no single material offers all of these attributes, so you need to weigh the drawbacks and advantages of each type. The following materials are the most commonly used; if possible, bring samples home and test them for durability.

Engineered stone: Made of quartz and polymers, this material has the look of stone in many different colors, with an evenly patterned surface that is extremely durable. The material resists heats, stains, scratches, and abuse, but it is expensive. It can be repaired.

 Dollar Stretchers

FREE KITCHEN DESIGN

Many home-store chains offer free computer-aided kitchen design and knowledgeable consultants. Take advantage of these services.

Kitchen Storage

Good storage can dramatically increase kitchen efficiency. Consider good-looking pots and pans part of the decor, and hang them in the open on a ceiling rack; a rolling cabinet can tuck into a corner and double as counter space or a cutting board. Use inexpensive trays and racks to organize cabinets, or try a custom pull-out door to make use of otherwise wasted space. For a multipurpose storage solution, consider a prefab or kit kitchen island.

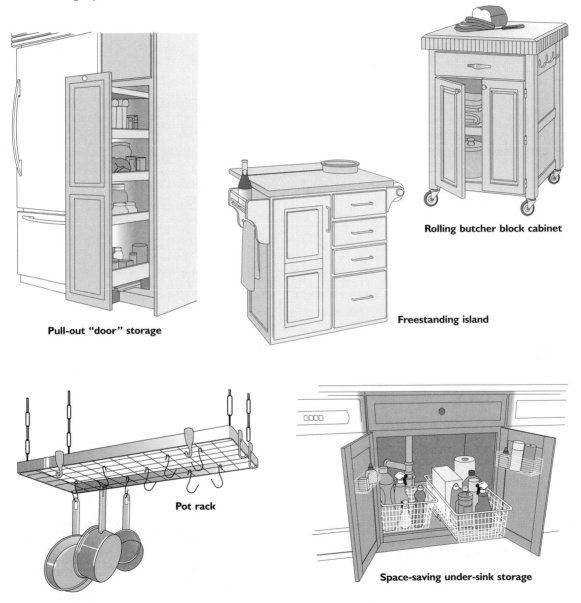

Pull-out "door" storage

Freestanding island

Rolling butcher block cabinet

Pot rack

Space-saving under-sink storage

Ceramic tile: Available in a wide selection of colors and patterns in an equally wide price range, tiles are somewhat prone to chipping and cracking and can cause dropped china and glass to break on impact. The tiles themselves are heat-resistant and easy to clean, but the grout tends to collect soil and food. The surface is expensive, but it lasts a long time.

Granite: Notable for its beautiful colors and markings, which can create an especially sophisticated look, granite comes as a single-surface material or in tiles. It is durable and heat-resistant, but it can stain. Dropped china and glass will break on impact. The cost is generally high, but this material lasts a long time.

Hardwood and butcher block: Natural maple, oak, or other hardwood surfaces need little care and are very durable. They do, however, burn easily. They can also stain, and readily absorb oils. Cutting on wood leaves marks that collect bacteria.

Laminate: This synthetic material is sold under various brand names. It offers the broadest range of colors, including solid and patterns—such as faux granite and marble finishes—and is among the most economical counter surfaces. It is highly stain-resistant, but can be damaged by heat and scratches, and is hard to repair.

Color-through laminate: This material is more expensive than regular laminate but without the edge seams. Scratches are less noticeable, and repairs are easier to make.

Marble: An elegant stone, with interesting graining patterns; it is durable and makes a cool, smooth surface for rolling and kneading pastry dough. It is heat-resistant, but it stains. China and glass will break on impact. It is expensive, but lasts a long time.

Solid surfacing: A manufactured material that mimics natural stone, and comes in white, neutrals, pastels, and faux marble and granite patterns. It is very durable and, unlike other counter materials, can be carved and shaped for various effects. For example, a long sweep of

Helpful Hints

A ROOM WITH A VIEW

Windowless kitchens are a common feature of modern apartments—even expensive ones. And they can be depressing! Glass-front cabinets with interior lighting and undercabinet lighting fixtures, are 2 ways to brighten up any kitchen.

counter can have a sink carved out of it, and it can have a rounded (bull nose) or beveled edge. You pay for these advantages, however; the material is expensive. Scratches can be buffed out with a nonabrasive pad, but heat can damage the surface.

Stainless steel: Favored for its sleek high-tech look, this shiny material is heatproof, easy to clean (use a cleanser meant for steel or it will streak or scratch) and stain resistant. It is prone to scratching, but scratch-concealing textured or brushed surfaces are available.

You may wish to design your counters with a combination of materials. A ceramic-tile or stainless steel surface adjacent to the stovetop is handy for resting hot pots and pans; a slab of butcher block will provide you with a built-in work area. When combining materials on the same counter, make sure the two will abut with flush seams at the same level; check with the manufacturer or your contractor.

Sinks

The location of your sink depends on the placement of the refrigerator, stove, and dishwasher (see pages 238–239); in all cases, however, it is important to have ample counter space on either side.

Faucets

The best kitchen faucets are made with an inner easing of cast or forged brass, which resists corrosion. Most new faucets are washerless, with a

Sink Materials

Stainless steel: the most popular type; solid. Cannot wear off, chip, or crack but can scratch—satin finish is a good choice to ensure wear and tear doesn't show. Easiest to keep clean with nonabrasive cleansers. Light and easy to install; lasts indefinitely.

Enameled cast iron: less expensive than stainless steel and available in many colors, but can chip. Prone to corrosion, loses heat rapidly, and is heavy and difficult to install.

Composite: less expensive acrylic-polyester blend can dent and nick, while quartz-resin type is hard and durable. Attractive, shiny finish available in many colors.

Solid surface: can be seamless part of countertop; many colors and patterns available, all easy to clean. Can nick, scratch, and dent, but blemishes can be repaired.

Porcelain: available in many colors. Heavy and more difficult to install. Can cause dishes to chip, and is susceptible to chips and rust stains.

cartridge or ceramic disc that virtually eliminates dripping (see pages 309–311). The best faucets carry lifetime warranties against failure and finish deterioration. Other features include temperature controls to save energy and prevent scalding.

When replacing a faucet, bring a template of your sink holes to check if the new model fits.

Faucets come in an array of finishes, including:

Chrome: remains the most popular finish for its brightness and durability.

PVD (physical vapor deposition) finishes: the finish of many high-end faucets. This is an extremely durable, plated synthetic finish that comes in a range of appearances, including nickel, brass, gold, copper, and colors.

Brushed metals: matte finishes such as brushed pewter, nickel, and satin-finish stainless steel hide fingerprints.

Copper: distinctive, especially when surface is antiqued. Not right for every kitchen but stunning in a country kitchen or one with other copper details or hanging copper pots and pans.

 ## How to Shop For...

LARGE APPLIANCES

If you have shallow cabinets and counters, be careful in selecting large appliances to ensure that they don't stick out too far. You'll also want to accommodate door swing in dishwashers, ovens, and refrigerators, all of which generally need 3 1/2 feet of free space for unfettered door swing. In the case of refrigerators, if your kitchen is narrow and cramped, opt for a side-by-side model that needs about half that swing space.

REFRIGERATORS

➤ As a rule of thumb, 2 people need a minimum of 12 to 14 cubic feet of food storage; add 2 cubic feet for every additional household member. Thus, the ideal refrigerator for a household of 4 would have a storage capacity of 16 to 18 cubic feet. This depends on how much you cook, how often you freeze meals, and how often everyone eats at home.

➤ When comparing refrigerators, always check the yellow energy guide label. This will tell you how energy efficient the unit is, and it even lists the anticipated yearly energy costs. Because refrigerators use a lot of energy, a more expensive, highly efficient unit can actually save you money over the life of the appliance (see box, page 69).

STAINLESS STEEL APPLIANCES

Of the 2 types of stainless steel—nickel and nonnickel bearing—nickel bearing is preferred because it resists wear better.

Sink Types

In small kitchens (less than 150 square feet), single-bowl sinks measuring 24 inches by 21 inches are recommended. Larger kitchens can accommodate double- or triple-bowl sinks, which are ideal for the dual purposes of preparing food and depositing dirty dishes as you put together a meal. Here are some options.

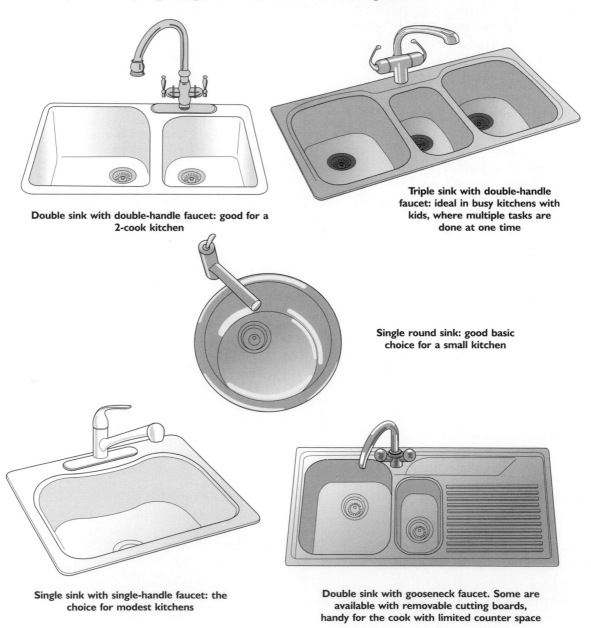

Double sink with double-handle faucet: good for a 2-cook kitchen

Triple sink with double-handle faucet: ideal in busy kitchens with kids, where multiple tasks are done at one time

Single round sink: good basic choice for a small kitchen

Single sink with single-handle faucet: the choice for modest kitchens

Double sink with gooseneck faucet. Some are available with removable cutting boards, handy for the cook with limited counter space

Brass: a traditional look in both kitchen and bath, especially antiqued brass. Not as durable as other finishes.

Gold plate: can add a colorful flash to the sink, but is expensive and can be scratched or dented.

Epoxy coated: a synthetic coating that comes in a range of colors, and black and white (letting you match sink and faucet more closely). Can scratch, but more durable finishes are now available than in years past, thanks to new bonding methods and materials.

Combinations, such as brass accent pieces on chrome faucets, are also popular. Finishes such as brass, which were once very susceptible to scratching and pitting, are now regularly coated with durable sealants that protect the surface.

Picking a new faucet can also involve choosing a neck type. In addition to the standard faucet neck, many manufacturers offer gooseneck varieties that provide a lot of room to maneuver under the faucet. Pull-out faucet spouts are increasingly popular, combining a sprayer right in the faucet neck and eliminating the need for a separate spray attachment.

Appliances

When choosing your refrigerator, cooktop, oven, or dishwasher, it is a good idea to visit many showrooms or dealers because the range of appliance styles and types is constantly expanding. Increasingly, manufacturers design appliances that are not only hardworking, but also good-looking. Appliances now come with sleek new profiles and a variety of finishes, including glass, enamel, and stainless steel. It is also possible to fit new appliances with panels to match your existing countertops, cabinets, or other appliances.

Major appliances come in standard sizes; your choice depends on your specific space allowances. Get help from a knowledgeable salesperson. Some appliances require 220 volts instead of the more common 120 volts. Check your home's voltage capacity before making a purchase.

Larger appliances that require connections, such as dishwashers and gas ranges, require professional installation. Your home center may have professionals who will install appliances for you at a lower cost than that charged by independent professionals.

The Bathroom

Any bathroom can be improved with simple updates. Even a few inexpensive touches, like a new shower curtain or towels, can make a big difference. Improving the lighting, faucets, and fixtures constitutes a bigger investment, of course, but repays you with efficiency and good looks.

Moisture-proof, easy-care surfaces are best for bathrooms. Ceramic tile can be coordinated with ceramic fixtures; marble and granite tiles are also popular choices because they, too, hold up well to moisture. While these are generally more expensive than ceramic tile, they can still be relatively economical in small areas. If you are using wallpaper, choose a good-quality vinyl or coated paper and have it installed professionally so it won't peel. Add a fungicide—available at most large paint stores and home centers—to the paint when painting a windowless bathroom or one with poor ventilation.

Fixtures

Like kitchen appliances, all types of bathroom fixtures come in attractive designs, and can be chosen as much for style as for efficiency and durability. Replacement fixtures can be found in a full range of finishes, from traditional chrome to pewter, brass, copper, and colors. Fixtures are simple to install with a few basic hand tools.

Tubs

The most common materials for tubs remain enameled cast iron and enameled metal, which are durable and attractive, if heavy to handle. Acrylic, fiberglass, and composite-material tubs are popular for their light weight and ease of installation. Molded in one piece, these make good replacement options when updating a bathroom. Measure first to make sure you can get the single piece through the door to your bathroom.

Whirlpool or Jacuzzi tubs are acrylic or fiberglass, and feature multiple jets that surround the bather in bubbling luxury. These are popular upgrades, but you should be sure your current plumbing and electrical system can accommodate the tub (check with your plumber and electrician or contractor). Deep-soak tubs are a good option for bathrooms that are too small for a regular tub. Ask a salesperson to let you get into a tub you are considering and test it for comfort; the way the back is sloped can make a big difference.

You can also avoid the need to tile or seal around the tub by selecting fiberglass or acrylic tubs that are molded as one piece with surrounds. Although these are not as elegant as tile, they are less work and can save money. Always check the water capacity and weight of a tub to make sure that your house framing can support it.

Showers

Most tubs can be fitted with a showerhead so you have both fixtures in one, but separate, independent shower enclosures are used in large well-appointed bathrooms or in those too small to accommodate a tub. One-piece shower enclosures range from simple shells with one showerhead, handles, and a drain to luxurious units with seating, multiple heads, variable temperature control, and steam-room features.

The key to a good shower is a good-quality showerhead that can be adjusted for angle, jet power, and stream. The right one for you is a matter of preference. Swing-arm units with flat heads can create the effect of rain coming down overhead; other heads create high-pressure streams for a brisk shower. If you like complete control over where the spray goes, consider one of the many handheld units.

Sinks

There are 3 basic types of bathroom sinks: pedestal, wall-mounted, and vanity. Some wall-mounted models are made to fit in corners, which helps make the most of a tight space. Vanities provide useful counter space and undercounter storage, and they can often accommodate more than one sink.

Pedestal or console sinks have an independent base that supports the sink. These come in a range of styles, from traditional to contemporary. Wall-mount and basin-style sinks are attached to the wall and hang off it with no visible support below; these create a sleek look. Vanity sinks can be flush-fit, self-rim with a lip that sits above the surface, or undermount, which is positioned underneath the surface. There are even sink bowls that rest like a bowl on top of a vanity.

Helpful Hints

TALL TALE

The comfortable bathroom-sink height for most adults is from 34 to 38 inches. You can mount a wall sink wherever you want it; vanity sinks can be built to any height.

Although the majority of sinks are porcelain, you can also choose from metal sinks, spun and cast glass, stainless steel, ceramic, and a small number of acrylic or resin models.

Hardware

Tub, shower, and sink faucets are usually a separate purchase. Some are installed in the fixture itself, some in the wall above. The same style and finish choices are available for bathroom hardware as for kitchen faucets. You can coordinate your faucets with towel racks, toilet paper holders, and grab bars.

Toilets

Toilets come in a variety of styles and colors, but the 2 basic styles are oval and round—choose depending on which feels most comfortable. Sleeker modern units are one piece with the tank and bowl forming a single unit. A standard 2-piece unit may be more appropriate in a traditional bathroom decor.

Perhaps the most important factor to consider is water use, determined by the flushing mechanism. Traditional gravity-feed toilets use about 5 gallons of water on average per flush.

Modern low-flush siphon-style toilets are quieter, and use about 1.5 gallons per flush. However, they can be weaker and may require more than one flush (but will probably still use less water than a gravity flush). If you're concerned about flushing power, opt for a pressure flush system, in which water is forced under pressure into the bowl. Although loud, pressure systems are highly effective.

The majority of toilets are white and porcelain. Special-order colors only if you are absolutely certain you are willing to live with the color for a long time—toilets last decades.

Bathroom Space Savers

- Consider buying the small-sized fixtures used on boats; you can shop for them through boating supply catalogs.
- Hang a triangular cabinet or shelves to take advantage of corner space.
- To minimize clutter, give each household member his or her own shelf or basket and label it.
- Keep individual blow dryers, toiletries, and grooming supplies in family members' bedrooms.
- Use hooks for towels. Four towels will fit in the space needed to hang 2 towels on a towel bar.
- Hang a vinyl-coated shower caddy from the showerhead to store shampoo bottles and soap neatly.
- Medicine cabinets are available in a wide range of styles. A deep version can increase storage.

Storage & Home Office Solutions

Earlier chapters have shown how to store clothes and accessories as well as where to stow items in the kitchen and the bathroom. This chapter explores the general principles behind successful storage, showing how to apply those principles throughout your house. Whether you're looking to store out-of-season items or display treasured objects, you'll learn how to find a place for everything. In addition, The Good Housekeeping Institute offers clever storage tricks.

Part of storing things properly is using all parts of a room wisely. And when you're looking to carve out part of a room for a home office, you'll find the advice in these pages invaluable. Here's everything you need to know about furnishings, lighting and ventilation, and electrical needs, as well as sanity-saving tips on separating your office space from your living space.

Storage Strategies

Whether your home is small or large, it will seem more spacious and work more efficiently if storage space is carefully planned and arranged.

While the prime goal of good storage is to stash possessions close at hand yet out of the way, organized storage spaces also help keep your possessions safe, in good working order, and readily available when needed.

Well-organized storage spaces can also help save precious time you might otherwise spend looking for misplaced objects, and can save you the money spent replacing items that cannot be located. Well-planned storage spaces can help you readily find things, even if you have a history of being disorganized.

For ultimate efficiency, plan different types of storage for different classes of objects:

- Easily accessed, convenient storage for the everyday items you use frequently, such as food, clothing, cooking gear, and laundry and bath supplies. Kitchen cabinets, linen closets, and bookshelves are prime examples of this type of storage.
- Out-of-the-way storage for items used seasonally or intermittently, such as lawn furniture, sports gear, and holiday decorations. Out-of-season item storage locations include the attic, basement, garage, or garden shed. Try to use the same area for all your seasonal items, like one closet or one section of the basement or garage. That way, since you're rotating the stuff in and out of use, there will always be a bit of space—snow skis replace water skis; ice skates replace Rollerblades.
- Convenient concealed storage for items you'll need at some time in the future, such as extra office supplies, batteries, hobby materials, wrapping paper, gifts, and cards. Opt for closets and drawers rather than open bookshelves, counters, and desktops.

- Accessible locations for everyday clutter, such as mail, bills, school papers, and current projects. Use baskets, cubbyholes, bins, and file cabinets to organize your ever-growing mounds of paper.
- Visible, safe display space for treasured objects. You might use shelves, open bookcases, built-ins, and the fireplace mantel.

The 5 Golden Rules of Convenient Storage

According to professional space planners and organizers, the basic principles of good storage apply to every item in every room of the home:

1. The most accessible prime storage is located in the space that corresponds with the area of your body between your shoulders and your knees—so your goal is to store the most frequently used objects there. Use the spaces above eye-level and below knee-level for infrequently used objects.
2. Group like items together. For example, put all the cooking utensils or wooden spoons in one pottery container adjacent to the range or cooktop. Likewise, stow the paddles and the life preservers in the kayak. Store the golf clubs, balls, and shoes on the same rack. Put the picnic baskets and coolers on the same shelf or in the same bin.
3. Plan to store items at the point of first or last use. For example, put dinner plates either near the table or the dishwasher; put the pasta pot near the sink, since that's where you fill it before using it.
4. Whenever possible, opt for adjustability, so that items can be moved as your needs change.
5. Use see-through storage boxes and labels liberally.

GARAGE GETUPS

➤ **Apply the 5 golden rules of storage to your garage, too. Clean out your garage, and then take inventory of what you plan to store there, taking care to measure any odd-shaped or bulky items. Next, visit your local home center, hardware store, or space-organizing store (or pore over its catalogs), and check out which storage gadgets best suit your gear.**

➤ **You'll find all kinds of solutions, from heavy-duty adjustable shelving and pegboards for tools to extra-large hooks designed to hold bikes and ladders. Look for oversized plastic bins and wire baskets to stash garden gear and sports equipment. You might even find a pulley system that allows you to hang large items like a canoe or bicycle from the overhead beams.**

➤ **You can also call in an expert who deals only in organizing garages.**

What Kind of Space is Available?

Search your home for storage space, assessing all the existing possibilities. As you do, think about the following:

Consider the access. Select your storage sites with care, especially for large and clumsy items and things used every day. Find another location if putting an item away means you must move other things to get to it. And don't block other functions of the storage site. For example, if you plan to store summer items like lawn furniture in the garage over the winter, maintain access to items you'll continue to need, like windshield cleaner and snow shovels.

Do you need it and is it in good condition? Before you store, purge items, such as kitchen gear, office files, linens, or toys. Discard or give away any that are broken, outgrown, or not used. And put things away in the best possible shape. Wash clothes, dust collectibles, hose off pool toys and lawn furniture and allow them to dry thoroughly before storing. Replace worn or broken items as necessary, or leave yourself a note in the storage container to, for example, buy a garden hose next spring.

What size space? Measure any large items before you bring them to the intended storage spot. There's no sense dragging an item to the attic only to find out it won't fit up the stairs, through the trap door, or to wherever you planned to store it.

Knowing the dimensions of smaller items will help you determine how to set up adjustable shelves. Deflate and fold what you can, but keep in mind that disassembling items wastes time (unless absolutely necessary). A prime example is an artificial Christmas tree, which (if you have the space) can be stored upright in a plastic bag

CHECK IT OUT

➤ **Make sure whatever storage site you select is dry and well ventilated. And before you actually put things away, inspect for signs of leaks in the storage area. Is mildew a problem? If so, use a dehumidifier and eliminate the leak and/or mildew, or find another location. If you elect to use the attic, be sure the floor can support the added weight of what you're storing.**

➤ **In the basement or garage, where items might come in contact with dirt, insects, or animals, store things off the floor in water-resistant storage containers (plastic, not cardboard), preferably those you can see through. Even if you can see the contents, label the outside of the box.**

COVER UP!

Stack out-of-season lawn furniture on the deck or patio under specially made heavy-duty plastic covers and tie the covers down around the legs. Since these covers really take a beating from the weather, plan to replace them every few years.

AN IDEAL CLOTHES CLOSET

AN IDEAL LINEN CLOSET

with the lights on it, ready for the next holiday season.

Buy storage devices. Look for ready-made solutions before considering custom-made, since these generally make more economic sense. Look for specialized bins, hangers, and racks for stashing all types of gear—from pot lids in the kitchen to shoes, ties, and scarves in the bedroom closet to sporting equipment in the garage.

Spend money on custom-made solutions only for the items and sites where you must. For example, to get the most out of unused basement or attic space, you might want to build shelves that fit under the stairs or eaves.

How much does it weigh? Be aware that most hooks and shelves and the bolts, screws, and anchors used to install them have weight limits. If the packaging says the hook will hold up to 15 pounds and you're not sure how much an item weighs, always err on the side of safety and choose the next larger size.

How to Organize Closets

Throw away, give away, or recycle items you have not used or worn in one year. Inventory the remaining contents—shoes, belts, scarves, folded items like T-shirts and sweaters, and your long and short hanging garments—to see what needs to be replaced.

Install a rod in one section of the closet to accommodate full-length items like robes and dresses. In the remaining section, install 2 rods, one above the other. One will accommodate your slacks or pants folded on a hanger, the other blouses or shirts. Determine the correct height for positioning these rods by measuring the length of your garments.

Hang hats and belts on hooks on the inside of the door.

Use the bottom and sides of the closets for shoes corralled in cubbies, bins, or see-through plastic boxes.

Fold T-shirts and sweaters and store them on shelves or in specially designed pull-out wire bins

Helpful Hints

CONNECT THE DOTS

Help children learn to put things away. Install a pegboard and paint it to match the space. Then trace the objects to be stored there (umbrellas, bike helmets, backpacks, and so on) with a dark colored marker. Kids can follow the outlines to hang the objects.

KID STUFF

In a child's room where new toys and paraphernalia seem to materialize almost daily, toy chests, under-bed boxes, clothes bags, and child-sized hangers are especially handy.

Safety First

PLAY IT SAFE

Keep safety in mind when planning storage in rooms occupied by children. Look for rounded edges and storage bins with safety hinges that can't close on small fingers. Keep toys on low shelves so your child need not climb to reach them. Attach (with bolts or anchors) tall bookshelves to the wall. Avoid hanging hooks or pegs at your child's eye level. (See pages 364–367 for additional child safety information.)

available in closet-organizing stores or catalogs.

Hang high shelves to store items that are used only occasionally or seasonally, leaving lower shelves and storage areas for more frequently used items.

Child's Play

Organizing a child's bedroom is rewarding, fun, and a unique challenge. Children's bedrooms are usually the smallest in the home and often must accommodate more than one child. To complicate matters, the room serves multiple functions, including sleep, storage, play, and study. Here are some ideas to simplify the situation:

Practical Storage Tips

- Stack china with paper or felt between the pieces to prevent scratching.
- Use soft paper towels or coffee filters between pots and pans for the same reason.
- Stash pot lids in a drawer or stack them on a shelf in a horizontal rack, from smallest to largest.
- Keep cleaning supplies in a plastic bucket ready to grab and take with you.
- Use see-through containers to help you easily identify the contents without opening the box.
- Label shelves to keep things organized and allow other family members to help maintain order.
- Convert space under the bed into storage space for out-of-season items.
- Use vertical space. Extend shelves to the ceiling. Select tall bookcases or an armoire to stash toys, office gear, and craft supplies nearby but out of sight.
- Be creative. Just because a product was made for the bathroom doesn't mean you can't use it in the office. Look in crafts and hardware stores as well as office-supply and organizational-equipment stores for ideas. In addition to cabinets, drawers, closets, and shelves, use racks, baskets, bins, buckets, boxes, dowels, pegs, and hooks.
- Store small items, which tend to clutter an area quickly, in baskets on grids hung on the wall instead of piled on the countertop or desk.

- Provide plenty of accessible, adjustable storage space that can grow along with your child.
- Include both open and closed shelves at varied heights for storing your child's books, games, and toys.
- Opt for the flexibility of adjustable shelves.
- Supply buckets, bins, and baskets for stashing smaller items.
- If space and budget allow, add an armoire to stash board games and other clutter out of sight.
- Invest in a closet organizing system that can be readjusted or reconfigured as the child, and his clothes, grow.
- Fill the space in the closet from the floor to the ceiling. Use the upper shelves to store out-of-season clothing in labeled bins or boxes and dedicate the lower half to in-season clothes. Include a hanging rod and a shelf within your child's reach. Install a shoe bag with pockets on the inside of the door for shoes, mittens, hats, and toys.
- Double the function of any furniture pieces you plan to buy; for example, consider a flip-top toy box that's also a window seat. Trundle beds provide the option of either an extra mattress for sleepovers or oversized drawers for storage.
- Keep favorite books or a collection on hand, but out of the way, with a narrow decorative ledge made from shelving.

Double-Duty Storage

If you have limited storage space, think in terms of multifunction pieces. Just as you might buy a trundle bed for a child's room, you should also consider the following:

- End tables in the bedroom, living room, or family room that also offer drawers or storage behind cabinet doors.

- Trunks, chests, bins, and boxes that double as tables or nightstands.
- Banquettes and window seats that also provide storage if the top is hinged.
- A bureau for the nursery topped by a changing pad mattress. Be sure to bolt the mattress pad to the back of the dresser and stand flush against the dresser when changing the baby.
- A tall, rather than a short, bookcase. It occupies the same amount of floor space, yet provides twice the storage.
- An armoire will provide much more storage space than a dresser, and takes up the same amount of floor space.

Kitchen, bathroom, and clothes storage all require specific accessories and detailed planning. See pages 237–245 for kitchen storage, pages 245–247 for bathroom storage, and pages 252–253 for clothes storage.

Displaying Collections

Any time you amass more than 2 of the same object, you're on the way to creating a collection. The secret to displaying a collection effectively is deceptively simple: group or mass like objects together, rather than scattering them all over the house. For example, hang your photographs together on one wall in the same room. While a collection is still small, display it in a small area, perhaps the foyer or a hallway.

The same rule of massing applies to large items like china, pottery, or a milk-glass collection. Create interest by varying the size and shape of the objects. Don't line items up in one straight line. Instead, stagger the pieces, placing the smaller and shorter items at the front of the display area and taller pieces behind. Shuffle the objects around in the display area until you are pleased with the effect. Experiment with groups of odd numbers; try putting 3 items on one shelf and 5 on another. Pull your collection together by creating a focal point with the largest object at the center.

As the collection gets larger, put some pieces away and occasionally rotate those on display. Consider painting the wall behind a collection that's displayed on a shelf in a contrasting color to make the items pop.

Specialized Storage

Store CDs, DVDs, and videotapes just one row deep, so you don't need to move one to get to another, and with the spines facing out. The simplest and least-expensive way to store CDs and DVDs, especially if you have a small collection, is to use photo album–type ringbinders with see-through plastic pockets. These albums take up little space and cost only a few dollars each.

Consider buying the albums in different colors, one for each type of music. Then organize the contents in each album according to a system that makes the most sense to you, such as one for vocals, another for instrumental, jazz, classical, country, and so on. Other storage options for CDs, DVDs, and videotapes include wicker baskets and cardboard or plastic boxes or bins available in many housewares, office-supply, and home-organizing stores. Free-standing racks and swiveling storage units are available in many styles and shapes, with and without doors. No matter which containers you choose, store the CDs, DVDs, and videotapes in a well-lit area or add appropriate lighting so you can see the tiny print on the cases.

Home Office Help

Whether you're a homemaker trying to keep tabs on your family's schedule, an entrepreneur managing a business, or a telecommuter for a large corporation working at home full or part time, chances are you could put a home office to good use. And an efficient home office, like efficient storage, takes planning.

The first step in planning a home office space is to consider carefully the kind of work you do, then search for the space that will accommodate it. For example, an occasionally used home mission-control center requires less space than an office where a full-time business is conducted.

Where can you set up a home office that won't interfere with other family activities? While the best-case scenario would be to turn an entire room over to office space, few homes boast that kind of unused extra space.

If you need a part-time office, try borrowing or stealing part of a room, such as the corner of a large kitchen, one wall in a dining or family room, or part of the laundry area. Or arrange a guest bedroom to do double duty as your home office. Investigate the possibility of using less obvious sites, such as a foyer, a large hallway, the space under the stairs, or even a closet.

For the business owner or telecommuter, remodeling the attic or the basement might provide the best solution. If you have enough headroom to use the attic without raising the roof, or if the basement is dry, both can be cost-effective to convert. They have the additional advantage of being out of the way and quiet. Before deciding on either location, consider how you'll add natural light and provide adequate heat and ventilation for you and your office equipment.

While you're evaluating a possible site, factor in the nature of your work. Must sensitive papers remain clean? Then don't even consider the kitchen, where splatters occur regularly. Do clients or suppliers visit your office? Then you need space away from the family areas, preferably with an entrance from the outside. If you need to keep many reference books, samples, or files on hand, a large space will be a necessity. If you require absolute quiet and total solitude, a remodeled attic or basement might work best. But if you're billing or word processing all day, you may need and want the hustle and bustle of family life going on around you to stave off boredom and provide opportunities for interaction with people.

Think ahead. What's critical today may not work tomorrow, and vice versa. You may not need space for an assistant or a copier now, but what about a year from now?

Putting It All Together

Plan the details of your home office on graph paper. Consider your furnishings, storage needs, lighting and ventilation requirements, and electrical needs.

Furnishings

You will increase your productivity if you choose comfortable, useful furnishings. Look for multifunction pieces such as a lateral file cabinet that serves as an extra work surface and an all-in-one printer, fax, and copier machine.

Choose flexible, modular, versatile furnishings. Stay away from built-ins, and always choose adjustable bookshelves because your needs may change. To eke more storage out of less space, choose office organization tools like storage containers and bins and baskets that are durable, attractive, and colorful.

A chair will be your most important piece of furniture. Buy a chair only where you can

The Ideal Office

A good home office is both comfortable and functional. Make sure that the chair and desk heights are suitable and that the lighting is good.

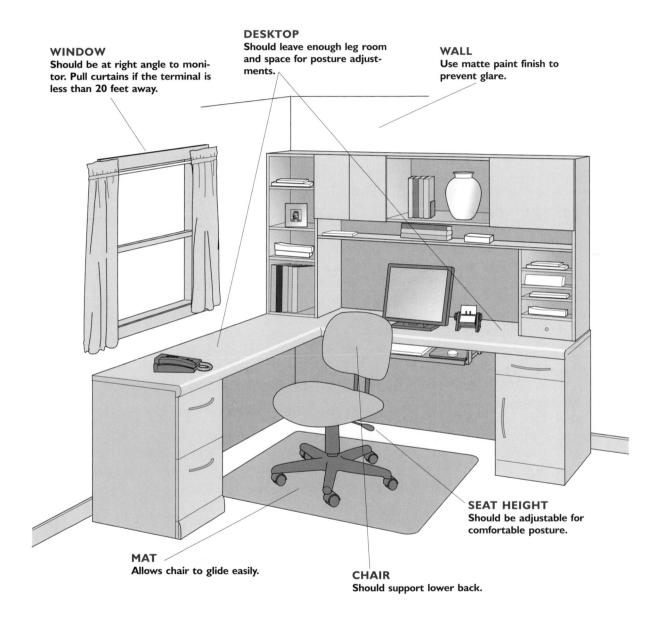

DESKTOP
Should leave enough leg room and space for posture adjustments.

WINDOW
Should be at right angle to monitor. Pull curtains if the terminal is less than 20 feet away.

WALL
Use matte paint finish to prevent glare.

SEAT HEIGHT
Should be adjustable for comfortable posture.

MAT
Allows chair to glide easily.

CHAIR
Should support lower back.

arrange an in-home trial; a catalog may not be the best place to shop for this important item.

Choose a model that adjusts forward and backward as well as up and down and that offers a lumbar support for the small of the back. If you opt for a spring-loaded back, select a model that is stiff enough for support and not too soft.

Be sure to buy a chair with no arms; this way your arms can hang correctly at your sides in a natural position.

Adjust the height of your chair so your forearms can rest on the surface of your desk or keyboard table. Again, try before you decide.

When you get the chair home, do not place it directly on a rug or carpet, since the drag caused by moving around on these surfaces can create stress on the lower spine. Instead, keep the chair on hard flooring or a plastic mat designed especially for chairs to glide on.

The work surface—whether a desk, table, or kitchen counter—needs to be a minimum of 20 inches from front to back, and closer to 36 inches deep if you plan to use a computer there. The work surface must be located at a proper height—generally from 28 to 30 inches off the floor, depending on your height.

If you plan to use a desk, the width will depend on the available space and the requirements for your work. But be aware that you won't be able to do much more than schedule appointments and pay bills at a desk less than 36 inches wide. Plan for a desk large enough to keep the supplies you need often close at hand so you don't waste time looking for a highlighter, message pad, or stapler.

To determine the best desk height for you, sit in your office chair with your feet on the floor in a working position. Bend your elbows. The desk surface should be just below your elbow. Ideally, the computer or keyboard would be 2 to 3 inches lower.

An L- or U-shaped desk is ideal. Choose a model with a minimum of 2 drawers: one shal-

Space-Saving Storage Expanders

Small home-office spaces demand careful organization. Here are some tips to maximize your space:

- Cork all or part of a wall to create another work surface. Tack up your calendar, family photos, and so on.
- Use labels—which are great organizational tools—throughout the office space.
- Set up a filing system that works for you. Then purge it once a year.
- Set up a desk system that includes a small vertical file for active projects.
- Locate bookcases in a hallway for reference books you don't need at hand.

low for pens and small supplies, another about 10 inches deep to hold files. If the desk offers no drawers, slide a file cabinet underneath it.

Pay careful attention to the position of your computer on your desk. Desk height and the height of the keyboard should allow your shoulders to remain in a natural position. Adjust the height of your monitor so you are not looking up or down but straight on to the screen. Positioning equipment correctly will add to your comfort and may help prevent eye strain, sore muscles, and carpel tunnel syndrome.

An angled footrest tucked beneath your desk will help reduce fatigue in the muscles of the back of thighs, knees, and hip joints.

Purchase a desk through a furniture or office-supply store or a catalog. Or build your own from a ready-made laminate countertop blank or a flush door supported by file cabinets, a drawer base, or open shelves. You can also cut a table down to your ideal desk height.

Storage Needs

Storage, too, should be personalized to accommodate your particular work needs. For example, the home-based interior designer, remodeling contractor, homemaker, and photographer will all require different types of storage.

Plan storage for the supplies you use. While it may be less expensive to buy office supplies in quantity, don't buy more than you can comfortably store. If necessary, keep one ream of paper in the office and stash the rest in another space.

No office can function without at least one file cabinet, and that should be located within arm's length of where you sit. Invest in the best-quality filing cabinets you can afford, even if you must buy just one at a time. Investigate used commercial-grade files, which are generally a good buy.

You'll find both lateral and vertical files. The choice can be dictated by personal preference and space—a tall vertical file takes up less floor space than a lateral cabinet.

Don't forget the "circular file". The trash basket is often your best friend when it comes to keeping your home office organized. If recycling regulations require you to separate trash, use 2 or 3 color-coded receptacles.

Lighting and Ventilation

Plan sufficient artificial light so your office can function after dark. Be sure there is enough light that you can see without squinting or leaning forward in your chair. Prolonged leaning will mean you slump or put a strain on the muscles in your neck and back.

Include both general illumination, to light your way into the space, and task-specific lighting, such as a lamp on your desk. Don't rely solely on overhead lighting, or you'll be working in your own shadow. The best artificial light for an office is often up light, such as sconces or a swivel desk lamp that lets you change the light's direction (see pages 194–197). Because you may require varying amounts of

Safety First

A WEIGHTY ISSUE

Look for weighted file cabinets that allow only one drawer at a time to open, so the cabinet can't tip. If you live with small children, bolt the cabinets to the wall. Drawers should open easily and quietly. Determine how much weight the tracks can support. If your business would be devastated if you lost your files, select fireproof units.

Create a Home Office with a Great Personality

Create a workspace that's not only functional but also a joy to be in and work in. Remember, once you've set up your office space, you'll probably be spending a lot of time there.

SOME TIPS:
- Pick the best—not the worst—room in the home.
- Pay attention to small details that will add up to big satisfaction: climate and noise control, air quality, the view, and access to the outside.
- Paint the walls your favorite color.
- Add life with plants and flowers.
- Provide shelves for a treasured collection.
- Hang favorite art or family photos.
- Keep a radio or CD player handy to provide pleasant background music.

light at different times, install lights on a dimmer and opt for 3-way lamps when possible.

Locate your desk so the window is not behind you, thereby eliminating glare on your computer screen.

Temperature and humidity need to be constant in an office, both for your comfort and the well-being of your computer and printer. Fluctuations will distract you and keep you jumping up and down to adjust the temperature or to add or subtract clothing.

If you work in a room with a ceiling fan, adjust the direction of the airflow away from your neck and back.

Electrical Needs

Be sure the office space you select includes sufficient electrical outlets for your needs. Plan for short-term growth with an adequate power supply for not only a computer but also additional items—an answering machine, a copier, lamps, a CD player or radio, and other small appliances. Be sure to include a surge suppressor in your computer setup to protect your electronic gear from power surges.

To figure power load, add up all amps on the labels on the rear panels of office equipment and appliances such as a radio. (If they're listed in watts, multiply by 1.4, then divide by 120 to convert to amps.) The average computer, monitor, and printer consume between 4 and 6 amps of electricity. The lowest rated house circuit is 15 amps.

To figure out what's connected to a circuit, go to the circuit breaker panel and turn off the breaker for the room. Now go back to see what's working. Be sure to check adjacent rooms.

Separate the Office from Home

As many telecommuters and home-based business owners can tell you, it's all too easy to become a workaholic when your office is 10 feet from the living room. Here's how to separate home from office when they are one and the same:

Shut the door. A door on the office is essential for separating work life from personal time. If your office doesn't have a door, have one installed—or move to a room that has one. If your office is carved out of another room, buy a decorative, portable screen or install a canvas shade or a pretty fabric curtain to conceal the work portion of the room during the hours your office is closed. You can even buy a desk that folds up into an armoire.

Determine your work hours and stick to them. Decide when you're at your best and work most effectively, or when you need to be at your desk to take calls, and schedule your in-office time then. If you have children at home, put in an hour or so of work before they are up for the day; then get them off to school, and then go back to work. That way you've put in a full workday by the time they come home.

Maintain physical boundaries. Open business mail and business packages only in your office. Keep business correspondence out of the rest of your home.

Put technology to work for you. Answering machines, pagers, faxes, cell phones, and e-mail are all wonderful tools that make telecommuting and home-based businesses possible. But those same tools can turn into monsters when you can't get away from them. Use the same technology to guard your time away from the office. The phone answering machine is your first line of defense, as long as you let it do its job. If your workday ends at 5PM, let the answering machine pick up starting then. If you can't bear to let a call go unanswered, install caller ID and use it to screen out all but the most crucial calls during the hours you're not officially working.

THE HOME WORKSHOP MENDING CHINA AND GLASS RESTORING WOOD FURNITURE WALL AND CEILING REPAIRS HOW TO HANG ANYTHING DOORS WINDOWS AND SCREENS FLOORS HEATING SYSTEMS COOLING SYSTEMS WEATHERPROOFING PLUMBING ELECTRICITY ROOF REPAIRS GUTTERS THE YARD THE HOME WORKSHOP MENDING CHINA AND GLASS RESTORING WOOD FURNITURE WALL AND CEILING REPAIRS HOW TO HANG ANYTHING DOORS WINDOWS AND SCREENS FLOORS HEATING SYSTEMS COOLING SYSTEMS WEATHERPROOFING PLUMBING ELECTRICITY ROOF REPAIRS GUTTERS THE YARD THE HOME WORKSHOP MENDING CHINA AND GLASS RESTORING WOOD FURNITURE WALL AND CEILING REPAIRS HOW TO HANG ANYTHING DOORS WINDOWS AND SCREENS FLOORS HEATING SYSTEMS COOLING SYSTEMS WEATHERPROOFING PLUMBING ELECTRICITY ROOF REPAIRS GUTTERS THE YARD THE HOME WORKSHOP MENDING CHINA AND GLASS RESTORING WOOD FURNITURE WALL AND CEILING REPAIRS HOW TO HANG ANYTHING DOORS WINDOWS AND SCREENS FLOORS HEATING SYSTEMS COOLING SYSTEMS WEATHERPROOFING PLUMBING ELECTRICITY ROOF REPAIRS GUTTERS THE YARD THE HOME WORKSHOP MENDING CHINA AND GLASS RESTORING WOOD FURNITURE WALL AND CEILING REPAIRS HOW TO HANG ANYTHING DOORS WINDOWS AND SCREENS FLOORS HEATING SYSTEMS COOLING SYSTEMS WEATHERPROOFING PLUMBING ELECTRICITY ROOF REPAIRS GUTTERS THE YARD THE HOME WORKSHOP MENDING CHINA AND GLASS RESTORING WOOD FURNITURE WALL AND CEILING REPAIRS HOW TO HANG ANYTHING DOORS WINDOWS AND SCREENS FLOORS HEATING SYSTEMS COOLING SYSTEMS WEATHERPROOFING PLUMBING ELECTRICITY ROOF REPAIRS GUTTERS THE YARD THE HOME WORKSHOP MENDING CHINA AND GLASS RESTORING WOOD FURNITURE WALL AND CEILING REPAIRS HOW TO HANG ANYTHING DOORS WINDOWS AND SCREENS FLOORS HEATING SYSTEMS COOLING SYSTEMS WEATHERPROOFING PLUMBING ELECTRICITY ROOF REPAIRS GUTTERS THE YARD THE HOME WORKSHOP MENDING CHINA AND GLASS RESTORING WOOD FURNITURE WALL AND CEILING REPAIRS HOW TO HANG ANYTHING DOORS WINDOWS AND SCREENS FLOORS HEATING SYSTEMS COOLING SYSTEMS WEATHERPROOFING PLUMBING ELECTRICITY ROOF REPAIRS GUTTERS THE YARD THE HOME WORKSHOP MENDING CHINA AND GLASS RESTORING WOOD FURNITURE WALL AND CEILING REPAIRS HOW TO HANG ANYTHING DOORS WINDOWS AND SCREENS FLOORS HEATING SYSTEMS COOLING SYSTEMS WEATHERPROOFING PLUMBING ELECTRICITY ROOF REPAIRS GUTTERS THE YARD THE HOME WORKSHOP MENDING CHINA AND GLASS RESTORING WOOD FURNITURE WALL AND CEILING REPAIRS HOW TO HANG ANYTHING DOORS WINDOWS AND ELECTRICITY GLASS RESTORING WOOD FURNITURE WALL AND CEILING REPAIRS HOW TO HANG ANYTHING

CHAPTER

6

Maintenance & Repairs

As any homeowner knows, repairs—to sinks, furniture, walls, and windows—can be incredibly expensive once a professional gets involved. And doing simple maintenance around the house—refinishing a floor, unclogging a gutter, putting in insulation—can be downright scary if you don't know what you're doing. But knowledge is power, and this chapter gives you the information you need to maintain and repair the many parts of your house. It explains which tools you need for which task, and shows how to use them safely and effectively. You'll find great advice on patching a hole in a plaster wall, repairing a carpet burn, maintaining your fireplace, fixing a leaky faucet, and much, much more. And if you decide that you do want a professional to handle the job, there's a list of helpful hints on the best ways to deal with repair people. Either way, this chapter will help you keep your house in top shape.

The Home Workshop

Do you think of yourself as "not the handy type"? Even if you do, you can take care of a surprising number of tasks—assembling toys, hanging pictures and shelves, repairing dripping faucets—if you have the right tools on hand (see pages 267–269).

Safety

Any tool, no matter how simple, can be dangerous if used without some safety precautions. To avoid problems, follow these safety rules:

- Always ask for help when you need it.
- If you're uncomfortable handling a tool, don't use it.
- Never work with children or pets nearby and never let children handle tools.
- Never draw any cutting tool toward your body, and always stand to one side as you work (if you're right-handed, stand to the left of your work as you saw, and vice versa).
- Keep your tools sharp. A dull tool is very dangerous because you often have to force it to get it to work—and that's when accidents happen.
- Wear safety glasses when using power tools and when there's a chance of flying debris.
- Safely secure long hair, loose-fitting clothing, and any dangling items that could get caught in a power tool or machine.

Tool Tips

- Use a tool only for its intended job and follow the manufacturer's instructions carefully. For example, don't use a screwdriver as a pry bar or a wrench as a hammer. A misused tool is often damaged and may later slip, jam, or bend, which could cause an injury.
- Don't leave tools, nails, and other sharp objects lying around the yard or on the floor

 Safety First

LADDER SAFETY TIPS

➤ Inspect the ladder before use; make sure all rungs are secure, clean, and intact.

➤ Be sure the ladder is stable and level before climbing it.

➤ Always face the ladder when climbing.

➤ Never stand higher than the second step from the top. To reach something high above your head, ask someone taller to help or get a higher ladder.

➤ Stand straight and stretch no more than an arm's length right or left. Can't reach what you want? Climb down and move the ladder.

➤ Don't climb and carry. Put your tools in your pocket or in a tool belt, or rest them on the swing-down shelf before you climb.

➤ Never use an aluminum ladder where it might come in contact with power lines.

➤ When using an extension ladder, the distance from the house to the ladder base should be about one-fourth the ladder's height.

LADDER RATINGS

All ladders come with a load-rating label noting how much weight they can carry. Types 2 and 3 are fine for most households.

➤ Type IAA (special-duty industrial): up to 375 pounds

➤ Type IA (extra heavy-duty industrial): up to 300 pounds

➤ Type I (heavy-duty industrial): up to 250 pounds

➤ Type 2 (medium-duty commercial): up to 225 pounds

➤ Type 3 (light-duty household): up to 200 pounds

What You Should Know About Ladders

Ladders are generally available in 3 materials: fiberglass, wood, and aluminum. Safe and strong, fiberglass ladders are used by professional workers, but they are more expensive; wood and aluminum are fine for home use. Wood ladders are less expensive than aluminum and are preferred because they feel stable underfoot. If you need an extension ladder, though, your best choice is probably aluminum, because the lightweight material makes the bulky ladder easier to handle. When buying a ladder, try to buy one that has been tested according to safety standards set by ASTM (American Society for Testing and Materials, www.astm.org) or ANSI (American National Standards Institute, www.ansi.org).

Stepladder

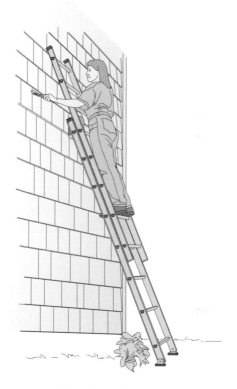

Extension ladder

Stepladders, which fold open (and stand on their own), are the most stable. They come in standard sizes. The smaller, 2- or 3-foot height is good for most indoor tasks, such as reaching shelves or replacing lightbulbs. You will need a 6- or 8-foot ladder for painting ceilings or pruning tall shrubs.

Extension ladders, which slide open (to double or triple length), are more cumbersome and less stable because they have to lean against something to stand up. They can, however, extend much longer than a stepladder (from 16 to 40 feet) and may be necessary for jobs like house painting or gutter cleaning.

of your garage or workshop. Even a rake can be dangerous if someone steps on it. Lean yard tools safely against a wall or fence with sharp edges pointed inward when they aren't in use.

- Any power tool you use in the yard should be equipped with heavy-duty cords approved for outdoor use. If your yard work requires an extension cord, make sure that it, too, is made for outdoor use.
- If a power tool jams, turn it off and unplug it before you look for the problem. Lawn mowers and snowblowers are power tools, and they can be especially dangerous—never try to unclog the blades or tinker with the motor unless the motor is switched off.

 Helpful Hints

PENNY NAILS
Phrases like "2 penny nail" have nothing to do with coins. The "penny" designator, represented by the symbol "d," is used to describe the length of the many nails sold in hardware stores and home centers. Here's a list of the length in inches of common penny nails.

2d=1 inch	8d=2 1/2 inches
3d=1 1/4 inches	9d=2 3/4 inches
4d=1 1/2 inches	10d=3 inches
5d=1 3/4 inches	12d=3 1/4 inches
6d=2 inches	16d=3 1/2 inches
7d=2 1/4 inches	20d=4 inches

Bolts, Nails, Screws, and Hooks

The fastener you use depends on the job; if you are in doubt, ask for advice at your local hardware store or home center. Keep on hand some of these basic types, which come in many sizes:

Bolt: Screws into nut or other threaded part to draw parts firmly together

Drywall screw: Threaded entire length; angled head sinks into drywall; can also be used in wood

Common nail: All purpose; good for general wood carpentry

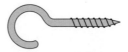

Screw hook: Wood screw with hook for hanging

Sheet-metal screw: Threaded entire length; creates own hole in wood; needs starter hole in metal

Wood screw: Tapered shank partially threaded; extra holding power for general wood use

The Basic Toolbox...

A good set of tools is a worthwhile investment that will save you money in the long run. Start with the basic tools listed here and invest in the best quality you can afford.

Abrasive pads: Fine to coarse grits

Anchors: For fastening items into drywall

Carpenter's pencil: Flat design keeps the pencil from rolling off a work surface

Caulk gun: Dispenses any adhesive or caulk that comes in a handy tube form

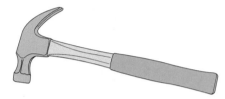

Claw hammer: 16-ounce

Duct tape

Electrical tape

Electric drill, cordless: No-cord convenience; batteries range in size from 7.2v, or volt, up to 24v

Extension cord

Glue: 4 types: all-purpose white, yellow carpenter's, 2-part epoxy, cyanoacrylate "instant"

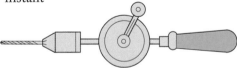

Hand drill and assorted bits: Ranging in size from 1/16-inch to 1/2-inch; for frequent use, consider an electric drill

Lubricant: Lightweight household oil

Masking tape

Nails and screws: Assorted

Paintbrushes: 4- or 8-inch for walls; 2-inch angled for corners and edges

Picture-hanging wire

Pliers

Plunger

Sandpaper: Fine to coarse grits

Scissors

Screwdriver, multibit: Holds various sizes of slotted and Phillips head tips in a single unit

Spirit level: Small torpedo level for hanging pictures, etc.; larger carpenter's level for most general construction projects

Staple gun and staples

Straightedge

Stud finder

Tape measure: 12-foot for small jobs, 25-foot for measuring rooms, etc.

Utility knife

Utility light

Wire: Assorted gauges

Wire cutters

Work gloves

Wrench: Adjustable

(continued on next page)

... and More

Consider adding these tools to your collection as you become more adept at repairs and tackle more complex jobs.

Allen wrench: To tighten bolts with recessed hexagonal heads

Awl: To make a starter hole
C-clamps: Assorted sizes; to hold objects in place while you work on them
Chisels: Assorted sizes; bevel-edged, to finish wood joints, firmer, for heavier work; paring, to finish long joints
Crosscut saw: Small; to cut smoothly across the grain of wood or to make a clean cut through plywood
Dust mask: To filter out fumes and dust
Files: Wood and metal; round, flat, and needle; to shape and smooth

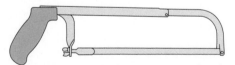

Hacksaw: To cut metal—a protruding nail, for example

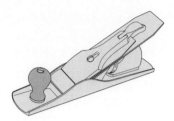

Jack plane: 12- to 15-inch; to shave wood, as on a sticking drawer
Keyhole saw: To make a straight cut through a bored hole and to cut in tight spaces where a crosscut saw won't fit
Locking pliers: Viselike jaws to grip and turn parts otherwise impossible to grab
Metal cutter: Tin snips

Monkey wrench
Nail set: To drive the head of a finish nail below a wood surface
Needle-nose pliers: For gripping in a tight spot
Notched trowel: To apply tile adhesive

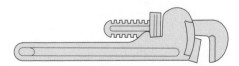

Pipe wrench: To loosen or tighten galvanized pipe and fittings
Plane: To remove thin shavings of wood from the surface of a board

Pry bar: To pull things apart, usually wood
Putty knife: To apply various patching compounds
Saber saw: To power-cut through metal and wood

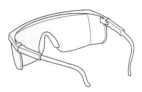

Safety goggles: To protect eyes from dust and debris

Slip-joint pliers: To grip pipes and other fittings; movable pivot increases the jaw capacity

Socket-wrench set: To loosen nuts and bolts; versatile and easy to handle
Tack rag: To pick up particles, such as dust or paint shavings, before applying a finish
Tool belt: To carry a few tools; ideal when working on a ladder

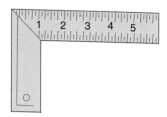

Try square: To mark a perfect right angle or check a corner for square
Vise: Metal or wood; To secure pieces of wood or metal when working on them

Mending China and Glass

epairing china or glass is never foolproof; any piece with great sentimental or dollar value is best repaired by a professional. When you mend simple breaks yourself, remember that the holding power of glue is weaker at stress points. Use pieces with repaired knobs, handles, and stems carefully, if at all, since the break may recur.

Applying Glue

Before gluing, lay out all the broken pieces in the exact pattern and order for reassembly. Work with 2 pieces at a time. Coat one edge of a piece, then press it gently to its mate and firmly secure the two parts until the adhesive cures (firm to the touch). You can secure 2 parts with masking tape, rubber bands, or a weight, like a book, if appropriate.

To keep pressure on a difficult patch—on the base of a goblet, for example—you may need to build a small frame to hold the item securely (ask for suggestions at the shop where you purchase the glue). You can also use sand, or prop the broken piece with books or other items, angling it so gravity holds the mended section in place.

After gluing, take a single-edge razor blade and scrape away the beads of hardened adhesive that will have been squeezed out of the mended joint.

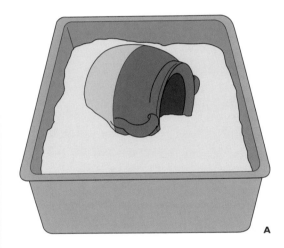

To hold a broken object at the necessary angle for gluing, work it gently into a container of sand (available at home centers) or cat litter. Set in the broken piece and let gravity hold it in place. **(A)**

What Kind of Glue?

For repairing most glass, porcelain, and earthenware, you can use one of 5 basic types of glue, available at craft or hardware stores. Follow the manufacturer's instructions and use a newspaper or cloth to protect your work surface. Avoid "instant" glues and quick-set epoxies: they set too quickly for this type of repair.

TYPE	PURPOSE
White glue (polyvinyl acetate: PVA)	For earthenware, porous crockery, and nonporous glass and porcelain. Don't use for stressed areas or on objects in contact with water. Dries in 24 hours.
Epoxy glue (slow-set, clear)	For earthenware, porous crockery, and nonporous glass and porcelain; especially good at stress points (handles, knobs). Cures by chemical reaction to create a very strong bond. Hardens in 40 to 60 minutes; cures in 48 hours.
Epoxy putty	Can be used to build up a missing piece, as if modeling clay, for porcelain or earthenware. Cures in 10 to 20 minutes.
Polyurethane glue	Contains no water, more convenient to use than epoxy; bonds well to porcelain. Wear gloves to keep the glue from staining your skin. Hardens in 1 to 4 hours; cures in 24 hours.
Urethane/silicone	For nonporous glass and porcelain. Flexible; will seal stress cracks and breaks; and holds up well to dishwasher heat and freezer cold. Impervious to water and soap. Sets in 20 minutes; cures in 3 days.

Restoring Wood Furniture

Before you consign a damaged or worn piece of furniture to the trash heap, consider whether you might be able to fix it yourself. Many pieces require nothing more than cleaning or regluing.

Dents, Scratches, and Stains

Any valuable piece of furniture, or one with major breaks, scratches, dents, or stains, should be repaired by a professional.

You can, however, take care of many minor repairs with such basic supplies as wood filler, stick shellac, and wax sticks. Most of these products come in colors to match different wood finishes and are generally available at paint or hardware stores and home centers. Carefully follow the manufacturer's instructions.

Shallow dents (where the finish is undamaged): Raise the grain with steam heat. Heat your iron to a high setting. Dampen 3 or 4 layers of cotton cloth and lay them over the dent. Press the hot iron over the cloth until it stops steaming. Repeat if the first application doesn't raise the grain.

Light scratches and blemishes: Rub using a thick paste of boiled linseed oil with pumice or rottenstone (see box, page 35). If the scratch is still noticeable, rub gently with a white abrasive pad moistened with paste wax or pure lemon oil. If that doesn't work, rub the scratch with a wax stick in a matching color.

Deep scratches: Fill with stick shellac in a matching color.

Deep dents and gouges: Pack with a pre-stained putty that matches the wood.

Burns: For surface burns, make a paste from rottenstone and linseed oil. Rub it in with a soft cloth (apply to the burn only) and polish with a clean cloth.

Water stains: Rub with a mixture of fireplace ashes, if available, and vegetable oil. Or rub gently with a white abrasive pad and a few drops of boiled linseed oil. Wipe clean with a dry cloth.

Loose Chair Rungs

When a chair rung or spindle has come loose and doesn't fit in its socket anymore, the problem may be old glue.

To soften and remove the old glue, daub it with a cotton swab soaked in warm white vinegar. Use a dull-bladed knife to scrape down to the bare, clean wood.

As you scrape, try not to shave any wood from the joint, because this will make the fit even looser.

If, after cleaning, the rung or spindle fits too loosely in its socket, wrap the end with thread until it fits snugly, then coat the end with white glue. Let the glue dry, coat the socket sides with glue, and insert the threaded end. Hold it in place using a piece of clothesline and a dowel (see box, page 274).

Restoring a Wood Finish

When you rescue furniture from the attic or snap up flea market bargains, the finish may be worn or scratched. Such pieces are often ideal for refinishing.

Sometimes, however, simple cleaning is all that's needed. Gently and quickly washing the piece with soap and water may be enough to restore the old finish to solid wood.

Dissolve a few chips of mild bar soap in a bucket of warm water. Dip a soft, clean rag in the water, squeeze it out well, and test a small corner of the piece to see if dirt comes off. If so, continue to wash the surface carefully, and quickly dry with a soft cloth.

Sanding and Polishing

Sandpaper and abrasive pads come in standard grits. The coarsest grits are for heavy-duty jobs, such as removing varnish or peeling paint; fine grits are for polishing and reaching into detailed areas.

Open-coat sandpaper has gaps between the grits that helps prevent clogging by giving the sawdust a place to go. Open-coat is most often used for woodworking. Closed-coat sandpaper is better for sanding metal and wood finishes but clogs easily with sawdust.

SANDPAPER GUIDE

600	Ultrafine
400 to 500	Superfine
320 to 360	Extrafine
220 to 280	Very fine
120 to 180	Fine
60 to 100	Medium
40 to 50	Coarse
25 to 50	Extracoarse

Abrasive pads are the modern equivalent of old-fashioned steel wool. Unlike their metal cousins, abrasive pads don't leave tiny slivers of steel behind. This is particularly important with today's water-based finishes because the steel slivers will combine with water in the finish to create rust, and then your project will be ruined. Abrasive pads are color-coded to indicate grit (see list below). It's important to note that although these colors are becoming more standard, they are specific to the manufacturer and you should always check the packaging to determine the grit or steel wool equivalent.

ABRASIVE PAD GUIDE

White	Extrafine (1200 grit)
Gray	Fine (400 to 600 grit)
Maroon	Medium (180 grit)
Green	Coarse (80 to 100 grit)

You can also remove the dirt with mineral spirits, a more aggressive detergent (such as trisodium phosphate or TSP), or denatured alcohol, which can generally be found at paint or hardware stores. When cleaning a wood veneer, always use a solvent; warm water alone may cause buckling.

Stripping Old Finishes

Stripping involves using a chemical solvent to soften paint or varnish so it's easy to scrape off. If you have never stripped a finish, start with a small piece of furniture that has a simple shape and flat surfaces; elaborate carving and turnings make it much more difficult to get off the old finish.

Chemicals in many removers are toxic and can burn your skin and clothing. If you apply solvents indoors, do it only in a well-ventilated space. Better yet, work outdoors—in your driveway, for example. Always wear gloves.

Electric hand sanders, which you can rent, save time and effort, and are great for removing finishes from flat surfaces (but don't try using them on detailed areas since they can cause damage). Choose a machine with orbital (circular) movement; for big jobs, try one with a 2-hand grip. A palm sander—a small orbital sander that you can hold in one hand—speeds your work on small areas and even helps around furniture legs and spindles. Fit the sanders with fine sandpaper in

How to Mend Chair Rungs

Mend unstressed broken, split, or loose furniture parts with any of 3 different types of glue: liquid hide glue (slightly amber in color), aliphatic adhesive (creamy), or polyvinyl acetate (known widely as white glue).

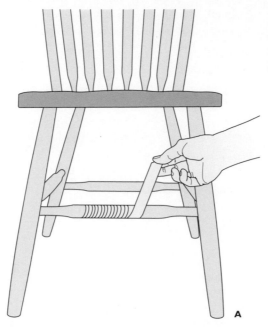

To repair a split rung, apply white glue, wipe off the excess, then wrap tightly with duct tape. **(A)** Remove the tape after the glue has set and within 24 hours. Otherwise, it will be difficult to peel off.

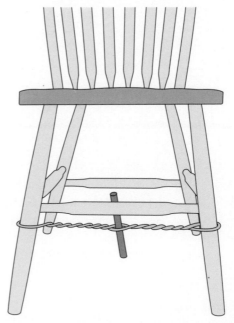

To hold rungs in leg sockets while glue dries, tightly wrap a piece of clothesline around the affected 2 legs just below the rung and tie. Insert a dowel and twist to tighten. **(B)**

the 180- or 220-grit range. Be sure to work carefully to avoid gouging the wood. Sand with, not against, the grain.

For protection, wear old clothes (long pants, long-sleeved shirt), protective gloves, and eye goggles, and tie your hair back. Make sure to wear chemical-resistant gloves, and avoid all solvent contact with your skin.

Scraping: Apply the remover following the manufacturer's instructions. Use an inexpensive throw-away paint brush, since chemicals can ruin a good brush.

When the finish has softened, scrape it away with a putty knife or a piece of wood; scrapers can gouge the wood.

Use a wire brush, a toothbrush, or a cotton swab in details and crevices, and burlap or abrasive pads on leg turnings, rubbing back and forth.

To remove solvent-loosened finishes in the finely detailed crevices of turnings, wrap a piece of jute (twine) around the turning and use a back-and-forth motion to rub the crevice clean.

As you scrape, deposit the material in a large juice or coffee can. Dispose of it with other household hazardous waste as your community directs.

The final steps: After scraping, rub gray or white abrasive pads (see box, page 273) over the entire surface to pick up any residue. Before refinishing, fine-sand the surface with 150- or finer-grit sandpaper, and vacuum away the dust.

 Green and Clean

ENVIRONMENTALLY FRIENDLY STRIPPERS

Conventional paint strippers use methylene chloride to dissolve finishes. Methylene chloride has been classified by the federal Environmental Protection Agency as a potential cause of cancer in humans. If you'd prefer an alternative, try one of the new environmentally friendly strippers that are water-based and solvent-free. These strippers tackle the problem differently: instead of trying to dissolve the finish, they work to break the bond between the finish and the underlying surface. Some of these are so safe to use, they've been certified for use by children.

Wipe the surface with a tack rag (a varnish-impregnated sticky cloth) to pick up specks the vacuum missed. Choose a finish from the chart on pages 276–277.

To get an extra-glossy paint finish, first apply a primer to a stripped or unfinished piece of furniture and let it dry. Apply a coat of alkyd enamel in a shade slightly lighter than the desired color. Let that dry, then lightly sand with 220- or higher-grit sandpaper. Add a second coat, if necessary. Finally, coat the piece with a clear polyurethane varnish, which will darken the color slightly (or use a water-based polyurethane, which will not darken the color).

Furniture Finishes

Choose among these treatments to refinish a stripped furniture piece or to finish a new untreated piece. Clear finishes and wax are best for enhancing wood grains, while opaque paints help camouflage flaws or inferior woods. Always try a test patch on a hidden area to be sure of the final effect. Follow the manufacturer's directions carefully, and be sure to work in a well-ventilated area. If you're sanding between coats, make sure to vacuum thoroughly or wipe with a tack cloth to remove all dust and abrasive residue.

TYPE	APPEARANCE	DRYING TIME	COATS	PROS & CONS
Enamel paint	Opaque; creates high-gloss finish.	24 hours	You may want 2 coats: check after applying first coat. Prime first for best results.	Wide color choices. Moderately expensive.
Natural-resin varnish	Clear; enhances wood grain; creates high- or low-gloss finish.	24 hours, perhaps more	Several. Between coats rub with gray abrasive pad; finish with white abrasive pad for high gloss.	Water- and alcohol-resistant. Resists scratches. Inexpensive.
Oil-based polyurethane varnish	Clear; enhances the wood grain; creates high- or low-gloss finish.	12 hours between coats	At least 2. Between coats rub with gray abrasive pad; finish with white pad for high gloss.	Water- and alcohol-resistant and has a durable finish. Expensive.
Water-based polyurethane varnish	Clear; imparts no color to the wood; creates high- or low-gloss finish.	4 to 6 hours between coats	At least 2. Between coats rub with gray abrasive pad; finish with white pad for high gloss.	Easy to apply, water cleanup. Not as tough as oil-based; slightly susceptible to water damage.

TYPE	APPEARANCE	DRYING TIME	COATS	PROS & CONS
Shellac	Creates clear finish with white shellac; darker with orange shellac.	2 hours between coats	4 to 6 coats. Between coats, sand with 400-grit open-coat sandpaper. Finish with wax.	Poor resistance to heat, alcohol, water. Not for table surfaces. Will stain, melt with heat. Inexpensive.
Oil-based wood stain	Darkens color; stain pigments obscure grain somewhat.	24 hours	1 coat. Fine-sand with 150-grit sandpaper; finish with varnish or shellac.	Can alter tone and color. Low to moderate cost.
Water-based wood stain	Darkens or colors wood without obscuring grain.	8 hours	1 coat. Since water raises grain, wet surface lightly before staining and sand lightly when dry with 220-grit sandpaper.	Raises grain, but leaves wood grain fully visible.

Wall and Ceiling Repairs

With a little know-how and the right materials, you can tackle minor wall and ceiling repairs, such as patching plaster or drywall.

For small holes and cracks use spackle, a puttylike vinyl or acrylic compound. Plaster, less forgiving but stronger, is necessary for large holes. Spackle shrinks as it dries. When the spackle dries, sand the surface with 180- to 220-grit sandpaper until the surface is smooth and flush with the wall. If necessary, apply more spackle, let dry, and resand. If you're patching with new plaster, don't paint it right away. Let it dry for 2 to 6 hours (depending on the thickness), or a powdery substance will form.

Patching Plaster

In order to repair your plaster wall, you must first determine if you're fixing a hairline crack, a small hole—such as one made by a picture hanger—or a large hole, and then follow the appropriate instructions that follow.

Small Hole

To repair a small hole in plaster, such as one made by a picture hanger, begin by brushing away any loose material.

1. Wet the area with a sponge. Apply ready-mix spackle, pressing it in with a putty knife or your finger. (A) Let it dry for 2 hours.
2. Using 150-grit sandpaper, sand the patch smooth.
3. Wipe clean. Apply primer before painting.

Use a putty knife to smooth spackle into a small hole.

A

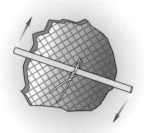

C

Hairline Cracks

1. Using an awl, dig out beneath the lines of the crack, then brush away any loose material. Wet the area with a sponge.
2. Press ready-mix spackle into the crack with your finger and smooth over with a putty knife. When dry, use 150-grit sandpaper to sand the patch smooth.
3. Wipe clean. Apply primer before painting.

Large Hole

1. Clean plaster dust from the hole, and check to see if plasterboard, wire, or wood is visible. If so, use it as backing for your patch. If not, cut a piece of heavy screening an inch larger all around than the hole.

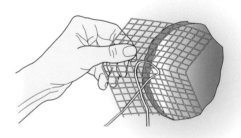

B

2. Loop a wire through the center of the screen; bend the screen through the hole (B) and, with the wire, pull it taut against the back of the plaster surface.

3. Fasten the 2 ends of the wire around a ballpoint pen or $3/8$-inch dowel longer than the hole is wide. Turn the pen or dowel (like winding the key for a toy) until the twisted wire holds the screen firmly in place. (C)
4. Apply plaster or spackle coat with a putty knife over the screen, working it under the dowel, and then smooth out.
5. Allow the plaster or spackle to dry according to the manufacturer's instructions. Then remove the pen or dowel and clip the exposed wire.
6. Apply a second coat so the patch will be flush with the wall and smooth it out. When this dries, sand the area smooth with 150-grit sandpaper and apply primer before painting.

Drywall Holes

Drywall, also called gypsum board, is a solid dry board covered on both sides with a special paper. It is commonly used in new construction or over old plaster walls that are in poor shape.

Small Holes and Dents

Patch a tiny hole not much larger than a nail with spackle, as you would for a plaster surface (see page 277).

Large Holes

Patching large holes requires joint compound, drywall tape, and extra drywall for making patches. If you've never worked with these materials, call a professional.

How to Replace a Broken Tile

Cracked or damaged ceramic tiles, such as in a kitchen or bathroom, are simple to replace. Be sure to wear goggles to protect your eyes and work gloves for your hands. Spread a drop cloth below your work area and seal doorways with drop cloths to deflect and catch tile shards. Follow the manufacturer's instructions for using adhesive and grout.

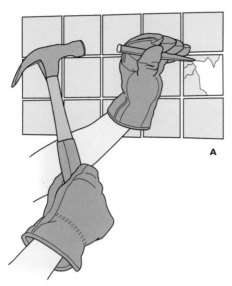

1. Using an awl or a grout saw, scrape out the grout surrounding the broken tile. Fit the blade of a cold chisel into a crack in the tile and tap it with a hammer until tile pieces break away. **(A)** If there are no visible cracks, hold the chisel perpendicular to the tile at the center and tap. Don't use a heavy hand; you don't want to puncture the material behind the tile.
2. Position the chisel blade at an angle and tap the blade between the tile and backing to force out the fragments.
3. Remove any adhesive or mortar with a paint scraper and rough sandpaper (60- or 80-grit).

4. Using a putty knife, spread tile adhesive or thin-set mortar evenly over the back of a new tile. **(B)** Press the tile in place.

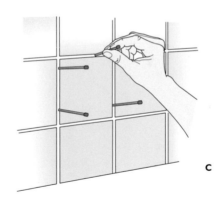

5. Insert toothpicks or pins (2 or 3 per side) into the space around the new tile so it stays centered until the adhesive cures. **(C)**
6. When the adhesive has set, remove the toothpicks or pins and use your fingers to press new grout into grooves. Wait 10 minutes. Wipe away excess grout with a clean, damp sponge.

How to Hang Anything

The key to hanging anything properly, whether it's a mirror, a plant, or a bookshelf, is to use the right anchor for the job.

First, match the anchor to your wall material. Toggle and expansion bolts are heavy duty and good for plasterboard, drywall, and wood paneling. A toggle bolt (**A**) has spiderlike expansion legs that spread against the back of the wall or ceiling, forming a brace that locks the bolt in place. The toggle drops behind the wall covering when you remove the bolt and can't be reused.

Expansion bolts are often called Molly bolts (**B**) after the brand that made them popular. This hanger has a metal sleeve that surrounds the bolt. As the bolt and sleeve are tightened in a predrilled hole, the sleeve expands, wedging itself against the wall material. If you remove the bolt, the sleeve stays in place. Special hardened steel masonry nails are available for working in concrete. You can also buy special anchors to prevent chipping plaster and concrete and to provide a "grip" for the hanger.

There's more to choosing the right hanger: Make sure it can carry the weight of the item. Commercially packaged hooks and other hangers give load recommendations.

To determine the best position for a picture or a mirror, see the suggestions on page 235.

Lightweight Objects

You can use a single regular picture hook to hang an item of 5 pounds or less on a plaster or plasterboard wall.

For an item weighing more than 5 pounds use 2 hooks, which distribute the weight, putting less strain on each nail point.

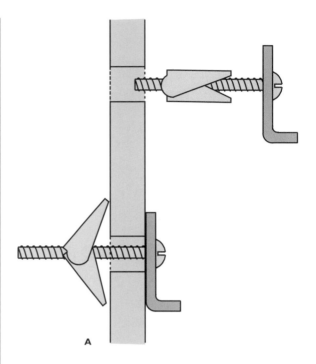

A

Toggle bolts

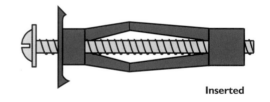

Inserted

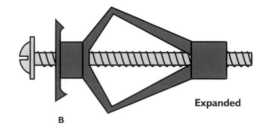

Expanded

B

Molly bolts

Stud Finders

Studs are the vertical framing timbers in walls. Whenever possible, fasten your hanger into a stud when you are hanging a heavy object to give it extra support.

If you live in an apartment building, the studs are probably steel. In that case, you will need metal screws and a drill bit strong enough to penetrate steel. Magnetic and electronic stud finders, available at most hardware stores, will help you locate steel studs. Magnetic stud finders work great for metal studs, but not very well on wood studs because they need to pass over a nail or screw in the stud to work. Electronic stud finders are very reliable because they sense density differences behind wall coverings to detect both metal and wood studs; on most a light will glow to indicate a stud. More deluxe versions also produce an audible tone when a stud is found.

If you don't own a stud finder, with your knuckles or a light hammer, rap the wall continuously, moving horizontally. When you reach a stud, the rap should sound a pitch higher and less hollow.

Here's a clue that may help: The baseboard should be nailed to the studs (although sometimes it isn't). The nail heads may be visible to help you locate the studs.

1. With a spirit level, mark 2 perfectly level points on the wall about one fourth of the way in from both sides of the object.
2. Cover the nail marks with small pieces of clear plastic tape so the nails won't cause hairline cracks.
3. Nail the hooks to the wall, making certain the hooks fall directly over your marks.

Suspended Objects

A screw eye or screw hook (see page 266) is best for hanging a lightweight item from the ceiling. Drill a hole to the same diameter as the screw shaft. Lightly tap in an anchor (a lightweight plastic one will suffice) and thread the eye or hook into the anchor.

Shelves and Other Heavy Objects

Putting up shelf brackets or hanging a big clay pot of geraniums calls for a fastener that can support up to 50 pounds, so consider toggle or expansion bolts.

Drill the recommended size hole for the fastener and insert the fastener into the wall or ceiling.

For objects that weigh 25 to 50 pounds, divide the load between 2 fasteners.

Place the hangers so you can make your drill hole in a stud (see box above). The strength of any hanger is at its maximum when hung at a right angle to the support.

Do not hang heavy objects from a wood joist in the ceiling; that could cause it to bow, resulting in a bad crack.

Putting Up Shelves

The simplest and most inexpensive form of shelving uses slotted metal standards (also called channels), metal brackets, and wood, plywood, or particleboard for shelves. For best results, attach the standards to wall studs and paint the standards and brackets to match the wall color before you start.

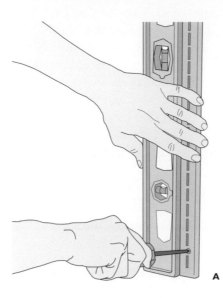

A

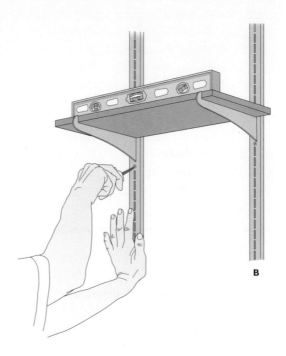

B

1. Start by locating the wall studs with a stud finder (see box, page 281). Drill a starter hole and lightly screw one standard into the wall at the top. Hold it straight and check for plumb with a spirit level. Mark for the bottom screw and secure it with a screw. **(A)** Drill starter holes for all the screws. Drive in wood screws at least 2 inches long.
2. To align the holes in the second standard with those in the installed standard, first loosely attach the standard to the wall with a nail so there is some up-and-down movement. Then lightly fasten the brackets, place a shelf board on the brackets, and lay a spirit level on the board.

3. Gently move the standard up and down; when the spirit bubble is dead center, drive a screw through one hole in the second standard to hold it in place. **(B)**
4. Remove the nail, shelf, and brackets. Check the standard for plumb with a spirit level, adjust if necessary, and fasten the standard with wood screws.
5. Insert the brackets and lay on the shelf boards.

Doors

Squeaking, scraping, and sticking doors are all relatively simple to fix. It's even fairly easy to remove and replace a faulty interior lock set. For exterior doors, however, you may want to hire a locksmith to ensure security.

Fixing Scraping and Squeaks

Straightening, or truing, a door not only stops scraping and squeaking, but also prevents damage to the floor, carpet, and door frame.

Tightening the Hinges
More often than not, a problem occurs when the top hinge has worked loose. This causes the door to tilt slightly down from the jamb, or frame. If one or both of the top hinge halves (called leaves) are loose, remove the screws and the leaves.

For a quick repair, replace the screws with screws that are 1 1/2 times longer. These will bite a little more deeply. Alternately, wipe glue on a couple of toothpicks and tap them into the stripped hole; these grip the threads as the screw is driven in.

For a longer-lasting repair, reinforce the original screw holes with wood dowels.
1. Clean out any dirt or wood shavings and measure the diameter of the hole. You will need a dowel that's a fraction smaller in diameter so it will fit tightly.
2. Insert the dowel in the hole and mark it for length. Remove and cut the dowel on the mark.
3. Dip a small brush in white glue and daub it inside the hole and on the dowel.
4. Insert the dowel so that the end is flush. Clean off any glue that squeezes out and wait until it dries.

5. Drill a pilot hole in the dowel for the screw. Repeat for all the screw holes and drive in the screws.

Shimming the Hinges
If the door scrapes along the floor or jamb, one hinge leaf may be set too deeply.
1. Place a spirit level on the door top to check that it is truly horizontal. If the level indicates a sag toward the floor, the lower jamb leaf is set back too far. A tilt toward the ceiling means the top jamb leaf needs adjustment.
2. Wedge a magazine under the outside corner of the door to prop it up. Remove the offending jamb leaf (see above). Place 1 or 2 sheets of cardboard or stiff paper (depending how much the door sags), cut to fit the leaf, between the leaf and jamb cutout.
3. Puncture the cardboard to meet the screw holes and reattach the leaf.

Anatomy of a Hinge

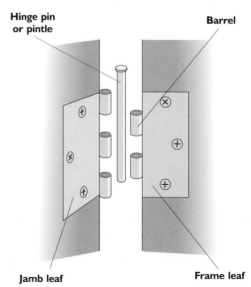

Hinge pin or pintle

Barrel

Jamb leaf

Frame leaf

Anatomy of a Door

While doors vary slightly, most will h284ave the basic parts illustrated here.

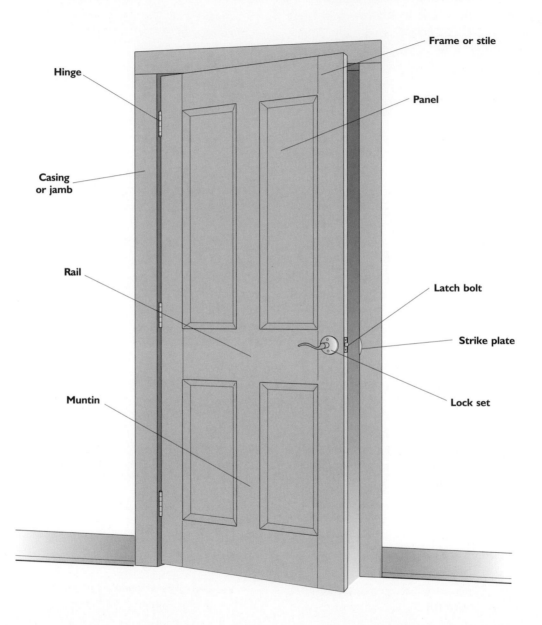

How to Install a Lock Set

Exterior doors need sturdy locks; check them often to make sure they're in good working order. If you need to install a new lock set on any door, here's how:

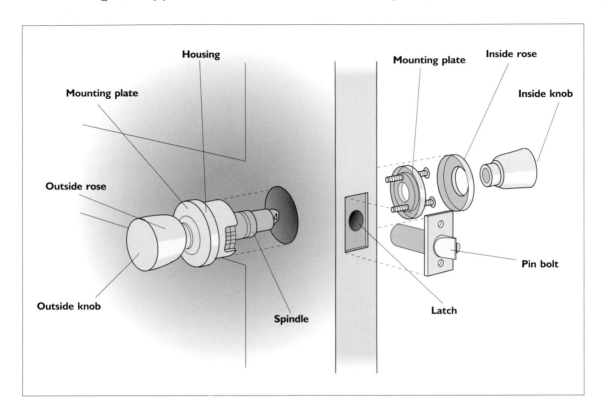

1. Using the manufacturer's template, mark on the door the areas to be cut.
2. Using a drill fitted with a hole saw, cut the back-set hole through the door. Change to a spade bit and drill a hole into the edge of the door for the latch.
3. Match the faceplate hole and the latch hole and, with a pencil, mark the faceplate outline. With a hammer and chisel, cut out this area to the depth of the faceplate.
4. Install the latch in the edge of the door.
5. Push through the outside knob assembly until its assembly engages with the latch mechanism.
6. Slip the mounting plate over the spindle and tighten bolts through the locking mechanism cylinder.
7. Place the inside rose over the mounting plate and attach the inside knob to the spindle (it connects with a spring catch).

Helpful Hints

RATTLING DOORKNOBS

Doorknobs often rattle because the small screw holding the knob to the shaft is loose. Tighten the screw with a small blade screwdriver. A loose knob may also be caused by a bent center spindle—the metal pin through the lock that holds inner and outer knobs. You can take apart the lock set (see page 285), remove the spindle, and try straightening it in a metal vise. If that fails, invest in a new lock set.

SILENCING A SQUEAKY DOOR

Most squeaks are caused by hinges. Here's how to restore quiet:

➤ Support the door and remove one hinge pin at a time. Clean all parts with an abrasive pad.

➤ Lubricate the pin and barrels with a petroleum-based product. Replace the pins.

➤ Sometimes squeaks occur inside the lock or in the latch as it slides past the strike-plate opening. Remove the lock from the door. (Refer to the manufacturer's literature for guidance, as models vary.) Lubricate the lock with an all-purpose oil or spray-on silicone and replace.

 DIY vs. the Pros

METAL DOORS

Many new exterior replacement doors are made of metal. Because you can't plane metal, and it's difficult to drill into, consider bringing in a locksmith if the door sticks or you need a new lock set. A pro will have the specialized tools to handle the job.

Planing Wooden Doors
If after checking the hinges and alignment the door still sticks, you may need to plane it (that is, remove thin shavings of wood from the edge or edges).

1. Make a pencil mark where it sticks. If the door scrapes at the top, stand on a ladder and plane the top, working inward from the outer corners.
2. Using a jack plane, shave only a small amount at a time, checking the fit as you work. Planing too much could leave an unsightly gap.
3. If the door scrapes at the bottom or side, you need to unhinge it. Plane, then sand the planed areas.
4. Wipe up the dust with a tack rag and apply 1 or 2 coats of clear wood sealer. This helps keep out moisture, which swells and warps wood.

Windows and Screens

When windows and screens aren't snug and tight in cold weather, warm air will escape; in hot weather, insects can find their way indoors. Whatever the weather, you can take care of minor repairs yourself.

Unjamming a Stuck Window

When you try to loosen a tight window, take care not to chip the frame or paint. Paint that has worked its way between the sash and jamb is often the culprit. Start by running the blade of a utility knife around all the edges of the sash to sever any existing paint bond. If this doesn't free the sash, you'll need to get a little more aggressive. Try holding a small block of wood against the sash and tap it with a hammer. Repeat at intervals around all sides. (Never strike the sash directly with a hammer—you'll dent the sash and possibly break the glass.)

If the window is still stuck, work a putty knife between the sash and the stop (the fixed wood molding holding the sash in place). Gently rock the knife back and forth, and repeat up and down on both sides and along the sill.

If that doesn't work, stand outside the window and insert a pry bar between the sash and sill at each end, and then the midpoint, to lever the sash open.

Screens

Patching Holes

Most hardware stores carry 2 types of patches to repair small screen holes or tears: aluminum mesh and fiberglass. Clean the screens before patching (see page 46).

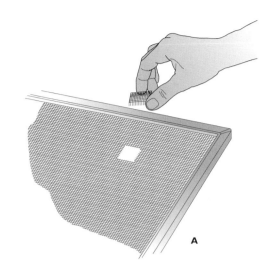

Placing an aluminum patch

1. Using scissors, trim the loose mesh ends around the edge of the hole in your screen.
2. Cut a square patch about 1 inch larger than the hole on all sides.

    a. For an aluminum patch, remove 2 or 3 outside wires on all 4 sides of the patch. Bend down the protruding wires around the patch over the edge of a small block of wood so that these strands are at right angles to the patch itself. **(A)** The patch should look like a short-legged spider.

    Center the patch over the hole and push the bent wire ends through the screen. While pressing the patch against the screen, bend down the wire ends on the opposite side of the mesh, toward the center of the patch.

    b. For a fiberglass patch, simply peel off the backing and press the patch in place over the hole, taking care to align the threads as much as possible.

Anatomy of a Window

While there are various window types—casement, pivot, louvered, and sash—the double-hung sash window illustrated here is most common.

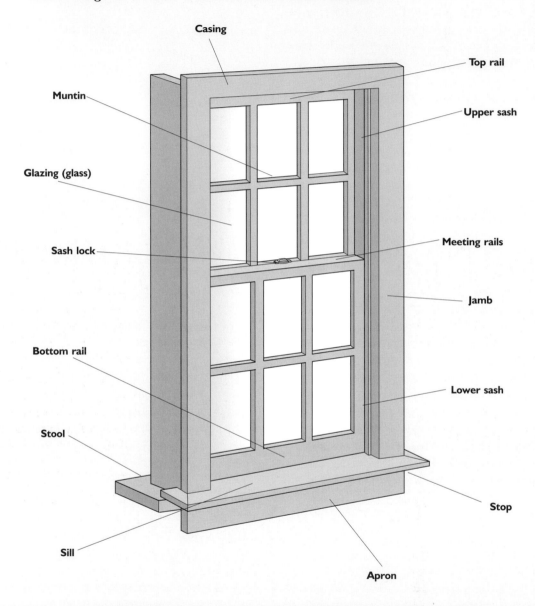

Casing

Top rail

Muntin

Upper sash

Glazing (glass)

Meeting rails

Sash lock

Jamb

Bottom rail

Lower sash

Stool

Stop

Sill

Apron

Replacing Screening

1. Pull out the old screening from the frame. On a wood-frame screen, pry off the molding and remove the tacks or staples using a slotted screwdriver. On an aluminum or vinyl frame, pull out the flexible rubber tubing, called splining.

2. Cut the replacement screen to measure at least 1 inch wider than the frame on all sides. In this way, it will reach beneath the moldings on a wood frame and into the grooves on a vinyl or aluminum frame.

    a. On a wood frame, fasten the replacement screen on one side with tacks and pull it taut and smooth over the opening.

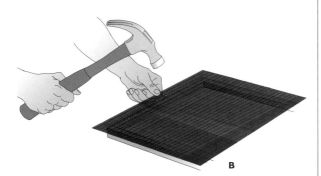

Pulling the screen taut

    Still holding the screen taut (**B**), drive the tacks in at a 45-degree angle with the heads toward the screen center. Repeat for the final 2 sides. Replace the molding and tack into place.

    b. On an aluminum or vinyl frame, place the screening over the opening and secure it with rubber spline and a splining tool. Pull the screening taut over to the opposite groove and, still holding the screen taut, press in the spline. Repeat for the final 2 sides.

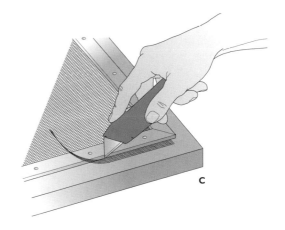

Trimming the edges around wood molding

3. With a sharp utility knife, trim away excess screening beyond the molding or splining. (**C**)

DIY vs. the Pros

DOUBLE-GLAZED WINDOWS

Most new construction and replacement windows are double-glazed (often referred to as double-insulated). Each sash has 2 panes and an insulating space between them to keep in warm air in the winter and cool air in the summer; the space also acts as a sound buffer. The space between the panes in many double-glazed windows is simply filled with air. Higher-tech versions are filled with argon and other gases that insulate better. Because of this, it's always best to let a professional repair your double-glazed windows—not only can pros handle the more complex double-pane glazing, but they can also refill the insulating space with the appropriate gas.

How to Replace Window Glass

Most windows made before about 1970 use putty (or glazing compound) to hold the panes in place. (To replace glass in older windows, see below.) To replace window glass in new windows, consult the manufacturer. Measure the opening exactly, show a piece of the glass to a salesperson, and buy glass cut to size. Use putty or caulk and glazier points to secure the new glass. Work on the outside of the window.

REPLACING GLASS IN OLD WOOD SASH WINDOWS

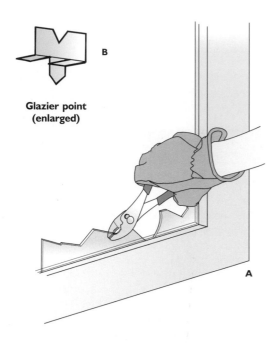

Glazier point
(enlarged)

4. Reinsert the glazier points and gently press them into the sash with the edge of a putty knife blade until they hold. (There's no need to sink them deeply into the wood.) For a typical 10-inch-by-10-inch or 12-inch-by-12-inch pane, 2 points per side are plenty.

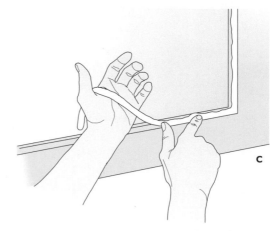

1. Wearing gloves, use pliers to pull out any remaining glass slivers from the frame (**A**) and remove the triangular metal glazier points (**B**) that hold the pane in place.
2. Scrape away the old putty (glazing compound) from the frame with a putty knife.
3. Spread a thin layer of new glazing compound around the frame—just enough to "grab" a newly inserted glass pane. Position the glass in the opening and gently press it into the layer of glazing compound.

5. Using your fingers, roll a 3/8-inch-diameter "rope" of glazing compound, and press it all around the glass perimeter next to the frame. (**C**)

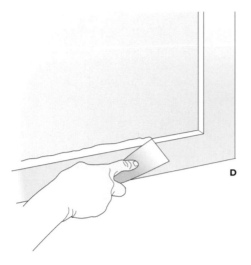

D

6. Smooth the compound by drawing the putty knife along the rope at a 45-degree angle between the frame and pane. (D) Clean off any excess.
7. If the compound doesn't form smoothly, dip the putty blade in linseed oil and try again.

REPLACING GLASS IN OLD METAL SASH WINDOWS

1. Glass in a metal sash—particularly a storm sash—is almost always held in place with a flexible vinyl spline that wraps around the glass edge. Remove the broken glass following the instructions on page 290 and lever out the spline with a slotted screwdriver blade.

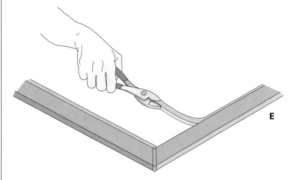

E

2. Once you have one end of a spline out, grab and pull it with your hands or pliers. (E) The rest will come right out.

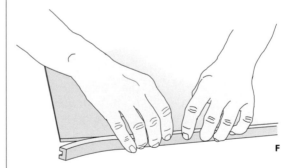

F

3. Wrap the new glass with the vinyl splines. (F) Reassemble the window in the order you took it apart.

Floors

The most commonly used household floor coverings—wood, vinyl, tile, and stone—don't require much special attention, but they shouldn't be ignored either.

Treat your floors kindly to lengthen their life, using doormats and protecting good wood floors with throw rugs.

Many materials also benefit from a protective sealer or wax. Don't leave chipped, peeling, or broken surfaces unattended as floor traffic will only make problems worse—and, in some cases, may cause injury.

Restoring Wood Floors

Wood floors treated with a penetrating sealer and still in reasonably good condition may be restored with a sealer or a reconditioning agent. A sealer won't flake when scratched, as varnish will, because it sinks below the wood surface rather than coating the top.

A floor finished with polyurethane may be lightly sanded and recoated. If possible, use the same brand and type of polyurethane as before; mismatched finishes may show discoloration.

Refinishing

If you are going to refinish (which can be a substantial undertaking), you must remove all traces of the old finish. You will need to rent an upright sander (for the main area) and a disc sander (for the floor edges). Both machines should have dust-collecting bags.

You'll also need sandpaper in coarse, medium, and fine grits (see box, page 273). Wear a paper breathing mask, seal off surrounding areas with drop cloths, and ventilate the work space when you begin sanding.

Board Floors

1. Remove all rugs and furnishings, including window dressings. Thoroughly vacuum the floor. Clean off any wax with a solvent remover.
2. Look for nail heads showing above the wood surface. Use a nail set and hammer to tap them below the surface. An exposed nail will rip up the sandpaper.

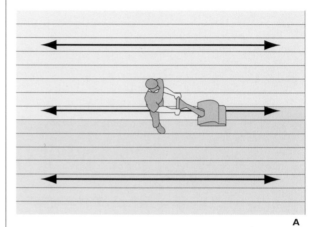

A

Sanding a board floor

3. Carefully remove the quarter-round wood moldings between the floor and baseboard with a pry bar or chisel. If there are no moldings, remove the baseboard. (This also gives you a chance to redo the moldings if desired.) Begin at one end of the room and carefully lower the sanding drum, fitted with the coarsest sandpaper, to the floor and begin guiding the machine across it. Don't stop until you reach the other end of the room. Overlap your sanding runs. Sand with the grain, which always runs the length of each board. (A) At the beginning and end of every run, tip the sander back on its wheel to lift the drum off the floor to prevent gouges.

4. Following the same procedure, make a second pass with medium-grit paper and a final run with fine-grit paper.
5. Use the handheld disc sander to finish the edges. For hard-to-reach corners, wrap sandpaper around a wood block and finish the job by hand.
6. Vacuum the floor and any other dirty surfaces. Pick up any remaining dust with a tack rag. If you're going to stain or bleach the wood floor (see box, page 294), this is the time to do so.

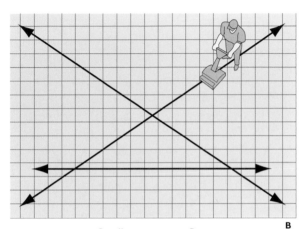

Sanding a parquet floor   **B**

Parquet Floors
1. Follow steps 1 through 3 for board floors. Then run the upright drum sander, fitted with medium-grit paper, on a diagonal across the full width of the room. **(B)**
2. On your second pass, run the sander along the opposite diagonal, across the full width of the room, using fine-grit paper.
3. Run a floor polisher fitted with a screen disc up and down the longest dimension of the room.
4. Finish the process by following steps 5 and 6 for board floors.

Treat a New Wood Floor

If not pretreated, a new wood floor needs to be sanded and finished. Sand with an upright machine fitted progressively with coarse, medium, and fine sandpaper. Then vacuum the floor and wipe with a tack rag.

After sanding, use a paste wood filler to treat oak, mahogany, walnut, and chestnut boards, which tend to have open pores. After the filler dries, sand lightly. To make new pine floors glow, seal the surface with shellac before applying varnish.

Three coats of any finish are recommended. After the first and second coats dry, sand the floor and then vacuum. After the third coat, buff the floor.

Repair Wood Floor Scratches

HAIRLINE SCRATCHES
Unsealed wood: Dip a white abrasive pad (see box, page 273) in pure lemon oil or paste wax. Rub the scratches gently, working with the grain. Polish with a soft cloth.

Polyurethane finish: Hand sand the scratches with 150- to 180-grit sandpaper (see box, page 273). Vacuum the dust and touch up the area with a new coat of polyurethane using the same brand as originally applied.

DEEP SCRATCHES
Hand-sand scratches with 150-grit sandpaper. Coat the scratch with a paste wood filler matching the wood tone, following the product instructions. Before the filler sets, wipe up any excess.

Let the filler dry for 24 hours. Sand the surface with 150-grit sandpaper. When the surface is smooth, switch to a finer grit paper (180- to 220-grit). Apply a finish to match the existing color.

Wood Floor Treatment Guide

To protect a new wood floor, you need to finish it (see box page 293). You may also want to refinish an older floor for a new, fresh look (see page 292). Oil-based finishes require 2 coats; water-based treatments need at least 3 coats. On pine and other soft woods, use a sealer (of the same brand) before varnishing.

FINISH	EFFECT	USEFUL INFORMATION	COST	DURABILITY
Oil-modified polyurethane (solvent-base)	Available in high-gloss and satin finishes.	Easy to apply. Buff first coat with gray abrasive pad, then wait 12 hours before applying second coat.	Moderate	Toughest of finishes, but will scratch. Will last 3 to 5 years.
Water-based polyurethane	Clear; maintains the wood's natural look without darkening. Available in moderate-gloss to satin finishes.	Available in 2 basic types (both require 3 to 4 coats): high acrylic—easy to apply, dries fast; and high urethane—also fast-drying, but harder to apply. Some require sanding between coats; check product label.	Moderate	Both basic types wear well. High urethane slightly more difficult to repair. Will last 2 to 3 years. Less resistant to some cleaners/ detergents.
Lacquers	Produces a high-gloss or matte finish in clear, black, or white.	Very difficult to apply. Hire a professional.	Moderate	Wears well but will scratch. Will last 2 to 5 years.

FINISH	EFFECT	USEFUL INFORMATION	COST	DURABILITY
Shellac	Creates a protective sheen.	Easy to apply. Don't allow to puddle; brush out smoothly. Sand lightly between each of 3 coats. Tends to chip; not resistant to water or alcohol spills, but is easily repaired. Can yellow.	Inexpensive	Wears fairly well but will scratch. Will last 1 to 2 years.
Penetrating sealer	Creates a subtle sheen; maintains the wood's natural look.	Very easy to apply. Penetrates rather than coats wood. Easily repaired.	Moderate	Wears fairly well, doesn't offer as much protection as above finishes. May dull in hard-wear areas; easy to repair. Lasts 1 to 2 years.
Paste wax	Polishes and protects floor finishes.	Easy to apply; must remove old paste wax with solvent-based cleaner before applying new. Buff with a soft cloth or electric polisher once dry.	Moderate	Hard-wear areas need retouching in 3 to 5 months. Will last 6 months.

CARPET COVER-UP

To repair burns and holes and replace stained areas, use a circular carpet cutter, a small can of seam sealer, and double-faced carpet tape, all available wherever carpet is sold.

A

1. **Gently rotate the cutter back and forth over the spot until a circular patch of carpet comes free. (A) Try not to cut the pad below the carpet. Cut a piece of carpet tape to fit the hole and press it into the opening.**

2. **Cut a patch the same size as the removed patch from a remnant of your carpet or from a hidden portion (in a closet, perhaps, or under a piece of furniture).**

B

3. **Carefully squirt a fine line of seam sealer around the edge of the hole. (B) Place the patch in the hole.**

Damaged Floors

Damaged flooring is not only unattractive, but it can also cause structural problems in the long run. A broken ceramic tile or a curled vinyl tile allows water to infiltrate, undermining the subfloor.

To replace parquet tiles and individual vinyl tiles, you'll need just a few simple supplies—a hammer, chisel, adhesive, and grout. Replacement tiles are available where flooring is sold.

Wood Parquet

Wood parquet, laid in squares, or blocks, adheres to a subfloor with adhesive. Most blocks are connected to one another with tongue-and-groove edges.

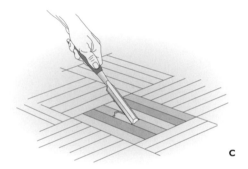

C

1. To replace a damaged block, work from the center out. With a sharp chisel at least an inch wide, cut away the center (**C**), then slide the chisel underneath the block.

2. Tap the chisel from the opened center toward the edges until the mastic bond is broken and the block is forced up. Don't be concerned about breaking the tongues. You'll be cutting them off anyway.

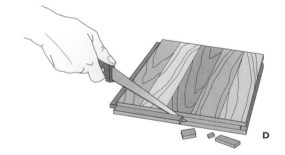

D

3. With a paint scraper, clean up the square of sticky subfloor. Using a keyhole saw, cut off the tongues from the blocks surrounding the open square. **(D)**

4. Lightly sand the subfloor so that the surface of the new parquet block will be flush with the existing flooring. Vacuum the square and rub a tack rag over the surface to pick up dust particles.

5. Make certain the new parquet block precisely fits the open square. The new block will have 2 tongues and 2 grooves. Cut off 1 of the tongues with a keyhole saw.

6. Apply a new coat of adhesive to the subfloor. Brush a thin coat of white glue over the 3 tongueless edges. Carefully fit the 1 remaining tongue into its groove and lower the block into place. Clean off any excess glue and weight the block with several books for at least 12 hours.

Ceramic Tiles

When chipping at ceramic tiles, wear goggles and work gloves.

1. Strike the tile's center with a cold chisel and hammer. Clear away the loose fragments and pry up any remaining tile by tapping the chisel beneath each piece.

2. Using a paint scraper and sandpaper, remove the old adhesive. Drop in the replacement tile, dry, to make certain it fits.

3. Remove the tile and coat the back with ceramic tile adhesive or thin-set mortar; set it into the floor space and, with toothpicks,

Helpful Hints

FLOORING TIPS

➤ **Whenever you have a new floor or covering installed, always ask for at least 12 extra tiles, plus 1 or 2 yards of extra carpeting or vinyl for future patching and repairs.**

➤ **Firmly nailed (tacked) tight-pile carpet is the safest stair covering. If you prefer a natural finish or paint on stair treads, avoid high-gloss finishes; they can be slippery.**

center it. Allow the adhesive or mortar to dry overnight.

4. Remove the toothpicks and fill the cracks with grout.

Vinyl Tile

1. To lift a broken or peeling tile, place a cloth over it and warm it with an iron on medium heat to soften the adhesive. Using a wide-blade putty knife, pry up the tile and scrape up the remaining adhesive. Lightly sand the subfloor and vacuum.

2. Set in the new tile, dry, to test the fit. If it is slightly large, remove it and rub the edges with 120-grit sandpaper, turning the tile so that all 4 sides are evenly shaved.

3. Using a notched trowel, spread new adhesive on the subfloor. Press in the new tile and weight it with books or bricks for at least 6 hours.

Heating Systems

A few simple preventive measures will help keep your heating system in top working order and can save you an emergency house call from a heating contractor.

Get to know the parts of your heating system and whether you have a furnace, boiler, heat pump, or space heater. Read the manufacturer's literature if it's available.

Thermostats

All central warm-air and hot-water heating systems are controlled by thermostats, which you set to the temperature you want your house to be. When the temperature reaches the setting, the heating system automatically shuts off, then restarts when the temperature drops below the setting. The thermostat should be located in a room in which the temperature is stable and the average conditions in your house are reflected. Setting the temperature is a matter of personal preference, but 68 degrees F is considered a good norm. Simply turning down a thermostat 10 degrees for 8 hours every night can save you 10 percent a year on your heating costs. Set it lower for an additional 6 hours a day while you're at work and you can save 15 percent. But who can remember to adjust a thermostat constantly? That's where programmable thermostats come to the rescue (see box, right).

Furnaces

There are 2 basic types of furnaces—gas- or oil-fired and electric. In each, a duct system carries warm air to *registers* in the rooms being heated.

Each fall, ask your heating contractor for an annual furnace checkup to make sure it is in good operating order and burning properly. If

Green and Clean

PROGRAMMABLE THERMOSTATS

Programmable thermostats offer the convenience of automatic temperature control along with the ability to suspend the program and manually control the temperature. Models range in complexity and cost—from simple thermostats (that use the same time and temperature settings that you program for every day of the week) to advanced units (where each day of the week can be programmed separately). More common are models that offer separate programming cycles for weekdays and 1 or 2 cycles for the weekend.

Most models allow you to program 4 different periods per day corresponding to waking, leaving, returning, and sleeping. Many models come preset with a typical energy-saving program, but it's very easy to custom-program it to match your own schedule. Two features to look for when shopping for a programmable thermostat are a manual setting that lets you override the program on days when your schedule changes and a vacation hold. A vacation hold lets you reset the temperature for a prolonged, indefinite period without reprogramming the thermostat.

you have a gas- or oil-fired furnace, have the contractor check carbon monoxide emissions and examine the flue for leaks, which can send carbon monoxide gas into your home.

If you have a gas-fired furnace, open the fire door periodically through the heating season when the gas flames are visible. The flames should be blue. If they are yellow tipped or streaked with yellow, tell your contractor. It's likely the air/gas mix is incorrect and needs adjustment.

Hot-Water Boilers

A hot-water boiler (also called a hydronic heater) heats water, which is sent by a pump through pipes to radiators or fin-tube convectors that release heat into the rooms.

- Before the cold season, have your boiler serviced to make sure it's running efficiently and that there are no air pockets.
- Excessive clanking soon after the boiler is turned on indicates there are air pockets in the water lines running to the radiator or convectors. Release the air by opening the petcocks (small faucets or valves) on each radiator or convector. Hold a glass beneath each petcock. When air stops and water flows evenly, close the petcock. This process is often called "bleeding the lines."
- On newer boilers, an air-eliminator valve is located on the boiler itself. When you have the boiler serviced, ask the contractor to open the valve to release the air.

Steam Boilers

A steam boiler heats water until it turns to steam, which travels through pipes to radiators throughout the house.

This system is often found in older homes. It requires annual maintenance.

- Dirt, lime deposits, and rust in the water tend to make the boiler sluggish, increase fuel use, and can eventually clog piping. Ask a heating contractor to check the system before the heating season.
- Air pockets can also impede the flow of steam to radiators; open radiator vents with a key that should accompany the system so that the air can escape. Be sure to do this when the system is not in use or has been shut down for several hours. Be careful; steam can cause serious burns.

Heat Pumps

A heat pump, also called a reverse-cycle air conditioner, cools air in hot weather and automatically reverses itself in cold weather to heat.

A fan draws air into the unit, where it is cooled or heated, depending on the season, and blown through vents to rooms in the house.

Follow these simple maintenance steps twice a year—before warm weather and at the beginning of the cold season:

- Change the filter.
- Call a contractor to clean the outside coils; they should be free of dirt, dust, leaves, and grass clippings.

Portable Space Heaters

Portable space heaters are small units you can move from room to room to help direct extra heat where it's needed. When buying a space heater, look for units that don't have exposed heating elements, do have an integral guard, can't tip over, and have an automatic shutoff.

There are 2 basic types: electric and kerosene.

Electric: Electric units include the newer fan heaters, which generate warmth throughout a room, and infrared heaters, which heat the body and not the room. Always keep electric heaters away from water and flammable items like curtains and blankets, and do not leave the heater unattended while sleeping.

The more old-fashioned models with electric resistance elements direct heat only to spot areas.

Kerosene: While new models of kerosene space heaters are safe, old ones can be dangerous because they produce carbon monoxide. If you use an old model, do so in a well-ventilated area. Always pay strict attention to the instructions and safety rules provided by the manufacturer.

Always open a window before lighting a kerosene heater. This type of heater requires a source of oxygen, and without a fresh supply of oxygen the heater will use up all the oxygen in the room. Also, kerosene smells bad, and the fresh air helps dissipate the smell.

Fireplaces

A fireplace has 5 basic parts: firebox, hearth, damper, flue, and chimney.

The firebox is where the fire is set, and its floor is the hearth.

The damper is the metal gate between the firebox and the chimney. Open it before lighting a fire. When a fire is lit, smoke travels through the damper and the flue-lined chimney out into the open air.

Before cold weather begins, take the following steps to be sure your fireplace operates properly and safely:

- Check the flue for obstructions such as leaves or birds' nests. On a sunny day, use a mirror and a powerful flashlight to look up the chimney through the open damper. If you see blockage, call a chimney sweep for help.
- Once a year, hire a chimney sweep to clean soot from the flue and inspect it for cracks. You want to be assured that no flame will find its way to your house's framing through a crack. Also, be certain that caked soot, which can cause a chimney fire, is cleaned away.

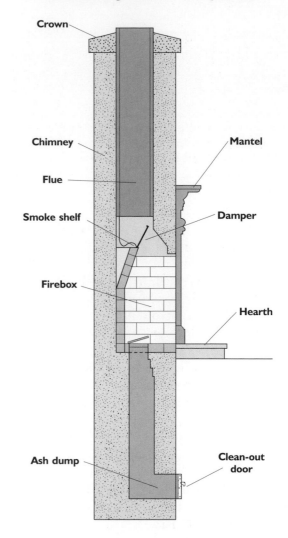

Anatomy of a Fireplace

- If your fireplace has warm-air circulators embedded in the firebox walls, vacuum the ducts at the beginning of each heating season.
- Have any cracks in the firebox and hearth repaired.

Lighting a Safe Fire
Before you lay a fire, check to see that the damper is open. Start with a bed of ashes about 1 inch thick. Over it place 2 or 3 crumpled news-

paper sheets, a layer of thinly cut kindling, and 1 small dry log. Light; when the log catches fire, add another.

How to Buy and Store Firewood

Invest in dense hardwood logs for firewood; oak, hickory, and beech are all prime choices. These burn more cleanly than softwoods, such as pine and cedar, and provide more heat per log. Avoid painted scrap lumber, which can give off fumes.

Most firewood should be aged for at least one year in a dry place outside your home. The drier the wood, the easier it will be to ignite.

Since logs burn more efficiently when dry, shelter outdoor stacks under a waterproof cover that allows air to reach the sides.

Firewood is sometimes sold by the cord (8-feet-by-4-feet-by-4 feet, or 128 cubic feet, or between 350 and 400 logs), but more often by the "face" cord, which can run anywhere from 32 cubic feet to 96 cubic feet. When comparing prices, make sure measurements are identical.

Since harmful insects such as ticks and termites can reside in or on the logs, always carefully inspect logs before bringing them into the house.

Gas Fireplaces

If you like the idea of having a cozy fire but aren't wild about the time and effort it takes to make one, you may want to get a natural-gas fireplace. Using either a traditional fireplace or one specially made for natural gas, you simply connect a gas line, press a button, and voila: instant fire.

 Safety First

FIREPLACE SAFETY

➤ **Do not put colored newspaper (or any paper with dyes), plastic, or laminated items into the fire. They will emit toxic gases when burned.**

➤ **Never burn pressure-treated wood; the gases emitted during burning contain copper chromated arsenate, recently classified as a hazard by the Environmental Protection Agency.**

➤ **Avoid burning softwoods like pine, since their high pitch content can cause chimney fires.**

➤ **Build an easy-to-tend small fire. This is safer than a big, 3- or 4-log blaze, which may send sparks and embers up and out the chimney.**

➤ **Keep a screen in front of the fireplace to prevent sparks and embers from shooting beyond the hearth.**

➤ **Always use fireplace tools to move a log. A basic set includes a poker, tongs, brush, and bellows.**

➤ **Do not leave a fire untended overnight. Douse it by shoveling ashes over the flames.**

A gas fireplace is cleaner and cheaper than a wood one, you have more control over the height of the flames and level of heat output, and you don't need to tend the fire continually. In fact, some gas fireplaces have controls and/or timers that automatically shut them off.

Call a professional for proper installation. Also, be sure to place a carbon monoxide detector nearby.

Cooling Systems

Cooling and ventilation are as important as heating, and there are many systems available, from fans to air conditioners. Choose carefully, according to your needs and the local climate, so you can regulate your home's temperature for both comfort and energy efficiency.

Energy Ratings

The more efficient the cooling equipment, the less power it needs to operate, which saves energy and money.

All room air conditioners have energy-efficiency ratings (EER). To check a unit's efficiency, always note this rating. A rating of 9 or more is quite good.

Central units are measured differently because they generally stay on for far longer periods than room units. They are rated over the entire season.

A central air conditioner or heat pump has a SEER number, which stands for seasonal energy-efficiency rating. A SEER of 10 or more is excellent.

All About Air-Conditioning

There are 2 types of air conditioners: central systems and room units.

A room air conditioner installed in a window cools only the room it is in. Buying 1 or 2 individual room units just to cool spaces used most often is far less expensive than installing a central system.

A central system circulates cool air throughout the house by way of ductwork and vents. Newer units offer whole-house air cleaning or purification systems. There are 3 basic types: filters, ion plates, and ion emitters. Filters such as HEPA filters can be added to the system, but these tend to restrict air flow and need to be changed frequently. Ion plates are installed within the system and are electrically charged to collect impurities. These don't restrict air flow and don't need to be cleaned as often. The highest-tech version of the 3 types, ion emitters, emit positive- and negative-charged ion particles into the room. These ions quickly dissolve and remove nitric oxide (which is contained in tobacco smoke), mold, viruses, and other pollutants. Ion emitters are effective, but they are also expensive.

Before working on either type, turn off the power or unplug the unit.

Room Unit Maintenance

- Change the filter several times during the cooling season. If the filter is permanent, soak it in warm, soapy water, rinse, and let it dry.
- At the beginning of the cooling season, vacuum the evaporator coils, which lie behind the filter (immediately behind the front grille).
- Using a spirit level, check to make sure that the rear of the unit slants slightly toward the ground, so that condensed water flows out.
- Off season, cover the outside of the unit to prevent rusting.

Central System Maintenance

- Change a disposable filter or wash a permanent one several times during the cooling season. If the filter is permanent, soak it in warm, soapy water, rinse, and let dry.
- Once a year, have a professional wash the condensing coils, oil the fan motor with motor oil, if required, and vacuum the evaporator coils located in the ducting above the furnace.
- Check regularly to make sure that leaves or fallen branches aren't covering the fan grille on the outdoor condensing unit.
- During cold months, cover the outdoor condensing unit with a waterproof tarp.

Built-in Fans

A few strategically located fans can effectively circulate air, distributing heat in the winter and cool air in the summer. Fans also curb mildew growth in damp areas like bathrooms.

Attic Fans

Attic fans—installed faceup in the attic floor in some newer homes—can provide comfort during hot months.

The same attic fan can work in 2 ways. You can run it during the day so the fan blades draw warm house air up into the attic, which then flows out through existing attic venting. Or you can operate the fan only at night so it draws cool air through open house windows. If no one

Attic fan

is at home, turn the fan off during the day and keep your windows closed and shades pulled.

For best results, establish the right ratio between fan speed (in cubic feet per minute, or CFM) and square footage of the living spaces. Your fan dealer can help you compute this ratio.

To maintain an attic fan:

- Clear bugs and dirt from the screening over attic vents (generally located either in the gable ends or along the roof ridge) so exhaust air can exit freely.
- Lubricate the fan motor and bearings once each season.

Ceiling Fans

Ceiling fans can help make your house energy-efficient throughout the year. In hot weather, the fan blades draw up cool air and recirculate it around the room. In cold weather, the fan gently forces down warm air. (A single switch reverses the direction.) To maintain a ceiling fan:

- Lubricate the motor once a year.
- Clean the blades and motor housing, which are located directly above the fan-blade shaft, monthly with a dry cloth.
- Check to make sure the blades are securely fastened to the fan arms; tighten if necessary.
- Call for service if the blades begin to wobble on the stem.

Helpful Hints

COOL TIPS

➤ **Switch on the power for the outside unit of a central air conditioner at least 24 hours before turning on the whole system. In that time, a small resistance element warms up the refrigerant, making it flow smoothly when given the first call for cooling.**

➤ **For long-term energy efficiency, plant trees or tall shrubs to provide afternoon shade on the south and west sides of your home.**

Exhaust Fans

Fans are particularly important in bathrooms and kitchens to remove both odors and mois-ture, which can cause mold and, over time, structural rot.

- Simple window units are available; you can also have a wall-mount unit professionally installed.
- Be certain the fan vents directly outdoors. If it vents into attic space, the attic insulation may become soggy.

To maintain an exhaust fan:

- Most new exhaust fans do not need lubrication, but a few older fans do, and they should be oiled once a year.
- About once a year, with a dry cloth, clean the grille, the blades, the shaft, and the motor housing above the blades.
- If the stem wobbles or the fan starts making a loud noise, call for service.

Weatherproofing

If your home isn't weathertight, it can leak as much as a month's worth of heated or cooled air in a year. Check for leaks, especially around windows and doors. Weather stripping and insulated windows are the keys to energy efficiency.

Weather Stripping

Weather stripping seals leaks around exterior doors and windows. It is found in nearly all houses built after World War II.

Old weather stripping is usually made of felt or aluminum, and if it is more than 25 years old, it needs to be replaced.

Weather stripping can be classified in 2 groups: self-stick tapes and nail-on strips. Self-stick tapes are either rubber- or foam-backed with adhesive, and covered with a peel-off back-ing. They are a good choice for metal or vinyl windows where nailing isn't an option, especially where parts press together instead of sliding against one another. Self-stick tapes can easily be cut with scissors and go on in minutes.

Nail-on V-strips are the best choice for sliding parts of wood windows because they don't rely on adhesive to hold them in place over time. Gaps less than 1/4 inch wide and relatively consistent in width are best sealed with spring bronze—a metal flange that's nailed in place and then "sprung" open the desired amount. Plastic V-strips work best between the sash and jambs and at the meeting rails on metal windows.

Plastic and metal V-strips are also used on the header and jambs of exterior doors.

You can also seal the door by attaching a door sweep over the threshold. Choose a brushlike sweep that attaches to the door bottom or a vinyl sweep that compresses between the door and the doorjamb.

Note: Felt weather stripping is also available, but it is for indoor use only—it will quickly rot if it gets wet. It should be used only as a stop-gap measure to seal leaks temporarily.

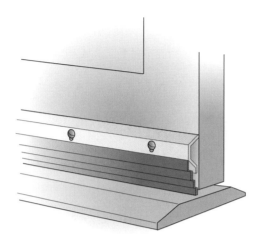

Door sweep

Insulated Windows

Tight, well-insulated windows are extremely important. Among the many energy-efficient options available are:

Storm windows: A well-installed storm window raises the insulating value of a single-glazed (one layer of glass) window between 80 percent and 100 percent.

As window insulating value rises, the need for storm windows decreases. Storm windows may increase insulating value of double- or triple-glazed windows by only 20 percent.

Double-glazed: In this type, 2 panes of window glass sandwich an air pocket, doubling the insulating value of a single-glazed window.

Windows

To make a window airtight, use rubber weather stripping on the top and bottom rails and V-strips between the sash and jambs.

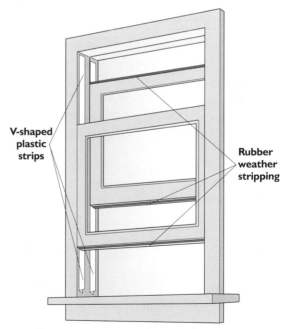

V-shaped plastic strips

Rubber weather stripping

Caulking Air Leaks

Caulks are sold in convenient cartridges with a pointed nozzle at one end. The cartridges fit into a caulking "gun" that presses caulk through the nozzle when you pull the trigger. For best results, use at a 45-degree angle.

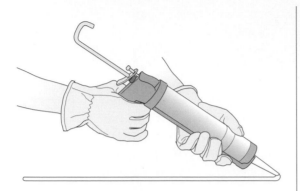

Caulking gun

Many types of caulk are offered in a variety of colors. If you can't find the right color, use a transparent formula. While less-expensive butyl and acrylic caulks work well, silicone caulks are recommended because they remain flexible over time and tend to shrink and crack less.

Some caulks cannot be painted over, so read the label before purchasing.

Caulk in the following places:

- Cracks between exterior siding and window and door frames.
- Thin cracks between wallboard and floors; remove the baseboard first.
- Slivers of air space at the point where piping passes through a wall.
- Along the joint between the wood sill plate and the top of the concrete foundation wall in the basement.

Triple-glazed: Three panes of glass sandwich 2 air pockets, which increases the insulating value by 60 percent over double-glazed windows. Triple-glazed windows cost more, but they also reduce sound transmission.

Low-emissivity glazed: These double- or triple-glazed windows are treated with an almost invisible film. They allow visible light to enter all year but keep reflected heat out during the summer and in during the winter. They are most effective if awnings or roof overhangs block the entry of direct sunlight in the summer.

Low-emissivity windows cost about 10 percent more than the others.

 Helpful Hints

PIPE INSULATION

To prevent freezing, insulate any pipes running through the unheated areas of your house with lengths of closed-cell foam tubes. These are split to slip easily over the pipes. Insulation also stops "sweating" in hot weather, and in time pays for itself by saving energy.

Insulating spaces: You can specify that the insulating spaces between glazing be filled with argon or krypton gas instead of air to further increase the window's insulating properties.

Where to Put Insulation

Whether you live in the North or South, your home will benefit from insulation. The reason is simple: insulation keeps warm air in and cool air out, or vice versa, depending on the season and climate. Good insulation can help you save significantly on fuel costs; here are some areas that typically need it.

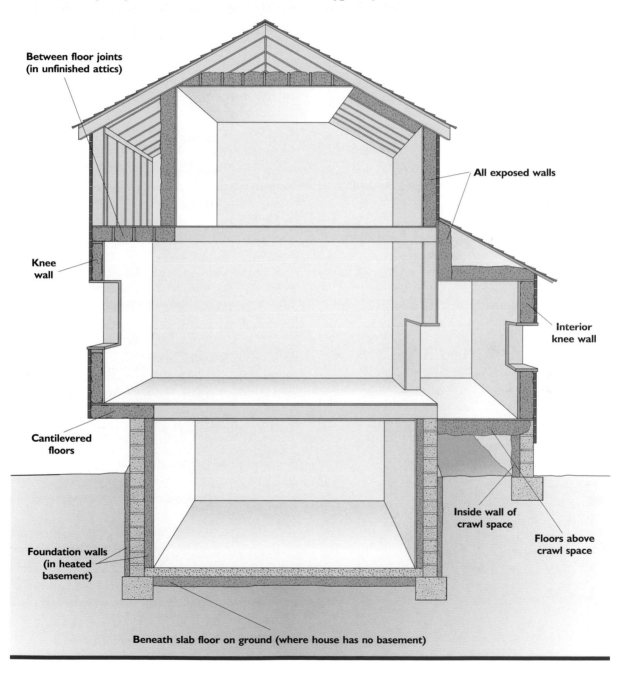

Between floor joints (in unfinished attics)

All exposed walls

Knee wall

Interior knee wall

Cantilevered floors

Inside wall of crawl space

Floors above crawl space

Foundation walls (in heated basement)

Beneath slab floor on ground (where house has no basement)

Plumbing

If you familiarize yourself with your home plumbing system, you can tackle many repairs, such as fixing leaky faucets and clearing blocked drains.

The Basic System

Simply put, plumbing delivers usable water—usually from a community reservoir, a spring, or a private well—and takes away wastewater. You'll find a main cutoff valve that turns the water on and off inside the house near the point where freshwater piping enters.

From the main cutoff, a pipeline branches off

Plumbing Dos and Don'ts

Most common plumbing problems result from careless housekeeping. Even the newest systems need to be treated kindly. Follow these pointers to avoid clogs and overflows.

DO:
- Know the location of all shutoff valves before an emergency arises.
- Protect drains with hair strainers and clean the strainers frequently.
- Keep drains clear of food.

DON'T:
- Pour liquid fat, which coagulates and clogs, down a kitchen drain. Let it solidify, and dispose of it with the garbage.
- Send anything but food scraps down an automatic food disposer.
- Flush anything down the toilet except bathroom tissue and human waste.

to a water heater (the tank is almost always located near the main cutoff valve). Cold water continues on in the original pipe. Hot and cold water travel through these separate pipes to every plumbing fixture in the house.

Each fixture should have its own shutoff valve. Beneath a sink, for instance, there should be one for the cold water line and another for the hot water. Toilets, which don't require hot water, have only one. When it's time for repair or replacement, these valves let you stop or start the flow of water to the fixture without having to shut off the water to the entire house. If any of your fixtures do not have their own shutoff valves, have them installed by a plumber.

Wastewater flows through a main soil pipe (often called a stack) either to a septic tank or to a city sewage system.

A trap, which is a U-shaped bend in wastewater piping, is located immediately below the point where water drains from a fixture (toilets have an integral trap that's part of the bowl).

Thawing Ice in Piping

Ice can build up inside an exposed, uninsulated, cold-water supply pipe during subfreezing weather, causing the pipe to burst.

The first indication of a frozen pipe is a dwindling supply of water from faucets. If you can, check any area where the freshwater supply piping is exposed to cold weather, such as near an exterior wall.

If there's ice inside the piping, the metal will be extremely cold. To prevent freeze burns, cover the piping with a cloth before checking the pipe.

If the pipe has burst, shut off the water supply using the shutoff valve, then call a plumber.

If the pipe has not burst, move quickly to thaw the ice.

- Do not use a blow torch or heat gun to thaw the pipe.
- Wrap the icy area with cloths soaked in boiling water. Repeat until the ice thaws and water runs freely from the faucets.

If you have electric heat tape, wrap the frozen area with it, and plug the tape into a GFCI-protected receptacle (see page 316 for more on GFCI-protected receptacles).

Fixing Leaky Faucets

All faucets work on the same premise—when the handle is activated, a valve inside the faucet turns the water on or off. A leaking faucet or dripping faucet usually indicates that a simple part is worn and needs to be replaced. The secret to fixing a faucet is to know what type of valve it uses to control the flow of water.

Once you've identified the problem, repairing any faucet is usually fairly straightforward and should take no more than 1 hour. Regardless of whether the faucet is located in the kitchen or bathroom, it will be 1 of 5 major types: ball, cartridge, compression, diaphragm, or disk. Compression and cartridge types are the most common.

If the kitchen faucet has a single handle, it's most likely a ball or cartridge type. You can tell which type it is by activating the handle: If the handle rotates, it's a ball faucet; if it goes up and down, the faucet is a cartridge type. For faucets with 2 handles, things get a little murky. If the handle rises and falls as you turn it, it's likely 1 of 3 types of compression faucet: modern, outdated, or reverse-compression. Or the faucet may be a disk type or diaphragm.

Sometimes the only way to figure out what's wrong is to turn off the water, disassemble the faucet, and take it to a home center or plumbing supply store for help.

Or, you could photograph the faucet and show the picture to the clerk at the plumbing supply store, and ask for a diagnosis.

To Fix a Faucet with a Washer (Compression Faucets)

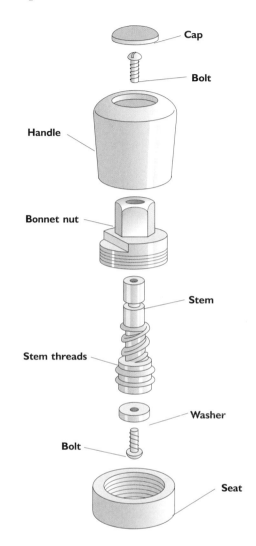

Faucet with a washer (compression faucet)

1. Close the shutoff valve (see page 308) so water won't spurt out when you begin disassembling the parts. As you disassemble the faucet, lay out the parts in order. Then when you're ready for reassembly, simply reverse the order.

2. Remove the screw holding the handle (sometimes beneath a Cold or Hot cap, which can be pried off with a small flat-blade screwdriver).

3. Remove the stem on a sink faucet, unscrew the nut beneath the handle with pliers or a small wrench, and lift out the stem (the working portion of the faucet beneath the handle). On a tub faucet, remove the first nut on the stem; then, using a socket wrench, loosen the larger nut that holds the bonnet (the cuplike metal cover to the tub stem).

4. At the bottom of the stem, you'll find the washer. Pry off the washer (or if it's held by a screw or a bolt, use a screwdriver or pliers to first remove the screw or bolt).

5. Take the washer to a plumbing supply shop. Buy 6 replacements exactly like it. (Next time the faucet leaks, you'll have a washer on hand.)

6. Attach the new washer, and reassemble the parts. Close the faucet to prevent water from spurting through the piping when the water is turned on.

7. Open the shutoff valve. Turn on the water faucet, let it run for a few seconds, then close it. If there's still a leak, call a licensed plumber.

To Fix a Cartridge Faucet

1. If you kept the repair instructions, follow the steps outlined. If not, begin by closing the shutoff valve (see page 308).

2. Pry off the handle or lever cap. If the cap is permanently connected to the lever, remove the screw holding the lever. In some cases, the lever and cap are held in place with a setscrew immediately below the lever. Use an Allen wrench to turn the setscrew.

3. If you see a nut, remove it and lift off the threaded sleeve. The cartridge is below the sleeve. Slip off the clip holding the cartridge in place; it lies at the base of the faucet housing. If you don't see a nut, your faucet has a different fastening system. To unseat it, remove the 2 long screws that go through the cartridge.

4. Slip in a new cartridge, available at hardware stores, designed for that faucet, and replace the parts in reverse order. If you run into trouble, call a plumber.

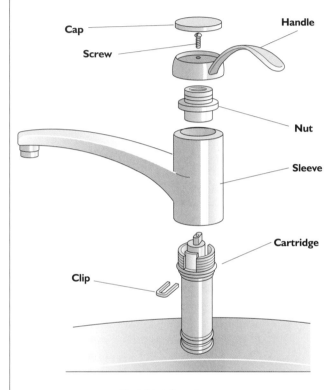

Cartridge faucet

 Dollar Stretchers

DROPS THAT ADD UP

Although a leaky faucet may seem like an insignificant problem, 1 drop every second adds up to more than 6 gallons of water daily—a good reason to make quick repairs.

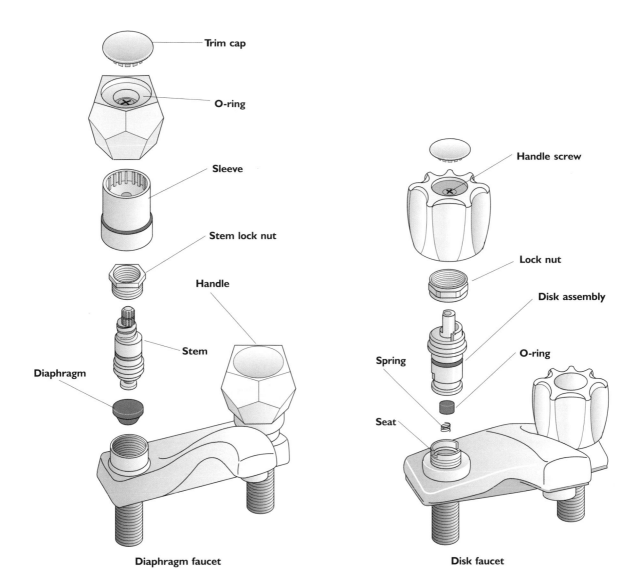

Trim cap

O-ring

Sleeve

Stem lock nut

Handle

Stem

Diaphragm

Diaphragm faucet

Handle screw

Lock nut

Disk assembly

Spring

O-ring

Seat

Disk faucet

 Dollar Stretchers

PURE HEAVEN

Some new faucets offer built-in water purification. Not only does this save you money (you won't have to buy a separate water-purification system) but it also saves space around and under the sink. Add-on purification systems require larger filters to be installed under the sink and some provide separate water spigots that mount to the sink. Both of these are unnecessary with a purification faucet.

Patching Pinhole Leaks

When a pipe springs a leak, turn off the water at the shutoff valve (see page 308). Have a professional make the repair. For small leaks, make these temporary patches while you wait for help. Dry the pipe surface first.

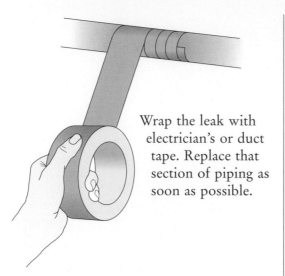

Wrap the leak with electrician's or duct tape. Replace that section of piping as soon as possible.

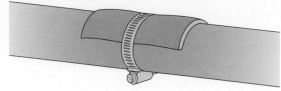

Cover the area around the leak with a section of rubber or garden hose held tightly with hose clamps, available at most hardware stores.

Clogged Drains

If your sink or tub drains slowly or is completely plugged, try pouring a quart of boiling water mixed with 1/4 cup of ammonia into the drain. If that doesn't work, try these suggestions in the following order:

1. If the sink or tub is full of water, bail it out. If your drain has a strainer, remove the screw and lift it off. Pour hot water over the drain to a depth of at least 3 inches in the sink or tub. Cover the drain tightly with the cup of a plunger, or "plumber's helper," and force the cup down hard 5 or 6 times. Lift the plunger to see if the water is draining. If not, plunge again.

2. If the drain is still blocked, the clog is probably in the trap—the U-shaped pipe just below the drain—which often has a clean-out plug at the bottom. The following method applies only to some traps.

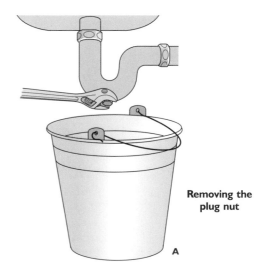

Removing the plug nut

A

Place a bucket beneath the trap. Fit a wrench snugly around the clean-out plug nut and remove the plug. **(A)** If you need to remove the blockage in the trap, use the hook end of a wire clothes hanger.

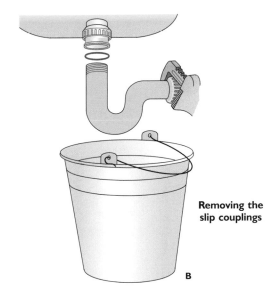

Removing the
slip couplings

B

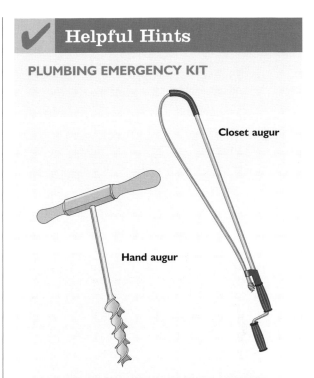

Closet augur

Hand augur

3. If the U-trap has no clean-out plug or the blockage doesn't budge, you will need to remove the trap.

First, measure the pipe diameter and buy several new gaskets (rubber rings) to fit the joints.

Place a bucket under the trap. You'll see 2 large nuts, one at either end of the trap pipe. These are slip couplings. Remove both with a large-jaw wrench using steady pressure so as not to strip the threads, and remove the old rubber gaskets. **(B)**

Clean out the trap and the drain pipe ends with a coat hanger bent into a coil to fit the pipe diameter.

When the trap is clear, place new gaskets on the trap joints and refasten the slip couplings.

4. If none of these solutions work, the clog is beyond the trap and lies within in the pipes. Call a drain-cleaning service.

It's a good idea to make a small plumbing emergency kit consisting of a closet auger (for stubborn toilet clogs), a hand auger (for clearing drain lines), epoxy putty, and a pipe repair kit (available at most hardware stores) for pinhole leaks and burst pipes. You'll be glad you've prepared in advance when trouble strikes—and Murphy's Law says it will at the absolute most inconvenient time, like just before a dinner party or during a family gathering around the holidays.

You can find epoxy putty at virtually any hardware store or home center. It's waterproof and easy to use. Most versions come in a Tootsie Roll–like log that consists of 2 differently colored inner and outer layers. When you cut off a piece and massage the 2 parts together, the epoxy is activated. Then simply apply it to the leak and let it set before turning the water back on.

Anatomy of a Toilet

Whether repairing a running toilet or replacing a tank ball, it helps to know the ins and outs of your toilet's interior.

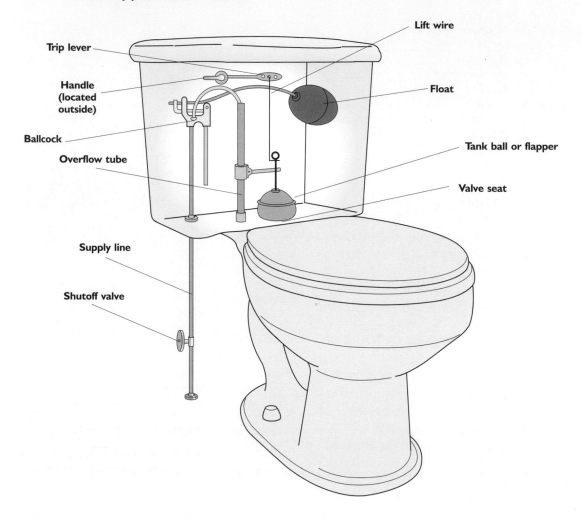

Lift wire

Trip lever

Handle (located outside)

Float

Ballcock

Tank ball or flapper

Overflow tube

Valve seat

Supply line

Shutoff valve

Toilet Problems

Clogs

You can usually open a clogged toilet drain with a plunger. Fit the rubber cup completely over the toilet bowl passage before plunging. Pump several times. If that fails, call a drain-cleaning service.

Continuous Running

Continuous running can frequently be traced to a tank ball or flapper that isn't seated properly in the discharge opening.

Remove the tank top and jiggle the lift wire. The ball or flapper usually falls into place.

If the ball doesn't fall properly, buy a replacement, which is inexpensive and easy to install; follow the manufacturer's instructions.

Less often, continuous running is caused by corrosion of the valve seat, permitting water to seep between it and the ball.

Close the shutoff valve (usually located on the wall beneath the tank), flush the toilet, and reach inside the tank to clean the valve seat with an abrasive pad until the parts work properly.

If water keeps running into the bowl, you may need to replace the ballcock. A ballcock is just a valve—what makes it special is that it's automatic. When a toilet is flushed, tank water flows into the bowl to force its contents down the waste line. As the water level drops, so does the float arm. This in turn pulls up a plunger inside the ballcock, letting water flow into and fill the tank. The water rises along with the float ball and arm, forcing the plunger down to shut off the water. Replacement ballcock kits are available at any hardware store or home center. This task is not as daunting as it may seem, but it does take patience and the ability to follow instructions closely. If you find it too difficult, call a licensed plumber.

Another possibility is that the tank float has

How to Soften Your Water

If you find that soap doesn't lather well in the shower, white clothing takes on a gray cast after laundering, and bathing always leaves a tub ring, your water is probably too hard.

Water is made hard when minerals like calcium and magnesium leach into ground water. Water softeners simply reverse the process by exchanging hard-water mineral ions for gentle sodium or potassium ions.

Water-softening equipment consists of either a single tank or 2 tanks, one for softening water and one for storing salt, which must be replaced periodically.

Purchasing the equipment and replacing the salt on your own is fairly simple and cost effective in the long run. (You will need to have the unit professionally installed.)

You can also rent from a water-softening service company, which will provide the unit, salt, and regular maintenance.

The treated water needs to go only to faucets for tubs, showers, and washing machines. A piping bypass installed by a plumber will send untreated water to toilets, outdoor faucets, and at least one supply of drinking water, if you wish.

sprung a leak. With water inside, the metal or plastic float is too heavy to float on top of the water. Stuck in a sinking position, the float continues to signal the supply valve for more water.

If this is the case, buy a replacement float and install it according to the manufacturer's instructions.

Electricity

Most of us take electricity for granted until it fails. Then the mystery and danger we associate with it often keep us from attempting repairs. There is danger, but if you approach problems with an understanding of the basic elements and follow a few simple safety rules, it's possible to do many small electrical repairs and improvements yourself.

Electrical Safety Rules

Yes, working with electricity can be dangerous. But what you really want to develop is a healthy respect for electricity—not a fear. Fear will only make you nervous and can lead to an accident. If you religiously follow the safety guidelines set out here, you'll greatly reduce the chance of receiving a shock.

The first thing to do whenever you need to work on part of your electrical system is to turn off power at the main service panel. Once you've shut off power, stick a piece of masking tape labeled "NO!" over the breaker or fuse. Then close the panel and attach a tag that warns everyone not to turn the breaker on. These steps can prevent a potentially dangerous situation: You're working on a circuit when someone else in the house realizes they don't have power. They go to the panel and flip the breaker "ON," energizing the circuit (and possibly you).

Even when you're positive that you've turned off the power, use a tester to double-check that it's off (see box, opposite).

Whenever you need to work in or around a service panel or on an appliance or device that's encased in metal, help insulate yourself from ground (an electrical path for the current) by wearing rubber-soled shoes and/or standing on a rubber mat. This is particularly important when a floor is wet or damp. If your basement tends to be damp, purchase a rubber floor mat and leave it on the floor under the service panel. (If you touch a hot wire or a switch and your feet are in a puddle of water, electricity will pass from the hot wire through your body.)

Never alter plugs. Altering a plug to fit an outlet is like playing Russian roulette—eventually someone is going to get hurt. When using a grounded plug—one that has a longer, third "prong," don't be tempted to break off the longer grounding prong so it'll fit into a 2-slot receptacle; that prong is there to protect you. Instead, use an adapter that's held in place with a cover plate screw. Note: An adapter like this will afford ground protection only if the receptacle is grounded. A plug-in circuit analyzer (available at hardware stores) will reveal the condition of a receptacle's wiring; lights on the tester will tell you if the receptacle is wired correctly and whether it is grounded.

For your electrical projects, use only parts that are listed with Underwriters Laboratories (UL), Electrotechnical Laboratory (ETL), or Canadian Standards Association (CSA). These organizations test electrical devices for safety. Check each part and look for the UL, ETL, or CSA label before you buy it.

Install GFCI (ground-fault circuit interrupter) receptacles. These devices monitor current flow and cut off power when it begins to flow where it shouldn't and protect you from potentially dangerous shock hazards. Install GFCI receptacles wherever they're called for by your local code—typically in bathrooms, kitchens, pool area, outdoors, and in garages.

Understanding Breakers and Fuses

Depending on the age of your home, the main service panel will be 1 of 2 types: a fused-based panel or, more commonly, a breaker-based panel. Both are designed to protect your home's wiring. Breakers and fuses are current-overload devices; circuit current flows through them continuously. When too much current flows, the breaker "flips" or the fuse "blows" and current stops flowing. Fuses and breakers can also be used as a convenient way to turn power on and off for repairs or emergencies.

1. Before resetting a breaker or replacing a fuse, try to determine what triggered the power cutoff. Most often, a power overload is the cause. For example, you may have plugged an iron into a circuit already taxed to its limit with lights, a TV, and a toaster.

Testing For Power

There are several ways to make sure that the power has been turned off (or that your power is back on).

A *circuit tester* has 2 pointed leads that you can touch to the ends of the wires or insert in the prongs of a receptacle. It will show (via a light) if there's power or not.

A *receptacle tester* is inserted into a receptacle. It will tell you whether you have power and will also indicate, via 3 lights, if the receptacle is wired correctly—in other words, that the polarity is correct and the receptacle is properly grounded.

A *multimeter* is the most complicated of the 3 testers, and has pointed leads that allow you to test for voltage, measure amperage, and resistance.

Helpful Hints

EASY IDENTIFICATION

Label your circuit breakers and fuses (often called circuit mapping) to show which appliances and switches are served by which fuses. Trip each breaker and loosen each fuse one at a time. Have a partner locate the corresponding appliances and switches that are without power. Write the information on a label next to the switch or fuse. Repeat for all circuits. Keep a flashlight and spare fuses handy.

2. Turn off switches and appliances on that circuit (see box, above), and unplug at least 1 of the offending appliances. If you don't, when you reset the breaker or replace a fuse, you'll overload the circuit again.
3. Reset the circuit breaker by flipping the tripped switch all the way off and then all the way on.
4. To replace a fuse safely, switch on a flashlight, then turn off the house power by pulling down the handle on the outside of the fuse box, or by pulling out the cartridge marked "MAIN" on the panel. Remove the blown fuse (its glass top will probably be clouded and the metallic filament inside the glass broken). Replace with one of proper amperage for the circuit, which should be indicated on the fuse box. Never touch the metal part of the fuse, whether removing an old one or inserting a new one.
5. Turn on the house power.

Rewiring a Lamp

Rewiring a lamp is a straightforward process. Follow the instructions provided here, using "Anatomy of a Lamp" (page 318) as a guide.

1. Unplug the lamp. Remove the shade fastener and lift off the shade; remove the bulb.
2. To remove the harp, squeeze the base of the harp and pull up.

3. Pull off the outer shell and insulating sleeve by working them back and forth.

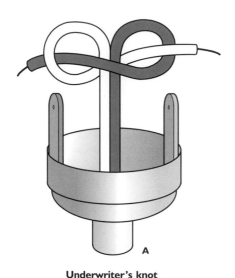

Underwriter's knot

4. Loosen the terminals. Untie the underwriter's knot (**A**) (if applicable) and straighten the wires.
5. Cut off the old plug. At the base of the lamp, splice the new cord to the old cord by cutting off some of the sheathing on each cord and twisting the exposed wires. Pull the old cord; as you do so, the new cord will be pulled into place. Detach the cords from one another and discard the old one.
6. Split the new wire and tie an underwriter's knot to relieve strain on the wire. Make certain enough wire remains above the knot to attach firmly to the terminals.
7. Remove insulation from the wire ends and hook the wires around the terminals in a clockwise direction, one at a time; tighten terminals.
8. Attach a new plug if necessary.
9. Reassemble the socket.
10. Slip the insulating sleeve and outer shell over the socket; reattach the harp and screw down the shade.

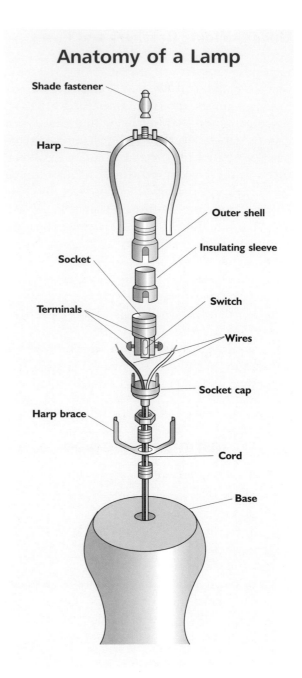

Anatomy of a Lamp

Shade fastener

Harp

Outer shell

Insulating sleeve

Socket

Switch

Terminals

Wires

Socket cap

Harp brace

Cord

Base

Switches

Replacing Switches

Replacing a switch is simply a matter of disconnecting the old switch, then rewiring the new switch exactly as the old switch was done. A foolproof method for this is to work on only

How to Replace a Receptacle

Most new homes are built with 3-blade grounded receptacles or ground-fault circuit interrupters (GFCI). A GFCI will quickly cut off misdirected electricity. You should replace old 2-blade outlets, which aren't grounded. It is especially important to do so in the kitchen, pantry, laundry, and bathrooms—wherever water is used—to reduce the chance of electrical shock.

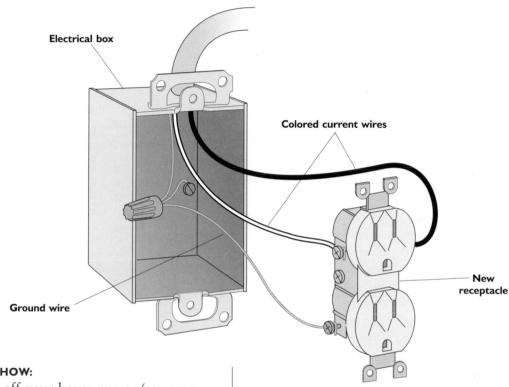

Electrical box

Colored current wires

Ground wire

New receptacle

HERE'S HOW:

1. Turn off your house power (see page 316).
2. Unscrew and remove the cover plate.
3. Unscrew and pull out the old receptacle.
4. Is a green or bare wire in the metal electrical box? If not, stop here: Ask an electrician to run a ground wire to the box or install a GFCI receptacle.
5. If yes: That is the ground wire. It should be secured to both the electrical box (if it's metal) and to the ground lug (or terminal) on the new receptacle. Ground lugs are generally green for easy identification.

6. Observe where the colored wires carrying current are attached. Make a note of their location, then attach wires to the new receptacle in the same way. Note: The terminals on switches and receptacles are colored silver and brass. As a general rule of thumb, white wires go to silver terminals and black wires connect to the brass terminals.
7. Replace the parts in reverse order.
8. Turn on your house power.

one wire at a time. That is, remove one wire from the existing switch and then attach it to the new switch; repeat as necessary.

1. Turn off your house power (see page 316).
2. Unscrew and remove the cover plate.
3. Unscrew the mounting screws and pull the switch out of the electrical box.
4. Replace the wires on the new switch exactly as they were located on the old switch.
5. Replace the parts in reverse order.
6. Turn on your house power.

Switch Types

Although most switches look the same from the outside, they may be 1 of 3 types: single-pole, 3-way, and 4-way. A single pole switch is the most common type of switch used. It controls a light fixture or receptacle from a single loca-

tion. It is easily identified by its 2 brass-colored screw terminals on one side and the clearly labeled "ON" and "OFF" positions on the switch lever. Three-way switches control a light fixture or receptacle from 2 locations. They are distinguishable from a single-pole switch in 2 ways. First, you'll find 3 screw terminals instead of 2—the 2 like-colored screws are "travelers" and the darker (or black) terminal is the common. Second, since these switches can be up or down for on or off, the switch lever has no markings. Four-way switches aren't as common—they're used to control a light fixture or receptacle from 3 or more locations. If your home has large rooms or long hallways, you may come across one. As with single-pole and 3-way switches, a 4-way switch is discernible by the number of screw terminals: it has 4—2 sets of "travelers." Four-way switches are always installed between a pair of 3-way switches.

Roof Repairs

A leaky roof can lead to expensive repairs, so it pays to keep your roof in good condition. All roof materials have limited lives, on the average of 15 to 20 years, but it's a good practice to check the roof annually and to contact a reputable roofing contractor when repairs are needed.

A typical roof consists of rafters (or roof trusses), sheathing (usually plywood), underlayment (tar paper), and tiles or shingles, which form the outermost layer.

The joints between the roof covering and chimneys, vent pipes, dormers, or skylights are closed with sheet metal or asphalt mats called flashing. Flashing is sealed with roof cement.

How to Locate Leaks

Many leaks are not located directly above the wet spot they cause. Rain or melting snow usually sneaks in through a crack drop by drop. Instead of falling immediately, droplets tend to run down the underside of sheathing or a rafter. When they hit a protruding nail or a knot, they fall.

Attic Leaks

Locating a roof leak is next to impossible if the attic is finished. Show the wet mark to a roofing contractor.

If your attic is unfinished, you can check for leaks yourself. On a rainy day, use a strong-beamed flashlight to locate the spot where water is dripping and carefully trace the wet water track to the leak. Mark the spot with chalk or spray paint.

On a bright sunny day, turn off all lights and look over the entire roof for a pinhole beam of sunlight. Mark the spot. Once you find the leak,

Safety First

ROOF SAFETY

If you're repairing or replacing the roof yourself, follow basic ladder safety rules (see box, page 264). In addition, be sure to:

➤ **Work only in mild weather.**

➤ **Never work in rain or high winds.**

➤ **For better footing, wear rubber-soled shoes such as sneakers if you have to step on the roof for a repair.**

➤ **Keep metal ladders away from power lines.**

generously fill the crack or hole with silicone caulk, working from the attic side of the roof.

Then cut a 3/8-inch-thick plywood patch 3 times as large as the hole. Coat 1 side of the plywood with white glue; from the ceiling side, press it over the hole and fasten it to the ceiling with 1/2-inch nails so that it stays put while the glue dries.

This should stop the leak, but keep in mind that a leak is usually a signal that a new roof will soon be needed.

Troubleshooting Roof Problems

Leaks aren't always a result of broken shingles. They also occur when a new roof is improperly flashed or when roofing is incorrectly installed.

To keep track of the condition of your roof, check it over once a year by looking through binoculars from the ground. If you spot any broken, bent, or missing shingles or tiles, or spots of mold, call a roofing contractor.

Anatomy of a Roof

The typical roof consists of these basic parts:

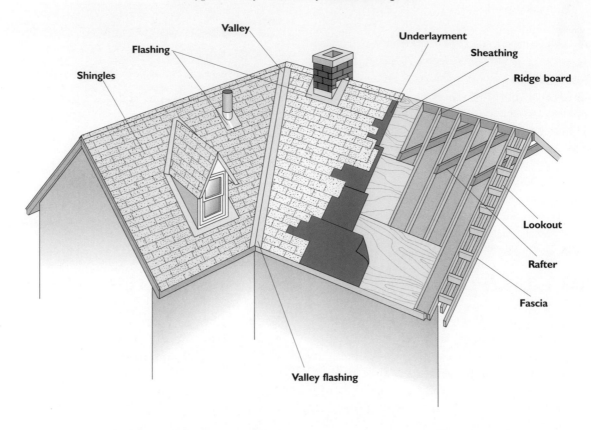

Shingles

Flashing

Valley

Underlayment

Sheathing

Ridge board

Lookout

Rafter

Fascia

Valley flashing

Gutters

Gutters help protect your house by collecting rainwater at the roof edge and funneling it away from your house via a downspout. Without them, runoff can erode the soil around your foundation and eventually cause basement leaks.

Gutters are usually made of aluminum, copper, steel, or vinyl. All materials perform well, but because vinyl gutters don't rust, peel, or corrode, they require less maintenance. Washed and painted as needed, a metal gutter can last for several decades.

At least twice a year, clear blockages.

Scrub all gutter and downspout surfaces with a stiff scrub brush and water. Inspect the inside of the gutter for signs of wear. Patch the smallest pinhole before it grows (see page 324). If a painted gutter is peeling, scrape it and repaint it using a latex paint specifically recommended for use on exterior metal. There's no need to paint copper or stainless steel. For unpainted gutters, apply 2 coats of a waterproofing sealer.

Clearing Blockages

Wet, decaying leaves packed in a gutter or a downspout not only cause blockages, but can also create another problem: Their weight may cause lightweight metals like aluminum to bend or break. Moreover, when evergreen needles and oak leaves rot, they can produce metal-eating acid. Also gutters can become distorted or can break when large amounts of snow or ice accumulate.

Here are 4 ways to clear blockages:
- Climb an extension ladder and remove the debris by hand.
- If you can reach the gutter safely from a window, dislodge the buildup with a broomstick. For snow and ice buildup, pour warm water through the gutter, which should also dislodge any ice in the downspout.
- Stay on the ground and use a special gutter cleaner, which you can attach to your garden hose. You can then aim a powerful spray at the blockage.
- Hire a gutter-cleaning service.

Anatomy of a Gutter

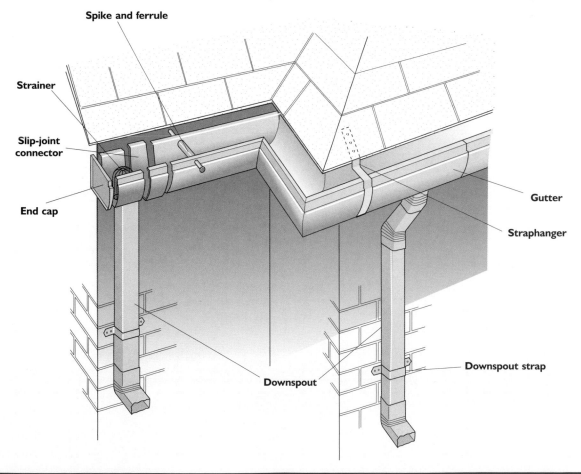

Spike and ferrule

Strainer

Slip-joint connector

End cap

Gutter

Straphanger

Downspout

Downspout strap

Fixing a Leaky Gutter

If your gutters leak, the water could cause damage to your house's foundation. Look for signs of leaks (rust stains on a house sidewall, for instance) at least twice a year. Always clean and dry the area around a hole before making repairs.

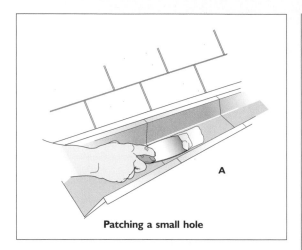

Patching a small hole

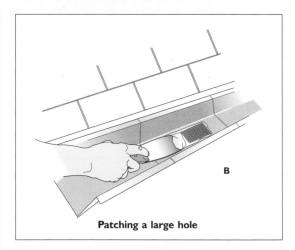

Patching a large hole

Aluminum gutter: Follow the manufacturer's instructions to patch a small hole. Apply plasticized aluminum and spread evenly **(A)**.

For a large hole, stretch fine aluminum screening or heavy aluminum foil into a thin bed of plasticized aluminum around the hole. Then apply a second coat over the screening or foil **(B)**.

Steel gutter: Patch a small hole with roofing cement.

Close a large hole by embedding a patch of galvanized steel flashing in a bed of roofing cement, followed by a layer of roofing cement over the patch.

Vinyl gutter: Close small holes with silicone caulk.

Cover a large hole with a vinyl patch imbedded in plastic adhesive.

Copper gutter: Plug a small hole with silicone caulk.

Embed a new patch of copper in roofing cement to close a large hole. Solder leaks at gutter joints.

Exterior House Painting

A good exterior paint job should last 5 to 7 years. Unless you are experienced, leave major repainting to a professional. But you can do minor touch-ups with the right paint and equipment:

- For wood exteriors, choose a good-quality exterior alkyd for the primer coat and a good-quality exterior latex for the finish coat (see page 198). One coat of each should be enough.
- Buy enough paint. Read the label to find out how much area a can covers.
- Use high-quality brushes and rollers.
- Never paint in rain, drizzle, mist, or fog. This could lock moisture into the paint film and later cause flaking. Nor should you paint in direct sunlight. Paint spreads poorly on a heated surface.

HOW TO PAINT

1. Scrape off all paint that has blistered or flaked. Fresh paint fails quickly when you apply it over a loose old coat.
2. Wash the surface you'll be painting; dirt prevents paint from clinging firmly. Remove mildew (dark green or black stains; often found on the north wall of a house near the ground) by scrubbing with a solution of 1 cup of household bleach to 1 gallon of water. Allow the surface to dry thoroughly before painting.
3. Lightly sand away any old, hardened paint drips.
4. Mask with tape areas you don't want painted.
5. Paint from the top down.
6. When painting, remove tape from masked areas as soon as possible; tape left overnight may be difficult to peel off. When painting window trim, many find it easier to scrape dried paint from window glass with a razor scraper rather than bother with masking tape.

Gutter Guards

A good way to reduce gutter cleaning is by using gutter guards. Buy them at hardware stores and home centers; install according to the manufacturer's directions.

Alternately, you can make your own:

1. Cut heavy screening 6 inches wide in lengths determined by the screening size. (Or buy 12-foot lengths of heavy screening already cut to a width of 6 inches for use as gutter guards.)
2. Wedge a screening piece lengthwise between the outer edges of the gutter (normal width 5 inches), so that the screening bows upward.
3. Repeat for the next piece of screening, overlapping the cut ends of both sections so that leaves don't fall in between.

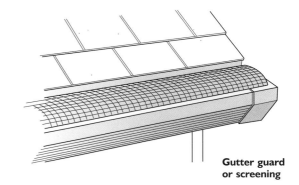

Gutter guard or screening

Contractor Checklist

If you are at all uncertian about how to fix something, hire a professional. However, do so with care: Complaints about home-improvement contractors and professional repair people are near the top of the list of problems reported to the Better Business Bureau and the U.S. Council of Consumer Affairs.

Most of these problems involve miscommunication: What customers wanted or expected was not what they received. These suggestions will help increase the likelihood that you'll be satisfied with the people you hire.

- Spend time getting the right person for your job. Ask your local builders' association or your friends for recommendations. When you have a list, ask your local Better Business Bureau or consumer-affairs office for information about the candidates' reputations.
- Get cost and time estimates from at least 3 contractors. Then ask the following questions:
  - ✔ Do they have a current license? (Not all states require licensing.)
  - ✔ Do they have workman's compensation and liability insurance? (The contractor may sue you if he or she is injured on the job.)
  - ✔ What is their business and/or home-phone number or address? (In case there's an emergency or disagreement about the bill. Also, this may help weed out questionable operators, who sometimes don't have a physical address to give.)
- Ask to see projects the contractor has recently completed that are comparable to yours—especially if you're planning a major job like remodeling a kitchen or adding a bathroom. Ask for the phone numbers of recent customers so you can call for references.
- Review the work-order form or contract to make sure you both understand what's expected. It should include:
  - ✔ A job definition
  - ✔ Starting and completion dates
  - ✔ A detailed list of services and/or materials (size, color, weight, brand name of parts)
  - ✔ The total price or an itemized estimate
  - ✔ A cancellation penalty, if applicable
  - ✔ The payment schedule (ideally, one third at the beginning, one third when half done, and one third when the job is satisfactorily completed)
- If the job includes replacing any parts, make sure you keep the old ones. Label them and put them where you can find them in case you have problems later and need to find out whether the part actually needed to be replaced.
- Don't pay cash. Why not? First, there's no record of the transaction. If you're financing the work, the bank will want a canceled check to prove payment was made (they often will not accept a cash receipt). Second, a check gives you a chance to stop payment if necessary. Third, an unscrupulous contractor could return the next day and say you shorted him on the payment. Also, you'll have a record of the payment with the canceled check. It's always wiser to have a paper trail.

The Yard

Yard and garden work can be a relaxing hobby. Here are some basic techniques and a few handy tools that will keep yard work under control.

Mowing

There are 2 basic mowers: power rotary and reel. Power rotary mowers come in 2 basic styles—walk-behind and rider. The manual reel mowers slice with a scissorslike action and give a smooth cut. While quiet and nonpolluting, they require substantial effort and are suitable only for small lawns.

Improper mowing can gradually ruin a lawn. These rules will keep you out of trouble:
- Mow when the grass is dry. A mower may crush wet grass.
- Mow before you use fertilizer, seed, or pesticides.
- Rake and bag clippings, or use a mulching mower designed to chop blades of grass into bits small enough to reenter the soil as a nutrient.
- Do your trimming before you mow with a string trimmer or edging tool. This way the clippings can be gathered in the grass bag as you mow or returned to the soil via a mulching attachment.
- Use a leaf blower for quick and easy cleanup.

Fertilizing

If you want to keep your lawn lush and green, you will need to fertilize it. In particular, grass needs the nitrogen, phosphorous, and potassium contained in commercial fertilizers.

Contrary to popular belief, lime, or calcium oxide, is not a grass food. It's used to neutralize soil that is too acidic.

If you planted a warm-season grass, wait until

Mowing Safely

Power mowers have a number of built-in safety features. Even so, you should take these added precautions.

DO:
- Mow across a slope rather than up and down when using a walk-behind machine. On a riding mower, up and down is fine.
- Turn off the motor if you need to inspect or work on it. Unfasten the spark plug to double your safety.
- Turn off the motor when you stop to empty the grass bag or unclog the discharge chute.
- Make sure grass is cleared of toys, large sticks, and stones before you begin mowing.
- Keep children and pets indoors when you mow.

DON'T:
- Let anyone stand in the line of the discharge chute. Flying stones and sticks can do serious harm.
- Add gasoline to the tank of a running mower. Turn off the machine, let it cool, and then add fuel.
- Carry youngsters on a riding mower.

summer to fertilize. Otherwise, spread fertilizer after the first spring mowing.

Follow the instructions on the bag to determine how much fertilizer to apply on a specific area. The amount you'll need depends on the dominant grass species and the area to be covered. You also need to check the nitrogen ratio

Mower Maintenance

While the setup may vary slightly, your power rotary lawn mower will likely have the basic parts illustrated here. Use the diagram and instructions as a guide when caring for your mower. If any of the directions require further explanation, refer to the owner's manual.

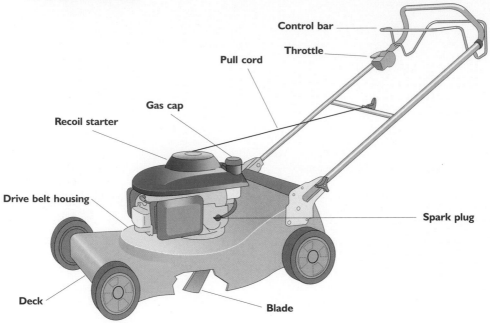

Control bar

Throttle

Pull cord

Gas cap

Recoil starter

Drive belt housing

Spark plug

Deck

Blade

AT THE BEGINNING OF THE SEASON

1. Change the oil (use only oil recommended by the mower manufacturer).
2. Fill the gas tank with fresh, unleaded gasoline.

THROUGHOUT THE SEASON

1. Check the belts and chain drives for wear and tightness.
2. Check that pull cords are not frayed.
3. Check blades for sharpness and clean out debris from under the deck.

AT THE END OF THE SEASON

1. Disconnect the spark plug and inspect for wear and corrosion. Replace if necessary.

2. With a screwdriver or putty knife, remove deck and scrape away hard-packed dirt and grass from the blade, wheels, and the deck's underside.
3. Clean and lubricate the choke and throttle linkages and apply grease to all the fittings.
4. Check the drive belt for wear. Replace a faulty belt that shows cracks or ply separations.
5. Check the blade. If the edges are nicked and dull in places (which is likely), have a professional sharpen them.
6. Reconnect the spark plug, and let the engine run until all gasoline is gone, as gas left in the tank over the winter may clog the motor.
7. Store the mower in a clean, dry location.

in your fertilizer. Nitrogen promotes growth and greenness, but too much can make your lawn susceptible to disease and insects. Consult the grass seed chart on pages 330–332, or review a chart in your local garden shop.

Seeding

To prepare an uncultivated area for new seed, lightly till the soil, removing any rocks. Rake it until the soil particles are no larger than peas.

Spread the seed on a windless day in early spring. Stroke the soil gently and only once with the back of a bamboo rake.

Fertilize and lightly water for 2 weeks, 2 or 3 times a day.

Do not begin to mow until the new grass is taller than 2 inches.

Reseeding

The best time to reseed thinning grass is in early fall, except in southern regions, where reseeding is done in spring.

If water use is restricted, try a seed mix with a high content of tall fescues, fine fescues, and perennial ryegrasses. Otherwise, use the same seed variety you have been using.

Groove the soil by drawing a rake across the

area to be seeded. (New seeds germinate better inside grooves.)

Spread the seed on a clear windless day, then cover it with a light layer of rich soil or peat moss.

Soak the area with water every 2 or 3 days for about 3 weeks.

Grass Seed

All grasses grow well in a balanced soil with a low clay content. To determine the balance of your soil, get it tested by calling your agricultural extension agent: Look in your local phone book under "Government Agencies." Then choose a seed or mixture of seeds to suit your needs. Check with your local garden center to determine fertilizer requirements.

VARIETY	NEEDS	MOWING HEIGHT	GOOD FOR	WHAT YOU SHOULD KNOW
Bahia	Warm nights, hot days	1 1/2 inches to 2 inches	Sunny or partly shady areas	Easy to grow, but coarse and not as tight as Bermuda or St. Augustine; adapts to sun or moderate shade.
Bermuda	Warm nights, hot days	1/2 inch to 1 1/2 inches	Sunny or shady areas	Hardy for southern climates; plant in sunny areas; attractive texture and deep color.
Centipede	Warm nights, hot days	1 inch to 2 inches	Low-maintenance areas	Often called "lazy man's grass"; requires little maintenance and tolerates very low soil fertility levels.
Fine fescue	Cool nights, warm days	1 inch to 2 inches	Shady areas	Attractive dark green color; easily adaptable to different soils; excellent shade grass.
Kentucky bluegrass	Cool nights, warm days	1 inch to 2 inches	Sunny areas	Most popular; hardy; pretty, dark green color; good in sun or light shade in north; shade in south.

VARIETY	NEEDS	MOWING HEIGHT	GOOD FOR	WHAT YOU SHOULD KNOW
Merion Kentucky bluegrass	Cool nights, warm days	$1/2$ inch to 1 inch	Sunny areas	Like Kentucky-bluegrass, but forms a denser growth, as on a golf course.
Perennial ryegrass	Cool nights, warm days	1 inch to 2 inches	Sunny or partly shady areas	Easily grown; coarser than bluegrass; may require reseeding after 2 years. Bright green.
Red fescue	Cool nights, warm days	$1^{1}/2$ inches to 2 inches	Partly shaded areas	Adaptable and undemanding; grows in sun, light shade; tends to be somewhat coarse.
St. Augustine	Warm nights, hot days	2 inches to 3 inches	Sunny or shady areas	For southern climates; dark green and coarser than Bermuda, but adaptable to sun or shade.
Tall fescue	Cool nights, warm days	1 inch to 3 inches	Sunny or shady areas	Not for fine lawns, but good for areas where growing other grasses is a problem. Does best in sunny areas; coarse.

(continued on next page)

(continued from previous page)

VARIETY	NEEDS	MOWING HEIGHT	GOOD FOR	WHAT YOU SHOULD KNOW
Zoysia	Warm nights, hot days	1 inch to 2 inches	Sunny or partly shady areas	Slow grower, but one of the most attractive varieties of southern grasses; requires little attention; adapts to sun, light shade. Tough; best cut with a reel mower.

Basic Gardening Tools

Start with a few basic tools that will help with the most basic garden chores. The best tools have wooden handles and one-piece solid-socket steel attachments. Handle tools safely. Clean, dry, and put them away after use. Store them indoors to avoid rust.

Claw or hand fork: For digging small amounts of soil and cultivating the ground before planting.
Gloves: For protecting hands against thorns, poison ivy, etc.
Hedge shears: Long-handled shears for trimming hedges and small shrubs.
Hoe: For turning soil.
Hose: For lawn sprinklers, extended watering, and reaching into difficult places.
Lopping shears: Long-handled shears for pruning limbs 1½ inches to 2 inches in diameter.

Pruners: For pruning branches or cutting back woody plants, such as roses.

Rake (fan): For moving leaves or grass.

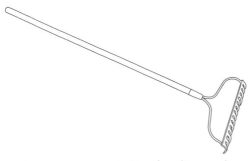

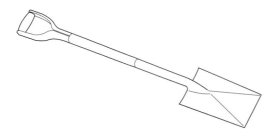

Rake (squareback): For leveling sod clumps or smoothing garden soil.
Shears: For cutting flowers and small branches.
Shovel: Cupped blade with rounded point for scooping and moving soil and loose materials, and for digging holes.

Spade: For digging and moving small amounts of earth, pebbles, or mulch. For transplanting and/or splitting perennials.
Spading fork: Four-tined fork for cultivating, loosening, and aerating soil.
Sprinkler: For even watering; attaches to the hose.

Trowel: For making small planting holes.
Watering can: For light sprinkling.
Wheelbarrow: For moving plants or weeds, soil, stones, bags of fertilizer.

 Safety First

UPROOTING POISON IVY

➤ **Wear a hat, gloves with long cuffs, a long-sleeved shirt, work pants, long socks, and sneakers.**

➤ **Work on a windless day. Use a spade or trowel to loosen dirt around the plants, then pull the plant stem up from the base. Pack the uprooted plants in a plastic bag, seal tightly, and dispose with your trash.**

➤ **Remove and wash your clothes, including your sneakers. Take a shower and use plenty of soap.**

➤ **Never burn poison ivy. Smoke from the fire will absorb and carry itch-inducing chemicals.**

Weed Killers

If weeds such as crabgrass crowd out your grass, attack them the next spring. Wait until the dandelions bloom, then spread a "weed-and-feed" mix, available at garden shops—most are inorganic. There are 2 types of weed-and-feed mixes—wet and dry. Both work well.

Apply a wet mix with a hose-end sprayer on a windless day. Hold the hose end at knee level and point it toward the grass. Avoid overspraying, which can kill flowers and shrubs.

Spread a dry mix on a windless day, and soak the mix into the soil with a good watering.

Do not apply weed-and-feed mixes when there is no apparent threat of weeds. The weed killer is potent, and repeated applications could kill the lawn.

Many homeowners worry about using weed killers, fertilizers, pesticides, and other chemically based concoctions because they contain toxins. To avoid them, you can use organic, nonchemical weed killers and fertilizers. New grass varieties, more resistant to weeds and insects, also lessen the need for weed killers.

A Seasonal Guide to Lawn Maintenance

Different types of weather mean different types of treatment for your lawn, which demands the most attention during warm months. Always use a sharp mower blade, since a dull blade damages the grass. Both rotary and reel mower blades are tricky to sharpen; get a mower-repair shop to do the job. Check the mower instructions if you're not sure how to raise and lower the blade.

SPRING

Dethatch: If you haven't dethatched your lawn within the last 3 years, do so now. Thatch is made up primarily of dead grass clippings that over time have become packed tightly between new blades of grass. A layer more than 1/2 inch deep impedes water and nutrients from reaching grass roots, and that's the cause of the majority of lawn problems.

You can rent a power dethatcher, buy a dethatching blade for your rotary power mower, or use a dethatching rake. Gather all loosened thatch and deposit it in the trash or on a compost pile.

Roll: Take one pass with a roller to help press the crowns back into the soil. If the ground is wet, rolling also smooths out frost bumps.

Mow lower: For the first spring cut, set the mower blade low but not so low that new plants are damaged. Cut from 1/2 to 2/3 of the new grass blade. A low cut makes the first spread of fertilizer and weed killer more effective.

Test the soil: Before fertilizing, which should be done after the first spring mowing, get a soil test. Do not overfertilize, which can burn out the root system. Add lime if the soil is in need of higher alkalinity, which the soil test will determine.

Water: Begin watering the lawn regularly immediately after the last frost. Do so between late morning and early afternoon. Watering in the evening encourages the growth of fungi. Soak the lawn.

Reseed: Spread new seed and weed killers after fertilizing.

SUMMER

Mow regularly: When the grass grows quickly, mow every few days. Mow grass in shaded and slower growing areas every week or two.

If water use is restricted in your community, let the grass grow taller for better protection from the heat.

If the grass turns brown, don't mow, but get rid of all weeds. (Sun-browned grass is often dormant, not dead.)

AUTUMN

Final mowing: Cut low on the last mowing of the growing season, and rake up the cuttings. This discourages insects and bacteria that thrive in the tall blades during the winter.

Reseed: If you intend to reseed, try to do so in the fall (for exceptions, see page 329).

Home Pest Control

Pests both indoors and out can do real damage, so inspect periodically to catch problems before it's too late. The following remedies are alternatives to chemical treatments. Most are essentially nontoxic and have minimal environmental impact. If pest problems persist, however, call in a reliable exterminator.

INSECTS

PEST	NASTY HABITS	WHAT TO DO
Ants	Invade kitchen cabinets, counters	Set out traps or bait containing boric acid. Pour boiling water into nest.
Carpenter ants	Bore into moist wood	Treat holes with boric acid. Check for structural damage and repair.
Carpet beetles	Larvae eat wool, fur	Have rugs professionally cleaned once a year. Dry-clean wools, furs; store in sealed containers.
Cockroaches	Invade kitchens and bathrooms; eat paste in book bindings	Spread pyrethrum (made from chrysanthemum blossoms); or use mix of $1/3$ borax, $1/3$ cornmeal, $1/3$ flour, dash of powdered sugar.
Houseflies	Buzz annoyingly and bite; can transmit disease	Secure screening; swat flies where they land and disinfect spot; use fly traps.
Mosquitoes	Buzz annoyingly and bite; can transmit disease	Secure screening; hang insect pest strips; use hair spray to stiffen wings, then kill.
Moths	Eat wool, fur, any clothes with stains	Have rugs professionally cleaned once a year. Dry-clean wools, furs, clothes before storage; store in sealed containers.
Silverfish	Eat paste in book bindings; invade damp areas, such as basements and bathrooms	Keep a dry basement; spread out pyrethrum (see Cockroaches).
Termites	Eat wood; can weaken house frame to point of collapse	Look for $1/2$-inch-wide mud tunnels along foundation; scrape them off. Fill with fresh dirt. Check for structural damage and repair.

(continued on next page)

The following precautions should help keep out pesky animals. If any do get into your home, call a professional game warden or exterminator for help.

PEST	NASTY HABITS	WHAT TO DO
Birds	Leave droppings; bring in fleas, other insects	Close all attic and basement access with strong screening after birds have gone.
Deer	Raid gardens; carry ticks, rabies	Secure garbage containers; place netting over plants.
Mice	Eat food scraps; travel through wall cavities; can bite if cornered; droppings can cause meningitis	Set traps.
Opossums	Get into garbage, bird feeders, and pet food; also work their way into basements, attics, sheds, and garages	Set traps; close openings in structures.
Raccoons	Nest in fireplaces; steal food; carry rabies	Close all attic, basement, and chimney access with strong screening after raccoons have gone.
Squirrels	May nest in attic insulation; leave droppings; can bite if cornered.	Close all attic and basement access with strong screening after squirrels have gone.

If you do use chemical products in your yard:
- Wear goggles and a nose and mouth mask while spraying or spreading fertilizers or pesticides.
- Read labels and follow instructions exactly.
- Keep pets and children away while you are working with any chemical.

Snowblowers

If you live in a climate that gets a lot of snow, a snowblower may be a good investment. Not only will a snowblower clear out the white stuff faster than a shovel, you'll also avoid the back pain that often accompanies snow removal.

There are 2 types of snowblowers: electric and gas. An electric-powered snowblower plugs into a standard outlet. Less expensive than a gas-powered snowblower, it also requires less maintenance. However, electric models are less powerful and their reach is limited to the length of the cord.

A gas-powered snowblower is better for long distances and can throw snow farther. However,

Insect-Borne Disease

- Deer ticks transmit Lyme disease, which usually begins with an enlarged bite or bull's-eye rash, fever, tiredness, headache, and stiff, achy joints. If you have any of these symptoms, particularly if you live in a wooded area where deer and ticks thrive, call your doctor. Antibiotics can be an effective treatment.
- A species of mosquito carries and transmits the West Nile virus. Symptoms are mild fever, headache, and body aches. West Nile encephalitis or menin-

gitis symptoms include headache, high fever, neck stiffness, stupor, disorientation, tremors, convulsions, muscle weakness, coma, and paralysis. It's estimated that only 1 in 150 people infected with West Nile virus will develop a more severe form of the disease. A blood test can confirm infection. There is no known treatment. For information call the Centers for Disease Control and Prevention, 800-311-3435.

you'll need to maintain the snowblower (follow the user's manual to clean the spark plugs, adjust the carburetor, and so on) and deal with occasional clogs. Since gas is involved, refer to the manufacturer's manual to avoid a fire or carbon monoxide hazard.

Preparing for Winter

Taking care of your house is a year-round process. Cold weather, however, calls for special jobs:
- Service your furnace (see page 298).
- Weather-strip leaky windows and doors (see pages 304–305).
- Check chimney flues (see page 300).
- Insulate water pipes against freeze-ups, as needed (see box, page 306).
- Stock firewood (see page 301).

 Helpful Hints

DON'T GET SNOWED

➤ Just before an expected snowfall, spread sand, rock salt, or cat litter on steps, sidewalks, and driveway to prevent snow from sticking.

➤ Use a rubber-tipped floor squeegee to remove light snow from porches and stairs. It's quicker than sweeping or shoveling and won't scratch paint surfaces.

➤ To keep snow from sticking to your shovel, coat both sides with salad oil, cooking spray, or any household wax.

➤ To avoid pulling a back or shoulder muscle, use a small shovel or fill only half of a large one.

➤ Consider replacing your old shovel with one of the new ergonomic designs that require less bending and make it easier to lift a full shovel.

➤ When heavy snows are forecast, shovel in stages as every 2 inches to 3 inches accumulate; waiting until it stops snowing can strain either your back, the snowblower, or both.

MANAGING YOUR MONEY EFFICIENTLY GETTING CREDIT HOW LONG SHOULD YOU KEEP YOUR FINANCIAL RECORDS? FRAUD AND IDENTITY THEFT MANAGING YOUR MONEY EFFICIENTLY GETTING CREDIT HOW LONG SHOULD YOU KEEP YOUR FINANCIAL RECORDS? FRAUD AND IDENTITY THEFT MANAGING YOUR MONEY EFFICIENTLY GETTING CREDIT HOW LONG SHOULD YOU KEEP YOUR FINANCIAL RECORDS? FRAUD AND IDENTITY THEFT MANAGING YOUR MONEY EFFICIENTLY GETTING CREDIT HOW LONG SHOULD YOU KEEP YOUR FINANCIAL RECORDS? FRAUD AND IDENTITY THEFT MANAGING YOUR MONEY EFFICIENTLY GETTING CREDIT HOW LONG SHOULD YOU KEEP YOUR FINANCIAL RECORDS? FRAUD AND IDENTITY THEFT MANAGING YOUR MONEY EFFICIENTLY GETTING CREDIT HOW LONG SHOULD YOU KEEP YOUR FINANCIAL RECORDS? FRAUD AND IDENTITY THEFT MANAGING YOUR MONEY EFFICIENTLY GETTING CREDIT HOW LONG SHOULD YOU KEEP YOUR FINANCIAL RECORDS? FRAUD AND IDENTITY THEFT MANAGING YOUR MONEY EFFICIENTLY GETTING CREDIT HOW LONG SHOULD YOU KEEP YOUR FINANCIAL RECORDS? FRAUD AND IDENTITY THEFT MANAGING YOUR MONEY EFFICIENTLY GETTING CREDIT HOW LONG SHOULD YOU KEEP YOUR FINANCIAL RECORDS? FRAUD AND IDENTITY THEFT MANAGING YOUR MONEY EFFICIENTLY GETTING CREDIT HOW LONG SHOULD YOU KEEP YOUR FINANCIAL RECORDS? FRAUD AND IDENTITY THEFT MANAGING YOUR MONEY EFFICIENTLY GETTING CREDIT HOW LONG SHOULD YOU KEEP YOUR FINANCIAL RECORDS? FRAUD AND IDENTITY THEFT MANAGING YOUR MONEY EFFICIENTLY GETTING CREDIT HOW LONG SHOULD YOU KEEP YOUR FINANCIAL RECORDS? FRAUD AND IDENTITY THEFT MANAGING YOUR MONEY EFFICIENTLY GETTING CREDIT HOW LONG SHOULD YOU KEEP YOUR FINANCIAL RECORDS? FRAUD AND IDENTITY THEFT MANAGING YOUR MONEY EFFICIENTLY GETTING CREDIT HOW LONG SHOULD YOU KEEP YOUR FINANCIAL RECORDS? FRAUD AND IDENTITY THEFT MANAGING YOUR MONEY EFFICIENTLY GETTING CREDIT HOW LONG SHOULD YOU KEEP YOUR FINANCIAL RECORDS? FRAUD AND IDENTITY THEFT MANAGING YOUR MONEY EFFICIENTLY GETTING CREDIT HOW LONG SHOULD YOU KEEP YOUR FINANCIAL RECORDS? FRAUD AND IDENTITY THEFT MANAGING YOUR MONEY EFFICIENTLY GETTING CREDIT HOW LONG SHOULD YOU KEEP YOUR FINANCIAL RECORDS? FRAUD AND IDENTITY THEFT MANAGING YOUR MONEY EFFICIENTLY GETTING CREDIT HOW LONG SHOULD YOU KEEP YOUR FINANCIAL RECORDS? FRAUD AND IDENTITY THEFT MANAGING YOUR MONEY EFFICIENTLY GETTING CREDIT HOW LONG SHOULD YOU KEEP YOUR FINANCIAL RECORDS? FRAUD AND IDENTITY THEFT MANAGING YOUR MONEY EFFICIENTLY GETTING CREDIT HOW LONG SHOULD YOU KEEP YOUR FINANCIAL RECORDS? FRAUD AND IDENTITY THEFT MANAGING YOUR MONEY EFFICIENTLY GETTING CREDIT HOW LONG SHOULD YOU KEEP YOUR FINANCIAL RECORDS? FRAUD AND IDENTITY THEFT MANAGING YOUR MONEY EFFICIENTLY GETTING CREDIT HOW LONG SHOULD YOU KEEP YOUR FINANCIAL RECORDS? FRAUD AND IDENTITY THEFT MANAGING YOUR MONEY EFFICIENTLY GETTING CREDIT HOW LONG SHOULD YOU KEEP YOUR FINANCIAL RECORDS? FRAUD AND IDENTITY THEFT MANAGING YOUR MONEY EFFICIENTLY GETTING CREDIT HOW LONG SHOULD YOU KEEP YOUR FINANCIAL RECORDS? FRAUD AND IDENTITY THEFT MANAGING YOUR MONEY CIENT

CHAPTER

7

Home Finances

Money may make the world go 'round, but it won't do you any good if you don't know how to handle it properly. This chapter teaches you the basics—and importance—of sound home finance. You'll learn how to make a household budget, designed with your particular financial goals in mind. You'll also discover ways to pay bills online, how to use credit to your advantage, the right ways to organize your financial files, where to keep your financial records (and for how long), and advice on staying safe in this age of identity theft. You'll even discover how to shop safely online and protect financial files on your computer. In short, this chapter will provide you with the keys to keeping your household running smoothly.

Managing Your Money Efficiently

Running a household smoothly means taking control of your time, your budget, and your paperwork. The key to financial control is organization.

Planning ahead for large expenditures will save both time and money in the long run—but make sure you actually follow through. A few simple budgets and some good filing systems—paper, and perhaps electronic—can be a surprising help.

Making a Budget

The first step in managing your money is to examine closely where it goes. The best way to do this is to make a budget—then stick to it (see sample budget, page 342). But before making that budget, you'll want to create an overview of your financial needs. Think of them in terms of simple, concrete goals—basic, everyday, short-term goals and more ambitious, long-term goals. You may find financial software helpful in creating a budget.

Basic Goals
Solvency: Aim to have enough income to cover your current yearly expenses— without going into debt or having to borrow (except for such serious expenses as a major home renovation, sending a child to college, or buying a home or a car).

Emergency reserve: It's always wise to have credit cards, a line of bank credit (perhaps a home equity credit line), or funds set aside in a bank account or money market mutual fund to cover unexpected bills; if possible, reserve at least 3 to 6 months' income.

Risk protection: While no one likes to plan for the worst, it's essential to have insurance protecting against financial loss due to long-term illness, disability, property damage, liability, or premature death. After all, anyone who is now depending on your income will need it no matter what happens to you, and if something cata-

strophic happens to your home or belongings, you'll want to be able to replace them easily.

Long-Term Goals
Home ownership: A home won't necessarily make you rich, but houses, condominiums, and cooperative apartments tend to grow in value over the long term. Also, few other investments offer the opportunity to boost their value while you get day-to-day enjoyment from them. What's more, you need to pay only a fraction of a home's price to buy it. Once you purchase the property, you can borrow against it and resell it, ideally for a profit.

Investment plans: Investing money in financial plans like IRAs or Keoghs, 401(k)s, 529 savings plans, mutual funds, savings bonds, and stocks lets you build savings for retirement or for major expenses, such as a child's education.

Estate plan: The best way to ensure the transfer of your property and valuables to the people you wish after you die is to have a lawyer draw up a will. You may also want to set up trust funds for your beneficiaries.

Month-by-Month Planning

For many people, a monthly budget is a smart way to manage finances because so many basic (essential) expenses, like rent and mortgage and car payments, are billed monthly. Such expenses are called fixed expenses because the amounts are always the same (an adjustable mortgage, however, may have monthly payments that fluctuate).

Variable expenses are also essential, such as groceries, utilities, and medical care, but are not set amounts month to month. It helps to break these out from fixed expenses because you must estimate them.

Discretionary expenditures are those you choose to make, but aren't absolutely essential,

✔ Helpful Hints

Any of these situations may alert you that it's time to take a closer look at your spending and make some adjustments:

➤ **You're going to the ATM (automatic teller machine) more often than usual to withdraw cash, or you're taking out more money from the ATM than in the past.**

➤ **Your bank statement balance is considerably lower than last month's balance.**

➤ **The amount you owe on your credit cards is significantly higher than the amount on last month's bills.**

➤ **You're paying only the minimum amount required on your credit cards.**

➤ **Your monthly credit card and loan payments (excluding mortgages and car loans) exceed 20 percent of your pay after taxes.**

➤ **You hold more than 8 credit cards.**

➤ **The amount you budgeted for walking-around money disappears faster than usual.**

➤ **Your utility bills are considerably higher than they were a year ago.**

such as hobbies, entertainment, vacation, children's camp, and health club membership. These can differ greatly from household to household and even from month to month for the same household.

4 Easy Steps

To set up your monthly budget, you must:

1. *Estimate your available income.* Total all sources of income, including take-home pay, interest, dividends, bonuses, and receipts from rental property. If your income fluctuates, give yourself a cushion by underestimating your income (and overestimating your expenses in the next steps). Don't include any bonuses or overtime pay you are not sure you'll receive in the future.

2. *List your basic fixed expenses.* (Prorate [that is, divide proportionately] quarterly or annual expenses.) Be sure to include daily expenses like transportation. Total the amounts.

3. *Estimate your basic variable expenses that you can control,* like food and clothing. Total the amounts.

4. *Add the amounts* in steps 2 and 3 and subtract from the total shown in step 1. If the sum is positive, you're in great shape! You can save or invest your surplus or increase the amounts you spend on discretionary items.

If the amount is negative, you'll have to cut back on your discretionary spending. You might postpone your vacation or cut down on some expenses, such as clothing, entertainment, or dining out, in order to get ahead.

Paying Bills Online

You may be able to avoid getting into financial trouble—and save a little money, too—by paying your bills online. By setting up these arrangements, you won't have to worry about forgetting to mail in your bills and will therefore steer clear of late-payment fees. Some utility companies

Easy Conversions

Most budgets are computed on a monthly basis. Here's how to convert weekly, biweekly, semimonthly, quarterly, or annual figures to monthly amounts.

If your budgeting amount is:
Weekly: multiply it by 4.33
Biweekly: multiply it by 2.16
Semimonthly: multiply it by 2
Quarterly: divide it by 3
Annually: divide it by 12

Sample Monthly Budget

If you've never made a budget, try using this sample as a model. It's easiest to start with fixed expenses because they're the same from month to month. You will probably have to estimate your variable expenses; round up to be safe.

INCOME

TAKE-HOME PAY _____
INTEREST/DIVIDENDS _____
RENTAL PROPERTIES _____
OTHER _____

TOTAL INCOME _____

BASIC (ESSENTIAL) EXPENSES

FIXED		VARIABLE	
CAR LOANS	_____	CAR CARE/GARAGE/GAS	_____
CHILD CARE	_____	CHARITABLE CONTRIBUTIONS	_____
HOME-EQUITY LOAN	_____	CLOTHING	_____
INSURANCE (CAR, DISABILITY, HEALTH, HOME, LIFE)	_____	CREDIT CARDS	_____
MORTGAGE/RENT	_____	DRY CLEANING/LAUNDRY	_____
PERSONAL LOANS	_____	GROCERIES	_____
SCHOOL TUITION/LOANS	_____	LIQUOR	_____
TAXES	_____	MAINTENANCE/REPAIRS	_____
TRANSPORTATION	_____	MEDICAL/DENTAL CARE	_____
OTHER (CABLE TV, INTERNET ACCESS, HOUSEHOLD HELP, HEALTH CLUB, ETC.)	_____	PERSONAL GROOMING (HAIR SALON, NAIL SALON)	_____
		PET CARE	_____
		TELEPHONE	_____
TOTAL FIXED EXPENSES	_____	TRAVEL & ENTERTAINMENT	_____
		UTILITIES	_____
		OTHER	_____
		TOTAL VARIABLE EXPENSES	_____

TOTAL INCOME	TOTAL BASIC EXPENSES (FIXED PLUS VARIABLE)	AMOUNT LEFT FOR DISCRETIONARY (OPTIONAL) EXPENSES
	−	=
_____	_____	_____

and insurance companies offer discounts for customers who pay bills online, since they get the money faster and can avoid some postage and paperwork costs.

By creating an online bill-paying program, you generally have money electronically transferred to the creditor automatically from a bank or brokerage account at a particular time each month.

Your bank may offer online bill payment services for free. Some online bill payment providers charge a monthly fee for this service, so you'll want to find out if there are any costs involved. If there are, determine whether the price of setting up an online plan is less than the cost of postage and checks if you paid your bills the old fashioned way.

Banks and Your Financial Privacy

Banks and other financial institutions have a lot of information about you and your money. The question is: What will they do with it? Sometimes, they'll share the data with other financial institutions. Sometimes, they'll try to sell you more products or services based on this information. If you don't like the notion of your financial data getting passed around, read the privacy notices you receive from your financial institutions and then, where possible, follow their instructions to stop them from sharing your information. This is known as "opting out."

Tax Software

Just as with online bill paying, your computer can also be a great help in preparing your tax return, even if you hire a pro to actually fill in the numbers. Today, sophisticated but inexpensive software programs can help ensure that you don't miss a deduction or tax credit. The software offers gentle reminders about expenses that could be deductible, if you have the backup to prove them. Tax software can also help you compare your current tax picture with last year's and project your tax situation a year ahead, so you can see if

Balancing Act

Balancing your bank statement each month will help you stay on a budget.

HERE'S HOW
Verify deposits and canceled checks by date and amount, making a check mark on the statement by each entry.

Compare the amount of each canceled check with your checkbook and the bank statement.

Check all deposits and withdrawals made at an ATM against your receipt slips.

CONFIRM YOUR BALANCE

1. Balance in your checkbook. _____

2. Subtract service charges on statement. − _____

= _____

3. Add any interest earned on account. + _____

4. New register balance. = _____

THEN ENTER

5. Balance shown on bank statement. _____

6. Add deposits not on statement. + _____

= _____

7. Subtract total of checks written but not cleared and ATM withdrawals since your last statement. − _____

8. New balance (should match line 4). = _____

Checkbook Security

Keeping a checkbook correctly and making sure it reconciles with your bank statement each month will help you catch any bank errors (and your own) and prevent overdrawn accounts. If you make a mistake on a check, correct it neatly and initial it; or, better yet, mark the check "void," rip it up, and start over. You might want to shred it to be safe (for more on shredders, see box, page 355). Always write in permanent ink; don't use pencil or erasable pen.

PAYEE
When writing a check for cash, write your own name, not "cash." Otherwise, if the check is lost or stolen, anyone can cash it. Draw a line after the payee; avoid abbreviations.

DATE
Most checks are valid for only a set period—usually 6 months. Postdating a check does not guarantee it won't be cashed sooner, because electronic scanners can't read the date.

CHECK NUMBER
Note this on the receipt when paying bills.

Jane Doe
300 Main Street
Anytown, USA

194

APRIL 5 20 04

PAY TO THE ORDER OF JANE DOE $ 24.95

TWENTY FOUR $ 95/100 DOLLARS

NATIONAL BANK

MEMO GROCERIES   Jane Doe

⑆ 198765432 ⑆ 987654 ⑈ 0194

MEMO SPACE
Use this for record keeping. It can come in handy at tax time.

AMOUNT
Print the written amount in capital letters starting at the extreme left, then draw a line through any space that remains on the line.

SIGNATURE
Always sign your name the same way. Write legibly and without flourishes, and be sure your signature matches your signature card on file at the bank. If the bank honors a forgery, usually it is responsible, not you.

FIGURES
Print as close to the dollar sign as possible to prevent anyone from altering the amount.

ROUTING NUMBER/ACCOUNT NUMBER/CHECK NUMBER
The first 9 digits identify your bank: this is the routing number. The next 6 or more digits are the number of your checking account. The last number (separated from the preceding digits by a space) is the number of of that particular check.

it will make sense to defer or accelerate some purchases for tax reasons.

More and more people are doing and filing their taxes electronically, too. This can save on the cost of hiring a professional preparer. And if you're due a refund, filing electronically will help get the money back to you faster than if your return is sent to the IRS by mail.

Overdraft Protection

Most banks offer overdraft protection, so you never have to worry about bouncing a check, which could harm your credit rating or sock you with a fee. Overdraft protection lets you write checks for more than the amount in your bank account. Some financial institutions offer this as a benefit if you sign up for their credit card, credit line, or savings account as well as their checking account. Check with your bank about its overdraft rules and any fees for this protection.

Safety First

SIGN HERE

If cashing a check, wait to endorse it until you're at the bank; otherwise, the check can easily be cashed if it falls into the wrong hands. When depositing a check, write "for deposit only" before you go to the bank. This helps to ensure that if the check gets lost, it can't be cashed, only deposited.

BE ATM ALERT

ATMs are convenient, but should be used with care.

➤ If the machine is in a secluded area, avoid it.

➤ Be aware of other users; if anyone looks suspicious, leave immediately.

➤ Always protect your PIN (personal identification number): Use your body to shield the machine when you enter your PIN; never tell anyone your PIN number; and don't carry it in your wallet.

➤ Be sure to put away your withdrawn cash before you leave the ATM.

Getting Credit

Credit can be a useful form of money management, but it can also get you into trouble if you're not careful. The chief advantage of credit is that you can pay for things when you don't have the cash on hand or prefer to spread the cost out over time.

But you'll pay for that privilege—sometimes dearly. Credit cards, mortgages, home equity lines, and car loans require you to pay interest. As a general guideline, financial advisers suggest limiting your total debt payments—excluding your mortgage—to 10 percent to 20 percent of your take-home pay. Including a mortgage, your debt payments shouldn't exceed 36 percent of your gross monthly income.

How Credit Works

Credit comes in 4 basic forms:

Credit cards and charge cards: Credit cards (Visa, MasterCard) are offered by banks, retail stores, and gasoline companies. Typically, the credit card has a minimum monthly payment. If you pay only the minimum, or less than the total amount of your balance, you'll owe interest. The card's interest rate may be fixed or may fluctuate from month to month. Credit cards generally have a specified limit on the amount you can borrow each month.

Charge cards or travel and entertainment cards, such as the traditional American Express card, require you to pay their balances in full each month and don't assess interest, though they do charge annual fees. They usually have no specified credit limit. American Express will, however, let you pay off over 36 months any air fare, cruise, or hotel charges booked through a travel agent with your American Express card; you'll owe interest and must make a minimum monthly payment.

Debit cards: A debit card looks like a credit card, but it's much different. When you use a debit card, the money you owe is automatically withdrawn from your bank checking account—so it's really more like a check. (Some banks issue debit cards that can also be used as ATM cards.) Unlike a credit card, there's no interest charge when you use a debit card. But remember, you get no grace period before making the payment. What's more, you can't withhold payment if you get into a dispute with the store where you used the debit card—the way you can with a credit card. Also, many banks and stores charge a fee whenever you use a debit card.

Loans: You might use a mortgage, car loan, home-equity loan, or a personal bank loan to help pay for a big-ticket purchase over time.

When you sign up for the loan, you know the exact number of payments and (aside from adjustable loans) the specific amount of each payment—usually spread over many months.

Interest rates can vary widely, so it pays to compare. Before signing for this type of loan, be sure to ask about options for prepaying it. Some banks charge a prepayment penalty if you pay off the balance sooner than the stated time.

Home-equity credit lines: Banks, brokerages, and finance companies offer home-equity credit lines. You borrow against your home, while you're living in it, and can use the money for whatever you want. The interest rate on a home-equity credit line typically fluctuates. You make monthly payments.

Your Credit Rating

How well you've used credit in the past will affect how easily you can get credit in the future and how much you'll pay for it.

Your credit history is based on how much income you have, how promptly you pay your bills, how long you have lived or worked in the same place, how much you owe, and your collateral—what you own that is worth more than the amount you want to borrow.

Credit Records

If you have obtained credit in the past, your credit records are probably on file at a credit bureau near you. (Look under "Credit Reporting Agencies" in the Yellow Pages of your phone book or on the Internet.)

These reporting agencies receive and file records of credit transactions plus information from public records such as a contract suit, judg-

Helpful Hints

WHICH CREDIT CARD IS BEST?

The best credit card for you depends on how you plan to use the card and how you intend to pay the bill.

If you are likely to use the card often and carry a balance from month to month, you should look for the lowest interest rate and longest grace period.

If you plan to pay off the balance in full every month, ignore the interest rate and look for a card with no (or a very low) annual fee.

ment, tax lien, or bankruptcy. They then make the information available to creditors to help them decide if you are a good credit risk, based on what's known as your "credit score" or "FICO score." As a rule, the higher your credit score, the more likely you'll be able to qualify for a loan or a credit card and the lower your interest rate will be.

It's a good idea to check your credit bureau file periodically for accuracy. The 3 national credit bureaus are Experian (888-397-3742), Equifax (800-685-1111), and Trans Union (800-888-4213). You may have to pay a small fee to get your credit report, unless you inquire within 30 days of being denied credit. If you think the information is incorrect, ask the credit bureau to investigate.

Information proven to be incorrect must be removed. If you and the creditor disagree about the accuracy of the information, you can file a 100-word statement telling your side. It must be added to your file.

Both spouses should develop separate credit records so each will have access to credit in case of divorce or death.

Credit bureaus often share personal financial data, which leads to your receiving unsolicited offers for credit cards and credit lines. If you want to opt out of getting these types of prescreened offers, call 888-5-OPTOUT.

All About Credit Cards

Credit cards are popular and easy to use. But you need to read the fine print about their terms, or you could wind up unpleasantly surprised with high fees or high interest rates. Be sure to consider the following:

Annual fee: the amount you pay once a year to use the card. Some cards have no annual fee, but their interest rates tend to be higher than cards with annual fees.

Grace period: the length of time after purchase before you're charged interest. Many cards have a 25-day grace period, but some

Helpful Hints

SOCIAL SECURITY ALERT

➤ **Don't assume the government is keeping a correct record of your Social Security benefits. To check, call Social Security at 800-772-1213 and ask for a Personal Earnings and Benefit-Estimate Statement request form (PEBS). When you receive your PEBS, make sure your work history is recorded correctly. The PEBS will also tell you how much money you can expect to receive at retirement (or in the event you become disabled), as well as the amount your spouse would collect if you died. This information will help you as you plan for your retirement.**

➤ **The Social Security Administration will not correct errors in records that are more than 39 months old, so it's to your advantage to complete the PEBS request form every 3 years.**

have no grace period at all—in which case your interest begins accruing from the moment you buy an item with the card.

Interest rate: the percentage rate of interest on the unpaid portion of your bill. Interest rates vary by card issuer and can be either fixed or variable. Issuers can change rates on a moment's notice, depending on state law. Generally, the interest rate on cards offered by retail stores is higher than the rate of Visa and MasterCards issued by banks.

Unauthorized use: by federal law, if your credit card is stolen and used by someone else, you are liable for only the first $50 in charges.

Dollar Stretchers

FREE OF FEES

If you are a good customer, you can ask the bank issuing your credit card to waive the annual fee.

How to Organize Your Files

The challenge in organizing your files is to keep the categories specific enough to be useful, yet general enough to be practical. Where you put items is less important than making sure material is returned to its designated spot. A good way to organize your files is to divide them into the following categories:

ACTION FILES

Set up separate files for: bills to pay, income/ expense records, correspondence, upcoming events, organizational activities, and current projects. These files need to be readily available, but not immediately visible.

Clean out action files yearly but save:
- The current year's tax records
- The current year's insurance premiums
- Real estate records
- Investments or property records
- Records of major purchases
- Automobile purchase and sale records

REFERENCE FILES

These are files for material you need to find less frequently. The files can be as diverse as your interests and will be most useful if you store them where you commonly use them. Typical categories include:
- Financial papers: Include canceled checks, receipts for tax deductible items, and tax returns.
- Insurance policies and records of claims.
- Education, health, and employment records.
- Household papers: Include records of home improvements, appliance warranties and manuals, and decorating ideas.
- Car and travel records: Include owner's manual, service records, maps, brochures, directions to friends' homes, and clippings about places you want to visit.
- Yard records: Include warranties for tools, landscaping plan, improvements made, trees planted.

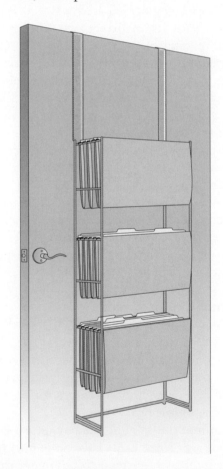

Hanging door files

FAMILY FILES
Depending on what's important in your household, you may want to create separate files for photographs and negatives, letters, recipes and party ideas, craft ideas and directions, personal writings, and genealogy lists.

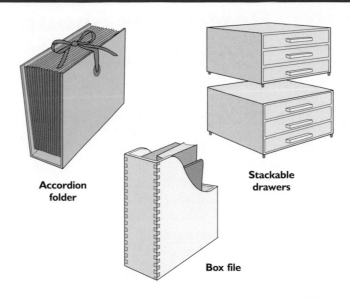

Accordion folder

Stackable drawers

Box file

Some Web sites extend this protection and say that you will not be responsible for *any* unauthorized purchases made with your card online.

Specialty Credit Cards
Two types of specialty credit cards are also available:

Affinity credit cards: may be offered from a university alumni association, a nonprofit organization, a charity, or another group. A small portion of the purchase price of items charged to the card (usually 0.5 percent) goes to the organization, or the organization may receive a flat fee for each member who signs up for the card.

Secured credit cards: These are offered by some banks for people who don't yet have a credit history or who want to erase a negative history due to past financial problems. To qualify for a secured credit card, you must keep a minimum balance—usually $500 to $1,000—on deposit. If you fail to pay the monthly bill, the bank withdraws the needed amount from your account. If you make the monthly payments, you can establish or improve your credit record and qualify for an unsecured card.

How Long Should You Keep Your Financial Records?

The length of time you should hold on to your financial records depends on their type:

Tax returns: After filing a tax return, keep substantiating records—tax returns, canceled checks, receipts for deductible expenses—for at least 7 years. The Internal Revenue Service (IRS) has 3 years after the year of filing to audit a return; 6 years if the taxpayer omits more than 25 percent of gross income; and unlimited time if fraud is found.

IRA contributions: You'll want to keep these records permanently. This is especially important for nondeductible IRA contributions, since you may need to prove that you already paid tax on the money at the time you withdraw the cash.

401(k) and other retirement plan statements: Keep your quarterly statements until you get the annual statement. Then you can discard the quarterly statements. Hold onto the annual statements until you retire or close the retirement plan account.

Bank records: At tax time each year, sort through your checks and keep the ones for deductible personal expenses, home renovations, business expenses, and your mortgage. Then toss the rest.

Brokerage and mutual fund statements: Be sure to hang onto all purchase and sales slips. This way, you can determine your gains and losses for tax purposes. As with retirement plans, keep your quarterly brokerage and mutual fund statements until your annual statements arrive. Keep end-of-year statements indefinitely.

Lose the Clutter

Storing file folders in a drawer or box works well for many people. Others prefer to use drawers, baskets, or other containers like those shown on pages 348–349. Use whatever works for you.

As you sort and organize, look for things you can throw out. Store the things you want in labeled containers. When possible, move them to the attic, basement, or a top or back closet shelf.

Many organizations that work with children welcome magazines and catalogs for cutting projects. Libraries often take books and magazines for their own collections or for fund-raising book sales.

Ask social agencies if they know of any local groups that might be able to use items. Or set up an exchange program with neighbors and coworkers.

Bills: The only ones you really need to keep are for large purchases such as home computers, jewelry, cars, and antiques. They'll come in handy if you need to prove the value of your belongings for insurance purposes.

Credit card receipts and credit card statements: You should keep the receipts until you get your monthly statement. Then you can discard the receipts, if everything matches up. Hold on to your credit card statements for 7 years, for tax purposes.

Paycheck stubs: You really need to keep these for just a year.

Home-related documents: Keep indefinitely records showing the purchase price, the cost of home improvements, and expenses for buying or selling the home. These will all be useful for tax purposes when you sell. Keep these records even after selling your house.

Insurance policies: Hold on to these as long as the policies are still in force.

Where to Keep Important Papers

It is extremely important to organize your financial and personal records well. Put whatever you don't need on hand into a bank safe-deposit box; often-used items should be neatly filed at home (see pages 348–349). Records you can toss: old, expired insurance policies; receipts for cars you no longer own; pay stubs from earlier years; expired product warranties.

WHERE	WHAT	WHY
Carry with you	Personal identification (name, address, phone number, e-mail address; the same for family members and friends)	For emergencies
	Auto insurance card (keep in your car)	To identify insurer in case of accident
	Credit cards, debit cards, ATM cards	For identification; to charge purchases or make transactions
	Driver's license, car registration	For identification; to prove your eligibility to drive
	Health insurance card	For identification; for hospital admittance
	Medical information (allergy, blood type, diseases, donor card)	For emergency treatment
	Physician's identification card (name, address, phone)	To contact in emergency
	Social Security card (or keep in your safe deposit box)	For identification

(continued on next page)

WHERE	WHAT	WHY
Home files	Checking and savings account information (canceled checks, deposit slips, phone and wire transfer numbers, extra checks, statements)	For tax and budget information
	Credit records (bills and receipts, copies of contracts, loan statements and payment books, notification forms for lost or stolen credit cards)	For reference: in case of loss or theft of a credit card, call the credit card company to report, then follow up with a letter; keep receipts to prove payment to return purchases
	Employment records (copies of employment contracts, benefits information, pay stubs or statements, resumé, Social Security records)	For reference
	Estate planning (instructions for survivors, unsigned copies of trusts, other legal documents, and a copy of your will)	For reference and referral
	Health information (insurance records, immunization history, surgery history, insurance forms, phone numbers of insurance companies)	For reference
	Household furnishings and appliances records (warranties, manuals, place and date of purchase, receipts, repair records, serial/model numbers)	For reference, use, and care; for insurance or warranty claims

WHERE	WHAT	WHY
Home files	Housing records (copies of lease or rental agreements, property tax records, receipts for home improvements, record of mortgage payments)	To compute capital gains/ losses or income-tax basis in your new residence
	Income tax records (copies of past returns, expenses in current year, records and receipts of income and deductible items, tax forms)	In case of audit
	Insurance records: auto, health, life, disability, property (policies, copies of claim forms, receipts of payment)	For reference of coverage until policies have expired
	Investment records (purchase, sale, and reinvestment statements for stocks, bonds, mutual funds, 401(k) plans, 529 plans, IRAs, Keoghs, SEPs, real estate earnings statements and transaction slips)	For reference
	Privacy statements from financial institutions	To keep a record of how your financial information can be shared
	Vehicle information (registration copy, repair and maintenance records)	To collect on a warranty, to resell car, in case of theft
Safe-deposit box	Appraisals, photos, receipts of valuables; inventory of household goods	For insurance claims
	Cemetery plot papers	To prove ownership and to aid family upon your death

(continued on next page)

WHERE	WHAT	WHY
Safe-deposit box	Contracts, leases, notes	To prove your debt or what is owed to you; for deductions on tax returns; and to prove that contract terms are fulfilled
	Jewelry	To avoid theft from your home
	List of insurance polices and agents	For reference when it's time to file a claim
	Military service records	For insurance, retirement, medical, and other benefits
	Mortgage documents, title and deeds for your home and other real estate	To prove ownership and to aid title examiner
	Motor vehicle titles and purchase receipts	To prove ownership; for sale, proof of collateral for a loan, and in case of theft
	Personal records for all household members (adoption, birth, citizenship, death, divorce, and marriage certificates; prenuptial agreements; passports; Social Security numbers)	For inheritance, insurance, and business matters; to prove citizenship or age (for Social Security questions, call the Social Security Administration at 800-772-1213)
	Stock, bond, and mutual fund certificates, and purchase and sales receipts (can be held by your broker)	To prove ownership; for tax purposes
	Tax assessments and records of home capital improvements	For tax purposes
	Wills (unsigned copies; leave the original signed copy with your lawyer and your signed "living will" with your doctor)	To record your bequests

Fraud and Identity Theft

If you're not careful, thieves can get their hands on your financial information and then steal your identity—and go wild using your credit cards, credit lines, and Social Security number to make purchases.

If you become an identity-theft victim, immediately contact the 3 credit bureaus. Call their fraud departments to place a fraud alert on your credit file. (Equifax's fraud number: 800-685-1111; Experian's fraud number: 888-EXPERIAN; TransUnion's fraud number: 800-680-7289.) This tells creditors to contact you before opening any new accounts or changing your existing credit accounts.

After a fraud alert, you'll receive your credit reports free. You should close accounts you think have been used fraudulently and then file reports both with the local police department and the Federal Trade Commission (877-IDTHEFT).

Shredders Can Protect You

While you can't protect all your financial information all the time, there are a few measures you can take to fend off identity theft. The first is to use a shredder to destroy any papers or computer disks that include your financial records or Social Security number before putting them out in the trash.

If you're in the market for a shredder, here's how to shop wisely:

- Determine whether you want a "strip-cut" shredder or a "cross-cut" version. A strip cut—also known as straight cut or spaghetti cut—will slice paper into long, thin strips. A cross-cut shredder cuts paper vertically and horizontally into small pieces, so it offers more security. Strip-cut shredders usually handle more paper at one time and cost less than cross-cut shredders.
- Compare the shred capacity. You'll want a shred capacity of at least 4 or 5 sheets at one time.
- Investigate additional features. Some shredders will tell you if there's a paper jam or the shredder basket is full. Some come with clear baskets or windows, so it's easy to see when it's time to empty the basket.
- Look for independent ratings. The Good Housekeeping Institute, for example, may have tested shredders recently. (Find this information at www.goodhousekeeping.com.)

Fending Off Telemarketers

Among life's top annoyances are telemarketers who call you during your dinner hour and interrupt family meals. You also need to watch out for fraudulent telemarketers, who attempt to find out your personal financial information through a series of legitimate-sounding questions. Never give out *any* personal information on the phone unless you've placed the phone

 Helpful Hints

TO SHRED OR NOT TO SHRED?

Although you may be tempted to shred everything—or nothing—here are the top 5 items you should shred in order to protect your financial information:

➤ **Anything you don't need that lists your Social Security number**

➤ **Unsolicited credit card offers**

➤ **Credit card statements and checks that you no longer need**

➤ **Bank, brokerage, and mutual fund statements you no longer need**

➤ **Insurance claim forms you no longer need**

What You Should Know About Warranties

Big ticket items like cars and appliances generally come with warranties, a policy that usually lasts for 3 years or 36,000 miles on automobiles and the first year of ownership on appliances. (The Good Housekeeping Seal is a 2-year limited warranty. If you buy a product with the Seal and it proves defective within 2 years, *Good Housekeeping* will replace it or refund your money. You can find a list of products with the Good Housekeeping Seal in *Good Housekeeping* magazine and on the magazine's Web site, (www.goodhousekeeping.com.)

Read all the terms of a warranty carefully and ask questions about any parts that need clarification.

Misunderstandings are common. Be sure to find out:

- What is or is not covered
- How long is the coverage
- Under what conditions is it covered

You must operate and maintain the car or appliance following the manufacturer's guidelines in order to be eligible for coverage on repairs.

Routine maintenance doesn't have to be done by the dealer, but replacements must meet or exceed the manufacturer's specifications.

An extended warranty is a form of insurance. Consider the extent of the manufacturer's warranty when deciding whether or not to buy it. You may find that you'll get a better return on your money by setting up your own repair fund.

---

call. You can sharply reduce these calls by signing up for the federal "Do Not Call Registry" at www.donotcall.gov or by calling 888-382-1222. This registry is managed by the Federal Trade Commission, the nation's consumer protection agency. Once your name has been on this list for 3 months, telemarketers are not supposed to call. If they do, you can file a complaint at the Do Not Call Web site (www.ftc.gov/donotcall/).

Shopping Safely Online

The Internet can be a terrific way to shop: It's convenient, quick, and prices are generally competitive with what you'll find in stores. But you need to be careful when shopping online. Otherwise, your credit card information and other financial data could wind up in the wrong hands, and you could wind up a victim of identity theft.

Be sure to read a Web site's online privacy policy before you buy anything from the site. The privacy policy should clearly explain what type of information the site collects about its users and how it uses the information. If the site doesn't tell you, find another one that does. Otherwise, your name and financial information could end up being passed around to many other merchants.

The Federal Trade Commission recommends thinking "ABC" to remember the privacy and security questions to ask about a company before buying items online:

A is for About Me. What information does the company collect about me and is it secure? How does it state that my information will be secure?

B is for Benefits. How does the company use that information and what is the benefit to me?

C is for Choices. What choices do I have about the company's use of information about me? Can I opt out of information uses and how?

You can also limit the chances of a bad online shopping experience by sticking with companies you know. If you've never heard of the online merchant, see if you can get a catalog or brochure from the company. This will give you an idea how reputable it is and how much it cares about its customers. Also, check out the company's refund and returns policy. This information should be on the Web site. If it's not, don't place an order.

Another online shopping tip: Be careful with your passwords. Try to use passwords that no one could guess and type in the password only on a site you know well. Don't use your Social Security number, phone number, or birth date as your password. If a hacker gets your password, he may now have access to key data that could be used to steal your identity. One common scam is an e-mail solicitation that may at first seem like it's from a legitimate organization or financial institution. Beware: If the e-mail message is asking you to "verify" your password to any of your online accounts, then it's a ruse to capture your private information and financial records.

Helpful Hints

COMPUTER SMARTS

➤ It's wise to update your computer's virus protection regularly, especially when you hear about a new virus alert, and to use a firewall program. Computer viruses can wind up sending out on the Internet some of your private financial files. A firewall program—especially if you have a high-speed Internet connection—helps prevent anyone from hacking into your computer and stealing your financial data.

➤ Before you toss out an old computer, try to delete any personal information on it. Start by saving any important financial information to a CD or floppy disk. Then, delete files on your hard drive normally. But since this may not be enough—your files with financial information may still be on your hard drive—buy what's called a "wipe" utility program to overwrite the whole hard drive and make all your files unrecoverable.

FETY BASICS   CHILDPROOFING YOUR HOME   SAFETY FOR THE ELDERLY   THE SAFE YAR
IERGENCIES IN THE HOME   INDOOR POLLUTANTS   HOME SECURITY   PREPARING FOR DISASTE
FETY BASICS   CHILDPROOFING YOUR HOME   SAFETY FOR THE ELDERLY   THE SAFE YAR
IERGENCIES IN THE HOME   INDOOR POLLUTANTS   HOME SECURITY   PREPARING FOR DISASTE
FETY BASICS   CHILDPROOFING YOUR HOME   SAFETY FOR THE ELDERLY   THE SAFE YAR
IERGENCIES IN THE HOME   INDOOR POLLUTANTS   HOME SECURITY   PREPARING FOR DISASTE
FETY BASICS   CHILDPROOFING YOUR HOME   SAFETY FOR THE ELDERLY   THE SAFE YAR
IERGENCIES IN THE HOME   INDOOR POLLUTANTS   HOME SECURITY   PREPARING FOR DISASTE
FETY BASICS   CHILDPROOFING YOUR HOME   SAFETY FOR THE ELDERLY   THE SAFE YAR
IERGENCIES IN THE HOME   INDOOR POLLUTANTS   HOME SECURITY   PREPARING FOR DISASTE
FETY BASICS   CHILDPROOFING YOUR HOME   SAFETY FOR THE ELDERLY   THE SAFE YAR
IERGENCIES IN THE HOME   INDOOR POLLUTANTS   HOME SECURITY   PREPARING FOR DISASTE
FETY BASICS   CHILDPROOFING YOUR HOME   SAFETY FOR THE ELDERLY   THE SAFE YAR
IERGENCIES IN THE HOME   INDOOR POLLUTANTS   HOME SECURITY   PREPARING FOR DISASTE
R SAFETY BASICS   CHILDPROOFING YOUR HOME   SAFETY FOR THE ELDERLY   THE SAFE YAR
IERGENCIES IN THE HOME   INDOOR POLLUTANTS   HOME SECURITY   PREPARING FOR DISASTE
FETY BASICS   CHILDPROOFING YOUR HOME   SAFETY FOR THE ELDERLY   THE SAFE YAR
IERGENCIES IN THE HOME   INDOOR POLLUTANTS   HOME SECURITY   PREPARING FOR DISASTE
FETY BASICS   CHILDPROOFING YOUR HOME   SAFETY FOR THE ELDERLY   THE SAFE YAR
IERGENCIES IN THE HOME   INDOOR POLLUTANTS   HOME SECURITY   PREPARING FOR DISASTE
FETY BASICS   CHILDPROOFING YOUR HOME   SAFETY FOR THE ELDERLY   THE SAFE YAR
IERGENCIES IN THE HOME   INDOOR POLLUTANTS   HOME SECURITY   PREPARING FOR DISASTE
FETY BASICS   CHILDPROOFING YOUR HOME   SAFETY FOR THE ELDERLY   THE SAFE YAR
IERGENCIES IN THE HOME   INDOOR POLLUTANTS   HOME SECURITY   PREPARING FOR DISASTE
FETY BASICS   CHILDPROOFING YOUR HOME   SAFETY FOR THE ELDERLY   THE SAFE YAR
IERGENCIES IN THE HOME   INDOOR POLLUTANTS   HOME SECURITY   PREPARING FOR DISAST
FETY BASICS   CHILDPROOFING YOUR HOME   SAFETY FOR THE ELDERLY   THE SAFE YAR
IERTY CIES IN THE HOME   INDOOR POLLUTANTS   HOME SECURITY   PREPARING FOR SA

CHAPTER

8

Safety

The best house is a safe and secure house. And because prevention is essential, the following pages are filled with vital information on averting falls, fires, and electrical mishaps; details on making your home safe for children and the elderly; and what to keep in a first-aid kit. The chapter also covers everything you need to know about safety in your yard. In addition, you'll learn the right steps to take if the unexpected strikes—what to do if a pipe bursts, if you smell gas, or if you find lead in your paint or in your soil. Plus, there are smart tips from The Good Housekeeping Institute on keeping your house secure—from locks to light timers to alarm systems. Finally, this chapter covers up-to-date directions for disaster-readiness, including how to make a disaster plan and what to keep on hand if your family must remain indoors for days without power or water. Armed with the knowledge in these pages, you'll be able to create a safe, secure home.

359

Safety Basics

Having a home that's safe is largely about prevention: knowing what can happen and how to avoid it. Falls, fires, and electrical mishaps are the major types of home accidents. By understanding these potential risks and taking the proper precautions, you can go a long way toward ensuring that your home is safe.

Avoiding Falls

Many household falls occur on wet floors and slippery or uneven sidewalks or when trying to reach high places. Here's how to avoid them:

Indoors
- Keep floors dry.
- Wipe up spills immediately.
- Keep stairs and other traffic areas free of obstacles.
- Place area rugs carefully. Don't use them at the top of the stairs, in entrance halls or other high-traffic areas, or in the bathroom, where a fall against ceramic surfaces can cause serious injury.
- Use a nonskid pad beneath area rugs or put nonskid adhesive strips on the backs to prevent slippage.
- Use only code-approved stepladders or step stools to reach high shelves, curtain rods, or light fixtures. Never use chairs, tables, or other unacceptable substitutes.

Outdoors
- Replace broken paving stones and fill in pavement cracks.
- Always keep sidewalks clear of snow.
- Salt icy walkways.
- Install sturdy railings on steps.
- Make sure walkways, porches, and steps are well lit and maintained.

- Don't let leaves gather on walks, steps, and porches.
- Use a sturdy nonslip doormat.
- Paint the edges of outdoor steps white so they are easy to see in the dark.
- To reach high places, use only code-approved ladders and carefully observe the rules on the caution decal (see page 264).

Preventing Fires

While fire is one of the most frightening and potentially devastating household disasters, basic, easy-to-implement prevention techniques

 Safety First

SAFE HOUSE DON'TS
➤ **Don't hang frequently used items at the back of the stove top, where you may have to reach across hot burners to grab them.**

➤ **Don't turn on a microwave oven if the door is damaged. Radiation leaks are possible if the door is damaged or doesn't seal properly. After heating anything in a microwave, open the containers carefully—the escaping steam can cause severe burns.**

➤ **Don't leave any pans unattended when cooking.**

➤ **Don't clutter the stairs or landings with objects.**

➤ **Don't polish wooden stair surfaces.**

➤ **Don't leave oily rags, wood shavings, and other flammable material lying around.**

CLOSE ENCOUNTERS
Equip an electric garage door opener with a monitor that stops or reverses the motor when the door encounters an object.

can be a powerful defense. (For information on what to do if fire does break out, see page 372.) Follow these basic recommendations:

- Place at least one smoke detector on every level of your house or apartment, including the basement. Remember to place it well away from your stove so you don't set off false alarms while cooking.
- Choose only a smoke detector that bears the label and approval of an independent testing lab, like the Underwriters Laboratories (UL), Electrotechnical Laboratory (ETL), Canadian Standards Association (CSA), or other organizations recognized by the Occupational Safety and Health Administration (OSHA) testing laboratory.
- Check the batteries regularly and change them twice a year. Remember: Change your clocks/change your batteries.
- Consider having your smoke detectors interconnected and hard wired to your house's electrical system. this way if one sounds off,

 Safety First

CALLING FOR HELP
Post these numbers near your telephone or on your refrigerator:

➤ **Emergency medical service (in many communities it's not 911)**

➤ **Fire department**

➤ **Police department**

➤ **Ambulance**

➤ **Nearest hospital**

➤ **Physician**

➤ **Pharmacist**

➤ **Poison control center (usually administered by your local health department)**

➤ **Gas, electric, and water companies (customer and 24-hour service numbers)**

➤ **Dependable neighbors**

 How to Shop For...

SMOKE DETECTORS
When you buy a smoke detector, look for these features for use in specific rooms:

➤ **In the kitchen: A silencer or "hush" feature lets you shut off the smoke detector during preset times when cooking may set off a false alarm. It will cycle back to "on" after the allotted time period.**

➤ **In hallways and bedrooms: Built-in emergency lights come on when the alarm is triggered.**

they all sound off, and dead batteries are no longer a factor.

- Test detectors every month. If more than 10 years old, replace.
- Be sure the alarm can be heard through closed doors. For the hearing impaired, smoke detectors with high-intensity strobe light plus sound are available.
- Have your furnace cleaned and checked for proper operation once a year (see page 298). Filters should be changed regularly (follow the manufacturer's recommendations) to avoid overheating. Fuel-burning appliances need to be checked for carbon monoxide and unburned hydrocarbon emissions.
- Keep broilers and other grease-gathering parts of your stove clean.
- Use fireplace screens and always make sure the chimneys are functioning properly (see page 300). Check the chimney every year for creosote and carbon buildups. Avoid burning "green" wood since the sap will stick on the chimney wall, build up over time, and present a fire hazard. You can collect green wood, but burn it only after it has been stored for a year.
- Store flammable paints and cleaning fluids well away from furnaces, fireplaces, and stoves. A detached garage or tool shed is the

Where to Get Safety Information

Numerous public agencies and councils provide valuable safety information free of charge. Keep their phone numbers on hand.

ASSOCIATION	INFORMATION	ASSOCIATION	INFORMATION
American Academy of Pediatrics 847-434-4000 www.aap.org	Toy safety, choking prevention	National Fire Protection Association 617-770-3000 www.nfpa.org	How to prevent household fires
American Council of Independent Laboratories 202-887-5872 www.acil.org	Lists labs that test for lead, radon, other contaminants around the house	National Lead Information Center Hotline 800-424-LEAD www.epa.gov	How to deal with lead; part of the EPA
American Red Cross 202-303-4498 www.redcross.org	First aid and disaster preparedness information	National Pesticide Information Center 800-858-PEST www.npic.orst.edu	How to use pesticides safely
Centers for Disease Control and Prevention 404-639-3534 www.cdc.gov	Preventing, treating and recognizing injury and disease; how to recognize symptoms of Lyme disease	National Safety Council 800-621-7619 www.nsc.org	Fire safety, radon, and other household hazards; accident prevention; first aid
Federal Emergency Management Agency 202-566-1600 www.fema.gov	How to protect your home from fire, severe storms, flooding, and other emergencies	Poison Control Center Hotline 800-222-1222	How to treat accidental ingestion of chemicals, drugs, and poisons
		Safe Drinking Water Hotline 800-426-4791 www.epa.gov	How to detect and deal with lead, radon, and other contaminants in drinking water; lists government-certified laboratories that test water and/or sell testing kits

ASSOCIATION	INFORMATION	ASSOCIATION	INFORMATION
Toxic Substances Control Act Hotline 202-554-1404 www.epa.gov	How to deal with asbestos and other toxic substances; part of the EPA	U.S. Environmental Protection Agency Public Information Center 202-272-0167 www.epa.gov	How to test for and handle asbestos, formaldehyde, lead, radon, and other household toxins
U.S. Consumer Product Safety Commission 800-638-2772 www.cpsc.gov	Potential hazards associated with products used around the home and how to avoid risks (does not handle boats, cars, food, drugs, cosmetics, firearms, or pesticides)	U.S. Environmental Protection Agency Radon Hotline 800-SOS-RADON www.epa.gov	How to test for and handle radon

safest place for them.

- Properly discard any rags saturated with furniture polish, oil, or other flammable material immediately after use.
- Never use space heaters to dry clothes.
- Make sure space heaters are throwing heat into the open room, not toward draperies or flammable furniture. Don't let children or pets play near space heaters.
- Avoid running electrical cords under a rug. Insulation can be worn away, resulting in an electrical short that ignites the rug.
- Exercise caution when using an electric blanket or heating pad. Set the timer or alarm to prevent burns.
- Be very careful with ashtrays and lit cigarettes. Use only large, stable ashtrays. Don't smoke when drowsy, drinking, or taking medications. Never smoke in bed.

- Don't dry oily rags in the dryer; the heat can ignite the rags if they aren't completely clean.
- Be sure the dryer is properly vented to avoid lint buildup.
- Tell children that matches and lighters are for grown-ups only, and be sure to store these items well out of reach.
- Don't cook near drapes or when wearing flowing sleeves.
- To minimize reaching over the stove, don't store frequently used items over it.
- Turn stove burners off when not in use. If you must leave the stove while cooking, carry a spoon or potholder with you as a reminder.
- Be careful when cooking if you have artificial fingernails; they can be flammable.
- Keep paper (including paper towels) away from toasters, toaster ovens, and the stove.

Preventing Electrical Mishaps

It's not necessary to know all the ins and outs of your home electrical system to operate it safely. Common sense and some basic knowledge will help you avoid burns, shocks, and fires, the most common electricity-related problems.

- If your lights flicker and your appliances run sluggishly, your electrical system might be overloaded or switches and outlets may be faulty. An electrician can correct this potential fire hazard. Never overload an outlet with extension cords, and be sure to use extension cords with the appropriate wattage rating for the appliance. Note that extension cords are temporary solutions. Multi-outlet extension bars, or power strips, are safer because they are equipped with built-in safety shutoffs that cut off power if the socket becomes overloaded.
- To avoid shocks, make sure your hands are dry before you use, plug in, or unplug appliances. Never use an electrical appliance near a tub, sink, or basin of water; if it falls into the water, even if it is turned off, the appliance can create an electrical field that will electrocute anyone who is in the water or who reaches into the water. If you do drop an electrical appliance in the water, shut off power to the circuit into which the appliance

Helpful Hints

HEALTH UPDATE

State and local health departments provide useful information on asbestos, formaldehyde, lead, radon, water, and other environmental concerns. Ask your state health department for a list of the agencies to contact in your area.

is plugged, unplug the appliance, drain the water and retrieve the appliance.
- In your bathroom and kitchen, install outlets with ground-fault circuit interrupters (see page 319). These outlets cut off power automatically as soon as they sense electrical current leaking from the power tool or appliance, as it does when dropped in water.
- When buying power tools and appliances, check to make sure they bear the label and approval of an independent testing lab, like the Underwriters Laboratories (UL), Electrotechnical Laboratory (ETL), Canadian Standards Association (CSA), or other organizations recognized by the Occupational Safety and Health Administration (OSHA) testing laboratory. This ensures they have met rigorous safety standards.
- Replace worn wires, cords and plugs.

Childproofing Your Home

Once babies learn to crawl, they want to explore and get into everything. All new parents need to look at the home from a baby's perspective, then childproof the house before the baby becomes mobile. Get down on your hands and knees for a baby's eye view, then follow the recommendations that follow. Childproofing doesn't have to be done by professionals; the tools and products needed are widely available. But remember, no amount of childproofing substitutes for proper parental vigilance.

Throughout the House:
- Put covers on unused electrical outlets.
- Be alert to young children who might chew

on cords. Biting through an electrical cord can cause severe burns.

- Use child safety gates with small openings at the top and bottom of stairways and install window guards in rooms above the ground floor. Look for products certified by the JPMA (Juvenile Products Manufacturers Association).
- Don't leave partially filled buckets of water around the house; a child can drown in them.
- Be alert to long cords on appliances, since children may pull on them. Do not allow small children access to cords over 12 inches, since they present a strangulation hazard.
- Cut window blind cords; the loops are strangling hazards for children; use safety tassels and inner cord stops.
- Be alert to small objects and parts within a child's reach. A child can choke on anything that can fit through a toilet paper roll (1$1/4$-inch diameter).
- Buy age-appropriate toys and furniture for children. Children under 6 should not sleep on the top of bunk beds, as there is a risk of falling out of bed in the night.
- Inspect your house for sharp edges and corners. Low-cost bumpers are available to pad sharp edges and corners of items like coffee tables and fireplace hearths.
- Be sure your baby's crib is safe. It should have a tight-fitting mattress and sheets. It should have no loose, missing, or broken hardware or slats. There should be no more that 2$3/8$ inches between each slat. (Cribs manufactured after 1974 must meet this safety standard.) The corner posts should not stick up more than 1/16 inch. There should be no designs or cutouts in the headboard or footboard.
- Never put a child in a bed next to a radiator.
- Use a cordless phone to make it easier to keep an eye on small children, especially when they are in the bathtub or near swimming pools or other dangers. Pool drownings are a leading cause of childhood fatalities. (As

Accidental Poisoning

If your child has swallowed something potentially poisonous, call the Poison Control Center at **800-222-1222**. You will be connected to the Poison Control Center serving your area. Do not try to make the child vomit unless advised to by a poison control specialist. Be prepared to give the following information:

- What the child swallowed, how much, how long ago
- The child's symptoms
- The child's name, age, and weight
- Whether the child has any serious medical problems such as asthma or a seizure disorder

with any electronic appliance, keep the phone well away from water.)
- Anchor freestanding bookshelves and bureaus to the wall so they can't fall on a child who may climb them or pull on them in search of a favorite toy or book.

In the Kitchen:
- Keep all sharp and breakable objects, as well as cleaners and other hazardous substances, in cabinets and drawers equipped with child-safety locks.
- Childproof appliance knobs; young children love to turn gadgets on.
- Try to use back burners, and turn pot handles toward the wall so a child can't reach up and grab a hot pot off the stove.
- Keep hot drinks and food away from the edge of the counter.
- When cooking, set up a safe place for a small child to play that's in sight but not underfoot.
- Don't consider high shelves or cabinets to be childproof—they may simply be

challenging an adventurous child to attempt a dangerous climb.

- Make sure the range is secured to the wall with an antitip bracket.

In the Bathroom:

- Don't leave the toilet seat up; young children can fall in and drown.
- Install child-safety locks on the medicine chest and on all other cabinets and cupboards.
- Never leave children unattended in the bathtub.
- Make sure the water heater is set to no higher than 120 degrees F to prevent scalds. The recommended temperature for a child's bath is between 90 and 102 degrees F.
- Teach children to test the water before washing their hands or climbing into the bath or shower.
- Face young children away from the tub faucets.
- Use a rubber mat or traction pads to reduce the likelihood of slipping and falling when entering or leaving the tub.

Preventing Choking

At Mealtime:

- Don't let young children eat alone. Insist that your children sit down as they eat. Encourage them to eat slowly and chew thoroughly.
- Hot dogs, grapes, and raw vegetables like carrots are choking hazards. Cut these foods into small pieces that are not round.
- Other foods that pose choking hazards include hard and sticky candy, nuts and seeds, popcorn, and spoonfuls of peanut butter.

At Playtime:

- Don't allow young children to play with toys for older children. Check packaging for age appropriateness.
- Check on floors, under furniture, and between cushions for small items like coins, marbles, batteries, pen and marker caps, and pieces of toys like rubber wheels.
- Never let children play with or chew uninflated balloons, which can be swallowed or inhaled.
- Inspect beanbag chairs periodically for holes and leaks. The chairs contain small foam pellets that can choke small children.
- Learn how to perform CPR in case of a choking emergency.
- Never let children play with plastic bags; they can suffocate a child.

Safety for the Elderly

Older people are vulnerable to falls and broken bones. Diminished vision and hearing can be a factor in their safety. Here's how homes can be made safer and more accommodating to the elderly:

Throughout the House:

- Install extra stair railings and secure carpets and rugs.
- Check for adequate lighting on stairs, landings, and porches. Consider installing light switches at the top and bottom of stairs.
- Consider installing an emergency response system which, when activated by pressing a button, contacts preprogrammed emergency numbers.
- Install photosensitive night-lights in the hallways and bathrooms.
- Make sure the house is warm in the winter to avoid the risk of hypothermia, which can be

Car Seats for Children

All 50 states require safety seats or belts for children riding in automobiles. Many states require car seats or booster seats for children, and safety experts recommend that children 12 and younger sit in the back seat.

Infants should sit in rear-facing seats until they weigh at least 20 pounds and are at least 12 months old.

Children who weigh between 20 and 40 pounds and are older than 12 months should sit in forward-facing car seats.

Children more than 40 pounds should sit in booster seats until they are 80 pounds or 4 feet 9 inches tall.

All car seats and booster seats must be placed in the back seat.

HOW TO SHOP FOR CAR SEATS

Infant-only seats: These rear-facing seats are designed for babies weighing up to at least 20 pounds and 12 months of age. Some have detachable bases so you can easily carry your baby in and out of your car without installing the seat each time. Look for an infant seat with a 5-point harness.

Forward-facing seats: Children who have passed the 20-pound/12-month-old mark can sit in forward-facing seats. This type cannot be used as a rear-facing seat.

Convertible seats: This handy type can be used rear-facing for infants and forward-facing for children over the age of 12 months and weighing more than 20 pounds. There are now convertible seats with higher rear-facing weight limits—up to 30 or 35 pounds—for bigger babies.

Booster seats: There are 2 common types of booster seats:

- Combination seats, which convert from a forward-facing child seat to a booster seat. They come with a harness that should be removed when the child reaches about 40 pounds. The booster can then be used in conjunction with the car seatbelt.
- Belt-positioning boosters, which simply raise a child up in the seat so that the car's seat belt fits correctly. High-backed and backless models are available.

Check the car's seat label to be sure the seat meets or exceeds National Highway Traffic Safety Administration (NHTSA) standards. Don't buy a used car seat, since it may not meet these standards.

Car seats are available in department and children's stores, and at some car dealers.

INSTALLATION

Make sure the seat belt that attaches to the car seat doesn't give too much slack.

Read the installation instructions carefully. Thoroughly understand how to install the car seat properly. Some communities have police checkpoints to confirm proper installation; take advantage of them.

The Safe House

You can go a long way toward preventing common household mishaps—which can lead to serious injury—by following these recommendations:

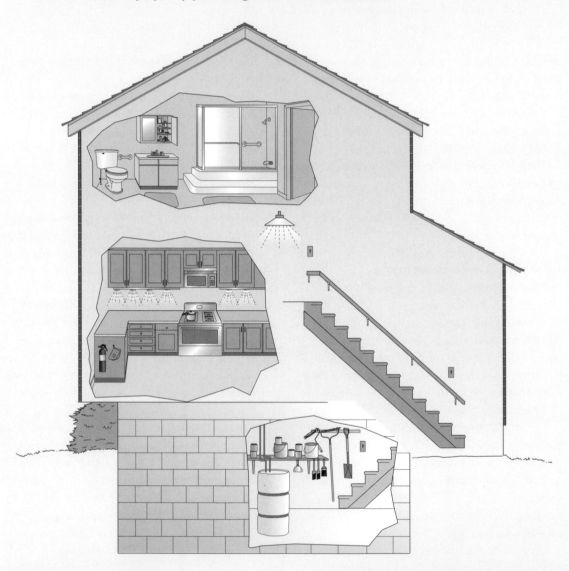

THE KITCHEN

- Keep all areas on and around the stove free of grease to avoid fires.
- Keep containers of drippings and grease well away from the stove.

- Check that your hot-water heater is set at 120 degrees F or less to prevent scalds.
- If you have a gas stove, make sure the pilot light, if there is one, is always lit.

- When cooking, use pot holders and oven mitts—a dishcloth won't protect you from a burn and can ignite easily.
- Keep your stove, sink, and countertops well lit.
- Keep a fire extinguisher handy.

THE STAIRS
- Use bright lights, and install light switches at the top and bottom of the stairs.
- Make sure handrails are secure and run the entire length of the stairs. For extra safety, install a handrail on each side of the steps.
- Carpeting must be tight-fitting and secure. Repair frayed and threadbare carpet immediately. Dense, short-pile carpet provides the surest footing.
- Metal or vinyl guards fitted onto the edge of steps make it easy to see each step and provide a nonslip surface.

THE BATHROOM
- Keep electrical appliances well away from water.
- Use nonskid rugs.
- Make sure medicines are clearly labeled. Look at expiration or use-by dates and dispose of all old medicine and cosmetics.

- Store all breakable bottles in places where they can't easily be knocked over. Use plastic whenever possible.
- Use a night-light to avoid stumbles in the dark.
- Use nonskid bath mats in both the bath and shower.
- Install a handrail near the bathtub to minimize the risk of falling as you climb in and out.

THE GARAGE AND BASEMENT
- For stairs in the basement and other dark places, paint the top and bottom steps yellow or white.
- Store paints, chemicals, and other toxins—such as pesticides—neatly in their original containers.
- Keep all tools, especially those with sharp edges, where they can't be stepped on or tripped over.
- Make sure light switches are easily accessible.
- Label gas and water lines and their shutoff points, and tag fuses or circuit breakers to show which rooms they control.

---

caused by temperatures less than 55 degrees F. Keep the house cool in summer to reduce the risk of heat exhaustion.
- Make sure the water heater is set to no higher than 120 degrees F to prevent scalds.

In the Kitchen:
- Use electric kettles, coffeemakers, and irons that switch off automatically, especially if anyone is forgetful.
- Kitchen utensils with sure-grip handles

make cooking easier and safer, especially for arthritis sufferers.
- Install lights that shine directly onto the stove and countertops to help avoid accidents.

In the Bathroom:
- Install lights that provide sufficient illumination for those with poor eyesight.
- Strategically place sturdy handrails and grab bars both inside and outside the shower and tub and near the toilet.

- Install shower seats.
- Replace shower curtains with heavy-duty doors, which prevent falls caused by loss of balance. Also, doors usually provide a bar for support.
- Make sure bathroom doors open outward; this way, if someone falls, he or she won't block the door and make assistance difficult.
- Provide sturdy and secured steps to help bathtub users get safely in and out of the tub.

- Use nonskid bath mats in both the shower and tub.
- Make sure all medications are in containers clearly marked with contents, doctor's instructions, expiration date, and patient's name. Properly dispose of all outdated medicines.
- Request non-child-resistant closures from the pharmacist only when the elderly person cannot open child-resistant containers. (If children visit, store medications out of reach.)

The Safe Yard

Cushion Their Fall

Most playground injuries occur from falls from climbing equipment or monkey bars. Install soft surfaces—such as wood chips, bark mulch, wood fibers, sand, pea gravel, shredded tires, or rubber mats—below all climbing equipment. Loose-fill surfaces should be approximately 12 inches deep. Avoid concrete, grass, and dirt. They are all too hard.

Jumping for Joy

Backyard trampolines have become increasingly popular in recent years. A few simple rules will keep bouncers safe:
- Supervise children on a trampoline.
- Allow only one person on a trampoline at a time.
- Do not attempt somersaults (landing on head or neck can cause serious injury, including paralysis).
- Do not use a trampoline without shock-absorbing pads that completely cover the springs, hooks, and frame.
- Place the trampoline away from structures, trees, and other play areas.

 Helpful Hints

STRINGS AND THINGS
Cut all drawstrings from children's clothing to avoid potential strangulation; strings can catch in play equipment like slides and swing sets. In winter, avoid scarves for the same reason.

- Keep all objects—especially balls—off trampolines. They could pose hazards.
- Do not allow any child under 6 to use a full-size trampoline. Do not use a ladder with a trampoline because it gives small children unsupervised access.
- Use a trampoline enclosure to help prevent falls off the trampoline.

Pool Safety

If you have a swimming pool, check local ordinances for proper safety regulations.
- Enclose the pool with a fence at least 6 feet high and with a locked gate to keep children out. Lawn chairs, trees, and shrubs should not be close enough to provide an easy

boost over the fence. Avoid using a side of the house as part of the fence; a child could wander through the house, out the door, and into the pool area.

- Use nonslip materials on the pool deck, diving board, and ladders.
- Install gates in the pool area that close and lock automatically.
- Install alarms on the gate or turn on pool alarms (which are activated when anyone falls in the water) when you are indoors or away. Use pool alarms that pass the ASTM F 2208-02 safety standard.
- Use perimeter or area alarms to alert you when someone enters the pool area.
- Keep the water level at least 3 inches from the top so a child can grasp the side and get air.
- Cover the pool during off season but remove the cover completely when the pool is in use.
- Keep a first-aid kit and phone near the pool.
- Take a course in CPR and water safety at your local YMCA or chapter of the American Red Cross.
- Keep electrical appliances and glass away from the pool area.

- Store pool chemicals in a locked cabinet.
- Never let children swim unsupervised; even adults should not swim alone.

Heading Off Head Injuries

Everyone, young and old, should wear a helmet while riding a bike or skating or scootering. Follow these simple rules to ensure the helmet does its job:

- Make sure the helmet fits snugly but comfortably. If you are buying a helmet for a child, bring the child along to the store to ensure a good fit.
- Wear the helmet flat on your head, not tilted back at an angle.
- Make sure chin strap fits securely and the buckle stays fastened.
- Make sure vision is not obstructed.
- Look for a label on the helmet stating that it conforms with CPSC (the Federal Consumer Product Safety Commission) safety guidelines.
- Use helmets designed specifically for the particular activity. For example, do not use a bike helmet for skiing.

Emergencies in the Home

Accidents can happen anytime. If you know what to do in case of an emergency, it may mean the difference between life and death for you and your family. Being prepared can also save your home from extensive damage.

Fire

Precautions: Everyone in your household should know the fastest routes out of the house. Have an escape plan and practice it at least twice a year.

When considering escape routes, be aware that any room in the house could be completely cut off by fire, trapping people inside. Know at least 2 ways out of the house. At least one window in every room must open wide enough so an adult can squeeze through it. All rooms on the second floor or higher should be equipped with a fire ladder or a knotted rope.

Think carefully about how you would get an elderly or handicapped member of the family

STOP, DROP, AND ROLL

If your clothes catch fire, do not run. Stop where you are, drop to the ground, and keep rolling over until the flames are extinguished. Cover your face with your hands to protect your face and your lungs. Everyone in the family needs to know this rule—even children.

WHAT TO DO AFTER A FIRE

If a fire has occurred in your home:

➤ Contact your insurance agent and the financial institution holding your mortgage.

➤ Secure your house against intruders.

➤ Itemize the damaged and destroyed items. Be sure to ask your agent how much detail is needed.

➤ If the electricity or gas has been turned off, call the utility to restore the service. Ask a service person to check your appliances for water and wiring damage before using them.

out in the event of a fire. Remember, it will take a disabled person much longer to get out, so plan accordingly.

If Fire Breaks Out

The most important thing to do in a fire is to get everyone out of the house quickly. No one should take the time to dress, gather valuables, or look for a family pet in another part of the house. Have an assigned meeting place outside the house, such as a tree or the end of the driveway. This way, you will be able to account for all family members at a glance. Call the fire department from a neighbor's house.

Beware of Smoke: Smoke and gases can be more deadly than flames. If you are surround-

Putting Out Fires

You should try to fight only small, contained fires that can be put out in less than 2 minutes. Call the fire department immediately for anything larger.

GREASE

Never throw water on a grease fire. Turn off the heat beneath the pan and smother the flames with a lid or a damp towel. You may also use a fire extinguisher that's filled with chemicals appropriate for flammable liquids.

ELECTRIC

Unplug the appliance and use a fire extinguisher intended to douse electric fires. If you don't have one, smother the burning appliance in a rug or heavy blanket. Don't throw water on a burning appliance, even if it's unplugged, because residual current could give you an electric shock.

MATTRESSES AND UPHOLSTERY

Pour water on a mattress or piece of upholstered furniture that is smoldering, then carry the burned item outside away from the house. If you are not able to control the fire, leave the house immediately because some upholstery contains material that emits lethal fumes when burning. Be aware that mattresses and upholstery can reignite if not completely doused.

ed by smoke, tie a rag (preferably wet) around your nose and mouth to filter the fumes. Smoke rises, so crouch on the floor on your hands and knees. Don't lie prone on the floor, however, because lethal gases can collect there, too.

Check Doors: If you are in a closed room, test the door before opening. Touch the door

Fire Extinguishers

A reliable fire extinguisher can put out a small fire before it becomes a disastrous blaze. Water-based extinguishers are for fires in upholstery, wood, and most other household materials. Chemical and foam extinguishers are for grease and electrical fires and should not be used on fabrics and wood.

- Keep an extinguisher on every level of the house, near the locations where a fire is most likely to occur—in the kitchen, for instance, or near the furnace.
- Keep extinguishers easily accessible; they are useless if tucked away in drawers or cluttered cabinets.
- Check extinguishers regularly, according to the manufacturer's instructions, to make sure nozzles aren't clogged, the pressure is high enough, and they are otherwise in good working order.

PROPER USE

Stand 6 feet from the flames and sweep the nozzle back and forth, aiming the spray at the base of the fire. If the flames don't go out by the time the fire extinguisher is empty, get out of the house and call for help.

HOW TO SHOP FOR A FIRE EXTINGUISHER

Fire extinguishers are rated with letters that correspond to the kind of fire they can put out. Any household fire can be put out by fire extinguishers marked with the letters ABC. Class A fires are when ordinary combustible materials such as cloth, wood, paper, rubber, and most plastics ignite. Class B fires involve flammable liquids like gasoline, alcohol, diesel oil, and oil-based paints and flammable gases. Class C fires involve energized electrical equipment.

An ABC-type fire extinguisher

with your hands to see if it's hot. Be sure to check the top of the door, because heat rises; if the door is hot, don't open it. Then check to make sure smoke isn't curling under the bottom. Be certain that everyone in your family knows how to check a door in this way.

If the Door Is Hot or Smoke Is Seeping Through the Cracks from the Other Side:

- Do not open it. Stuff towels, blankets, rugs, or whatever else is on hand at the bottom of the door to keep out smoke and fumes.
- Hang a sheet out the window to alert firefighters that someone is trapped inside. Get down on your hands and knees to avoid

smoke and fumes. As a last resort, you can tie sheets together to use as a ladder, attaching them firmly to a radiator or other fixture. Before you do so, however, throw a mattress, pillows, or even coats out the window to cushion a fall.

- Don't believe that you can breathe in a smoky room. It's like trying to breathe underwater.

If It Seems Safe to Open the Door:
- Do so cautiously and pay careful attention to the air temperature on the other side—if it isn't suspiciously hot, you can leave the room and take the fastest route out of the house.

Floods

Water can be very destructive, so it is important to act quickly during flooding. Even a minor flood in your home can destroy furniture, floors, and structural elements. Water has disastrous effects on electric circuits, gas lines, and appliances, triggering fires and gas leaks and posing the risk of electrocution. Know the location of your main water valve.

If a Pipe Bursts:
- Turn off water at the main valve.
- Close the doors to the room where the pipe has burst and put towels over the doorjamb to keep water out.
- Repair the pipe if you know how, or call a plumber (see pages 308–313).

Fire Safety in Apartments

Make sure you know the layout of your floor and where the closest stairways and exits are located. All stairway doors should be self-closing and unlocked on both sides. If you are escaping a fire in your apartment, be sure to close all doors behind you, but don't lock them. Closed doors help keep fires from spreading too fast.

If there is a fire in your building but not in your apartment:
- Stay inside; don't enter a smoke-filled hallway.
- Keep your door closed.
- Seal the door with duct tape or wet sheets or towels. Seal vents and other openings.
- Turn off air conditioners.
- Fill your bathtub with water. If the front door gets hot, wet it down with water from the tub.
- Open your windows a few inches from the top or bottom, unless smoke comes in. Don't break the windows; they may need to be closed later.
- Call the Fire Department; give your apartment number and describe what's going on in your apartment.
- If you feel you are in grave danger, wave a bed sheet out your window so firefighters will see you.

- Mop up the water; thick towels are especially efficient because they are so absorbent. Then use a wet vacuum.
- Use a portable, submersible pump if the water is extensive.

If Water Floods Outside:
- Turn off gas and electricity to the house.

- Put rolled up blankets and towels (and sand bags, if available) at the bottom of doors to the outside to keep as much water out of the house as possible.
- If there's time, move valuables to an upper floor.
- If it's prudent, leave the house by a safe route to dry land. If not, take food, bottled water, a flashlight, candles and matches, and a battery-operated radio to an upper floor and wait for help. If the telephone is still working, alert your local emergency service of your situation and whereabouts.

Gas Leaks

To avoid gas leaks, gas furnaces, water heaters, stoves, and other appliances should be serviced regularly, according to the manufacturer's recommendations. It's also important that gas appliances such as a gas dryer are installed properly. Gas furnaces, for instance, require sufficient air space around them so there is enough oxygen for the gas to burn properly. Some gas appliances may require vents or flues. Follow the manufacturer's installation instructions carefully, and if in doubt call your local utility company. Know where the main gas valve is located.

If You Smell Gas:
Don't take the smell of gas casually—a gas leak can cause an explosion, start a fire, or cause asphyxiation. Calmly follow these steps:
- If the odor is strong, get everyone out of the house at once. Immediately call your utility company from a neighbor's house.
- If the odor is relatively slight, open doors and windows to air out the house.
- Put out fires, cigarettes, candles, and other open flames.
- Don't operate electrical appliances, use the telephone, or turn on lights.
- Check pilot lights. If one has gone out, wait for the gas smell to diminish, then relight.
- If the source is unknown, call for emergency service.

Carbon Monoxide Poisoning

Every year, more than 200 people die from carbon monoxide poisoning in the United States. Thousands more go to the hospital because of it. Carbon monoxide is invisible, odorless, and tasteless, so you are not likely to know if it is building up until you begin suffering from its ill effects. The symptoms of carbon monoxide poisoning are sometimes mistaken for the flu, and can be misdiagnosed even by doctors. They include nausea, fatigue, headache, dizziness, confusion, lethargy, and difficulty breathing. Sometimes, a victim's skin may appear pinker or redder than usual.

A surprising number of household devices—including wood-burning stoves, fireplaces, furnaces, grills, kerosene lamps, and gas-fired water and space heaters—can release carbon monoxide if they burn without enough oxygen. When fresh air is restricted, carbon monoxide can build up in your home. This gas is especially threatening in winter, when your house is often sealed up tight against the cold.

The best precaution against carbon monoxide poisoning is installing carbon monoxide detectors/alarms. Choose one that meets the requirements of an independent testing lab (see page 361) which will be indicated on the packaging.

Install a carbon monoxide detector/alarm in the hallway near every separate sleeping area of the house. Make sure the alarms are not covered by furniture or draperies.

If your carbon monoxide alarm goes off, call emergency services and move to fresh air, either by a window or outside.

A carbon monoxide detector/alarm is no substitute for the proper use and upkeep of carbon monoxide–producing appliances. It is important to take the following precautions, whether or not you have a detector:

- Be sure adequate air is available to any room containing a gas-burning appliance. If in doubt, have your building code inspector check.
- Have a trained professional inspect, clean, and tune up your central heating system (furnace, chimneys, and flues) annually. Repair leaks promptly.
- When buying a wood-burning stove, choose one that meets EPA safety standards. (The stove should be labeled as such; if not, ask the retailer or dealer.) It should be installed to meet all local installation codes.
- Make sure the door and stovepipe connections on all old wood-burning stoves fit tightly.
- Use a range hood with a fan if you have a gas range, or install an exhaust fan in a nearby window.
- When using a space heater that operates on oil, gas, or kerosene, open a window slightly or make sure a door is open to the rest of the house. Use proper fuel in a kerosene heater. Purchase a vented space heater when replacing an old one.
- Do not idle a car inside a garage, especially if it's an attached garage.

Indoor Pollutants

Pollutants around the house can trigger coughs, runny noses, watery eyes—and, in some cases, even serious illness. Be familiar with common pollutants so you can protect yourself.

Mildew, Molds, and Dust Mites

These organisms grow in bathrooms, the kitchen, the basement, and in other areas of your home with high humidity. They often account for persistent sneezing, watery eyes, and other allergy like symptoms.

For prevention, keep a window open or use a ventilation fan to keep bathroom tiles and other surfaces free of mildew, clean air conditioners and humidifiers frequently, and open a window or install a fan in bathrooms and the kitchen to reduce humidity. (If your window panes sweat, the humidity in your house is too high and you are creating ideal living conditions for these irritants.)

Many allergy sufferers react to dust mites—tiny creatures that live in carpets, bedding, and upholstered furniture and require moisture to survive. Regularly clean furniture, cushions, and mattresses to eliminate them (see box, page 24), and reduce the level of humidity in your house.

Have your house tested for mold by a professional.

Formaldehyde

Formaldehyde is used in insulation, paneling, pressed plywood, carpeting, fabrics, cabinets, and countless household products, including facial tissue and toothpaste. While formaldehyde is often not a problem, it does emit a gas that can cause skin rashes, runny noses, watery eyes, and other reactions.

Green and Clean

NATURE'S POLLUTION FIGHTERS

Houseplants—especially spider plants—offer some help in your fight against household air pollution, according to NASA scientists who have been investigating ways to clear the air in space stations. A philodendron can absorb much of the formaldehyde that builds up in a room, while a chrysanthemum will reduce some of the harmful chemicals in tobacco smoke.

Spider plant

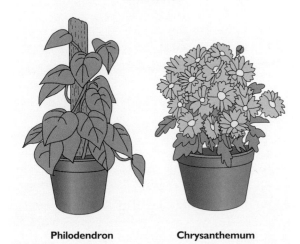

Philodendron   Chrysanthemum

You can usually lower formaldehyde levels considerably by keeping windows open to circulate fresh air. Your state health agency or local EPA office can also inspect your home or recommend private inspectors.

It may be necessary to remove material containing formaldehyde or cover paneling that emits formaldehyde with a vinyl wall covering. Airing dry cleaning before putting it in the closet helps, too.

Asbestos

This durable, fibrous material was once widely used in flooring, ceiling tiles, shingles, and insulation. Because prolonged exposure to asbestos fibers has been found to cause cancer, the material was banned 20 years ago. If your home was built before then, it's quite possible that the pipes and heating ducts are wrapped in asbestos.

However, the asbestos in your house is not necessarily dangerous. If the material is in good condition and is not leaking fibers as it crumbles and flakes, the rule of thumb is to leave it in place. Be extremely careful when working around asbestos, however.

• Never tear the asbestos coating from around a pipe, for instance, when brushing or vacuuming it, and don't saw or drill into asbestos when remodeling.

• Never remove the material yourself. If you are concerned that asbestos in your home poses a hazard, contact your state health agency or local EPA office (see page 363) for a list of inspectors and contractors who specialize in asbestos removal.

Lead

Lead is a highly toxic element. Exposure to it can result in damage to the brain, kidneys, blood, central nervous system, and reproductive system. Children are especially vulnerable to its ill effects, and lead has been linked to learning disabilities and behavioral problems. Lead poisoning can occur when this metallic element leaches into drinking water and soil through lead pipes. Dust particles from flaking lead paint are another hazard.

If you live in a house built before 1978, when lead paint was banned, have the paint tested. Have the water tested for lead if your house was built prior to 1988, when the government prohibited the use of lead in plumbing materials. See pages 362–363 for lead-testing resources or contact the National Lead Information Center Hotline (see page 362).

Even if your home is equipped with copper water pipes, your water is not necessarily lead free. Pipe connections may contain lead solder, and brass and bronze faucets often contain lead that can leach into the water.

Check with your local health department or pediatrician to see if you are living in a high-risk area.

Get the Lead Out

If There Is Lead Paint in Your House:

• Don't remove it yourself, because you risk exposing yourself and your family to harmful lead-dust particles. Ask your local health department for names of contractors who specialize in lead paint removal.

Green and Clean

SPARKLING AND SAFE

Some cleaning products contain chemicals that can pose a hazard to children and even sensitive adults. As alternatives, consider the following "green" cleaning products.

Baking soda

Borax (dangerous if ingested, so keep out of reach of children)

Distilled white vinegar

Lemon juice

Liquid soap (perfume and dye free; available at health food stores)

Salt

Scouring powder (look for a brand without chlorine)

- Don't simply paint over lead paint, because the lead will continue to chip and fill the air with particles.
- Always clean up paint chips immediately.
- Don't sweep floors. Wash them with a wet mop so you stir up as little dust as possible.
- Clean floors, window frames, and windowsills weekly.
- To keep children away, use furniture to block windowsills and other areas where paint might be chipping; repair as soon as possible.
- Have children wash their hands often, especially before meals, naps, and bedtime.
- Install vinyl siding over exterior lead paint as a less-expensive alternative to costly scraping and repainting.
- Wash toys and any large objects children might put in their mouths. (Beware of old, brightly painted toys; they may have lead paint even if your house does not.)
- Wash bedding and stuffed animals to keep them free of dust.
- Have your children tested for blood lead levels by a physician.

If There Is Lead in Your Water:
- Run tap water for 30 to 60 seconds to drain off lead that accumulates in the pipes in your house. (If lead is entering your water supply from street mains and connections—many municipalities used lead in water systems up until the 1930s—you will not be able to flush lead from your pipes simply by letting the water run for a while. Use bottled water for drinking and cooking or install a water filter registered for lead reduction.)
- Use cold water rather than hot for cooking and drinking. Hot water accumulates more lead from pipes.
- When in doubt, call the EPA Safe Drinking Water Hotline: 800-426-4791.

If There Is Lead in Your Soil:
- Clean or remove your shoes before entering the house to avoid tracking dirt in.
- As an interim measure, plant grass to cover high lead levels.
- Hire a certified lead-abatement contractor to reduce lead levels permanently. (Contact the National Lead Information Center Hotline at 800-424-LEAD to help find certified contractors in your area.)

Radon

This odorless, colorless, tasteless gas occurs naturally when uranium in rocks and soil decays. It is found all over the United States and may be entering your house undetected through cracks in the basement floor, pores in concrete-block basement walls, and through other openings between the earth and the house.

Radon can occur randomly. Just because a neighbor's house is free of radon doesn't mean that yours is. According to the EPA, one in 15 homes in the United States has a high level of radon.

Recent studies indicate that exposure to high levels of radon over extended periods is linked to lung cancer. Both the U.S. Surgeon General

Disposing of Toxic Household Products

Many communities now sponsor programs to recycle and/or safely dispose of household waste materials that can be dangerous if not taken care of properly. Some communities support recycling centers where home owners can bring drain cleaners, car batteries, motor oil, paints and thinners, pesticides, household cleaners, and other potentially hazardous materials.

Ask your local health department or EPA office (see page 363) to provide information and advise you on services available in your community to get rid of questionable substances. While you are waiting to dispose of these items, store them safety:

- Keep flammable items in the garage or tool shed, where they will be far from the furnace, stove, and other heat sources.
- Lock up hazardous materials securely to keep them out of the reach of children.
- Keep materials in their original containers so you don't confuse them with other products.

and the EPA recommend that every home be tested for radon. Fortunately, it's easy to identify a radon problem, and it's usually easy and fairly inexpensive to lower levels.

All states now have offices that provide information on radon, and some states will test your home for radon free of charge (call your local health department to locate the nearest office). Inexpensive, do-it-yourself radon test kits, usually less than $50, are also available at hardware stores and other retail outlets. Your state radon office can provide a list of test-kit companies that have met EPA requirements for reliability or are state-certified.

There are 2 kinds of radon-testing kits: short-term, which measure radon in the home for between 2 days and 90 days, and long-term, which give you a yearly average. The EPA recommends first doing a short-term test. You should close your windows and doors 12 hours before beginning the test and leave them closed as much as possible for the duration. Place the testing kit in the lowest lived-in level of the house, in a room that is used regularly (but not the kitchen or bathroom). To avoid drafts and other disturbances, the kit should be at least 20 inches off the floor. Leave it in place for the recommended length of time, and when finished, reseal and send it immediately to the lab noted in the kit. You should have the results within a few weeks. If your radon reading is higher than 4 picoCuries per liter of air, you should do a follow-up test.

If you do have radon, you can try to correct the problem by caulking cracks in basement concrete and masonry where the gas can enter (see page 306) and sealing floors and walls with latex paint. Sometimes you can reduce radon levels by keeping your basement windows open or installing fans to circulate fresh air from outside. Be sure to test again. Be aware, however, that the EPA cautions against do-it-yourself repairs, so you may want to have these problems fixed by a qualified contractor. In general, radon levels can be reduced for between $800 and $2,500. If the problem persists, consult the state's radon office to determine the best way to respond.

Home Security

In order to make your home secure, you need to understand your options when it comes to alarm systems and locks.

Professional Home Alarm Systems

Besides making your home safer, a professionally installed home alarm system can lower your homeowner's insurance bills by 5 to 15 percent. The alarm can be connected directly to your community's police or fire station or, more commonly, directly to the alarm company. With a central-station system, the alarm company tells the police that the alarm has sounded. If there's a false alarm, you can notify the alarm company before the police are called.

Anatomy of a Lock

The locks on your doors are your first line of defense against a break-in.
Check the following in all locks:.

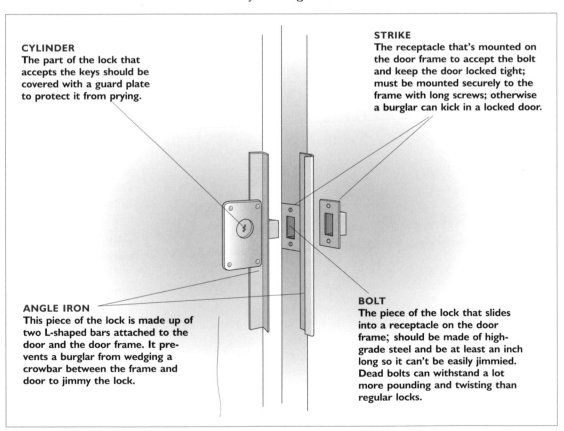

CYLINDER
The part of the lock that accepts the keys should be covered with a guard plate to protect it from prying.

STRIKE
The receptacle that's mounted on the door frame to accept the bolt and keep the door locked tight; must be mounted securely to the frame with long screws; otherwise a burglar can kick in a locked door.

ANGLE IRON
This piece of the lock is made up of two L-shaped bars attached to the door and the door frame. It prevents a burglar from wedging a crowbar between the frame and door to jimmy the lock.

BOLT
The piece of the lock that slides into a receptacle on the door frame; should be made of high-grade steel and be at least an inch long so it can't be easily jimmied. Dead bolts can withstand a lot more pounding and twisting than regular locks.

The Secure House

No house is 100 percent burglarproof. It's reassuring to know, though, that the more precautions you take to prevent a break-in, the less likely a burglar will be to target your house. This illustration shows some basic ways to increase the security of your house. If you are frequently away from home, live in an isolated area or one where break-ins are common, a burglar alarm system may be in order.

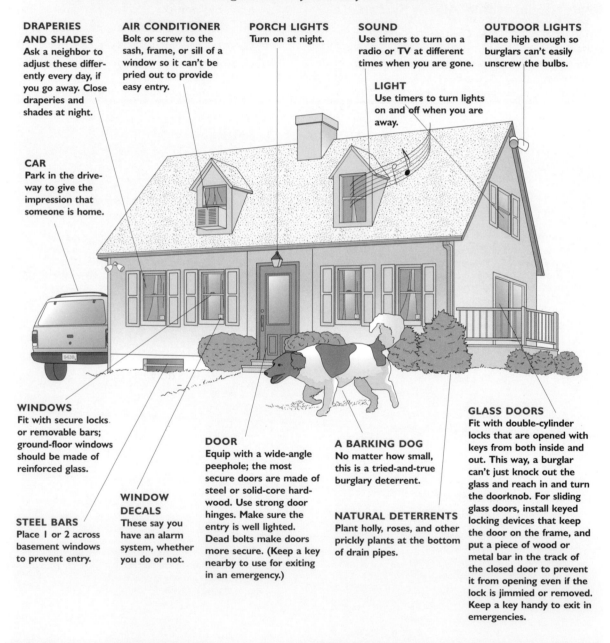

DRAPERIES AND SHADES
Ask a neighbor to adjust these differently every day, if you go away. Close draperies and shades at night.

AIR CONDITIONER
Bolt or screw to the sash, frame, or sill of a window so it can't be pried out to provide easy entry.

PORCH LIGHTS
Turn on at night.

SOUND
Use timers to turn on a radio or TV at different times when you are gone.

OUTDOOR LIGHTS
Place high enough so burglars can't easily unscrew the bulbs.

LIGHT
Use timers to turn lights on and off when you are away.

CAR
Park in the driveway to give the impression that someone is home.

WINDOWS
Fit with secure locks or removable bars; ground-floor windows should be made of reinforced glass.

STEEL BARS
Place 1 or 2 across basement windows to prevent entry.

WINDOW DECALS
These say you have an alarm system, whether you do or not.

DOOR
Equip with a wide-angle peephole; the most secure doors are made of steel or solid-core hardwood. Use strong door hinges. Make sure the entry is well lighted. Dead bolts make doors more secure. (Keep a key nearby to use for exiting in an emergency.)

A BARKING DOG
No matter how small, this is a tried-and-true burglary deterrent.

NATURAL DETERRENTS
Plant holly, roses, and other prickly plants at the bottom of drain pipes.

GLASS DOORS
Fit with double-cylinder locks that are opened with keys from both inside and out. This way, a burglar can't just knock out the glass and reach in and turn the doorknob. For sliding glass doors, install keyed locking devices that keep the door on the frame, and put a piece of wood or metal bar in the track of the closed door to prevent it from opening even if the lock is jimmied or removed. Keep a key handy to exit in emergencies.

There are 2 types of alarm systems: hardwired and wireless. A hardwired system, where wires are attached to windows and doors with alarm sensors, generally costs less than a wireless system. It takes longer to install this type of system, however, and the wires must be hidden carefully so they aren't easily disabled. A wireless system allows you to have the same coverage but without having to run the wiring throughout your house.

Don't forget to change the batteries, or the alarm might not work when you need it. It is recommended that you change the batteries twice a year, when the clocks are changed from daylight savings and back again, just as with smoke alarms and carbon monoxide detectors.

Less-expensive options to a burglar alarm system include:

- Sound-detecting sockets that plug into a light fixture and make the light flash when it detects noise.
- Motion-sensing outdoor lights that turn on when someone approaches.
- Lights with photo cells that turn on when it's dark and off when it's light.

Dead Bolts

Strengthen the door to your home with a dead bolt lock. This type of lock bolts deeper into the door jamb than the bolt in an ordinary lock, and therefore makes your home more secure. You can buy a single-cylinder dead bolt, which locks with a key from the outside and a thumb turn on the inside, or a double-cylinder lock, which is keyed inside and out. (Check local building codes to make sure   double-cylinder dead bolts are not prohibited where you live.)

Look for a bolt that:

- Extends at least 1 inch in the locked position, to resist ramming and kicking.
- Has steel inserts to prevent bolt from being sawed off.
- Has a reinforced strike plate with extra-strong mounting screws to anchor the lock well.

The First-Aid Kit

Always keep a well-stocked first-aid kit in an easily accessible place, making sure everyone in the family knows where it is. Keep a complete first-aid manual handy. Also assemble a kit for your car. The kits should contain the following items:

BANDAGES	MEDICATIONS	EQUIPMENT

• Adhesive bandages of assorted sizes (for minor cuts or scrapes)
• Bandages and gauze pads of assorted sizes (to dress wounds)
  • 2 rolls of 3-inch-by-3-inch sterile gauze pads (for large wounds)
  • Two 4-inch-by-4-inch sterile gauze pads (for large wounds)
  • 1 roll 3-inch cohesive bandage (for sprains)
• Triangular bandages (to make a sling)
	• Activated charcoal (use only if Poison Control Center recommends it)
	• After-sun lotion
	• Antacid
	• Antibiotic ointment
	• Antidiarrhea medication
	• Antiseptic solution and wipes (to clean wounds)
	• Aspirin or a nonaspirin pain killer like acetaminophen
	• Calamine lotion (to apply to insect bites)
	• Cough syrup
	• Eyewash (sterile saline solution)
	• Insect repellent
	• Laxative
	• Petroleum jelly
	• Soap
	• Sunscreen
	• Syrup of ipecac (use to induce vomiting only if Poison Control Center recommends it)
		• Adhesive tape
		• Blanket made of Mylar or some other lightweight material
		• Cotton balls and swabs
		• Duct tape
		• Latex gloves
		• Matches (to sterilize instruments)
		• Needle (to remove splinters)
		• Paper cups (for fluids, to flush wounds, to use as a protective covering for eyes or wounds)
		• Plastic sheeting
		• Safety pins (to fasten bandages)
		• Scissors (to cut bandages)
		• Thermometer
		• Tweezers (to remove splinters and objects from wounds

Preparing for Disaster

Disasters, both natural and man-made, can strike anywhere and anytime. Unfortunately, winter storms, hazardous spills, earthquakes, and terrorist attacks are all possible. Depending on the nature of the disaster, your family may be confined at home or forced to evacuate quickly. All families need to be prepared ahead of time for either scenario.

Create a Plan

Every family needs a plan in the event of a disaster.
- Discuss with your family the types of disasters that could occur.
- Discuss what you would do if you were advised to evacuate. Make a plan.
- Practice the plan.
- Pick 2 meeting places outside of your home, one at a safe distance from your home in case of fire, one outside your neighborhood in case you can't return home.
- Choose an out-of-state friend or relative as a contact for everyone to call. Make sure everyone has the number.
- Post emergency telephone numbers by every phone, and carry the numbers with you when you're away from home.
- Show responsible family members how and when to shut off water, gas, and electricity at main switches.

Create a Kit

The American Red Cross recommends storing the following basics in your home in the event of a disaster in which you and your family must remain indoors while power and water are out. You should have 3 days' worth of supplies for each person in your family. The items with an asterisk (*) should also go into your smaller, portable disaster kit that you have packed and ready to go at a moment's notice in the event of an evacuation. Store your kit somewhere convenient and let everyone in your household know where it is. Every 6 months to a year, replace batteries and freshen water and food supplies.

Water
- One gallon of water per person per day (2 quarts for drinking, 2 quarts for food preparation and sanitation.)*

Food
Should require no cooking, no refrigeration, little water. If you must heat food, pack a can of sterno.
  Select from the following:
- Canned food*: meats, fruits, vegetables
- Canned juices, milk, soup*
- Staples*: sugar, salt, pepper
- Energy foods*: peanut butter, jelly, crackers, granola and protein bars, trail mix
- Vitamins*
- Foods for infants, elderly persons, or those on a restricted diet*
- Comfort food: cookies, hard candy, sweetened cereal, lollipops, instant coffee, tea bags

Clothing and Bedding
- One complete change of clothing and footwear per person*
- Sturdy shoes or work boots*
- Rain gear*
- Blankets or sleeping bags*
- Hat and gloves
- Thermal underwear
- Sunglasses

A Kit for the Car

Whether you're on the road a lot or a little, here's a list of items that will help you get to your destination safely—and keep you safe along the way.

TOOLS TO CARRY
Flashlight
Funnel (flexible neck)
Ice scraper
Jack
Jumper cables
Locking pliers
Lug wrench
Penknife
Pliers (adjustable)
Screwdrivers (slotted blade and Phillip's head)
Tire pressure gauge
Tow strap or chain
Wrench set (small)

SUPPLIES TO HAVE
Aerosol tire inflator (nonflammable brand)
Antifreeze (or 50/50 coolant mix)
Blanket
Board (to put under jack on soft ground)
Brake fluid (new, unopened can)
"Call Police" sign (for window)
Can opener
Drive belts (assorted sizes specified for your car model)

Fire extinguisher
First aid kit (see page 384)
Flares
Gallon jugs (empty; to hold water or gas in an emergency)
Gloves
Hand cleaner (foil packs or a tube)
Paper towels
Safety glasses
Spare tire

DOCUMENTS TO KEEP HANDY
Auto club membership card
Credit card or emergency cash
Driver's license (keep on person)
Emergency phone numbers
Insurance ID card
Maps
Owner's manual
Service record or log
Vehicle registration

Tools and Supplies

- Mess kits or paper cups, plates, and plastic utensils*
- Emergency-preparedness manual*
- Battery-operated radio and extra batteries*
- Flashlight with extra batteries*
- Cash (including change): at least $400, or enough for 2 to 3 days*
- Nonelectric can opener*
- Utility knife*
- Fire extinguisher: small cannister, ABC type
- Tube tent
- Pliers
- Duct tape
- Compass
- Matches in a waterproof container
- Aluminum foil
- Plastic storage containers

- Signal flare
- Paper, pencil
- Needles, thread
- Medicine dropper
- Shut-off wrench to turn off household gas or water
- Whistle
- Plastic sheeting
- Map of the area (for locating shelters)
- Gas-powered generator (to keep space heater operating in case of severe cold)

Sanitation
- Toilet paper*
- Soap, liquid detergent*
- Feminine supplies*
- Personal hygiene items*
- Plastic garbage bags, ties
- Plastic bucket with a tight lid
- Disinfectant
- Household chlorine bleach

Special Items:
- Formula*
- Diapers*
- Bottles*
- Powdered milk*
- Medications*

For Adults:
- Heart and high blood pressure medication*
- Insulin*
- Prescription drugs*
- Denture needs*
- Contact lenses and supplies*
- Extra eyeglasses*

*First Aid Kit** (as described on page 384)

Entertainment
- Games and books

Important Family Documents
Keep the following records in a waterproof, portable container:
- Will, insurance policies, deeds, contracts, stocks and bonds
- Passports, Social Security cards, immunization records
- Bank account numbers
- Credit card account numbers and companies
- Inventory of valuable household goods
- Important telephone numbers
- Family records (birth, marriage, death certificates

Appendix

Here are the formulas to convert measurements commonly used in the United States to the metric system, which is used as the measurement standard in many countries worldwide.

LINEAR MEASUREMENTS

USA	Metric
Inches	*Millimeters*
1/16	1.5875
1/8	3.2
1/4	6.35
3/8	9.5
1/2	12.7
5/8	15.9
3/4	19.05
7/8	22.2
1	25.4

Inches	*Centimeters*
1	2.54
2	5.1
3	7.6
4	10.2
5	12.7
6	15.2
7	17.8
8	20.3
9	22.9
10	25.4
11	27.9
12	30.5

Feet	*Centimeters*	*Meters*
1	30.48	.3048
2	61	.61
3	91	.91
4	122	1.22
5	152	1.52

Feet	*Centimeters*	*Meters*
6	183	1.83
7	213	2.13
8	244	2.44
9	274	2.74
10	305	3.05
50	1524	15.24
100	3048	30.48

1 yard = .9144 meters
1 mile = 1.6 kilometers
1 nautical mile = 1.852 kilometers

VOLUME

USA	Metric
1 teaspoon	5 ml
1 tablespoon	15 ml
1/4 cup	60 ml
1/3 cup	80 ml
1/2 cup	120 ml
2/3 cup	160 ml
3/4 cup	180 ml
1 cup	240 ml
1 pint	475 ml
1 quart	.95 liter
1 quart plus 1/4 cup	1 liter
1 gallon	3.8 liters

WEIGHT

USA	Metric
Ounces	*Grams*
1	28.3
2	56.7
3	85
4	113
5	142
6	170
7	198
8	227
9	255
10	283
11	312
12	340
13	369
14	397
15	425
16	454

Pounds	*Kilograms*
1	.45
2	.9
3	1.4
4	1.8
5	2.3
6	2.7
7	3.2
8	3.6
9	4.1
10	4.5

AREA

USA	Metric
1 sq in	6.45 sq cm
1 sq ft	929 sq cm = .093 sq meters
1 sq yd	.84 sq meters
1 acre	4,047 sq meters
1 sq mile	2,589,988 sq meters = 2.589 sq kilometers

TEMPERATURE

To convert from Fahrenheit to Celsius: subtract 32, multiply by 5, then divide by 9

To convert Celsius to Fahrenheit: multiply by 9, divide by 5, then add 32

32°F	0°C
212°F	100°C
250°F	121°C
325°F	163°C
350°F	176°C
375°F	190°C
400°F	205°C
425°F	218°C
450°F	232°C

FLUID MEASUREMENTS

Milliliters [ml] and cubic centimeters [cc] are equivalent, but it is customary to use milliliters for liquids.

USA	Metric
1 fl oz	29.6 ml
1 cup	237 ml
1 pint	473 ml
1 quart	946 ml = .946 liters
1 gallon	3785 ml = 3.785 liters

SMALL VOLUME

Tablespoons	Cups	Fluid Ounces
1 tablespoon = 3 teaspoons		1/2 fluid ounce
2 tablespoons	1/8 cup	1 fluid ounce
4 tablespoons	1/4 cup	2 fluid ounces
5 tablespoons plus 1 teaspoon	1/3 cup	2 2/3 fluid ounces
6 tablespoons	3/8 cup	3 fluid ounces
8 tablespoons	1/2 cup	4 fluid ounces
10 tablespoons plus 2 teaspoons	2/3 cup	5 1/3 fluid ounces
12 tablespoons	3/4 cup	6 fluid ounces
14 tablespoons	7/8 cup	7 fluid ounces
16 tablespoons	1 cup	8 fluid ounces

LARGE VOLUME

Cups	Fluid Ounces	Pints/Quarts
1 cup	8 fluid ounces	1/2 pint
2 cups	16 fluid ounces	1 pint
3 cups	24 fluid ounces	1 1/2 pints = 3/4 quart
4 cups	32 fluid ounces	2 pints = 1 quart
6 cups	48 fluid ounces	3 pints = 1 1/2 quarts
8 cups	64 fluid ounces	2 quarts = 1/2 gallon
16 cups	128 fluid ounces	4 quarts = 1 gallon

Index